TEXTILE
MATHEMATICS

TEXTILE MATHEMATICS

By

THOS. H. QUIGLEY
Georgia Institute of Technology
Atlanta, Georgia

BRUCE COX
Georgia Institute of Technology
Atlanta, Georgia

and

CHARLES A. DUKE
Georgia Institute of Technology
Atlanta, Georgia

W. R. C. SMITH PUBLISHING CO.
Atlanta, Georgia

LIBRARY OF CONGRESS CATALOG CARD NUMBER: 73–89909
INTERNATIONAL STANDARD BOOK NUMBER: 0–912476–05–2

To

you who have so emphasized the need,
and to the memories of

THOS. H. QUIGLEY

and

JAMES H. GROVES

who tried to satisfy that need with
the preparation of this book, it is
sincerely dedicated.

ACKNOWLEDGMENTS

Space does not permit enumeration of all the individuals and companies from whom information, assistance, criticisms, suggestions, and encouragement have been received. Indebtedness to each of them and all of them is hereby gratefully acknowledged.

CONTENTS

PART ONE

PART TWO

Part One

Chapter I

READING NUMBERS

Each day many calculations are made in a textile plant involving all kinds of numbers from very small ones to very great ones. It is essential, therefore, for your study of textile mathematics to begin with a firm understanding of how to recognize and read numbers.

All numbers are composed of *digits*. The digits are 0, 1, 2, 3, 4, 5, 6, 7, 8, and 9.

Consider the number 6,259,347. It is composed of seven digits. The last or right-hand digit in any number is called the *units* digit. In this case 7 is the units digit. The next to the last digit is called the tens digit. In this case 4 is the tens digit. The second from the last digit is called the *hundreds* digit. In this case 3 is the hundreds digit. The next digit is called the *thousands* digit. In this case 9 is the thousands digit. Then next is the *ten thousands* digit which is 5. Next is the *hundred thousands* digit which is 2. Next is the *millions* digit which is 6. Usually, as in this case, commas are put into a number to separate the digits into groups of three, thereby making the number easier to read.

The number 6,259,347 is read: six million, two hundred fifty-nine thousand, three hundred forty-seven. In other words, to read a number we separate the last three digits off from the rest by a comma, then the next three digits, and so on until we have the whole number separated into groups of three digits. Then we read the first digit or group of digits just as though there were no other digits in the number. In this case there is only one digit in the first group, so we simply say "six." Then we say the name of the digit, "million." Then we read the next group of digits just as though there were no other digits in the number. We say "two hundred fifty-nine" and then we say the name of the last digit in the group, "thousand." Then we read the last group, "three hundred forty-seven," but do not call the names of the last two digits.

PROBLEMS. **Put in the commas and read the following numbers:**

1. 122	**7.** 11122	**13.** 1111122
2. 236	**8.** 32236	**14.** 6532236
3. 999	**9.** 99999	**15.** 9999999
4. 1122	**10.** 111122	**16.** 11111122
5. 2236	**11.** 532236	**17.** 76532236
6. 9999	**12.** 999999	**18.** 99999999

After the millions digit comes the *ten millions* digit, then the *hundred millions* digit and then the *billions* digit.

19. 143256793	**21.** 769832456	**23.** 11456666732
20. 650763941	**22.** 3896743226	**24.** 27567891429

If any group of digits has a zero, 0, in it, we do not say the name of the zero at all. Consider the number 709,690,032,001. We read it like this: seven hundred nine billion, six hundred ninety million, thirty-two thousand, one.

25. 1001	**28.** 500009	**31.** 90120304
26. 10001	**29.** 1000000	**32.** 9000000002
27. 100000	**30.** 900000000	**33.** 100001001001

Write in digits the numbers that are given in the following statements:

34. A specialized textile fabric used for race driver's suits will withstand temperatures in excess of four thousand four hundred seventy five degrees.

35. There are thirty-two thousand textile and apparel plants in the United States.

36. One million forty six thousand four hundred people are employed in the American textile mill products industry.

37. One million four hundred sixteen thousand five hundred fifty Americans are employed in the apparel industry.

38. In 1971, the value of shipments produced by the American textile industry was more than twenty-two billion two hundred eighty million dollars.

39. The textile industry supplies more than twenty two thousand items for the United States Armed Forces.

40. Total Cotton spindles in the United States reached a peak of thirty-seven million nine hundred twenty-nine thousand in 1925.

41. The American textile industry consumes more than nine billion one hundred forty million nine hundred thousand pounds of natural and man-made fibers annually.

Chapter II

ADDITION
OF
WHOLE NUMBERS

The process of finding a number equal to two or more numbers taken together is called *addition*. Thus, to *add* 3 yards of cloth and 6 yards of cloth is to find the number of yards in both pieces taken together.

To signify that numbers are to be added together, we use the sign + which is read "plus." We could signify that the above pieces of cloth are to be added by writing thus: 3 yards + 6 yards. We would read it like this: "three yards plus six yards."

To signify that the numbers when added together are the same as, or equal to, another number, we use the sign = which is read "equal" or "equals," whichever is proper. Thus, in the above case, 3 yards + 6 yards = 9 yards. We would read it thus: "three yards plus six yards equal nine yards."

When we add two or more numbers together we find their *sum*. Thus, the sum of 3 yards and 6 yards is 9 yards.

ADDITION OF NUMBERS CONTAINING ONE DIGIT

EXAMPLE: *Find the sum of* 2, 3 *and* 5.

$2 + 3 + 5 = 10$

EXAMPLE: *Find the sum* of 5, 6 *and* 7.

$5 + 6 + 7 = 18$

PROBLEMS. Find the sum of the following, using plus and equal signs:

1. 2 and 3	**4.** 5 and 6	**7.** 8 and 9	**10.** 6, 7 and 8
2. 3 and 4	**5.** 6 and 7	**8.** 9 and 9	**11.** 7, 8 and 9
3. 4 and 5	**6.** 7 and 8	**9.** 4, 5 and 6	**12.** 9, 9, 9 and 0

ADDITION OF NUMBERS CONTAINING MORE THAN ONE DIGIT WHEN THE SUM OF SIMILAR DIGITS DOES NOT EXCEED NINE

The easiest way in which to add numbers of more than one digit is to place the numbers under each other, keeping the units digit of each

32   number in a straight line, the tens digits in a straight line, the hundreds
21   digits in a straight line and so on. Suppose we wish to add 32, 21, and
16   16. We would do it as follows:

32   Adding the units digits (6 + 1 + 2) first, the sum is 9. Place the
21   9 below the line.
16
 9

32   Adding the tens digits (1 + 2 + 3), the sum is 6. Place the 6
21   below the line.
16   Therefore, the sum of 32 + 21 + 16 = 69. The answer is 69.
69

EXAMPLE: *Find the sum of 22, 36 and 41.*

22
36
41
99   **Answer: 99.**

PROBLEMS:

13. Add 11, 23 and 51.
14. Find the sum of 13, 26 and 40.
15. What is the sum of 11, 31, 26 and 10?
16. What does 1, 2, 11, 22, 21 and 32 equal?
17. What does 2, 21, 30 and 136 equal?
18. How much is 23 plus 105 plus 201 plus 670?

ADDITION OF NUMBERS OF MORE THAN ONE DIGIT WHEN THE SUM OF SIMILAR DIGITS IS GREATER THAN NINE

Suppose we wish to add 540, 449, and 331. We proceed as we did before.

1
540   Adding the units digits (1 + 9 + 0) first, the sum is 10. Place
449   the 0 of the 10 below the line and place the 1 of the 10 above the
331   tens digits.
 0

1 1
540   Add the tens digits and the 1 we have placed above the tens
449   digits (3 + 4 + 4 + 1). The sum is 12. Place the 2 of the 12 below
331   the line and the 1 of the 12 above the hundreds digits.
 20

1 1
540   Add the hundreds digits and the 1 we have placed above the
449   hundreds digits (3 + 4 + 5 + 1). The sum is 13. Place the 12 below
331   the line.   **Answer: 1320.**
1320

EXAMPLE: *Six laps are delivered from the picker weighing* 70
pounds, 72 *pounds,* 71 *pounds,* 73 *pounds,* 70 *pounds* and 74 *pounds.*
What is the total weight of the six laps?

¹
70
72
71
73
70
 74
430   **Answer:**   430 pounds.

19. If there are 840 looms in room No. 1 and 810 in room No. 2
and 290 in room No. 3, how many looms in the plant?

20. If a weaver weaves 660 yards of cloth the first day, 702 the
second day and 967 the third day, how many yards did he weave in
three days?

21. The sizing tallow report for the week is as follows: Monday,
398 pounds; Tuesday, 310 pounds; Wednesday, 356 pounds; Thursday,
324 pounds; Friday, 342 pounds, Saturday, 88 pounds. How many
pounds were used during the week?

22. In a certain plant, 1080 looms make sheeting, 460 looms
make drills, 380 looms make sateen. How many looms in the plant?

23. A buyer buys three bales of cloth, the first containing 1128
yards, the second 1242 yards and the third 1080 yards. How many
yards in all?

24. A plant sold five bales of thread waste weighing as follows:
the first bale 622 pounds, the second 608 pounds, the third 684 pounds,
the fourth 700 pounds and the fifth 667 pounds. How many pounds
did the five bales weigh?

25. A company sells a certain amount of sheeting for $7524,
drills for $8241, twills for $1260, sateens for $2408 and print cloth
for $3008. What was the amount of this sale?

26. The weekly report of a cloth room is as follows: Monday,
baled 77,600 yards; Tuesday, 81,004 yards; Wednesday, 74,666 yards;
Thursday, 80,422 yards; Friday, 78,948 yards; Saturday, 30,024 yards.
How many yards are there in all?

27. A plant purchased five boxes of drop wires, the first box containing 50,000, the second 62,420, the third 30,020, the fourth 28,960
and the fifth 40,000. How many drop wires in the five boxes?

28. A picker produced the following amounts of 14-ounce lap:
Monday, 2271 pounds; Tuesday, 2286 pounds; Wednesday, 2296
pounds; Thursday, 2285 pounds; Friday, 1149 pounds. How many
pounds did this picker produce in a week?

29. A spinning room report showed the following amounts of
warp yarn spun during the week: number 13 yarn, 15,160 pounds;
number 12 yarn, 32,082 pounds; number 21 yarn, 14,900 pounds;
number 23 yarn, 13,550 pounds; number 11 yarn, 13,162 pounds;
number 9 yarn, 22,818 pounds. How many pounds of warp were
produced?

30. A spinning overseer's report for the week showed the following made during the week: 111,672 pounds of warp yarn; 94,100 pounds of filling yarn; 247 pounds of spooler waste; 18 pounds of filling waste; 2714 pounds of cleaners' waste; 184 pounds of beam waste. How many pounds of yarn were produced and how many pounds of waste?

Chapter III

SUBTRACTION OF WHOLE NUMBERS

The process of finding the difference between two numbers is called *subtraction*. Thus, to *subtract* 3 yards from 9 yards is to find the difference between 3 yards and 9 yards.

To signify that one number is to be subtracted from another number, we write the larger number, then write the sign −, which is read "minus," then write the smaller number. We use the equal sign as we did in addition. Thus: 9 yards − 3 yards = 6 yards. This would be read "9 yards minus 3 yards equal 6 yards."

SIMPLE SUBTRACTION

EXAMPLE: *Subtract 7 from 8.*

$8 - 7 = 1$

EXAMPLE: *Subtract 7 from 18.*

$18 - 7 = 11$

PROBLEMS. Find the difference between the following numbers, using the signs for minus and equal:

1. 3 and 7	**2.** 5 and 9	**3.** 13 and 2
4. 15 and 3	**5.** 19 and 4	**6.** 25 and 2
7. 69 and 6	**8.** 117 and 5	

9. If we take away 7 from 19, what is left?
10. 5 subtracted from 48 equals what number?
11. 0 subtracted from 25 equals what number?
12. What is the difference between 41 and 0?
13. 9 subtracted from 9 equals what number?

Find the difference between the following numbers:

14. 12 and 8	**17.** 7 and 11	**20.** 8 and 17
15. 6 and 13	**18.** 8 and 13	**21.** 9 and 18
16. 9 and 15	**19.** 14 and 7	**22.** 10 and 4

SUBTRACTION OF NUMBERS INVOLVING SUBTRACTION OF SIMILAR DIGITS FROM EACH OTHER

Usually in subtracting numbers of more than one digit, it is easiest, especially while you are still learning, to write the larger number above the smaller number. Suppose we wish to subtract 21 from 35. We should do it as follows:

$$\begin{array}{r} 35 \\ \underline{21} \end{array}$$

Starting with the units digits, subtract the 1 from the 5. The difference is 4. Place the 4 below the line.

$$\begin{array}{r} 35 \\ \underline{21} \\ 4 \end{array}$$

Next subtract the tens digit. The difference is 1. Place the 1 below the line.
Therefore, $35 - 21 = 14$.   **Answer:**. 14.

$$\begin{array}{r} 35 \\ \underline{21} \\ 14 \end{array}$$

PROBLEMS.   Find the difference between the following numbers:

23. 27 and 12   **25.** 36 and 26   **27.** 79 and 35
24. 35 and 24   **26.** 45 and 15   **28.** 199 and 98

SUBTRACTION OF ANY NUMBERS

Suppose we wish to subtract 469 from 658. Place the larger number above the smaller.

$$\begin{array}{r} 658 \\ \underline{469} \end{array}$$

Not being able to subtract 9 from 8, we will *borrow* 10 from the tens digit column, thereby reducing the 50 to 40 (that is, reducing the 5 to a 4), and increasing the 8 to 18, and then subtract the 9 from the 18 and place the difference, 9, below the line, like this:

Again, we see we cannot subtract the 60 in the tens digit column from the 40 above it (that is, the 6 from the 4). So we borrow 100 from the hundreds column, thereby reducing the 600 to 500 (that is, reducing the 6 to 5), and increasing the 40 to 140 (that is, increasing the 4 to 14).

Then, we subtract the 60 from the 140 (that is, the 6 from the 14) and place the difference, 80 (that is, 8), below the line, like this:

Then we subtract the 400 from the 500 (that is, the 4 from the 5) and place the difference, 100 (that is, 1), below the line, like this:

Therefore, $658 - 469 = 189$.

EXAMPLE: *If a spinning room has 26,614 spindles, and 11,125 spindles are running warp yarn and the rest of them are running filling yarn, how many are running filling yarn?*

$$\begin{array}{r} 26\,614 \\ \underline{11\,125} \\ 15\,489 \end{array}$$

Answer: 15,489 spindles are running filling yarn.

29. A plant has 940 drill looms and 690 sheeting looms. How many more drill looms than sheeting looms?

30. From a bale of burlap containing 1034 yards, 360 yards have been cut. How many yards remain in the bale?

31. 62,847 pounds is the weekly production of a certain spinning room. If 38,117 pounds of this are warp, how much is filling?

32. A cut of certain style of cloth weighs 14 pounds. If it contains 8 pounds of sized warp, what is the weight of the filling?

33. A cut of a certain style of cloth weighs 15 pounds. The filling weighs 6 pounds. What is the weight of the warp and sizing?

34. The cut marks on the warp for a certain style of cloth are 124 yards apart as the warp comes from the slasher. The cut marks in the woven cloth are 118 yards apart. How much has the warp contracted during weaving?

35. 25,000 pounds of cotton were manufactured into cloth, making 21,987 pounds of cloth. How many pounds were lost in manufacturing?

36. Arkwright patented the first ring spinning frame in the year 1769. How many years has it been in use up to 1972?

37. In 1894 the present type of automatic loom was put on the market. How many years has it been in use up to 1972?

38. An order comes to the plant for 251,570 yards of a certain style of cloth. The warehouse has 544,000 yards of the cloth in storage. After filling the order, how many yards will be left in the storage?

39. An order calls for 208,000 yards of a certain style of cloth. 199,788 yards have been made. How many yards must be made to complete the order?

40. The weights of ten section beams before being slashed are as follows: 478 pounds, 475 pounds, 479 pounds, 471 pounds, 474 pounds, 475 pounds, 476 pounds, 474 pounds, 474 pounds, and 477 pounds. After being slashed, this same yarn has a total weight of 5206 pounds. How many pounds of sizing has the slasher put into the yarn?

Chapter IV

MULTIPLICATION OF WHOLE NUMBERS

Multiplication, or *multiplying,* is a short method of adding. Thus, to find out how many yards there are in three pieces of cloth if each piece contains 2 yards, we can *add,* like this: 2 yards + 2 yards + 2 yards = 6 yards. Or we can shorten this by *multiplying,* using the multiplication sign, ×, like this: 3 × 2 yards = 6 yards. This would be read as follows: "3 times 2 yards equals 6 yards," or like this: "3 multiplied by 2 yards equals 6 yards," or like this: "2 yards multiplied by 3 equals 6 yards," or like this: "2 yards times 3 equals 6 yards."

The result of multiplying is called the *product.* Thus: "6 is the product of 2 times 3"; or "6 yards is the product of 3 yards multiplied by 2"; or "the product of 2 times 3 yards is 6 yards." Or you may say it any way that makes common sense.

The preceding problem may be written in any one of the following ways:

$$3 \times 2 \text{ yards} = 6 \text{ yards}$$
$$2 \text{ yards} \times 3 = 6 \text{ yards}$$
$$6 \text{ yards} = 3 \times 2 \text{ yards}$$
$$6 \text{ yards} = 2 \text{ yards} \times 3$$

Hence, we see that it is shorter to multiply 2 yards by 3 than to add 2 yards plus 2 yards plus 2 yards, provided we already know that 2 times 3 is 6. And the only way to find out what 2 × 3 is, is to add 2 + 2 + 2.

EXAMPLE: *Find the product of* 6 × 4.

$$4 + 4 + 4 + 4 + 4 + 4 = 24 \quad \text{or}$$
$$6 + 6 + 6 + 6 = 24$$

EXAMPLE: *Find the product of* 7 × 4.

From the preceding example we see that 6 × 4 = 24. Therefore, 7 × 4 must = 6 × 4 + 4 = 28.

PROBLEMS: Find the product of the following numbers. Do as little work as possible to find the products. Look closely and you may see that the product of one problem will make another one easy. For

instance, the answer to problem 1 will help you with problem 2, and the answer to problem 3 will help you with problem 7.

1. 5×6	**5.** 9×3	**9.** 5×5	**13.** 0×9
2. 6×6	**6.** 4×9	**10.** 8×10	**14.** 7×0
3. 6×7	**7.** 7×6	**11.** 9×1	**15.** 1×0
4. 8×3	**8.** 7×10	**12.** 1×5	**16.** 3×12

Note to Teachers. It will be observed that this book provides only a minimum of drill exercises in the handling of abstract numbers. The number of additional drill exercises you should give the individual members of your class depends on that individual's age, academic advancement and motives for learning. For adult people who have a daily need for the strictly textile mathematics of part II of this book, only such a minimum of drill should be provided as will enable them to barely master the handling of abstract numbers, since subsequent matter in the book will provide the incentive and occasion for mastering the handling of abstract numbers.

MULTIPLICATION INVOLVING PRODUCTS OF DIGITS NOT EXCEEDING NINE

One easy way to multiply numbers containing more than one digit is to set the number with the more digits directly above the number with less digits. Suppose we wish to multiply 24 by 2.

24   To multiply these numbers, place them one directly under the
 2   other, the same as in addition and subtraction.

24   Multiplying the units digit of the larger number, 4, by the units
 2   digit of the smaller number (4×2), the product is 8. Place the 8 below
 8   the line.

24   Multiplying the tens digit in the top line by the units digit in
 2   the lower line (2×2), the product is 4. Place the 4 below the line.
48   Therefore, the product of $24 \times 2 = 48$.

EXAMPLE: *What is the product of* 33×3?

33
 3
99

PROBLEMS.   Find the products of the following numbers:

17. 11 and 2	**19.** 13 and 3	**21.** 14 and 2
18. 12 and 3	**20.** 23 and 3	**22.** 44 and 2

MULTIPLICATION INVOLVING PRODUCTS OF DIGITS EXCEEDING NINE

634   Suppose we wish to multiply 634 by 5. Arrange the numbers
 5   as before.

²
634   Multiply the 4 by the 5. The product is 20. Place the 0 of the
_5_   20 below the line directly under the 5. *Carry* the 2 of the 20 directly
0   above the 3.

^{1 2}
634   Multiply the 3 by the 5. The product is 15. Add the 2. The sum
_5_   is 17. Put the 7 of the 17 below the line directly under the 3. *Carry* the
70   1 of the 17 over the 6.

^{1 2}
634   Multiply the 6 by the 5. The product is 30. Add the 1. The sum
_5_   is 31. Put the 31 below the line.
3170   Therefore, 634 × 5 = 3170

EXAMPLE: *What is the product of 752 and 8?*

752
_8_
6016

PROBLEMS.   Find the products of:

| **23.** 123 × 9 | **25.** 841 × 3 | **27.** 7 × 9516 |
| **24.** 456 × 7 | **26.** 8 × 9121 | **28.** 9 × 9999 |

MULTIPLICATION OF ANY WHOLE NUMBERS

^{1 2}
634   Suppose we wish to multiply 634 by 745. We place one
_745_   number directly above the other and then we multiply the 634 by
3170   the 5 of the 745, just as we did before.

^{1 1}
634   Then we erase the little figures above the top number and
_745_   multiply by the 4, setting this product down under the 3170, but
3170   moved one space to the left.
2536

^{2 2}
634   We again erase the little figures and multiply by the 7, moving
_745_   the product another space to the left. Then, we add these products.
3170   Therefore, 634 × 745 = 472,330.
2536
_4438_
472330

Suppose we wish to multiply 258 by 240.

258   But this result is the same as if we merely put one   258
_240_   zero under the line and put the 1032 in front of the zero.   _240_
000   Hence, we would multiply these numbers as shown at the   10320
1032   right.   _516_
_516_   61920
61920

Suppose we wish to multiply 258 by 204.

258   But this is the same as if we left out the row of zeros.   258
204   Hence, we multiply as shown at the right.   204

```
 258        But this is the same as if we left out the row of zeros.      258
 204        Hence, we multiply as shown at the right.                     204
1032                                                                     1032
 000                                                                      516
 516                                                                    52632
52632
```

Suppose we wish to multiply 462 by 200.

```
 462                          But this is the same as:       462
 200                                                         200
 000                                                       92400
 000
 924
92400
```

EXAMPLE: *A spinning department has* 508 *spinning frames. Each frame has* 216 *spindles. How many spinning spindles in the department?*

```
   508
   216
  3048
   508
  1016
109728     Answer:   109,728 spindles.
```

PROBLEMS:

29. Each yard of lap from a certain picker weighs 15 ounces. What is the weight of a 48-yard lap?

30. What would be the value of 220 bales of cloth at $150 a bale?

31. If one bale of cloth contains 20 pieces of cloth, 25 yards each, how many yards are there in 24 bales?

32. A reed 41 inches long has 24 dents to the inch. How many dents in the reed?

33. How many bobbins are required to fill 1940 batteries, if each battery contains 23 bobbins?

34. The weight of yarn on a full spinning bobbin with 6-inch traverse is about 2 ounces from a $1\frac{3}{4}$-inch ring. How many ounces should a doff weigh from a 320-spindle frame?

35. A buyer sends an order to a mill for 512 bales of cloth, each bale to contain 20 forty-yard pieces. The plant ships him 162 bales. How many yards remain of the order?

36. A company buys 300 bales of cotton, the average weight being 490 pounds per bale; 14,000 pounds of this cotton go to waste. How many pounds of cloth are produced from this cotton?

EXAMPLE: *If the hank clock registers* 15 *hanks per spindle made in a day, how many hanks would be made on* 2 *frames of* 92 *spindles?*

If each hank of this size roving weighs 4 pounds, how many pounds are produced in a day?

$$
\begin{array}{r}
92 \\
2 \\
\hline
184 \\
15 \\
\hline
920 \\
184 \\
\hline
2760 \text{ hanks}
\end{array}
\qquad
\begin{array}{r}
2760 \\
4 \\
\hline
11040 \text{ pounds}
\end{array}
$$

37. 200 looms on a certain style of goods weave 52 yards per loom per day; 180 looms on another style weave 48 yards per loom per day. How many yards will the 380 looms weave in six days?

38. In a weave room there are 834 looms. There are 2 harnesses on each loom and each harness contains 890 heddles. How many heddles on all the looms?

39. A cloth woven with 8 harnesses requires 350 heddle eyes to each harness. How many heddle eyes will be required for 275 looms?

40. How many dollars will it cost for supplies for 28 sections for a year, if the average cost is $187 a month per section?

41. On a loom running 182 picks per minute how many times will it pick in 8 hours if it does not stop?

42. A loom runs 7 hours on the first shift, $6\frac{1}{2}$ hours on the second shift and $7\frac{1}{4}$ hours on the third shift. How many total picks did it make if it ran at a speed of 160 picks per minute.

Chapter V

DIVISION OF WHOLE NUMBERS WITHOUT FINAL REMAINDERS

Division, as its name suggests, is the process of finding how many times one number is contained in another number. Division is denoted by the division sign, ÷, which is read "divided by." Thus, 6 yards ÷ 3 yards is read "six yards divided by three yards." This means "How many 3-yard lengths are contained in a 6-yard length?" We readily see that the answer is 2. Hence, 6 yards ÷ 3 yards = 2. Not 2 yards, but just plain 2.

Now then, what is the meaning of 6 yards ÷ 2? This is read "6 yards divided by 2," and means "How long is each piece when a 6-yard length is divided into 2 equal lengths?" We readily see that the answer is 3 yards. Not plain 3, but 3 yards.

From the above instances we see that division is the reverse of multiplication. Hence, 6 yards ÷ 3 yards also means "What number multiplied by 3 yards = 6 yards?" And hence, 6 yards ÷ 2 means "What number of yards multiplied by 2 = 6 yards?"

PROBLEMS. What is the meaning of and the answer to the following:

1. 10 pounds ÷ 5	**4.** 16 yards ÷ 2
2. 12 yards ÷ 3	**5.** 16 yards ÷ 2 yards
3. 15 inches ÷ 5 inches	**6.** 8 boxes ÷ 4

The number divided is called the *dividend.* The number that does the dividing is called the *divisor* and the result is called the *quotient.* Thus, in the expression "6 yards ÷ 3 yards = 2," 6 yards is the dividend, 3 yards is the divisor and 2 is the quotient.

What is the meaning of 6 ÷ 3? This may mean only one of the following:

(a) How many parts are contained in 6 when the size of each part is 3? Or:

(b) What is the size of each part when 6 contains 3 equal parts? Or:

(c) How many times is 3 contained in 6? Or:

(d) How many times does 3 go into 6? Or:

(e) What number multiplied by 3 equals 6?

Regardless of the meaning, however, the quotient is 2.

PROBLEMS. Tell which is the dividend, the divisor and the quotient in the following problems, and using the multiplication table, find the quotient:

7. $42 \div 6$ **13.** $54 \div 9$
8. $45 \div 5$ **14.** $81 \div 9$
9. $2 \div 1$ **15.** $100 \div 10$
10. $2 \div 2$ **16.** 72 shuttles $\div$ 8 shuttles
11. 49 bobbins $\div$ 7   **17.** $100 \div 100$
12. $49 \div 49$ **18.** 100 heddles $\div$ 100 heddles

SHORT DIVISION

An easy way to divide a number of two or more digits by a number of one digit when we can't find the quotient at a glance, is by **short division.** Suppose we wish to divide 287 by 7. Set them down like this:

$7 \overline{)287}$

We see that the divisor, 7, is not contained in 2, the first digit of the dividend. Then we try the first two digits of the dividend. 7 is contained in 28, 4 times. Set the 4 above the line directly over the 8.

$\dfrac{4}{7 \overline{)287}}$

We now see that 7 is contained in 7, 1 time, or once. Set the 1 above the 7 of the dividend and the job is done. Therefore, the quotient of $287 \div 7 = 41$.

$\dfrac{41}{7 \overline{)287}}$

To prove that 41 is the quotient of $287 \div 7$, multiply 41 by 7 and the product is 287.

$\begin{array}{r} 41 \\ \underline{7} \\ 287 \end{array}$

EXAMPLE: *How many times is 9 contained in 81,999?*

$\dfrac{9111}{9 \overline{)81999}}$ **Answer:**   9111 times.

EXAMPLE: *How many times does 3 go into 666?*

$\dfrac{222}{3 \overline{)666}}$

PROBLEMS.   Find the quotients of:

19. $355 \div 5$ **21.** $396 \div 3$
20. $468 \div 2$ **22.** $7299 \div 9$

Suppose we wish to divide 6080 by 8. Set the dividend and divisor down as before.

$8 \overline{)60\ 80}$

$\dfrac{7}{8 \overline{)60^4 80}}$

8 is not contained in the six. 8 is contained in 60, but not "evenly." What is the nearest number to 60, but smaller than 60, into which 8 goes "evenly"? $8 \times 7 = 56$; $60 - 56 = 4$. So 8 goes into 60, 7 times with a *remainder* of 4. Put the 7 over the 0 of the 60 and "carry" the remainder, 4, in front of the 8 of the dividend.

$\dfrac{7\ 6}{8 \overline{)60^4 80}}$

8 goes into 48, 6 times "evenly." Put the 6 over the 8 of the dividend.

How many times does 8 go into 0? In other words, how

$\frac{7\ 60}{8)\,60^4 80}$

many times is something contained in nothing? No times, or zero times, of course. Put the 0 over the 0 of the dividend and we have the answer, 760.

EXAMPLE: *How many times does 6 go into 320,430?*

$\frac{53405}{6)\,320430}$

PROBLEMS.   Find the quotients of:

23. 7350 ÷ 5	**27.** 1673 pounds ÷ 7
24. 1442 ÷ 7	**28.** 1728 yards ÷ 6 yards
25. 1791 ÷ 9	**29.** 720320 ÷ 8
26. 8040 ÷ 8	**30.** 818271 ÷ 9

LONG DIVISION

When the divisor contains more than one digit, another easy way to divide is by *long division.*

$13)\,\overline{20865}$

Suppose we wish to divide 20,865 by 13. We set the divisor and dividend down as before. 13 will not go into 2. It will go into 20, 1 time.

$\frac{1}{13)\,20865}$
$\underline{13}$
7

Place the 1 over the 0 of the 20. Multiply the 1 by the divisor, 13, and set the product under the 20 of the dividend. Subtract the 13 from the 20. The difference, or remainder, is 7.

$\frac{16}{13)\,20865}$
$\underline{13}$
78
$\underline{78}$

Bring down the next digit of the dividend, 8, and place it after the remainder, 7. We see that 13 goes into 78, 6 times. Put the 6 over the 8 of the dividend. We multiply the divisor, 13, by the 6, placing the product under the 78 as we do our multiplying. The product is 78. Subtracting 78 from 78, we have no remainder.

$\frac{160}{13)\,20865}$
$\underline{13}$
78
$\underline{78}$
6

Bring down the 6. 13 goes into 6, 0 times. Put the 0 over the 6. We could multiply the 13 by 0. The product would be 0. Then we could subtract the 0 and get a remainder of 6. Then we would be no further along than we are now. So bring down the next digit, 5, putting it after the 6.

$\frac{1605}{13)\,20865}$
$\underline{13}$
78
$\underline{78}$
65
$\underline{65}$
0

We see that 13 goes into 65, 5 times. Put the 5 over the 5 of the dividend and multiply as before, obtaining 65 for a product. Subtracting 65 from 65, there is no remainder. There are no more digits in the dividend. Hence, the division is completed.

EXAMPLE: *Divide* 324,000 *by* 150.

$$\begin{array}{r} 2164 \\ \hline 150\overline{)324600} \\ 300 \\ \hline 246 \\ 150 \\ \hline 960 \\ 900 \\ \hline 600 \end{array}$$

PROBLEMS:

31. If 504 looms are divided equally between 12 weavers, how many looms will be each weaver's share?

32. If a loom will weave 225 yards of cloth in a week, how many weeks will be required for it to weave 9675 yards?

33. A cloth of 48 warp threads per inch contains 1728 warp threads. How wide is the cloth?

34. 840 yards of number one yarn weigh one pound. How many pounds in 74,760 yards?

35. A 60,032 spindle plant is equipped with spinning frames containing 224 spindles to a frame. How many spinning frames are there in the plant?

YARN AND ROVING NUMBERS

The number of yarn is found by dividing 1000 by the number of grains that 120 yards weigh.

EXAMPLE: *120 yards of a certain size of yarn weigh* 10 *grains. What is the number of the yarn.*

$1000 \div 10 = 100$. The number of the yarn is 100.

36. What is the number of the yarn if 120 yards weigh 20 grains?

37. What is the number of the yarn if 120 yards weigh 25 grains?

38. What is the number of the yarn if 120 yards weigh 40 grains?

39. What is the number of the yarn if 120 yards weigh 50 grains?

The number of roving is found by dividing 100 by the number of grains that 12 yards weigh.

40. What is the number of the roving if 12 yards weigh 10 grains?

41. What is the number of the roving if 12 yards weigh 20 grains?

42. What is the number of the roving if 12 yards weigh 25 grains?

43. What is the number of the roving if 12 yards weigh 50 grains?

44. What is the number of the roving if 12 yards weigh 100 grains?

45. If a certain frame produces 4576 pounds of a certain size roving in a day, how many days will be required for it to produce 13,728 pounds?

46. 70 spinning frames, 224 spindles to each frame, spin 62,720 pounds in a week. How many pounds does each spindle run?

47. A plant runs 300 days in a year, and manufactures 12,400 bales of cloth averaging 1260 yards per bale. Find the average yards manufactured per day.

48. A 64 yard piece of picker lap weighs 4 pounds. How many ounces does each yard of lap weigh?

49. A picker lap weighs 14 ounces per yard. How many yards should there be in a lap weighing 84 pounds?

Chapter VI

MULTIPLES, PRIME NUMBERS, & FACTORS

Even Numbers. Any number that can be evenly divided by 2 is an *even number*. Thus, 2, 4, 6, 8, 10 and any number whose right-hand digit is 2, 4, 6, 8 or 0 is an even number because it is divisible by 2.

Odd Numbers. All numbers that are not even numbers are *odd numbers*. Therefore, all numbers whose right-hand digit is 1, 3, 5, 7 or 9 are odd numbers.

Multiples. A product of two or more numbers is a *multiple* of those numbers. 2 × 3 = 6. Therefore, 6 is a multiple of 2. Therefore, also, 6 is a multiple of 3. 30 is a multiple of 2. 30 is a multiple of 15. 30 is also a multiple of 3. 30 is also a multiple of 10. 30 is also a multiple of 5 and also of 6.

Prime Numbers. Any number that is not a multiple of other numbers is a *prime number*. In other words, a number that cannot be divided by another number (except itself and 1) is a prime number. Thus, 1, 2, 3, 5, 7, 11, 13, 17 and many other numbers are prime numbers.

Factors. Numbers which multiplied together make another number are *factors* of that number. In other words, a multiple has factors. A prime number has no factors. Thus, 2 and 15; 3 and 10; 5 and 6; and 2, 3, and 5 are factors of 30. 2 is a factor of 30; 15 is a factor of 30; 3 is a factor of 30, and so on.

Prime Factors. The prime numbers which multiplied together make another number are *prime factors* of that number. Thus, the prime factors of 30 are 2, 3 and 5.

Multiples of 2. All even numbers, as we have seen, are multiples of 2. That is, 2 is a factor of all even numbers.

Multiples of 3. A number is divisible by 3 if the sum of its digits is divisible by 3. The sum of the digits of 129 = 1 + 2 + 9 = 12. 12 is divisible by 3. Therefore, we shall find that 129 is a multiple of 3.

Multiples of 5. Any number ending in 5 or 0 is a multiple of 5.

The finding of factors and multiples is of very frequent necessity in textile calculations.

FINDING THE PRIME FACTORS

In factoring we use the division sign made like this:)_____ instead of like this:)

EXAMPLE: Find the prime factors of 420.

420 is a multiple of 2 because it is an even number.   2)420

210 is a multiple of 2 because it is an even number.   2)210

105 is a multiple of 5 because it ends in 5.   5)105

21 is a multiple of 3 because the sum of its digits is divisi- 3)21
ble by 3.

7 is a prime number because it cannot be divided by any   7
other number except itself and 1.

Therefore, the prime factors of 420 are 2, 2, 3, 5 and 7.
Proof: $2 \times 2 \times 3 \times 5 \times 7 = 420$.

EXAMPLE: *Find the prime factors of 6006.*

2)6006
3)3003   11
7)1001   13)143
13)143   13
    11   13

The prime factors are 2, 3, 7, 13 and 11.

PROBLEMS.   Find the prime factors of:

1. 120	**4.** 175	**7.** 540	**10.** 1001
2. 128	**5.** 210	**8.** 239	**11.** 3432
3. 150	**6.** 291	**9.** 840	**12.** 31416

Least Common Multiple.   The smallest number that is a multiple of two or more numbers is their *least common multiple*. Thus, the least common multiple of 4 and 6 is 12.

FINDING THE LEAST COMMON MULTIPLE

EXAMPLE: *Find the least common multiple of 24, 30 and 36.*

We must first find the prime factors of each number.

2	24	2	30	2	36
2	12	3	15	2	18
2	6		5	3	9
	3				3

The least common multiple since it is to contain 24, 30 and 36 must contain all the prime factors that make up each number. We start with the smallest number, 24. The least common multiple to contain 24 must therefore contain 2, 2, 2, and 3. We set down 2, 2, 2 and 3.

The prime factors of 30 are 2, 3 and 5. Therefore, the least common multiple must contain 2, 3 and 5. But we have already set down a 2 and a 3. Hence, for 30 we set down the 5 only.

The prime factors of 36 are 2, 2, 3 and 3. We have already set down two 2's and one 3. Hence, for 36 we set down one 3.

Hence, the least common multiple $= 2 \times 2 \times 2 \times 3 \times 5 \times 3 = 360$.

Find the least common multiple of the following groups of numbers:

13. 12, 16 and 24   **18.** 24, 36, 48 and 72
14. 8, 12 and 24   **19.** 10, 12, 18 and 24
15. 5, 9, 10, 15 and 30   **20.** 39, 52 and 91
16. 7, 9, 14 and 21   **21.** 36, 144 and 180
17. 7, 11 and 13   **22.** 12, 18, 24, 36 and 42

Chapter VII

THE MEANING OF FRACTIONS

UNITS

When we are talking about yards, the **unit** is *one yard*. The word **unit** means *one*. In other words, when we are thinking of yards, one means one yard. That is, in all calculations dealing with yards, one yard is the unit. On the other hand, in all calculations dealing with feet, the **unit** is *one foot*. And when we are dealing with inches, the **unit** is *one inch*. So we must always keep clearly in mind the unit with which we are dealing, for we see that the yard unit is 3 times as large as the foot unit and the foot unit is 12 times as large as the inch unit. When we are calculating with yards, the whole number 2 means 2 yards. When we are calculating in inches, the whole number 2 means 2 inches. Now then, when we are calculating in yard units and we wish to express 2 inches, how shall we do it? This brings up the subject of *fractions*.

THE FRACTION AS A PART OR PARTS OF A UNIT

So far in this book we have learned to add, multiply, divide, and subtract whole numbers; that is, whole units. The word *fraction* means a *part* of a *unit*. A fraction consists of a number directly above another number with a line between. Thus, $\frac{1}{4}$ is a fraction. This fraction is called "one-fourth" or "one-quarter." If we are dealing with inches, $\frac{1}{4}$ means a length that is equal to 1 part when the inch unit is divided into 4 equal parts.

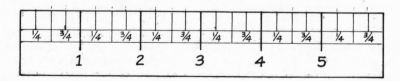

On the ruler shown above, $\frac{1}{4}$ would therefore mean one of the smallest lengths, spaces or distances. That is, $\frac{1}{4}$ would mean the distance between any two adjacent cross lines.

The fraction $\frac{2}{4}$, when we are dealing with inches, would mean a length that is equal to 2 parts when the inch unit is divided into 4 equal parts. Hence, on the ruler $\frac{2}{4}$ means any length equal to 2 of the smallest spaces. That is, $\frac{2}{4} = \frac{1}{4} + \frac{1}{4} = 2 \times \frac{1}{4}$.

Similarly, $\frac{4}{4}$, when we are dealing with inches, means a length that is equal to 4 parts when the inch unit is divided into 4 equal parts. Hence, on the ruler $\frac{4}{4}$ means any length equal to 4 of the smallest spaces. That is, $\frac{4}{4} = \frac{1}{4} + \frac{1}{4} + \frac{1}{4} + \frac{1}{4} = 4 \times \frac{1}{4}$. But 4 of these spaces = 1 inch. Hence, $\frac{4}{4} = \frac{1}{4} + \frac{1}{4} + \frac{1}{4} + \frac{1}{4} = 4 \times \frac{1}{4} = 1$.

We see that the fraction $\frac{1}{2}$, when we are dealing with inches, means a length that is equal to 1 part when the inch unit is divided into 2 equal parts. This fraction is called "one-half." Hence, on the ruler $\frac{1}{2}$ means any length that is equal to the distance between one of the longest cross lines and the adjacent next to the longest line. But we also see that this length is equal to two of the smallest spaces. Hence, $\frac{1}{2} = \frac{1}{4} + \frac{1}{4} = \frac{2}{4}$.

The fraction $\frac{8}{2}$, when we are dealing in inches, means a length equal to 8 parts when the inch unit is divided into 2 equal parts. Hence, on the ruler $\frac{8}{2}$ means any length equal to 8 of the spaces between any one of the longest cross lines and the adjacent next to longest cross line. Hence, $\frac{8}{2} = \frac{1}{2} + \frac{1}{2} + \frac{1}{2} + \frac{1}{2} + \frac{1}{2} + \frac{1}{2} + \frac{1}{2} + \frac{1}{2} = 8 \times \frac{1}{2}$. But, by counting, we see that 8 of these spaces equals 4 inches. Hence, the fraction $\frac{8}{2} = \frac{1}{2} + \frac{1}{2} + \frac{1}{2} + \frac{1}{2} + \frac{1}{2} + \frac{1}{2} + \frac{1}{2} + \frac{1}{2} = 8 \times \frac{1}{2} = 4$.

Numerator and Denominator. From the preceding discussion, we see that in a fraction the number above the line shows the number of parts of the unit to be considered, while the number below the line shows the total number of parts into which the unit is divided. For this reason, the number above the unit is called the **numerator**, which means "*numberer*"; while the number below is called the **denominator**, which means "*namer*," that is, it names the size of the parts, whether they are halves, fourths and so on.

PROBLEMS. **Locate the cross lines of the ruler that show the distances from the left end of the ruler expressed by the following fractions or whole numbers:**

1. $\dfrac{1}{4}$	4. $\dfrac{4}{4}$	7. $\dfrac{5}{4}$	10. $\dfrac{7}{4}$	13. 2	16. $\dfrac{11}{4}$
2. $\dfrac{1}{2}$	5. $\dfrac{2}{2}$	8. $\dfrac{6}{4}$	11. $\dfrac{8}{4}$	14. $\dfrac{6}{2}$	17. $\dfrac{12}{4}$
3. $\dfrac{3}{4}$	6. 1	9. $\dfrac{3}{2}$	12. $\dfrac{4}{2}$	15. 3	18. $\dfrac{10}{2}$

READING OF FRACTIONS

There is a certain method of reading fractions which you will "pick up" from the following:

$\dfrac{1}{2}$ is read one-half; $\dfrac{2}{2}$ is read two-halves; $\dfrac{7}{2}$ is read seven-halves; $\dfrac{3}{4}$ is read three-fourths or three-quarters; $\dfrac{1}{5}$ is read one-fifth; $\dfrac{1}{3}$ is read one-third; $\dfrac{4}{3}$ is read four-thirds; $\dfrac{1}{4}$ is read one-fourth or one-quarter; $\dfrac{7}{5}$ is read seven-fifths; $\dfrac{1}{6}$ is read one-sixth; $\dfrac{5}{6}$ is read five-sixths; $\dfrac{1}{7}$ is read one-seventh; $\dfrac{1}{10}$ is read one-tenth; $\dfrac{1}{20}$ is read one-twentieth; $\dfrac{1}{21}$ is read one twenty-first; $\dfrac{1}{22}$ is read one twenty-second; $\dfrac{31}{31}$ is read thirty-one thirty-firsts; $\dfrac{25}{42}$ is read twenty-five forty-seconds; $\dfrac{50}{100}$ is read fifty one-hundredths; $\dfrac{2}{261}$ is read two two-hundred-sixty-firsts; $\dfrac{11}{1000}$ is read eleven one-thousandths.

PROBLEMS.   Read the following fractions:

19. $\dfrac{15}{2}$	23. $\dfrac{13}{15}$	27. $\dfrac{140}{44}$
20. $\dfrac{33}{6}$	24. $\dfrac{7}{8}$	28. $\dfrac{3}{23}$
21. $\dfrac{40}{5}$	25. $\dfrac{333}{33}$	29. $\dfrac{10}{24}$
22. $\dfrac{44}{4}$	26. $\dfrac{33}{13}$	30. $\dfrac{15}{11}$

31. $\dfrac{21}{109}$ **33.** $\dfrac{55}{545}$ **35.** $\dfrac{101}{1000}$

32. $\dfrac{7}{112}$ **34.** $\dfrac{91}{100}$ **36.** $\dfrac{2}{2000}$

MEANING OF MIXED NUMBERS

A *mixed number* is a number composed of a whole number and a fraction. Thus, $1\frac{1}{2}$ is a mixed number. It means $1 + \frac{1}{2}$. It is read "one and one-half."

If the unit being considered is inches, $1\frac{1}{2}$ means one whole inch plus one-half an inch. On the ruler $1\frac{1}{2}$ inches would mean any distance equal to the distance from the left end of the ruler to the $\frac{1}{2}$-inch cross mark between the 1-inch and 2-inch marks. We see that this distance is also equal to $\frac{1}{2}+\frac{1}{2}+\frac{1}{2}$. Hence, $1\frac{1}{2}=$ $\frac{1}{2}+\frac{1}{2}+\frac{1}{2}=3\times\frac{1}{2}$. Similarly, $3\frac{1}{4}$ yards means 3 yards plus $\frac{1}{4}$ of a yard.

PROBLEMS. Read the following mixed numbers and locate the cross lines of the ruler that show the distances from the left end of the ruler expressed by these mixed numbers:

37. $1\frac{1}{4}$ **40.** $2\frac{2}{4}$ **43.** $4\frac{1}{4}$ **46.** $5\frac{3}{4}$

38. $1\frac{3}{4}$ **41.** $2\frac{1}{2}$ **44.** $5\frac{1}{2}$ **47.** $3\frac{3}{4}$

39. $2\frac{1}{4}$ **42.** $5\frac{3}{4}$ **45.** $5\frac{1}{4}$ **48.** $3\frac{1}{4}$

Express the following numbers in the form of digits and fractions; that is, in the form of mixed numbers:

49. Ten and eleven-sixteenths.

50. Two hundred twenty-five and thirty-seven two-hundred-and-firsts.

51. One hundred sixteen and one-hundred-forty-one one-thousandths.

52. Seventeen and two-hundred-twenty-two two-thousandths.

THE FRACTION AS AN INDICATED DIVISION

So far from our own study of fractions we see that $\frac{4}{4}=1$; that $\frac{8}{2}=4$; that $\frac{2}{2}=1$; and that $\frac{8}{4}=2$. We see also that $\frac{4}{2}=2$; that $\frac{6}{2}=3$; that $\frac{12}{4}=3$; that

$\frac{10}{2} = 5$. We see from our study of division, however, that if we divide the numerator of any one of these fractions by the denominator we obtain the same result as locating the point on the ruler. That is, $4 \div 4 = 1$; $8 \div 2 = 4$; $2 \div 2 = 1$; $8 \div 4 = 2$; $4 \div 2 = 2$; $6 \div 2 = 3$; $12 \div 4 = 3$; $10 \div 2 = 5$. Hence, we see that a fraction also means that the numerator is to be divided by the denominator. Therefore, $\frac{4}{4}$ means $4 \div 4$; $\frac{8}{2}$ means $8 \div 2$; $\frac{12}{4}$ means $12 \div 4$; $\frac{5}{7}$ means $5 \div 7$; $\frac{9}{11}$ means $9 \div 11$, and so on. Now then, we can divide 4 by 4 and get 1; we can divide 8 by 2 and get 4; but we cannot divide 5 by 7, or 9 by 11 and get anything simpler than $\frac{5}{7}$ or $\frac{9}{11}$. In other words, we cannot *perform* the division, we can only *indicate* it. Hence, we say that a fraction is an *indicated division*. Sometimes in textile plant calculations, as we shall see later, even though we can *perform* the division and find a simple quotient, it is convenient merely to *indicate* the division by making the dividend and the divisor the numerator and denominator of a fraction.

Indicate the following in fractional form:

53. Fifty-seven divided by sixteen.

54. One thousand six hundred eighty divided by eight hundred forty.

55. The number of pieces when a piece of belting 57 inches long is cut into 16-inch lengths.

56. The length in inches of each piece when 57 inches of belting is cut into 16 pieces.

57. The number of 840-yard lengths contained in 1680 yards.

58. The number of times 120 yards is contained in 840 yards.

59. The number of times 840 yards is contained in 12 yards.

60. The weight of one yard of cloth when 7 yards weigh 1 pound.

Finding the Value. *Finding the value* of an expression means actually performing the operations indicated. Thus, to find the value of 2×2 we actually multiply 2×2 and obtain the product, 4. To find the value of the fraction $\frac{16}{2}$ we actually divide 16 by 2 and obtain the quotient, 8.

Find the value of the following fractions:

61. $\frac{10}{5}$ **63.** $\frac{30}{5}$ **65.** $\frac{1}{2}$ **67.** $\frac{100}{25}$ **69.** $\frac{97}{11}$

62. $\frac{12}{3}$ **64.** $\frac{42}{7}$ **66.** $\frac{3}{4}$ **68.** $\frac{99}{11}$ **70.** $\frac{1000}{40}$

THE MEANING OF A DENOMINATOR OF 1

Since a fraction indicates that the numerator is to be divided by the denominator, the fraction $\frac{2}{1}$ means $2 \div 1$ which, of course, equals 2. Hence, the value of any fraction with a denominator of 1 equals the numerator. Thus, $\frac{30}{1} = 30$. And, therefore, we can make any number into a fraction by making it the numerator of a fraction whose denominator is 1. Thus, $4 = \frac{4}{1}$ or $100 = \frac{100}{1}$.

Chapter VIII

REDUCTION OF FRACTIONS, CANCELLATION & DIVISION WITH FRACTIONAL REMAINDERS

Let us consider the fraction $\frac{12}{6}$. We see at once that the value of $\frac{12}{6}$ is 2.

Now let us multiply both the numerator and denominator of $\frac{12}{6}$ by 5. We then

have $\frac{12 \times 5}{6 \times 5}$ or $\frac{60}{30}$. Dividing 60 by 30 we see that the value of the fraction $\frac{60}{30}$ is

2. Hence, *we can multiply both numerator and denominator of a fraction by the same number without changing its value.* That is,

$$\frac{12}{6} = \frac{5 \times 12}{5 \times 6} = \frac{60}{30}; \quad \text{or} \quad \frac{1}{2} = \frac{5 \times 1}{5 \times 2} = \frac{5}{10};$$

or

$$\frac{3}{500} = \frac{3 \times 10}{500 \times 10} = \frac{30}{5000}, \text{ and so on.}$$

Let us consider the fraction $\frac{40}{8}$. The value of this fraction is 5. Now let

us divide both numerator and denominator of $\frac{40}{8}$ by 4. We then have $\frac{40 \div 4}{8 \div 4}$ or

$\frac{10}{2}$. The value of the fraction is still 5. Hence, *we can divide both numerator and denominator of a fraction by the same number without changing its value.*

Reducing a fraction to higher terms means multiplying the numerator and denominator by the same number. Reducing a fraction to lower terms means dividing both numerator and denominator by the same common factor. Reducing a fraction to lowest terms means dividing both numerator and denominator by their largest common factor. (See chapter VI.)

EXAMPLE: *Reduce $\frac{3}{4}$ to higher terms so that the fraction will have*

a denominator of 48.

First, we must find what number multiplied by 4 will give 48.

$4)\overline{48} \qquad 4 \times 12 = 48. \qquad 3 \times 12 = 36$
$\quad\overline{12}$

Therefore, $\dfrac{3}{4} = \dfrac{36}{48}$.

EXAMPLE: *Reduce $\dfrac{5}{71}$ to a fraction with a denominator of* 284.

$$71\overset{\displaystyle 4}{\overline{)284}}$$
$$\underline{284}$$
$$0 \quad \text{Therefore, } \dfrac{5}{71} = \dfrac{20}{284}.$$

PROBLEMS: Reducing to higher terms:

1. Reduce $\dfrac{1}{25}$ to a fraction with a denominator of 75.

2. Reduce $\dfrac{3}{4}$ to a fraction with a denominator of 36.

3. Reduce $\dfrac{7}{8}$ to a fraction with a denominator of 96.

4. Reduce $\dfrac{5}{4}$ to a fraction with a denominator of 100.

5. Reduce $\dfrac{7}{20}$ to a fraction with a denominator of 120.

EXAMPLE: *Reduce $\dfrac{10}{5}$ to lowest terms.*

We see at once that the largest factor common to both numerator and denominator is 5. $10 \div 5 = 2$. $5 \div 5 = 1$. Therefore, $\dfrac{10}{5} = \dfrac{2}{1} = 2$.

EXAMPLE: *Reduce $\dfrac{12}{3}$ to lowest terms.*

$$\dfrac{12}{3} = 4$$

EXAMPLE: *Reduce $\dfrac{6}{8}$ to lowest terms.*

2 is the largest number that will divide both numerator and denominator. Therefore, $\dfrac{6}{8} = \dfrac{3}{4}$.

Reduce the following fractions to lowest terms:

6. $\dfrac{2}{4}$ 7. $\dfrac{3}{6}$ 8. $\dfrac{2}{8}$ 9. $\dfrac{2}{6}$ 10. $\dfrac{3}{9}$

11. $\dfrac{4}{12}$ 13. $\dfrac{3}{15}$ 15. $\dfrac{25}{5}$ 17. $\dfrac{39}{3}$ 19. $\dfrac{36}{21}$

12. $\dfrac{15}{3}$ 14. $\dfrac{4}{20}$ 16. $\dfrac{13}{39}$ 18. $\dfrac{3}{39}$ 20. $\dfrac{12}{36}$

In order to reduce fractions with large numerators and denominators to lowest terms when we cannot see their largest common factor at a glance, it is necessary to use longer methods.

EXAMPLE: *Reduce* $\dfrac{240}{504}$ *to lowest terms.*

First, find the prime factors of 240 and 504. (See chapter VI.)

```
2)240        2)504
2)120        2)252
 2)60        2)126
 2)30         3)63
 3)15         3)21
   5            7
```

The common prime factors are three 2's and one 3. Hence, we divide both numerator and denominator by $2 \times 2 \times 2 \times 3$. But instead of dividing, we merely keep the factors that are left in the numerator and denominator after the common factors are removed. Hence, reduced to lowest terms, $\dfrac{240}{504} = \dfrac{2 \times 5}{3 \times 7} = \dfrac{10}{21}$.

Reduce the following fractions to lowest terms:

21. $\dfrac{21}{189}$ 23. $\dfrac{288}{512}$ 25. $\dfrac{756}{1140}$

22. $\dfrac{250}{550}$ 24. $\dfrac{154}{198}$ 26. $\dfrac{851}{1219}$

REDUCTION BY CANCELLATION

This method is called *cancellation* because we *cancel,* or scratch out, the numerator and denominator as we divide.

EXAMPLE: *Reduce* $\dfrac{26}{182}$ *to lowest terms.*

$\dfrac{26}{182}$ We see at a glance that both numerator and denominator are divisible by 2.

$\dfrac{13}{\cancel{26}}$
$\dfrac{\cancel{182}}{91}$ Divide each by 2; cancel out the 26 and 182 and replace them with 13 and 91. We see that the new numerator and denominator are divisible by 13.

$$\begin{array}{c} 1 \\ \cancel{13} \\ \cancel{26} \\ \cancel{182} \\ \cancel{91} \\ 7 \end{array}$$

Divide each by 13; cancel out the 13 and 91 and replace them with 1 and 7.

Therefore, $\dfrac{26}{182} = \dfrac{1}{7}$.

EXAMPLE: *Reduce* $\dfrac{44}{198}$ *to lowest terms.*

$$\begin{array}{c} 2 \\ \cancel{22} \\ \cancel{44} \\ \cancel{198} \\ \cancel{99} \\ 9 \end{array} = \dfrac{2}{9}$$

Canceling Final 0 Digits.   Suppose we wish to reduce $\dfrac{10}{120}$. Dividing both numerator and denominator by 10, we would have $\dfrac{1}{12}$. But this has the same effect as if we merely canceled out the 0's.

EXAMPLE: *Reduce* $\dfrac{250}{3600}$.

$\dfrac{25\cancel{0}}{360\cancel{0}}$ **Answer:** $\dfrac{25}{360} = \dfrac{5}{72}$.

EXAMPLE: *Reduce* $\dfrac{2500}{3600}$ *to lowest terms.*

$\dfrac{25\cancel{0}\cancel{0}}{36\cancel{0}\cancel{0}}$ **Answer:** $\dfrac{25}{36}$.

Reduce the following fractions by cancellation to lowest terms:

27. $\dfrac{1001}{91}$ 29. $\dfrac{210}{540}$ 31. $\dfrac{45}{495}$

28. $\dfrac{7000}{840}$ 30. $\dfrac{540}{7000}$ 32. $\dfrac{840}{31416}$

REDUCTION OF MIXED NUMBERS TO FRACTIONS

We have seen that $1\dfrac{1}{2}$ means $\dfrac{1}{2}+\dfrac{1}{2}+\dfrac{1}{2}$. From the definition of a fraction, the numerator shows the number of parts to be considered while the denominator shows the kind of parts. Hence, $\dfrac{1}{2}+\dfrac{1}{2}+\dfrac{1}{2}=\dfrac{3}{2}$. Similarly, we can show that $1\frac{1}{4} = 1 + \frac{1}{4} = \frac{4}{4} + \frac{1}{4} = \frac{5}{4}$; and also that $2\frac{3}{4} = 2 + \frac{3}{4} = \frac{8}{4} + \frac{3}{4} = \frac{11}{4}$. These conclusions can easily be verified by counting off spaces on the ruler. Now we see that since $1\frac{1}{2} = \frac{3}{2}$ and $1\frac{1}{4} = \frac{5}{4}$ and $2\frac{3}{4} = \frac{11}{4}$, all we have to do to reduce a mixed number to a fraction is to multiply the whole number by the denominator of the fraction and add the numerator to the product. Thus, in the case of $1\frac{1}{2}$, $1 \times 2 + 1 = 3$; put the 3 over the 2 and we have the answer, $\frac{3}{2}$. In the case of $2\frac{3}{4}$, $2 \times 4 + 3 = 11$; put the 11 over the 4 and we have the answer, $\frac{11}{4}$.

EXAMPLE: *Reduce $5\frac{5}{6}$ to a fraction.*

$5 \times 6 + 5 = 35$.   **Answer:** $\frac{35}{6}$.

Reduce the following mixed numbers to fractions:

33. $2\frac{1}{4}$ **35.** $7\frac{1}{11}$ **37.** $10\frac{6}{7}$ **39.** $25\frac{4}{5}$

34. $5\frac{3}{4}$ **36.** $9\frac{3}{13}$ **38.** $13\frac{1}{12}$ **40.** $10\frac{3}{100}$

REDUCTION OF FRACTIONS TO MIXED AND WHOLE NUMBERS

From the definition of a fraction we know that the numerator shows the number of parts to be considered, while the denominator shows the kind of parts. Hence, $\frac{15}{4} = \frac{12}{4} + \frac{3}{4}$. But $\frac{12}{4} = 3$. Therefore, $\frac{15}{4} = 3 + \frac{3}{4}$. From the definition of a mixed number, $3\frac{3}{4}$ means $3 + \frac{3}{4}$. Therefore, $\frac{15}{4} = 3\frac{3}{4}$. This can be verified on the ruler by counting off 15 one-fourth-inch spaces and finding that the distance from the left end of the ruler is 3 inches plus 3 one-fourth-inch spaces. Hence, to reduce a fraction to a mixed number, we divide the denominator into the numerator and keep the remainder as a new numerator. Of course, when there is no remainder, the fraction is reduced to a whole number.

EXAMPLE: *Reduce $\frac{235}{4}$ to a mixed number.*

We see that the numerator and denominator have no common factors. We, then, divide by short division.

$\begin{array}{r} 5\ 8 \\ 4\overline{)23^3 5^3} \end{array}$ We see that after dividing 4 into 35 we have a remainder of 3.

$$\text{Hence:} \quad \frac{235}{4} = 58\frac{3}{4}.$$

EXAMPLE: *Reduce* $\dfrac{3245}{16}$ *to a mixed number.*

$$\begin{array}{r} 202 \\ 16\overline{)3245} \\ \underline{32} \\ 45 \\ \underline{32} \\ 13 \end{array}$$

Answer: $202\dfrac{13}{16}.$

EXAMPLE: *Reduce* $\dfrac{7000}{840}$ *to a mixed number.*

We see at a glance that numerator and denominator have common factors.

$$\begin{array}{r} 25 \\ \cancel{100} \\ \cancel{7000} \\ \hline \cancel{840} \\ \cancel{12} \\ 3 \end{array}$$

$$3\overline{)25} \quad \overset{8}{}$$

Answer: $8\dfrac{1}{3}.$

EXAMPLE: *Reduce* $\dfrac{1358}{14}.$

$$\begin{array}{r} 97 \\ \cancel{679} \\ \cancel{1358} \\ \hline \cancel{14} \\ \cancel{7} \end{array}$$

Answer: 97.

Reduce the following fractions to mixed or whole numbers:

41. $\dfrac{6}{2}$	44. $\dfrac{7}{4}$	47. $\dfrac{147}{16}$	50. $\dfrac{6400}{720}$
42. $\dfrac{9}{3}$	45. $\dfrac{10}{3}$	48. $\dfrac{200}{40}$	51. $\dfrac{70000}{31416}$
43. $\dfrac{20}{5}$	46. $\dfrac{19}{5}$	49. $\dfrac{694}{7}$	52. $\dfrac{38750}{2500}$

LONG AND SHORT DIVISION WITH FRACTIONAL REMAINDERS

In Chapter V we learned how to divide numbers when there is no final remainder. We are now prepared to divide numbers with fractional remainders.

EXAMPLE: *Divide 88 by 5.*

$$1\ 7\frac{3}{5}$$
$$5\overline{)8^38^3}\qquad \textbf{Answer:}\quad 17\frac{3}{5}.$$

EXAMPLE: *Divide 1255 by 27.*

$$46\frac{13}{27}$$
$$27\overline{)1255}$$
$$\underline{108}$$
$$175$$
$$\underline{162}$$
$$13\quad \textbf{Remainder.}$$

Answer: $46\dfrac{13}{27}$

PROBLEMS: If necessary review Yarn and Roving Numbers, Chapter V.

53. Ten bobbins of roving weigh 39 pounds. What does each bobbin weigh?

54. If 120 yards of yarn weigh 75 grains, what is the weight of each yard?

55. If a piece of cloth 60 yards in length is cut into 4 equal parts, how many yards will each part contain?

56. A reed 42 inches long contains 945 dents. How many dents are there to an inch?

57. A picker lap containing 50 yards weighs 45 pounds. How many ounces does each yard weigh?

58. 6 yards of card sliver weigh 351 grains. What is the weight of the card sliver per yard?

Chapter IX

ADDITION
&
SUBTRACTION
OF FRACTIONS
& MIXED NUMBERS

ADDITION OF FRACTIONS

From the definition of fractions we have seen that the numerator shows the number of parts to be considered and the denominator shows the kinds of parts. Hence, if we wish to add two or more fractions all of which have the same denominator, we merely add their numerators. Thus, $\frac{1}{4} + \frac{2}{4} = \frac{3}{4}$; $\frac{1}{2} + \frac{3}{2} + \frac{2}{2} = \frac{6}{2} = 3$. These conclusions can easily be verified by counting off spaces on the ruler. This is just as simple as adding 1 bobbin and 2 bobbins and getting 3 bobbins for an answer.

PROBLEMS. Add the following fractions and reduce your answers to lowest terms. If the numerator is larger than the denominator, reduce your answer to a mixed or whole number. Check your answers by counting spaces on a ruler:

1. $\frac{1}{4} + \frac{3}{4}$ 3. $\frac{2}{4} + \frac{7}{4} + \frac{1}{4}$ 5. $\frac{3}{4} + \frac{5}{4} + \frac{1}{4} + \frac{3}{4}$

2. $\frac{2}{4} + \frac{5}{4}$ 4. $\frac{1}{2} + \frac{7}{2} + \frac{3}{2}$ 6. $\frac{2}{4} + \frac{3}{4} + \frac{5}{4} + \frac{7}{4}$

Least Common Denominator. Fractions to be added must have the same denominator; that is, a *common denominator*. Fractions not having the same denominator, must be reduced to a common denominator; and in order to save work should be reduced to their *least common denominator*.

EXAMPLE: *Add* $\frac{6}{4} + \frac{1}{2}$.

We see at once that $\frac{6}{4} = \frac{3}{2}$. Therefore, $\frac{6}{4} + \frac{1}{2} = \frac{3}{2} + \frac{1}{2} = \frac{4}{2} = 2$.

Answer: 2.

EXAMPLE: *Add* $\dfrac{3}{10} + \dfrac{1}{5}$.

We see at once that $\dfrac{1}{5} = \dfrac{2}{10}$. Therefore, $\dfrac{3}{10} + \dfrac{1}{5} = \dfrac{3}{10} + \dfrac{2}{10} = \dfrac{5}{10} = \dfrac{1}{2}$.

Answer: $\dfrac{1}{2}$.

EXAMPLE: *Add* $2\dfrac{4}{9} + \dfrac{2}{3}$.

$$2\dfrac{4}{9} + \dfrac{2}{3} = 2\dfrac{4}{9} + \dfrac{6}{9} = 2\dfrac{10}{9} = 2 + \dfrac{10}{9} = 2 + 1\dfrac{1}{9} = 3\dfrac{1}{9}.$$

Answer: $3\dfrac{1}{9}$.

In the two preceding examples, the common denominator to which the fractions were reduced was also the least common multiple of the separate denominators. When we cannot at once see the least common multiple of the separate denominators, we must find it by the usual process as shown in chapter VI.

EXAMPLE: *Add* $\dfrac{5}{24} + \dfrac{7}{30} + \dfrac{1}{48}$.

```
2)24        2)30        2)48
2)12        3)15        2)24
2)6          5          2)12
 3                      2)6
                         3
```

Least common denominator $= 2 \times 2 \times 2 \times 3 \times 5 \times 2 = 240$. $\dfrac{5}{24}$ reduced to a fraction with a denominator of 240 gives us $\dfrac{50}{240}$. $\dfrac{7}{30}$ reduced to a fraction with a denominator of 240 gives us $\dfrac{56}{240}$. $\dfrac{1}{48}$ reduced to a fraction with a denominator of 240 gives us $\dfrac{5}{240}$. Adding the numerators $(50 + 56 + 5)$, we obtain the new numerator 111. Hence $\dfrac{5}{24} + \dfrac{7}{30} + \dfrac{1}{48} = \dfrac{111}{240}$. Reducing $\dfrac{111}{240}$, we obtain $\dfrac{37}{80}$.   **Answer:** $\dfrac{37}{80}$.

PROBLEMS: Add the following by the method most suitable to each problem:

7. $3\dfrac{1}{6} + \dfrac{3}{6} + \dfrac{8}{12}$ 9. $\dfrac{5}{22} + \dfrac{3}{11} + \dfrac{9}{99}$

8. $2\dfrac{3}{8} + \dfrac{5}{16} + \dfrac{1}{24}$ 10. $11\dfrac{1}{4} + 14\dfrac{1}{8} + 1\dfrac{1}{5}$

11. $\dfrac{3}{40} + \dfrac{1}{16} + \dfrac{3}{32}$ **14.** $\dfrac{3}{40} + \dfrac{6}{35} + \dfrac{3}{25}$

12. $\dfrac{1}{24} + \dfrac{3}{28} + \dfrac{4}{36}$ **15.** $10\dfrac{1}{13} + 3\dfrac{1}{5} + 8\dfrac{1}{12}$

13. $\dfrac{3}{28} + \dfrac{4}{30} + \dfrac{5}{36}$

A convenient way of adding mixed numbers is to set them down in a column as in ordinary addition.

EXAMPLE: *Add* $13\dfrac{1}{4}$, $22\dfrac{1}{2}$, $45\dfrac{1}{3}$, *and* $64\dfrac{2}{3}$.

$13\dfrac{1}{4}$ $\dfrac{3}{12}$

$22\dfrac{1}{2}$ $\dfrac{6}{12}$

$45\dfrac{1}{3}$ $\dfrac{4}{12}$

$64\dfrac{2}{3}$ $\dfrac{8}{12}$

$\overline{144}$ $\dfrac{21}{12} = 1\dfrac{9}{12}$

$1\dfrac{9}{12}$

$145\dfrac{9}{12}$

Add the whole numbers.
Find the common denominator of the fractions. We see that the common denominator is 12. Convert the fractions to 12ths and put the new numerators in a column at the right. Add the numerators, put the sum over the common denominator and reduce to a mixed number. Add the mixed number to the sum of the whole numbers. This sum is the answer.

Answer: $145\dfrac{9}{12}$.

16. Section No. 1 made $3\dfrac{1}{4}$ pounds of filling waste in one day; section No. 2 made $3\dfrac{3}{4}$ pounds; section No. 3 made 4 pounds; and section No. 4 made $2\dfrac{1}{2}$ pounds. How many pounds of waste did the four sections make?

17. What would be the total weight of 4 pieces of cloth weighing as follows: the first, $10\dfrac{1}{4}$ pounds; the second, $9\dfrac{1}{4}$ pounds; the third, $12\dfrac{3}{4}$; and the fourth, $14\dfrac{1}{2}$ pounds?

18. Four balls of waste weighed as follows: first ball, $12\dfrac{1}{2}$ pounds;

second ball, $13\frac{3}{4}$; third ball, $9\frac{1}{4}$ pounds; and the fourth ball, $10\frac{1}{2}$ pounds. What was the total weight of the four balls?

19. The friction on a slasher was run too tight and made 4 bad warps with waste as follows: first beam, $10\frac{3}{4}$ pounds; second beam, $9\frac{1}{4}$ pounds; third beam, $12\frac{1}{2}$ pounds; and the fourth beam, $13\frac{1}{2}$ pounds. What was the total waste?

SUBTRACTION OF FRACTIONS

EXAMPLE: *Find the difference between $\frac{5}{4}$ and $\frac{2}{4}$.*

$$\frac{5}{4} - \frac{2}{4} = \frac{3}{4} \qquad \textbf{Answer:} \quad \frac{3}{4}$$

EXAMPLE: *Find the difference between $\frac{4}{16}$ and $\frac{3}{8}$.*

$$\frac{4}{16} = \frac{2}{8} \qquad \frac{3}{8} - \frac{2}{8} = \frac{1}{8} \qquad \textbf{Answer:} \quad \frac{1}{8}.$$

EXAMPLE: *Subtract $\frac{1}{5}$ from $\frac{3}{10}$.*

$$\frac{1}{5} = \frac{2}{10} \qquad \frac{3}{10} - \frac{2}{10} = \frac{1}{10} \qquad \textbf{Answer:} \quad \frac{1}{10}.$$

EXAMPLE: *Subtract $\frac{2}{9}$ from $2\frac{3}{9}$.*

$$2\frac{3}{9} - \frac{2}{9} = 2\frac{1}{9} \qquad \textbf{Answer:} \quad 2\frac{1}{9}.$$

EXAMPLE: *What is the difference between $\frac{2}{3}$ and $2\frac{4}{9}$?*

$$2\frac{4}{9} - \frac{2}{3} = \frac{22}{9} - \frac{6}{9} = \frac{16}{9} = 1\frac{7}{9} \qquad \textbf{Answer:} \quad 1\frac{7}{9}.$$

EXAMPLE: *Find the difference between $8\frac{25}{30}$ and $5\frac{7}{36}$.*

$2\overline{)30}$ $2\overline{)36}$ Least common denominator is $2 \times 3 \times 5 \times 2 \times 3 =$

$3\overline{)15}$ $2\overline{)18}$ 180.

   5      $3\overline{)9}$

           3

$$8\frac{25}{30} \qquad 150$$

$$-5\frac{7}{36} \qquad -\ 35$$

$$\overline{3} \qquad \frac{115}{180} = \frac{23}{36}$$

$$+\ \frac{23}{36}$$

$$\overline{3\frac{23}{36}}$$

Subtract the whole numbers. Convert the fractions to 180ths and put the new numerators in a column to the right. Subtract the new numerators, put the difference over the common denominator and reduce. Add the difference of the fractions to the difference of the numerators.

Answer: $3\frac{23}{36}$.

EXAMPLE: *Find the difference between* $8\frac{25}{30}$ *and* $5\frac{35}{36}$.

Least common denominator is 180.

$$\overset{7}{\cancel{8}}\frac{25}{30} \qquad 180$$

$$\qquad\qquad 150$$

$$-5\frac{35}{36} \qquad \overline{330}$$

$$\overline{2} \qquad -\ 175$$

$$+\ \frac{31}{36} \qquad \frac{155}{180} = \frac{31}{36}$$

$$\overline{2\frac{31}{36}}$$

Explanation: $8\frac{25}{30} = 8\frac{150}{180} = 8 + \frac{150}{180} = 7 +$

$1 + \frac{150}{180} = 7 + \frac{180}{180} + \frac{150}{180} = 7\frac{330}{180}$.

Proceed as in the previous example.

Answer: $2\frac{31}{36}$.

Find the difference between the following numbers by the method most suitable to each problem. Do as much of the work in your head as possible.

20. $\frac{3}{2}$ and $\frac{9}{2}$

21. $\frac{7}{8}$ and $\frac{3}{8}$

22. $1\frac{1}{8}$ and $1\frac{5}{8}$

23. $3\frac{3}{16}$ and $4\frac{1}{16}$

24. $5\frac{3}{16}$ and $7\frac{1}{8}$

25. $10\frac{1}{8}$ and $9\frac{7}{8}$

26. $12\frac{15}{16}$ and $12\frac{3}{8}$

27. $13\frac{6}{7}$ and $21\frac{1}{3}$

28. $21\frac{13}{95}$ and $\frac{4}{19}$

29. $10\frac{23}{36}$ and $29\frac{11}{30}$

30. 32 and $26\frac{19}{31}$

31. $101\frac{1}{18}$ and $93\frac{5}{6}$

32. A certain warper beam when full weighs $517\frac{1}{4}$ pounds. The

empty beam weighs $98\frac{3}{4}$ pounds. What is the weight of the yarn on the beam?

33. The weight of warp in a cut of cloth is $9\frac{3}{4}$ pounds. If the weight of the cut is $15\frac{1}{2}$ pounds, what is the weight of the filling?

34. The width of the finished cloth on a certain loom is $34\frac{1}{2}$ inches. The width of the warp in the reed is $36\frac{1}{16}$ inches. How much does the cloth contract in width during weaving?

35. A certain cut of warp as it came from the slasher was $63\frac{1}{12}$ yards long. The cloth woven from this warp measured $59\frac{1}{2}$ yards long. How much did the warp contract during weaving?

Chapter X

MULTIPLICATION OF FRACTIONS

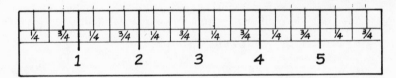

Multiplication of Fractions and Whole Numbers. Multiplication always means adding a number to itself a certain number of times. Hence, $4 \times \frac{1}{2}$ must mean $\frac{1}{2} + \frac{1}{2} + \frac{1}{2} + \frac{1}{2}$. From what we have learned of addition of fractions, $\frac{1}{2} + \frac{1}{2} + \frac{1}{2} + \frac{1}{2} = \frac{4}{2}$. Therefore, $4 \times \frac{1}{2} = \frac{4}{2} = \frac{4 \times 1}{2} = 2$. By counting off $4 \frac{1}{2}$-inch spaces on the above ruler, we arrive at the 2-inch mark. Similarly, $4 \times \frac{3}{4}$ means $\frac{3}{4} + \frac{3}{4} + \frac{3}{4} + \frac{3}{4} = \frac{12}{4} = \frac{4 \times 3}{4} = 3$. We can verify this also by counting off $\frac{3}{4}$-inch spaces on the ruler. Hence, *to multiply a fraction by a whole number we multiply the numerator by the whole number and place the product over the denominator.*

Meaning of the Word "Of" after a Fraction. When we say "a fourth of 4 inches," we really mean the length of one of the parts when 4 inches are divided into 4 equal parts, which, of course, is a 1-inch length. When we say "three quarters of 4 inches," we really mean 3 times one of these 1-inch lengths, which, of course, is a 3-inch length. That is, $\frac{1}{4}$ of $4 = 1$; $\frac{3}{4}$ of $4 = 3$.

But from the preceding paragraph $\frac{1}{4} \times 4 = 1$ and $\frac{3}{4} \times 4 = 3$. Hence, $\frac{1}{4}$ of $4 = \frac{1}{4} \times 4$ and $\frac{3}{4}$ of $4 = \frac{3}{4} \times 4$. Therefore, "of" between a fraction and another number means to multiply the number and the fraction together.

Multiplication of a Fraction by a Fraction. When we say "$\frac{1}{2}$ of $\frac{3}{2}$ of an inch" we really mean the length of one of the parts when $\frac{3}{2}$ of an inch is divided into 2 equal parts. Looking at the ruler we see that this is $\frac{3}{4}$ of an inch. From the preceding paragraph we see that $\frac{1}{2}$ of $\frac{3}{2} = \frac{1}{2} \times \frac{3}{2}$. Therefore, $\frac{1}{2} \times \frac{3}{2} = \frac{3}{4} = \frac{1 \times 3}{2 \times 2}$. Hence, *to multiply one fraction by another, we multiply the numerators together and the denominators together.*

EXAMPLE: *Multiply 4 by* $\frac{3}{5}$.

$$4 \times \frac{3}{5} = \frac{4 \times 3}{5} = \frac{12}{5} = 2\frac{2}{5}$$

EXAMPLE: *Multiply* $\frac{4}{5}$ *by* $\frac{3}{5}$.

$$\frac{4}{5} \times \frac{3}{5} = \frac{4 \times 3}{5 \times 5} = \frac{12}{25}$$

PROBLEMS. **Perform the following multiplications, reducing and checking your answers on the ruler:**

1. $5 \times \frac{1}{2}$ 4. $\frac{1}{2} \times 7$ 7. $\frac{1}{2} \times \frac{2}{2}$ 10. $\frac{3}{2} \times \frac{5}{2}$

2. $6 \times \frac{1}{2}$ 5. $10 \times \frac{1}{4}$ 8. $\frac{1}{2} \times 1$ 11. $\frac{4}{2} \times \frac{3}{2}$

3. $7 \times \frac{1}{4}$ 6. $\frac{1}{2} \times 10$ 9. $\frac{5}{2} \times \frac{1}{2}$ 12. $\frac{4}{2} \times \frac{5}{2}$

Cancellation.   Suppose we wish to multiply $\frac{6}{5}$ by $\frac{10}{9}$.

$$\frac{6}{5} \times \frac{10}{9} = \frac{6 \times 10}{5 \times 9} = \frac{60}{45} = 1\frac{1}{3}$$

Instead of multiplying and then reducing, let us reduce first, $\frac{6}{5} \times \frac{10}{9} = \frac{6 \times 10}{5 \times 9}$. We see that we can divide both numerator and denominator of this fraction by 3 and by 5, as follows:

$$\frac{\overset{2}{\cancel{6}} \times \overset{2}{\cancel{10}}}{\underset{1}{\cancel{5}} \times \underset{3}{\cancel{9}}} = \frac{2 \times 2}{1 \times 3} = \frac{4}{3} = 1\frac{1}{3}.$$

5 divides into 5, 1 time. It is not necessary, however, to put down the 1. We now see that we could have canceled when our problem was in the form of $\frac{6}{5} \times \frac{10}{9}$ as follows:

$$\overset{2}{\cancel{\frac{6}{5}}} \times \underset{3}{\overset{2}{\cancel{\frac{10}{9}}}} = \frac{4}{3} = 1\frac{1}{3}$$

EXAMPLE: *Multiply* $4 \times \frac{3}{4} \times \frac{5}{6} \times \frac{3}{5}$.

$$4 \times \frac{\cancel{3}}{\cancel{4}} \times \frac{\cancel{5}}{\cancel{6}} \times \underset{2}{\frac{3}{\cancel{5}}} = \frac{3}{2} = 1\frac{1}{2}$$

Perform the following multiplication, using cancellation:

13. $\dfrac{10}{13} \times \dfrac{25}{3} \times \dfrac{13}{30} \times 12$ **15.** $\dfrac{2}{3} \times \dfrac{7}{5} \times 30 \times \dfrac{10}{21}$

14. $\dfrac{1}{26} \times \dfrac{39}{70} \times \dfrac{35}{42} \times 10$ **16.** $840 \times \dfrac{4}{7000} \times \dfrac{60}{16}$

MULTIPLICATION OF MIXED NUMBERS

Multiplication of a Whole Number and a Mixed Number.   Suppose we wish to multiply $142\frac{3}{8}$ by 117.

$$142\frac{3}{8} \times 117 = \frac{1139}{8} \times 117 = \frac{133262}{8} = 16657\frac{7}{8}$$

$$
\begin{array}{r}
142\frac{3}{8} \\
117\frac{8}{} \\
\hline
994 \\
142 \\
142 \\
\hline
43\frac{7}{8} \\
\hline
16657\frac{7}{8}
\end{array}
\qquad
\begin{array}{r}
117 \\
3 \\
\hline
8)351 \\
43\frac{7}{8}
\end{array}
$$

We can also do this problem as shown to the left. Set the numbers down in the usual manner for multiplication. Multiply the whole part of the mixed number and the whole number. Then find the value of $\frac{3}{8} \times 117$. Then add. This is usually an easier method when the mixed number is large.

Suppose we wish to multiply 239 by $112\frac{2}{3}$.

$$239 \times 112\frac{2}{3} = 239 \times \frac{338}{3} = 26927\frac{1}{3}$$

239

$112\frac{2}{3}$

$\frac{}{478}$

239

239

$159\frac{1}{3}$

$\frac{}{26927\frac{1}{3}}$

239

2

$\frac{}{3)478}$

$159\frac{1}{3}$

We can also do this problem by setting the numbers down in the usual manner for multiplication. This method is usually the easier method when the mixed number is large.

Multiplication of Mixed Numbers by Fractions and Mixed Numbers. Suppose we wish to multiply $14\frac{1}{2}$ by $\frac{1}{2}$.

$$14\frac{1}{2} \times \frac{1}{2} = \frac{29}{2} \times \frac{1}{2} = \frac{29}{4} = 7\frac{1}{4}$$

Suppose we wish to multiply $239\frac{1}{2}$ by $12\frac{2}{3}$.

$$239\frac{1}{2} \times 12\frac{2}{3} = \frac{479}{2} \times \frac{\overset{19}{\cancel{38}}}{3} = 3033\frac{2}{3}$$

We could set this problem down in the usual manner for multiplication and perform the work, but it is not practical to do so.

Multiply the following numbers by the more suitable method:

17. $1\frac{1}{2} \times 3$ **19.** $240 \times 12\frac{3}{5}$ **21.** $1\frac{1}{2} \times 4\frac{1}{2}$

18. $3\frac{3}{4} \times 7$ **20.** $477 \times 24\frac{2}{3}$ **22.** $15\frac{2}{3} \times 14\frac{3}{8}$

EXAMPLE: *There are 16 ounces in a pound. How many ounces in three-quarters of a pound?*

$$\frac{3}{4} \times \overset{4}{\cancel{16}} = 12$$ **Answer:** 12 ounces in $\frac{3}{4}$ of a pound.

PROBLEMS:

23. (a) How many ounces in seven-eighths of a pound?
    (b) How many ounces in eleven-sixteenths of a pound?
24. There are 36 inches in a yard.
    (a) How many inches in two-thirds of a yard?
    (b) How many inches in three-quarters of a yard?

25. There are 7000 grains in a pound. How many grains in four-sevenths of a pound?

26. There are 60 minutes in one hour.

    (a) How many minutes in three-quarters of an hour?

    (b) How many minutes in two-thirds of an hour?

27. How many yards of cloth will 420 looms weave in 48 hours if one loom weaves $4\frac{1}{4}$ yards per hour?

28. The knock-off motion on a picker is set to make lap rolls containing 68 yards of lap. If the lap weighs $13\frac{3}{4}$ ounces per yard, how many pounds and ounces should the full lap roll weigh?

29. If a lap roll containing 48 yards of what is supposed to be $14\frac{1}{2}$-ounce lap (that is, $14\frac{1}{2}$ ounces per yard) weighs $42\frac{3}{4}$ pounds, how many pounds is it short of what it is supposed to weigh?

30. If a reed has $22\frac{1}{4}$ dents in one inch, how many dents in 40 inches?

31. If it costs $28\frac{3}{4}$ cents to manufacture one yard of cloth, what will it cost to manufacture 12 yards?

32. How many ends would there be in the warp of a certain kind of cloth if the cloth is $34\frac{3}{4}$ inches wide and has 64 warp ends per inch?

33. The front roll of a roving frame is delivering $596\frac{8}{10}$ inches of roving per minute and the spindle puts $1\frac{1}{2}$ twists per inch in the roving; how many turns is the spindle making in a minute?

NOTE: Each turn of the spindle puts one turn in the roving.

34. A weaver earned $112 in a week and another weaver earned $\frac{6}{7}$ as much. What did the last weaver earn?

35. A certain cloth weighs one-seventh of a pound per yard. What should be the weight of a $58\frac{1}{2}$-yard cut?

36. A mill receives the following castings from the foundry: 27 gear blanks; $3\frac{1}{8}$ pounds each; 42 treadle rolls, $\frac{1}{2}$ pound each; 90 treadles, $4\frac{1}{16}$ pounds each. Find the number of pounds of casting received.

37. An alloy used for machine bearings is $\frac{24}{29}$ copper, $\frac{4}{29}$ tin and $\frac{1}{29}$ zinc. How many pounds of each in 261 pounds of alloy?

Chapter XI

DIVISION OF FRACTIONS & REDUCTION OF COMPLEX FRACTIONS

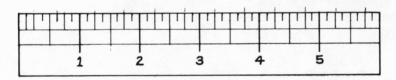

Division of Fractions and Mixed Numbers by a Whole Number. We have seen that $\frac{3}{4}$ means the same thing as $3 \times \frac{1}{4}$. Therefore, $\frac{3}{4}$ divided by $3 = \frac{1}{4}$ just like 3 yards divided by 3 means 1 yard. By taking the first $\frac{3}{4}$ of an inch on the ruler and then taking one of the 3 equal parts into which it is divided, we see we have $\frac{1}{4}$ of an inch. Hence, $\frac{3}{4} \div 3 = \frac{1}{4}$. Similarly, $2\frac{1}{2} \div 5 = \frac{5}{2} \div 5 = \frac{1}{2}$.

PROBLEMS. Find the value of the following expressions and check your answers on the ruler:

1. $\frac{6}{8} \div 2$ 3. $\frac{7}{8} \div 7$ 5. $\frac{12}{8} \div 4$ 7. $2\frac{1}{4} \div 3$

2. $\frac{6}{8} \div 3$ 4. $\frac{5}{8} \div 5$ 6. $1\frac{1}{8} \div 3$ 8. $4\frac{3}{8} \div 7$

Complex Fractions as Indicated Divisions. There is another way of setting down the above problems. We have learned that a fraction is also an indicated division. Hence, we can indicate the division of a fraction by a whole number by making the fraction the numerator and the whole number the denominator. Thus, we can put down $\frac{3}{4} \div 3$ in this manner: $\frac{\frac{3}{4}}{3}$. This is one kind of a *complex fraction* or *complicated fraction*. In our textile calculations we shall have all kinds of complex fractions. We have seen that $\frac{3}{4} \div 3 = \frac{1}{4}$.

Therefore, $\dfrac{\dfrac{3}{4}}{3} = \dfrac{1}{4}$. Similarly, $\dfrac{1\dfrac{1}{8}}{3} = \dfrac{\dfrac{9}{8}}{3} = \dfrac{3}{8}$.

Find the value of the following expressions, checking your results on the ruler:

9. $\dfrac{\dfrac{10}{8}}{2}$ 12. $\dfrac{1\dfrac{1}{4}}{5}$ 15. $\dfrac{3\dfrac{3}{4}}{5}$ 18. $\dfrac{2\dfrac{5}{8}}{3}$

10. $\dfrac{\dfrac{12}{4}}{4}$ 13. $\dfrac{3\dfrac{1}{4}}{13}$ 16. $\dfrac{6\dfrac{3}{4}}{3}$ 19. $\dfrac{2\dfrac{5}{8}}{7}$

11. $\dfrac{\dfrac{12}{4}}{3}$ 14. $\dfrac{3\dfrac{3}{4}}{3}$ 17. $\dfrac{6\dfrac{3}{4}}{9}$ 20. $\dfrac{3\dfrac{1}{8}}{5}$

There is another way of dividing a fraction by a whole number. $\dfrac{3}{4} \div 3 = \dfrac{1}{4}$. We could have gotten the same result by multiplying the denominator of the fraction by the whole number. Thus, $\dfrac{3}{4} \div 3 = \dfrac{3}{4 \times 3} = \dfrac{3}{12} = \dfrac{1}{4}$. That is to say, multiplying the denominator has the same effect as dividing the numerator. Putting the problem in the form of a complex fraction,

$$\dfrac{\dfrac{3}{4}}{3} = \dfrac{3}{3 \times 4} = \dfrac{1}{4}.$$

Multiplying the denominator is the only way we can divide a fraction by a whole number when the numerator of the fraction is not divisible by the whole number. For instance,

$$\dfrac{\dfrac{1}{2}}{4} = \dfrac{1}{4 \times 2} = \dfrac{1}{8}.$$

We can verify this on the rule by taking one of the parts resulting from dividing $\dfrac{1}{2}$ an inch into 4 equal parts and finding that it is $\dfrac{1}{8}$ of an inch.

Find the value of the following expressions:

21. $\dfrac{1}{2} \div 2$ 22. $\dfrac{3}{4} \div 2$ 23. $\dfrac{\dfrac{5}{8}}{2}$

24. $\dfrac{\frac{5}{8}}{3}$ **26.** $1\frac{1}{8} \div 2$ **28.** $9\frac{7}{10} \div 24$

25. $\dfrac{\frac{7}{16}}{5}$ **27.** $\dfrac{2\frac{5}{9}}{3}$ **29.** $\dfrac{45\frac{17}{100}}{22}$

Oftentimes we can divide some mixed numbers without reducing them to fractions. What is the value of $4\frac{1}{2} \div 2$? Since $4\frac{1}{2} = 4 + \frac{1}{2}$, we see at once that $4\frac{1}{2} \div 2 = 2 + \dfrac{1}{2 \times 2} = 2\frac{1}{4}$. Similarly, $3\frac{3}{8} \div 3 = 1\frac{1}{8}$.

Find the value of the following without putting any work on paper:

30. $2\frac{1}{2} \div 2$ **32.** $3\frac{3}{4} \div 3$ **34.** $\dfrac{15\frac{3}{7}}{3}$ **36.** $\dfrac{100\frac{1}{2}}{25}$

31. $4\frac{3}{4} \div 2$ **33.** $\dfrac{10\frac{5}{8}}{5}$ **35.** $\dfrac{18\frac{7}{8}}{3}$ **37.** $\dfrac{50\frac{1}{2}}{50}$

Inversion and Reciprocals.   To *invert* means to turn upside down. Thus, $\frac{2}{3}$ *inverted* is $\frac{3}{2}$. $\frac{3}{2}$ is the *reciprocal* of $\frac{2}{3}$; and $\frac{2}{3}$ is the reciprocal of $\frac{3}{2}$. To state it another way, $\frac{2}{3}$ and $\frac{3}{2}$ are reciprocals. $\frac{4}{5}$ inverted is $\frac{5}{4}$; $\frac{4}{5}$ and $\frac{5}{4}$ are reciprocals. In the last paragraph, chapter VII, we learned the meaning of a denominator of 1. That is, $\frac{2}{1} = 2$, $2 = \frac{2}{1}$; $5 = \frac{5}{1}$, $\frac{5}{1} = 5$. Hence, 2 $\left(\text{that is, } \frac{2}{1}\right)$ inverted is $\frac{1}{2}$; or $\frac{1}{2}$ is the reciprocal of 2.

Dividing Whole Numbers by Fractions and Mixed Numbers.   Suppose we wish to divide 2 by $\frac{1}{2}$. Looking on the ruler, this means the number of $\frac{1}{2}$-inch lengths contained in a 2-inch length. We see at once that there are $4\frac{1}{2}$-inch lengths in a 2-inch length. Hence, $2 \div \frac{1}{2} = 4$. Or since a fraction is an indicated division, we can make the whole number the numerator and the fraction the denominator of a complex fraction. We can, therefore, set the problem down this way:

$$2 \div \frac{1}{2} = \dfrac{2}{\frac{1}{2}} = 4.$$

Similarly, we can show on the ruler that $\dfrac{3}{\frac{3}{8}} = 8$, since there are $8\frac{3}{8}$-inch

lengths in a 3-inch length. From this we see that $\dfrac{2}{\frac{1}{2}}$ is the same as $2 \times \dfrac{2}{1}$,

because $\dfrac{2}{\frac{1}{2}} = 4$ and $2 \times \dfrac{2}{1} = 4$. Similarly, $\dfrac{3}{\frac{3}{8}}$ is the same as $3 \times \dfrac{8}{3}$, because

$\dfrac{3}{\frac{3}{8}} = 8$ and $3 \times \dfrac{8}{3} = \dfrac{\cancel{3} \times 8}{\cancel{3}} = 8$. Hence, *to divide a whole number by a fraction,*

we merely invert the divisor and multiply.

EXAMPLE: *Divide 5 by* $1\frac{1}{4}$.

$$\frac{5}{1\frac{1}{4}} = \frac{5}{\frac{5}{4}} = 5 \times \frac{4}{5} = 4$$

Find the value of the following expressions, checking the answers of the first three problems on the ruler. Do as many as possible without paper and pencil:

38. $\dfrac{1}{\frac{1}{2}}$ 41. $\dfrac{3}{\frac{1}{8}}$ 44. $\dfrac{6}{2\frac{1}{8}}$ 46. $100 \div 1\frac{1}{9}$

39. $\dfrac{1}{\frac{1}{4}}$ 42. $\dfrac{4}{1\frac{1}{2}}$ 45. $\dfrac{7}{\frac{7}{8}}$ 47. $\dfrac{1000}{71\frac{3}{7}}$

40. $2 \div \dfrac{1}{8}$ 43. $5 \div 1\dfrac{3}{4}$

Division of Fractions and Mixed Numbers by Fractions and Mixed Numbers. Suppose we wish to divide $\frac{3}{4}$ by $\frac{3}{8}$. On the ruler this means the

number of times that a $\frac{3}{8}$-inch length is contained in a $\frac{3}{4}$-inch length. At once

we see that this is 2 times. Hence, $\frac{3}{4} \div \frac{3}{8} = 2$. But we see that $\frac{3}{4} \div \frac{3}{8}$ is the same

as $\frac{3}{4} \times \frac{8}{3}$, because $\frac{3}{4} \div \frac{3}{8} = 2$, and $\frac{3}{4} \times \frac{8}{3} = \dfrac{\cancel{3} \times \overset{2}{\cancel{8}}}{\cancel{4} \times \cancel{3}} = 2$. Therefore, to divide a frac-

tion by a fraction, we invert the divisor and multiply.

EXAMPLE: *Divide* $5\frac{1}{4}$ *by* $2\frac{1}{16}$.

$$\frac{5\frac{1}{4}}{2\frac{1}{16}} = \frac{\frac{21}{4}}{\frac{33}{16}} = \frac{\cancel{21}^{7}}{\cancel{4}} \times \frac{\cancel{16}^{4}}{\cancel{33}_{11}} = \frac{28}{11} = 2\frac{6}{11}$$

EXAMPLE: *Find the value of the following expressions, checking the answers to the first four problems on the ruler:*

48. $\dfrac{\frac{1}{2}}{\frac{1}{4}}$ 52. $\dfrac{6\frac{1}{4}}{\frac{5}{8}}$ 56. $101\frac{2}{3} \div 11\frac{1}{4}$

49. $\dfrac{\frac{1}{4}}{\frac{1}{8}}$ 53. $\dfrac{8\frac{1}{8}}{1\frac{1}{4}}$ 57. $\dfrac{102\frac{7}{18}}{204\frac{7}{9}}$

50. $\dfrac{4\frac{1}{2}}{\frac{3}{4}}$ 54. $2\frac{1}{6} \div 10\frac{1}{9}$

51. $\dfrac{3}{8} \div \dfrac{1}{8}$ 55. $7\frac{2}{9} \div 17\frac{1}{7}$

General Rule for Division of All Numbers.   The following instances of division show that the general rule of inverting the divisor and multiplying applies to all numbers:

(a) $\dfrac{6}{2} = 3, \cancel{6}^{3} \times \dfrac{1}{\cancel{2}} = 3$ (c) $\dfrac{2}{\frac{6}{2}} = \dfrac{2}{3}, \cancel{2} \times \dfrac{2}{\cancel{6}_{3}} = \dfrac{2}{3}$

(b) $\dfrac{\frac{6}{2}}{2} = \dfrac{3}{2}, \dfrac{\cancel{6}^{3}}{2} \times \dfrac{1}{\cancel{2}} = \dfrac{3}{2}$ (d) $\dfrac{\frac{3}{2}}{\frac{6}{2}} = \dfrac{\frac{3}{2}}{3} = \dfrac{1}{2}, \dfrac{\cancel{3}}{\cancel{2}} \times \dfrac{\cancel{2}}{\cancel{6}_{2}} = \dfrac{1}{2}$

Therefore, remember that when you cannot divide in any other manner, invert the divisor and multiply.

Averages.   Finding the average is common in the testing of material in a textile plant. The meaning and use of averages is evident from the following:

EXAMPLE: *The rolls of lap from a certain picker are supposed to weigh* 50 *pounds. 4 laps weigh as follows:* $70\frac{1}{2}$ *pounds,* $69\frac{3}{4}$ *pounds,*

$70\frac{1}{4}$ *pounds,* $69\frac{1}{2}$ *pounds. What is the average weight of the laps?*

$70\frac{1}{2}$ $\left(\frac{2}{4}\right)$

$69\frac{3}{4}$ $\left(\frac{3}{4}\right)$

$70\frac{1}{4}$ $\left(\frac{1}{4}\right)$

$\underline{69\frac{1}{2}}$ $\left(\frac{2}{4}\right)$ $4\overline{)280}^{\,70}$ Average weight = 70 pounds.

278        $\left(\frac{8}{4}=2\right)$ Thus, the average weight gives us a more
$\underline{2}$ accurate idea of the weight of the run of the laps
280   than if we took the weight of one lap.

58. Find the average weight of a cut of cloth if four cuts weigh as
follows: $15\frac{7}{8}$ pounds, $15\frac{3}{4}$ pounds, 16 pounds, $15\frac{7}{8}$ pounds.

59. It is desired to find the average weight of some roving frame
bobbins. We find that 12 bobbins weigh $4\frac{1}{2}$ pounds. What is the average
weight (in pounds) of these bobbins?

60. A certain cloth $30\frac{3}{4}$ inches wide between selvages contains 12
repeats of the warp pattern.
(a) How wide is each repeat of the warp?
(b) If there are 205 warp ends in each repeat, how many warp
ends are there in one inch?

61. A $59\frac{1}{2}$-yard cut of a certain cloth weighs 18 pounds. How
many yards are there to the pound?

62. 6 yards of sliver weigh $313\frac{1}{2}$ grains. What is the weight per
yard?

63. If one yard of cloth weighs $\frac{3}{16}$ of a pound, how many yards
should there be in a 57-pound roll?

64. If a loom weaves $3\frac{3}{4}$ yards of cloth in one hour, how long will
be required to weave a cut of 120 yards?

65. There are $3\frac{2}{10}$ yards of a certain kind of cloth to a pound.
What is the weight of one yard?

66. How many yards of picker lap weighing $15\frac{1}{2}$ ounces per yard are there in a 68-pound roll of lap?

67. If a picker lap weighs $14\frac{3}{4}$ ounces per yard, how many yards are there in a $66\frac{1}{2}$-pound roll of lap?

68. A reed $43\frac{3}{4}$ inches long contains 980 dents. How many dents are there per inch?

69. A piece of ply yarn 12 inches long placed in the twist counter requires 270 turns to untwist it. What is its twist per inch?

Chapter XII

THE MEANING OF DECIMALS; ADDITION & SUBTRACTION OF DECIMALS

All of our previous study of fractions has concerned *common fractions*. We now take up *decimal fractions*, or *decimals*. Decimals are fractions, the denominators of which are 10 or multiples of 10. However, in the decimal system of fractions we write $\frac{1}{10}$ as follows: .1. The dot before the 1 is called the *decimal point,* or *point.* Our starting place, therefore, in the study of decimals is that $\frac{1}{10}$ is written .1. From this we shall reason out everything about decimals. Practically all textile calculations are in the form of decimals rather than common fractions, because decimals are much more convenient to use.

We know that $100 \div 10 = 10$; that $10 \div 10 = 1$; that $1 \div 10 = .1$. That is to say, whenever we divide a number by 10, the first digit of the quotient "moves" one "place" to the right. How can we express in decimal form the fraction $\frac{1}{100}$? In other words, what is the quotient of $.\frac{1}{10}$? $\left(\frac{1}{100} = \frac{\frac{1}{10}}{10} = .\frac{1}{10}\right)$. We have seen that whenever we divide by 10 we "move" the first digit of the quotient one place to the right. Therefore, $\frac{1}{100}$ in the decimal system would be written .1, leaving one blank place between the point and the digit. But we are apt to misunderstand how many places are intended to be left between the point and the digit. So, for each blank place intended, we put in a zero. Thus, $\frac{1}{100}$ is written .01. Similarly, $\frac{1}{1000}$ is written .001; and $\frac{1}{10000}$ is written .0001. Now we see that we can make this statement: To divide a number by 10, we "move" the decimal point one place to the left. That is, $.1 \div 10 = .01$; $.01 \div 10 = .001$; $.001 \div 10 = .0001$.

Since to divide by 10 we move the decimal point one place to the left, and since $1 \div 10 = .1$, therefore, the decimal point with a whole number must be placed directly after its right-hand digit. That is, the decimal point with the whole number 1 must be placed like this: 1. Therefore, 1. means the whole number 1; 2. means the whole number 2; 10. means the whole number 10, and so on.

Since .1 means $\frac{1}{10}$, .2 must mean $\frac{2}{10}$, .9 must mean $\frac{9}{10}$; and since .01

means $\dfrac{1}{100}$, .09 must mean $\dfrac{9}{100}$. Similarly, .003 must mean $\dfrac{3}{1000}$, and .009 must mean $\dfrac{9}{1000}$.

What is the meaning of .10? It cannot mean $\dfrac{10}{10}$, because 1. means $\dfrac{10}{10}$. We know that .09 means $\dfrac{9}{100}$. Therefore, .10 must mean $\dfrac{10}{100}$. Similarly, .11 means $\dfrac{11}{100}$ and .99 means $\dfrac{99}{100}$.

Therefore, we see that one digit to the right of the decimal point means tenths; two digits to the right of the decimal point means hundredths; three digits to the right of the decimal point means thousandths; four digits to the right means ten-thousandths, and so on.

EXAMPLE: *Read the following decimal and write down its meaning as a common fraction:*   .5590.

This decimal has four digits to the right of the decimal point. Therefore, it is read "five thousand five hundred ninety ten-thousandths." It means $\dfrac{5590}{10000}$.

PROBLEMS.   Read the following decimals and write their meanings in the form of common fractions. Reduce the common fractions. Do not confuse a period after a number with a decimal point:

1. .9.	**11.** .98.	**21.** .09.	**31.** .990.	**41.** .099.
2. .8.	**12.** .97.	**22.** .07.	**32.** .977.	**42.** .081.
3. .7.	**13.** .91.	**23.** .06.	**33.** .800.	**43.** .075.
4. .6.	**14.** .77.	**24.** .05.	**34.** .750.	**44.** .050.
5. .5.	**15.** .75.	**25.** .04.	**35.** .500.	**45.** .025.
6. .4.	**16.** .50.	**26.** .03.	**36.** .499.	**46.** .010.
7. .3.	**17.** .45.	**27.** .02.	**37.** .390.	**47.** .009.
8. .2.	**18.** .25.	**28.** .01.	**38.** .250.	**48.** .005
9. .1.	**19.** .11.	**29.** .999.	**39.** .101.	**49.** .001
10. .99	**20.** .10.	**30.** .998.	**40.** .100.	**50.** .0009.

Reduction of Decimals.   From the preceding problems we see that .500 means the same thing as .5, because both mean $\dfrac{1}{2}$. Similarly, .1500 means the same as .15. Hence, to reduce a decimal ending in 0 or several 0's, we "drop" the final 0 or 0's. We could reduce, as we have seen, .15 to $\dfrac{3}{20}$. But $\dfrac{3}{20}$ is harder and more awkward to write than .15, and we would lose the advantage that the decimal system gives us.

Mixed Numbers in Decimal Form.   1.1 means $1\dfrac{1}{10}$; 2.5 means $2\dfrac{5}{10}$ or

$2\frac{1}{2}$; 4.75 means $4\frac{75}{100}$ or $4\frac{3}{4}$; 5.90 means $5\frac{90}{100}$ or $5\frac{9}{10}$; 100.999 means

$100\frac{999}{1000}$.

Read the following numbers. Reduce them to shorter decimals and then read your answer:

51. 10.10.	**54.** 1.8400.	**57.** 19.080.
52. 12.20.	**55.** .50.	**58.** 2000.020200.
53. 25.290.	**56.** 7.0500.	

From the preceding problems we see that final 0's can be dropped without changing the value of the decimal. Since 1.1 means $1\frac{1}{10}$, 0.1 must mean

$0 + .1$, which merely means .1 or $\frac{1}{10}$. Similarly, 01. merely means 1.; 0005.5 merely means 5.5; 00009.9000 merely means 9.9. Hence, we see we can add or drop as many zeros before a whole number, or at the end of a decimal as we please without changing the value of the number.

EXAMPLE: *Change (or reduce) .8 to thousandths.*
Answer: .800.

59. Reduce .500 to tenths.
60. Reduce 7.5 to hundredths.
61. Reduce 08.4020 to the shortest decimal.
62. Reduce 080.400 to the shortest decimal.
63. Reduce 099.7000 to the shortest decimal.

United States and Canadian Money.   The unit (see chapter VII) of United States and Canadian money is the *dollar*. The dollar is made up of 100 *cents*. The *nickel* is 5 cents. The *dime* is 10 cents. The *quarter* of a dollar is, of course, 25 cents. The *half dollar* is, of course, 50 cents. The sign, $, preceding a number means dollars; the sign, ¢, following a number means

cents. Thus, $2.10 means 2 dollars and $\frac{10}{100}$ dollars, but is read "2 dollars and

10 cents." We also see that it means 210 cents, but is never read this way. 10 cents can be written either $.10 or 10¢. 1 cent could be written $.01 or 1¢.

.1¢ would mean $\frac{1}{10}$ of a cent.

Write the following amounts of money in the form of decimals, using the dollar sign:

64. Five dollars and one cent.
65. Six dollars and sixty-six cents.
66. One hundred and fifty-nine cents.
67. 269 cents.
68. Twenty-two dollars and eighty-nine cents.
69. 28 dollars and seven cents.

70. Five hundred fifty-seven dollars and eleven cents.
71. One thousand nine hundred six dollars and six cents.
72. Ten dollars ten and five-tenth cents.
73. Nineteen dollars nineteen and nine-tenths cents.
74. Ten dollars.
75. Ninety dollars.
76. Ten thousand five hundred ninety-six dollars.

Read the following:

77. $10\frac{1}{2}¢$ **78.** $.105   **79.** $14.56   **80.** $5146.567

ADDITION OF DECIMALS

Suppose we wish to add $10.3 + 145.873$. $10.3 = 10.300$.

Hence, $10.3 + 145.873 = 10\frac{300}{1000} + 145\frac{873}{1000}$. Adding these we have:

$$10\frac{300}{1000}$$

$$145\frac{873}{1000}$$

$$155\frac{1173}{1000} = 1\frac{173}{1000}$$

But we see that this gives the same sum as this:

$$+ 1\frac{173}{1000}$$

$$\begin{array}{r} {}^{1}\\ 10.3 \\ \underline{145.873} \\ 156.173 \end{array}$$

$$156\frac{173}{1000} = 156.173$$

Therefore, to add decimals and mixed decimals, place the decimal points under each other and add as in adding whole numbers.

EXAMPLE: *Add* 101.15, 549.675 *and* 1120.7593.

$$\begin{array}{r} 101.15 \\ 549.675 \\ \underline{1120.7593} \\ 1771.5843 \end{array}$$

PROBLEMS.   Add the following:

81. 8.3 and 7.92
82. 101.113 and .896
83. 1.2, 14.57 and 146.399
84. The labor cost of equipping a weave room with tape selvage motion was as follows: first week, $38.15; second week, $33.07; third week, $28.54; fourth week, $56.71. What was the total cost?
85. In one yard of a certain style of cloth the warp and size weigh .0915 pound and the filling .0845 pound. What is the weight of one yard?

SUBTRACTION OF DECIMALS

Suppose we wish to subtract 5.3 from 10.22. $5.3 = 5\dfrac{30}{100}$, $10.22 = 10\dfrac{22}{100}$.

$$\begin{array}{r} 1\cancel{0}\overset{9}{}\dfrac{22}{100} \\ - \quad 5\dfrac{30}{100} \\ \hline {}^{4}\,\dfrac{92}{100} \\ + \quad \dfrac{}{100} \\ \hline {}^{4}\dfrac{92}{100} \end{array}$$

$$\begin{array}{r} 100 \\ 22 \\ \hline 122 \\ 30 \\ \hline 92 \\ 100 \end{array}$$

$= 4.92$

But we see that this gives the same result as this:

$$\begin{array}{r} \overset{9}{1\cancel{0}}.{}^{1}22 \\ 5.\;3 \\ \hline 4.\;92 \end{array}$$

Subtract the following:

86. 27.89 from 32.011

87. $5.06 from $6.01

88. .891 from 1.0001

89. If the warp and size in 1 yard of a certain style of cloth weighs .0809 pound and 1 yard weighs .1427 pound, what is the weight of the filling?

90. If the cost of supplies for section No. 19 of the weave room was $39.17 and for section No. 22, having the same number of looms and making the same cloth, was $21.90, what was the difference in the cost of supplies for the two sections?

Chapter XIII

MULTIPLICATION OF DECIMALS

Suppose we wish to multiply 42.2 by 53.12. First, let us change these numbers to common fractions and multiply:

$$42.2 = \frac{422}{10} \qquad 53.12 = \frac{5312}{100}.$$

Therefore, $42.2 \times 53.12 = \frac{422 \times 5312}{10 \times 100}.$

```
      53.12                              664
      42.2                    2241 ———— = 2241.664
     10624                             1000
     10624           1000) 2241664
    21248                  2000
   2241.664                2416
                           2000
                           4166
                           4000
                           1664
                           1000
                            664
```

Hence, $42.2 \times 53.12 = 2241.664$. But we see that this product is exactly the same as would be obtained by multiplying the numbers 42.2 and 53.12, as in ordinary multiplication and then placing a decimal point between the 1 and the 6, as shown at the left below:

```
   53.12
   42.2
  10624
  10624
  21248
 2241.664
```

We notice that 53.12 has two places to the right of the decimal point and 42.2 has one place to the right of the decimal point. We notice that 2241.664 has three places to the right of the decimal point. Hence, to multiply one decimal by another, we count the places to the right of the decimal point in both decimals and then "point off" the same number of places at the right of the product.

EXAMPLE: *Multiply 52 by 12.6.*

$$
\begin{array}{r}
1\ 2\ 6 \\
5\ 2 \\
\hline
2\ 5\ 2 \\
6\ 3\ 0 \\
\hline
6\ 5\ 5.2
\end{array}
$$

Answer: 655.2.

PROBLEMS.   Multiply the following:

1. 1.2×5 **3.** 13.723×1.1 **5.** 11.1×242.3745

2. 3.7×4.2 **4.** 15.4×11.32 **6.** 1.25×3.1416

Powers of Numbers. $2 \times 2 = 4$; $2 \times 2 \times 2 = 8$; $10 \times 10 = 100$; $10 \times 10 \times 10 = 1000$.

4 is the *second power* of 2; 8 is the *third power* of 2; 100 is the *second power* of 10; 1000 is the *third power* of 10. That is, the second power of a number is the product resulting from multiplying two of that number; the *third* power is the product resulting from multiplying three of that number.

The *second* power is often spoken of as the *square* of a number. Thus, 100 is the *square* of 10; or 10 *squared* is 100. The *third* power of a number is often called the *cube* of that number. Thus, 1000 is the *cube* of 10, or 10 *cubed* is 1000.

There is a short method of *indicating* powers, as follows: the second power or square is indicated by a ^{2} placed after the number, the third power by a ^{3}, and so on. Thus, $2^2 = 2 \times 2 = 4$; $10^3 = 10 \times 10 \times 10 = 1000$. 3^2 is read "3 squared," or "3 to the second power"; 10^3 is read "10 cubed," or "10 to the third power." 2 is the first power of 2; 10 is the first power of 10.

It will be observed that the first power of 10 has one 0; the second power has two 0's; the third power has three 0's, and so on.

It will also be observed that the first power of .1 has one decimal place; the second power of .1 ($.1 \times .1 = .01$) has two decimal places; the third power of .1 (.001) has three decimal places, and so on.

EXAMPLE: *Read the following and find the value of:* 3.2^3.

It is read "3 and two-tenths cubed" or "3 and two-tenths to the third power." The value $= 3.2 \times 3.2 \times 3.2 = 32.768$.

EXAMPLE: *Find the value of* $.10^3$.

Without putting anything on paper we see at once that $.10 = .1$; that $.10^3 = .1^3$; that since the third power is indicated, the result must have three decimal places; and that the answer must be .001.

Read and find the value of the following. Do as much work as possible in your head:

7. 3^3 **9.** 1^1 **11.** $.1^4$ **13.** $.100^2$ **15.** 10^4

8. 9^2 **10.** 1^3 **12.** $.2^3$ **14.** $.01^2$ **16.** 100^2

To Multiply by Powers of 10.   If we perform the following multiplications, we shall obtain the products shown:

(a) $10 \times 2 = 20$ (c) $1000 \times 4.21 = 4210$
(b) $100 \times .21 = 21$ (d) $10000 \times 5.96712 = 59671.2$

From these multiplications we see that to multiply a number by a power of 10 we move that number's decimal point as many places to the right as the power of 10 has 0's.

EXAMPLE: *Multiply* 21 *by* 10.   **Answer:**   210.

EXAMPLE: *Multiply* 32.536 *by* 100.   **Answer:**   3253.6.

Find the product of:

17. 52 and 100   **20.** 1000 and .02
18. 3.1416 and 100   **21.** .830 and 100
19. 437.5 and 1000   **22.** .007 and 10000

To Multiply by Powers of .1.   If we perform the following multiplications, we shall obtain the products shown:

(a) $.1 \times 2 = .2$ (c) $.001 \times 4215 = 4.215$
(b) $.01 \times .21 = .0021$ (d) $.0001 \times 59671.2 = 5.96712$

From these multiplications we see that to multiply a number by a power of .1 we move that number's decimal point as many places to the left as the power of .1 has decimal places.

Find the products of:

23. 52 and .1   **26.** .840 and .001
24. 3.1416 and .01   **27.** 769.2 × .1
25. 7000 and .001   **28.** 120 × .00001

EXAMPLE: *A certain loom is making* 180 *picks per minute. How many yards will it produce in* 9.5 *hours if the cloth has* 50 *picks per inch?*

If this loom makes 180 picks in one minute, it will make 60×180 picks in 60 minutes or 1 hour. It will, therefore, make $9.5 \times 60 \times 180$ picks in 9.5 hours. But each inch has 50 picks. Therefore, each yard contains 36×50 picks. And, therefore, the number of yards produced in 9.5 hours is the number of times that 36×50 is contained in $9.5 \times 60 \times 180$.

$$\frac{9.5 \times \overset{}{\cancel{60}} \times \overset{36}{\cancel{180}}}{\cancel{36} \times \cancel{50}}$$

$$\begin{array}{r} \overset{3}{9.5} \\ \underline{6} \\ 57.0 \end{array} \quad \textbf{Answer:}\ \ 57\ \text{yards.}$$

In the following problems use cancellation wherever possible:

29. If during the day a picker delivered 48 rolls of lap, each roll containing 69 yards and each yard weighing 14.5 ounces, how many pounds of lap did the picker produce during the day?

30. How many pounds will the picker in the preceding problem produce in 6 days?

31. How many pounds of sliver will a drawing frame of 3 heads, each head containing 4 deliveries, produce in 6 days, if each delivery delivers 154.25 pounds of sliver in a day?

32. A certain roving frame producing number one roving fills all its bobbins 4.4 times a day. How many pounds will it produce in a day if it has 96 spindles and each bobbin holds 56 ounces of roving?

33. If each spindle of a spinning frame produces .3 of a pound of number 23 warp in 6 hours, how much will be produced in 6 hours on the following frames: 10 frames equipped with 216 spindles and 10 frames equipped with 224 spindles?

34. The weight of yarn on a full spinning bobbin of a certain size is 2.875 ounces. How many pounds will there be in one doff on a 320 spindle frame?

35. If 2.5 yards of cloth weigh one pound, how many yards will it take to weigh 25 pounds?

36. How many dents in a reed 40.5 inches long, if it has 22 dents per inch?

37. A piece of cloth counts 48 warp ends per inch and the cloth is 44.75 inches wide. How many warp threads in the cloth?

38. How many yards of cloth in a bale that weighs 420.25 pounds, if 2.5 yards of cloth weigh one pound?

39. If a tying-in machine will average tying 200.5 knots per minute, how many knots will it tie in .25 hours?

40. How many teeth in a gear 55 inches around, if there are 2.2 teeth per inch?

41. If a certain kind and size of filling bobbins cost $.134 each, how much money is invested in filling bobbins by a plant that has 50,000 of them on hand?

42. At $8.93 each, how much will shuttles cost a plant per year if it uses 175 shuttles each month?

43. What will be the cost of 22 barrels of sizing wax @ 23 cents per pound, the barrels averaging 466 pounds each?

44. A workman getting $1.78 cents per hour worked $37\frac{1}{2}$ hours. How much did he earn?

45. On a certain style of cloth, seconds are worth $2\frac{1}{2}$ cents less per yard than first-quality cloth. How much will the plant lose on a 120-yard roll of seconds?

46. Drop wires for a loom are shipped 5 thousand per box @ $8.32 per thousand. What will 30 boxes cost?

47. A certain type of lug strap cost $2.13. How much will 250 cost?

48. If 280 pounds of starch at $6\frac{3}{4}$ cents per pound and 18 pounds of sizing wax at 23 cents per pound are used to make one kettle of size, what will be the cost of 8 kettles?

49. If it costs $12\frac{3}{4}$ cents a yard to manufacture a certain style of cloth, how much would a plant lose on 250 bales of seconds, 1010 yards to each bale sold at $12\frac{1}{4}$ cents a yard?

50. A plant sold 100 bales of seconds at a loss of $2\frac{1}{4}$ cents a yard. The bales contained 825 yards each. How much was the loss?

51. A and B wove 4220 yards of cloth each in one week. $87\frac{1}{2}$ yards of A's cloth was second quality, and 426 yards of B's cloth was second quality. How much more was A's worth to the mill that week than B's, if the first-quality cloth sold at $13\frac{3}{4}$ cents a yard and the second-quality cloth sold at $3\frac{1}{4}$ cents a yard less than first quality?

52. A worker makes $2.14 per hour. During the week he worked as follows: Monday, 9.5 hours; Tuesday, 10.5; Wednesday, 9.25; Thursday, 8; Friday, 8; and Saturday, 16. How much did he earn during the week if he was paid 1.5 time for all over 40 hours worked?

Chapter XIV

DIVISION OF DECIMALS & REDUCTION OF FRACTIONS TO DECIMALS

Division of Whole Numbers with a Decimal Quotient. Suppose we wish to divide 4 by 50 so that the quotient will be in decimal form.

$$\frac{4}{50} = \frac{4 \times 2}{50 \times 2} = \frac{8}{100} = .08$$

We see, however, that this same result might be obtained by setting the 4 and the 50 down in the usual manner for division as follows:

$$50\overline{)4.}$$ Place the decimal point after the 4 in its proper position. Place a decimal point above the line and directly above the decimal point after the 4.

$$50\overline{)4.00}$$ Add 0's after the decimal point of the 4.

$$\underset{50\overline{)4.00}}{.08}$$ Then divide as with ordinary division.

Suppose we wish to divide 75 by 4.

$$4\overline{)7^3 5^3 4}\,\,{1\,8\tfrac{3}{4}}\,;\qquad \frac{3}{4} = \frac{3 \times 25}{4 \times 25} = \frac{75}{100} = .75$$

Therefore, $75 \div 4 = 18.75$. But we could have obtained this same result by dividing as we did above:

$$4\overline{)7^3 5.\,^3 0^2 0}\,\,{1\,8.\,7\,5}$$

Suppose we wish to divide 239 by 17. We proceed as before.

We could keep on adding 0's to the dividend, but with this divisor and dividend we would never come to an end of the quotient. Each decimal place we would add to the quotient would make our quotient more nearly accurate, but we would never get an exactly accurate quotient. We can, however, get a quotient sufficiently accurate for any purpose "carrying" the quotient out

```
     14.0588
17) 239.0000
    17
    ──
     69
     68
    ────
    1 00
      85
    ────
     150
     136
    ────
     140
```

to enough decimal places. This quotient, as will be observed, is "carried" to 4 decimal places. Suppose that 3 decimal places are sufficient for our purpose. We would carry the division to 4 decimal places and find that an 8 would occupy the 4th decimal place. Since 8 is larger than 5 we put down the result as 14.059. If, however, the 4th decimal place would be occupied by a number less than 5, we would put down the result as 14.058.

EXAMPLE: *12 yards of roving weigh 66 grains. What is the number of the roving? Carry the number to 2 decimal places.*

```
       1.515
66) 100.000
    66
    ────
    34 0
    33 0
    ────
    1 00
      66
    ────
     340
```

Answer: The number of the roving is 1.52.

PROBLEMS.   If necessary, review yarn and roving numbering, chapter V:

1. What is the number of the roving if 12 yards weigh 40 grains?
2. What is the number of the roving if 12 yards weigh 30 grains?
3. What is the number of the roving if 12 yards weigh 16 grains?
4. What is the number of the yarn if 120 yards weigh 60 grains?
5. What is the number of the yarn if 120 yards weigh 15 grains?

Reduction of Common Fractions to Decimals.   It is always advisable to keep in mind the *decimal equivalents* of fractions that occur often in textile calculations. Practically all fractions in textile calculations are finally reduced to decimals.

EXAMPLE: *Reduce $\frac{1}{3}$ to a decimal.*

```
     .3 3 3 3
3) 1.0¹0¹0¹0
```

Answer: .333.   This is called a repeating decimal. Why? Why does it repeat?

Reduce the following fractions to decimals:

6. $\frac{1}{8}$ 8. $\frac{1}{2}$ 10. $\frac{3}{4}$ 12. $1\frac{1}{8}$

7. $\frac{1}{4}$ 9. $\frac{5}{8}$ 11. $\frac{7}{8}$ 13. $1\frac{1}{4}$

Division of All Numbers.   Suppose we wish to divide 4.5 by 5.

$$4.5 \div 5 = 4\frac{5}{10} \div 5 = \frac{45}{10} \div 5 = \frac{9}{10} = .9$$

$$\begin{array}{r} .9 \\ 5\overline{)\,4.5} \end{array}$$ But we could have obtained this same result by dividing as shown at the left.

Suppose we wish to divide 420.864 by 51.2.

$$420.864 \div 51.2 = 420\frac{864}{1000} \div 51\frac{2}{10} = \frac{420864}{1000} \div \frac{512}{10} =$$

$$\begin{array}{c} 822 \\ \dfrac{\cancel{420864}}{\cancel{1000}} \times \dfrac{10}{52} = \dfrac{822}{100} \\ 100 \end{array} \qquad \begin{array}{r} 8.22 \\ 100\overline{)\,822.00} \\ 800 \\ \hline 22\ 0 \\ 20\ 0 \\ \hline 2\ 00 \\ 2\ 00 \\ \hline 0 \end{array}$$

Hence, $420.864 \div 51.2 = 8.22$.

But we could have obtained this same result by dividing as follows:

$$51.2\overline{)\,420.864}$$

$$\begin{array}{r} 8.22 \\ 51.2.\overline{)\,420.8.64} \\ 409\ 6 \\ \hline 11\ 2\ 6 \\ 10\ 2\ 4 \\ \hline 1\ 0\ 24 \\ 1\ 0\ 24 \\ \hline 0 \end{array}$$

There is one decimal place in the divisor. "Move" the decimal point of the divisor and dividend one place to the right. Place the decimal point of the quotient directly above the "moved" decimal point of the dividend. Remember that this moving of the decimal points merely multiplies the divisor and dividend by 10 which does not change the value of the quotient. Then divide as in ordinary division. We observe that our answers agree.

Division by Powers of 10 and Powers of .1.

14. Prove that to divide any number by a power of 10 we merely move its decimal point to the left as many places as the power of 10 has 0's.

15. Prove that to divide any number by a power of .1 we merely move its decimal point to the right as many places as the power of .1 has decimal places.

EXAMPLE: 120 *yards of yarn weigh 50.22 grains. What is the number of the yarn? Carry the answer to two decimal places.*

$$
\begin{array}{r}
19.912 \\
50.22.\overline{)\,1000.00.000} \\
502\ 2 \\
497\ 80 \\
451\ 98 \\
45\ 82\ 0 \\
45\ 19\ 8 \\
62\ 20 \\
50\ 22 \\
11\ 980
\end{array}
$$

Answer: Number of yarn is 19.91.

16. What is the number of the yarn if 120 yards weigh 35.5 grains?

17. If the calender roll of a picker is 28.27 inches around, how many times must it turn to deliver a yard of lap?

18. A box full of bobbins weighs 250 pounds. The box weighs 75 pounds. How many bobbins are there in the box if a bobbin weighs 2.5 ounces?

19. If 198 cuts of cloth weigh 4009.5 pounds, how many pounds does each cut average?

20. How many yards of cloth will it take to weigh one pound, if 60.75 yards weigh 13.5 pounds?

21. How many belts 20.8 feet long will 312 feet of belting make?

22. If a tying-in machine ties on the average 250.5 knots per minute, how many minutes will be required to tie a warp with 3507 ends?

23. A certain size loom picker weighs .125 pounds. How many pickers in an 80-pound lot?

24. A cloth counts 47.8 in the sley and has 1673 ends in the warp. How many inches wide is the cloth?

25. A reed contains 969 dents, spread on 42.5 inches. How many dents per inch?

26. If a bale of cloth weighs 312.8 pounds and it takes 4.5 yards of this cloth to weigh one pound, how many yards are in the bale?

27. A piece of ply yarn 12 inches long placed in the twist counter requires 310 turns to untwist it. What is the number of twists per inch?

On a certain style of cloth the plant makes a profit of $\frac{1}{8}$ of a cent per yard. On this basis solve the following problems:

28. The profit on how many yards of cloth is lost when 2 bobbins costing 12 cents each are run over by a truck and smashed?

29. When 2 inches of 2-inch belting @ 47.9 cents a foot is wasted, the profit on how many 60-yard cuts of cloth is lost?

30. When a reed costing $2.95 is smashed, the profit on how many 60-yard cuts is wiped out?

31. On first-quality cloth of a certain style, a plant is making a profit of $\frac{1}{8}$ of a cent per yard. For second-quality cloth of the same style, the plant receives $2\frac{1}{4}$ cents less per yard than it does for first quality.

This cloth has 60 picks per inch and the looms that weave this cloth make 180 picks per minute. How many 120-hour weeks will one loom have to run to make enough first quality cloth to make up for the loss due to a weaver making 700 yards of seconds in one week?

Chapter XV

EQUATIONS, ANALYSES, FORMULAS, & POLYNOMIALS

Equations. *Equations* often simplify the thinking necessary in applying our knowledge of mathematics to practical textile plant problems. An equation is a statement that two things (or *quantities* or *terms* or groups of things, quantities, or terms) are equal to each other. An equation contains the equal sign, =, with which you are already familiar. Indeed any expression containing = is an equation. Hence from the beginning of learning to add, you have used equations.

Let us see what can be done to true equations and keep the results true: From our study in previous chapters we know that (a) $\frac{1}{10} = .1$ and (b) $1 = 1.00$. Add 1 to each side of equation (a). But from (b) common sense tells us we can express the result as (c) $\frac{1}{10} + 1 = .1 + 1.00$. Again we know that (d) $\frac{3}{10} = .3$ and common sense tells us we can subtract $\frac{3}{10}$ from each side of (c) and write the result as (e) $\frac{1}{10} + 1 - \frac{3}{10} = .1 + 1.00 - .3$. We know (f) $1 = \frac{10}{10}$ and (g) $.1 + 1.00 = 1.10$ and common sense tells us we ought to be able to *substitute* the *value* of 1 from (f) and the value of $.1 + 1.00$ from (g) into (e), obtain (h) $\frac{1}{10} + \frac{10}{10} - \frac{3}{10} = 1.10 - .3$, and still have a true equation. Let us *perform* the addition and subtraction that are only indicated in equation (h) and obtain (i) $\frac{8}{10} = .8$. Thus we see that equal values added to, subtracted from, and substituted into each side of a true equation results in a true equation. Let us multiply each side of (i) by 20 and obtain (j) $20 \times \frac{8}{10} = .8 \times 20$. We know that (k) $20 = 10 \times 2$ and (m) $4 \times 5 = 20$. Substitute the values of 20 from (k) and (m) into each side of (j) and obtain (n) $10 \times 2 \times \frac{8}{10} = .8 \times 4 \times 5$. Divide one of the terms on each side of (n) by 2 and obtain (o) $10 \times 2 \times \frac{8}{10} \div 2 = .8 \times 4 \div 2 \times 5$. Perform the multiplication and division indicated and obtain (p) $8 = 8$.

1. From the foregoing and similar calculations establish for future reference the following principle:

Equal operations indicated or performed upon both sides of a true equation give a true equation.

Analysis of Problems.   Already in previous chapters of this book you have used this principle many times.

EXAMPLE 1:   *A sample of duck 12 inches long weighs 6 ounces. What is the weight of 1 yard?*

We know (a) weight of 12 inches = 6 ounces; (b) 36 inches = 1 yard. Add the left and right sides of (a) twice to the right and left sides of (a) and obtain (c) weight of 36 inches = 18 ounces. Substitute the value of 36 inches from (b) into (c) obtain (d) the weight of 1 yard = 18 ounces. Or we might solve this problem by "unitary analysis" as follows: dividing both sides of (a) by 12 obtain (e) weight of 1 inch = $\frac{6 \text{ ounces}}{12} = \frac{1}{2}$ ounce. Multiplying both extreme sides of (e) by 36 obtain (f) weight of 36 inches = $36 \times \frac{1}{2}$ ounce − 18 ounces. Substituting the value of 36 inches from (b) into (f) obtain (g) weight of 1 yard = 18 ounces.

The sign ∴ means "therefore."

EXAMPLE 2:   *A $3\frac{1}{4}$-yard sample of cotton yarn weighs .65 of a grain. What is the yarn number?*

We know weight of $3\frac{1}{4}$ yards = .65 grains ∴ (b) weight of 1 yard =

$$\frac{.65 \text{ grains}}{3\frac{1}{4}} = \frac{.65 \text{ grains}}{\frac{13}{4}} = \frac{.65 \text{ grains} \times 4}{13} \therefore \text{ (c) weight of 120 yards} =$$

$$\frac{120 \times .\overset{.05}{\cancel{65}} \text{ grains} \times 4}{\cancel{13}} = 24 \text{ grains. From our previous study} \therefore \text{ (d) yarn}$$

number $= \frac{1000}{24} = 41.7$.

2. A sample of cloth $\frac{3}{4}$ of a yard long weighs 640 grains. What are the grains per yard?

3. A 100-pound bag of dry sizing compound holds just about $26\frac{2}{3}$ measuring cups full. How many cups full to make 15 pounds?

4. A cloth sample $\frac{3}{4}$ yard long weighs 750 grains. Find the yards per pound.

5. A certain cloth is woven 18″ wide. A sample 18″ long weighs 218 grains. What are its yards per pound?

6. From a small cloth sample received by a plant, warp yarn is picked out, straightened, $5\frac{1}{3}$ yards long and weighs 1.92 grains. What is its number?

7. If 10 2–0 spinning travellers weigh 8 grains and the contents remaining in a box of these weigh $15\frac{1}{2}$ ounces, how many are in the box?

8. From a sample of cloth 4 inches by 4 inches, containing no sizing, and weighing 14.95 grains the warp is picked out, weighs 9.72 grains, 10 pieces are straightened, laid end to end, and measure 42 inches. The filling is similarly treated and 10 pieces measure $42\frac{7}{16}$ inches. If there are 50 ends (i.e., strands of warp) and 40 picks (i.e., strands of filling) per inch, what is the yarn number of the (a) warp (b) filling?

Literal Equations and Formulas.   Each equation discussed under the side head "Equations" at the start of this chapter is a *numerical equation;* which means that every *term* (i.e., the value, quantity, thing, or idea about which the statement is made) is numerical (i.e., expressed by the kind of numbers you have already studied). But under the side head "Analysis of Problems" the examples involve equations having at least one term composed of a word or words, or letter or letters standing for such word or words.

EXAMPLE 3:   *A certain stock going through a roving frame contracts .025 of its length after its delivery by the front roll and before being wound onto the bobbin. What length must the front roll deliver to make 840 yards on the bobbin?*

To shorten our equation let the abbreviation "f" stand for "length the front roll must deliver to make 840 yards on the bobbin."

(a) f = 840 yards + .025 × f	Subtracting .025 from
(b) f − .025 × f = 840 yards	both sides of equation (a).
Therefore *(c)* 1 × f − .025 × f	Because f is the same
= 840 yards	as 1 × f.
Therefore *(d)* .975 × f = 840 yards	Perform the indicated subtraction on the left side.
(e) f = $\dfrac{840}{.975}$ yards = 861.54 yards	Divide both sides of (d) by .975.

In Example 3 we let f stand for many words as well as a number and without knowing exactly how much f is we make an equation which states that we do know about f, and then we deal with f just as if it were a numerical term. Such terms composed of a word or words, or a letter or letters standing for such word or words are *literal terms*. Equations having literal terms are *literal equations*. In textile manufacturing mathematics you will make and use literal equations frequently. In making and using literal equations to solve a problem, the original understanding of the words or letters must be kept in mind throughout the solution.

EXAMPLE 4:   *Write a literal equation dealing with feet and inches.*

If we understand "feet" to mean number of feet in the dimension of an object and inches to mean the number of inches in the same dimension we must write: $\text{feet} = \dfrac{\text{inches}}{12}$. If we want to know the value of one foot in relation to one inch we must write: 1 foot is 12 times greater in value than 1 inch, or we may write it in literal equation form as:

1 foot = 12 × 1 inch.

Write a literal equation containing each set of words or letters that stand for such words in the following problems. (You may have to obtain some basic information for some of the problems.)

9. The number of inches and the number of yards.
10. Value of one skein in relation to one yard.
11. The number of pounds and the number of ounces.
12. The number of yards and the number of hanks.
13. The number of grains and the number of pounds.
14. The number of hours and the number of minutes.
15. Cotton yarn numbers, yards, and grains.

You will notice that the literal equations which you have written as your answers to the preceding problems (1) are true of any problem whatever involving the words, or letters that stand for the words, so long as the understanding of the words remain the same, and (2) can be used repeatedly. For instance, we need to know the yarn number of a piece of yarn 10 yards long and weighing 4 grains.

10 yards = 4 grains

$$120 \text{ yards} = \frac{120 \times 4}{10} \text{ gr.} = 48 \text{ gr.}$$

$$\text{cotton yarn number} = \frac{1000}{48} = 20.8$$

Using the literal equation of your answer to a preceding problem.

Formulas.   In this book a literal equation which will be referred to after being written sometimes is identified by a number in parenthesis preceding it; and if it is to be referred to repeatedly it is in black face on a line by itself and is called a *formula*. The reasoning involved in writing a literal equation, especially a formula, is often called *deriving* or *derivation*. The rest of this book is largely occupied with deriving, writing and using formulas that frequently save tremendous effort in textile manufacturing.

Polynomials.   Occasionally in textile manufacturing mathematics it is necessary to deal with the indicated sum or difference of two or more terms as if they were merely one term. Such an indicated sum or difference of two or more terms is called a *polynomial*.

EXAMPLE 5:   *Derive a formula for the length of any stock with any amount of contraction required to be delivered by the front roll of a roving frame for the bobbin to wind any length.*

Immediately we see that such a formula, if it had been available, could have been used to solve the specific problem in Example 3. As in Example 3 let f = number of yards the front roll must deliver; and in addition let cn = hundredths of f that the stock contracts and bo = number of yards wound onto the bobbin.

(1) $f = bo + cn \times f$ Just as in Example 3 except we do not have specific numbers for bo and cn.

(2) $1 \times f - cn \times f = bo$ Subtracting cn × f from both sides of (1).

Unlike Example 3, we cannot perform the subtraction on the left side of (2), and can only indicate it. Comparing with Example 3, the hundredth of f left after contraction must be the polynomial $1 - cn$. To express that $1 - cn$ is a polynomial to be dealt with as a single term, let us enclose it in parenthesis, thus: $(1 - cn)$. Then the number of yards of f that are left after contraction must be $(1 - cn) \times f$; and $1 \times f - cn \times f$ must be the same as $(1 - cn) \times f$.

∴ (3) $(1 - cn) \times f = bo$ Substituting into equation (2).

∴ (4) $f = \dfrac{bo}{(1 - cn)}$ Dividing both sides of equation (3) by $(1 - cn)$.

Or since the parenthesis are no longer needed; and, in case someone is in a hurry to use equation (4) and does not wish to take the time to see the meaning of f, bo, and cn, equation (4), we can derive:

(5) yards delivered by front roll $= \dfrac{\text{yards on bobbin}}{1 - \text{hundredths of contraction}}$

EXAMPLE 6:   *Verify formula (5), Example 5, by using it in solving the problem in Example 3.* By formula (5): yards delivered by front roll $= \dfrac{840}{1 - .025} = \dfrac{840}{.975} = 861.54$.

Factoring Out and Inserting Parenthesis.   From the two terms of the polynomial $1 \times f - cn \times f$ in equation (2), Example 5, we *factored out* their common factor, f, and obtained a new polynomial $1 - cn$ and enclosed it in parenthesis to make sure we would deal with it as a single term. And evidently we dealt with these polynomials correctly for we verified our result in Example 6.

Rewrite the following equations by factoring the largest common factor out of each polynomial and enclosing each new polynomial in parenthesis:

16. $2 \times 3 - 2 \times 1 = 4$
17. $6 - 2 = 4$

18. $2 \times 3 + 2 \times 1 = 8$
19. $5 = 25 - 20$
20. $4 = 20 - 12 - 4$
21. $9 + 12 - 18 = 3$
22. $6 = 30 - 26 + 2$
23. $108 = 500 - 300 - 92$
24. $60 - 40 - 20 = 0$
25. $a \times 3 - a \times 1 = 4$
26. $6 \times b - 2 \times b = 4$
27. $2 \times c + 2 = 8$
28. $5 = 25d - 20d$
29. $6 = 15 \times yz - 13 \times yz + yz$
30. $108 \times a = 500 \times bc - 300 \times bc - 92 \times bc$
31. $60 \times c \times d - 40 \times c \times d - 20 \times c \times d = 0$
32. $60 \times c \times d \times y - 40 \times c \times y - 20 \times d \times y = 0$
33. $\dfrac{1}{2} \times 3 - \dfrac{1}{2} = 1$

34. $6 \times \dfrac{1}{4} - 2 \times \dfrac{1}{4} = 1$

35. $\dfrac{6}{4} - \dfrac{2}{4} = 1$

36. $\dfrac{2}{3} \times C + \dfrac{2}{3} = 1$

37. $5 = \dfrac{25 \times d}{m} - \dfrac{20 \times d}{m}$

38. $6 = \dfrac{15 \times yz}{f} - \dfrac{13 \times yz}{f} + \dfrac{yz}{f}$

39. $d = \dfrac{500 \times ef}{e \times f} - \dfrac{300 \times ef}{e \times f} - \dfrac{92 \times ef}{e \times f}$

40. $\dfrac{60 \times a \times d \times y}{b \times r \times c} - \dfrac{40 \times a \times y}{b \times c} - \dfrac{20 \times d \times y}{c \times r} = 0$

41. $\dfrac{3 - 1}{2} = 1$

42. $1 = \dfrac{3}{3 + 4} + \dfrac{4}{3 + 4}$

43. $L = \dfrac{5 \times 5 \times y}{p + c} + \dfrac{10 \times 5 \times a}{p + c}$

Removing Parenthesis and Fraction Bars. Sometimes a fraction bar makes unnecessary parenthesis around a polynomial numerator or denominator. For instance, in equation (4), Example 5, we can hardly understand otherwise that $1 - cn$, whether or not enclosed in parenthesis, is to. be dealt with as one term. So we removed the parenthesis. The answers to the last two preceding problems also have unnecessary parenthesis.

EXAMPLE 7:   *Remove the parenthesis from* $(a + b) \times \dfrac{1}{(c - d)} = 1$.

There is no mistaking that $c - d$ is to be treated as one quantity.

$\therefore$ (a) $a + b \times \dfrac{1}{c - d} = 1$

As we learned in previous chapters, to multiply a fraction by a whole number we multiply the numerator by the whole number and place the product over the denominator; and the product of 1 and any other number is that number.

$\therefore$ (b) $\dfrac{a + b}{c - d} = 1$

EXAMPLE 8:   *Remove the parenthesis from* $a \times (b + c) \times \dfrac{1}{d + e} = 2$.

(a) $\dfrac{a \times (b + c)}{d + e} = 2$ For the same reasons leading up to equation (b) Example 7.

Since, as you have seen in your answer to the problems under the side head "Factoring Out and Inserting Parenthesis," the polynomial $a \times b + a \times c = a \times (b + c)$, $a \times (b + c) = a \times b + a \times c$. That is to remove parenthesis enclosing a polynomial we multiply each term within the parenthesis by whatever the polynomial is multiplied. $\therefore \dfrac{ab + ac}{d + e} = 2$.

Remove parenthesis from the following:

44. $2 \times (3 + 4) = 14$
45. $3 \times (4 - 3) = 3$
46. $5 \times (6 + 7) = 7 \times (10 - 1) + 2$
47. $2 \times \left(\dfrac{1}{2} + \dfrac{3}{2}\right) = 3 \times \left(\dfrac{2}{3} - \dfrac{4}{3} + \dfrac{6}{3}\right)$
48. $2 \times 3 \times (4 + 5) \times \dfrac{6}{7(10 - 6)} = \dfrac{81}{7}$
49. $a \times (b + c) = 14$
50. $(b - c) \times a = 3$
51. $5 \times (6 + b) = b \times (10 - 1) + 2$
52. $a \times \left(\dfrac{1}{a} + \dfrac{b}{a}\right) = b \times \left(\dfrac{a}{b} - \dfrac{c}{b} + \dfrac{d}{b}\right)$
53. $a \times b \times (c + d) \times \dfrac{e}{f \times (h - g)} = z$

54. $(3 + 4) \times (3 + 4) = 49$ Hint: Do this in 3 steps: First step, remove one set of parenthesis. Second step, remove the other set of parenthesis.

55. $(5 - 3) \times (5 - 3) = 4$

56. $(a + b) \times (a + b) = 49$

57. $(c + d) \times (c + d) = 36$

58. $(a - b) \times (a - b) = 4$

59. $(r - s) \times (r - s) = 25$

EXAMPLE 9:   *Remove the fraction bar from under the polynomial numerator of* $2 \times \dfrac{3 + 4}{7 - 5} = 7.$

(a) $2 \times \dfrac{(3 + 4)}{7 - 5} = 7$ 　　　　Because $(3 + 4)$ is the same as $3 + 4$.

(b) $\dfrac{2 \times (3 + 4)}{7 - 5} = 7$ 　　　　Because to multiply a fraction by a whole number we multiply the numerator by the whole number and place the product over the denominator.

$\therefore \dfrac{2 \times 3 + 2 \times 4}{7 - 5} = 7$

We have learned previously that to add or subtract fractions all of which have a common denominator we place the sum or difference of the numerators over the denominator. Hence to remove a fraction bar from under a polynomial numerator we separate the original fraction into fractions with the original denominator and terms of the polynomial as numerator and indicate the addition or subtraction of the fractions as the terms of the polynomial are indicated.

$\therefore$ (d) $\dfrac{2 \times 3}{7 - 5} + \dfrac{2 \times 4}{7 - 5} = 7$

EXAMPLE 10:   *Remove the fraction bar from under the polynomial numerator of* $3 \times \dfrac{6 - 4 + 5}{9 - 7} = 10.5.$

$\dfrac{3 \times 6}{9 - 7} - \dfrac{3 \times 4}{9 - 7} + \dfrac{3 \times 5}{9 - 7} = 10.5$

Remove the fraction bar from under each polynomial numerator of the following:

60. $10 \times \dfrac{4 + 5 - 6}{7} = 4\dfrac{2}{7}$

61. $9 \times \dfrac{7 - 5 + 3 - 2}{13} = 2.08$

62. $a \times \dfrac{b + c - d}{e + f} = g$

63. $s = (b + p) \times \dfrac{b + p}{r}$

64. $x = (y - z) \times \dfrac{y - z}{y + z}$

Negative Subtrahends, Multipliers, and Divisors and Removing Parenthesis and Fraction Bars.   Negative numbers and other quantities (i.e., those preceded by the minus sign, −) require more study given them than thus far in this book and more than positive quantities (i.e., those which, when necessary to distinguish them from negative quantities, are preceded by the plus sign, +).

A plant ships a customer 10 4800-yard bales of cloth. The customer rejects the shipment because using 1 bale as a sample, he claims that in a quarter of the shipment the allowable defects exceed the specified number per 100-yd. cut. The plant and the customer agree to submit this bale, as a fair sample of the whole, to an impartial inspector who decides that 900 yards of the questionable yards did meet specifications. Therefore, there must take place some such thinking as expressed by the following equation:

(*a*) Customer claims acceptable yds. $= 10 \times 4800 - 10 \times \dfrac{4800}{4}$.

(*b*) Inspector decides acceptable yds. $= 10 \times 4800 - 10 \times \left(\dfrac{4800}{4} - \right.$
$\left. 900\right) = 48000 - 10 \times (1200 - 900) = 48000 - 12000 + 9000 = 45000$; or (c)

inspector decides acceptable yds. $= 10 \times 4800 - 10 \times \left(\dfrac{4800}{4} - 900\right) = 48000 -$
$10 \times \left(\dfrac{4800 - 3600}{4}\right) = 48000 - 10 \times \dfrac{4800 - 3600}{4} = 48000 - 10 \times \dfrac{4800}{4} +$
$10 \times \dfrac{3600}{4} = 48000 - 12000 + 9000 = 45000$.

Thus we see: From equations (b) and (c) that $-(-9000) = 9000$; and ∴ that *subtracting a negative quantity makes it positive.* From equation (b) that $-10 \times -900 = 9000$; ∴ that $-1 \times -1 = 1$, ∴ that $\dfrac{1}{-1} = -1$, and ∴ that *multiplying or dividing a quantity by a negative quantity changes the sign of the result from that of the quantity multiplied or divided.* From equation (b) that *removing parenthesis preceded by a minus sign changes the sign of each quantity within.* From equation (c) that *removing a fraction bar preceded by a minus sign changes the sign of each quantity in either the numerator or denominator.*

65. A certain weave room each week for each weaver running the same style uses this formula: qr. $= \dfrac{p - sw}{mc}$ in which qr means quality rating, p means total lbs. produced, sw means lbs of seconds and waste, and mc means maximum capacity in lbs. of the weaver's looms. For one week a weaver made a total of 50 lbs. more production and 5 lbs. less in seconds and waste than the week before. (a) Make an equation showing her change in quality rating. (b) If maximum capacity was 3400 lbs. per week, find her change in rating.

66. For warp spinning frames the following true equation sometimes is used: RPM bow $= \dfrac{\text{RPM f} \times \text{dia. f}}{\text{dia. bo}}$ in which RPM bow means revolutions per minute that the bobbin is devoting to winding the yarn onto itself at any given instant; RPM bo means revolution per minute of the bobbin at that same instant; RPM f and dia. f mean the unchanging revolutions per minute and thickness in inches, respectively, of the front roll. (a) Write an equation showing the CRPM bow, change in RPM bow to full bobbin thickness of 2 inches from bare bobbin thickness of $\dfrac{3}{4}$ of an inch. (b) If RPM = 168 and dia. f = 1 inch, find CRPM bow. (c) What does the sign preceding CRPM bow indicate?

Remember that terms can be expressed in different ways without changing their value.

$$-(a - b) = -a + b = b - a = +(b - a) = +(-a + b),\text{ and}$$

$$-\frac{a - b}{c} = -\frac{a}{c} + \frac{b}{c} = \frac{b}{c} - \frac{a}{c} = +\frac{b - a}{c}$$

EXAMPLE 11.   *Solve the following equation for a:* $\dfrac{2a}{d} = b + c$.

(a) $2a = d(b + c)$ Multiply both sides by d.

(b) $a = \dfrac{d(b + c)}{2}$ Divide both sides by 2.

EXAMPLE 12.   *Solve the following equation for a:* $\dfrac{2a}{4} = 5 + 3$.

(a) $2a = 4(5 + 3)$ Multiply both sides by 4.

(b) $a = \dfrac{4(5 + 3)}{2}$ Divide both sides by 2.

(c) $a = 16$ Reduced to the lowest term.

Note: Example 12 is the same as Example 11 except numbers are used in the place of the letters b, c, and d.

Solve the following equations for a:

67. $5a = 10 + 4a$

68. $4a - 5 = 3a + 2$

69. $4(a - 2) = 2(a + b)$

70. $4a + b = c$

71. $a = \dfrac{10(a - b) - 5(b - a)}{(a - b)}$

72. $-b - a = \dfrac{10(a - b - c)}{15} - \dfrac{2(b - c + a)}{3}$

Chapter XVI

PERCENTAGES

The word *percent* means "by the hundred." Thus, when a card makes 5 percent waste, 5 out of every hundred pounds is waste. If a man's wages are increased 6 percent, for every hundred cents he was receiving he now receives 6 cents more.

To put it another way: when a card makes 5 percent waste, $\frac{5}{100}$ of all the cotton fed is waste. If a man's wages are increased 6 percent, $\frac{6}{100}$ of his former wages are added to his former wages.

Hence, 5 percent means .05; 6 percent means .06. The sign % means percent and is read "percent."

EXAMPLE: 360 *pounds of stock are fed to a card. If the card makes 5% waste, how much waste may we expect?*

5% of 360 pounds means .05 × 360 pounds = 18 pounds.

EXAMPLE: *A spinner is to receive an increase of 6% in her hourly pay. If she now makes* $2.50 *per hour, what will she make with the increase?*

6% of $2.50 means .06 × $2.50 = $.15 or 15 cents.

∴ she will receive $2.50 + $.15 = $2.65.

PROBLEMS:

1. A spinner earns $123.65 a week and saves $33\frac{1}{3}$% of it. How much does she save in a week?

2. If a plant makes 880,220 yards of cloth in a week, 95% of it first quality, how many yards of seconds were made?

3. The gearing of a spinning frame is figured to put 28.5 twists per inch into a certain yarn. But the yarn contracts 3% due to twisting. (a) How long are 28.5 twists after twisting? (b) Therefore, how many twists per inch are put into the yarn?

4. A certain plant from its experience figures on $12\frac{1}{2}$ % of its stock going into waste and seconds. How much first-quality cloth does it expect from a 500-pound bale of fiber?

100 Percent.   Since 90% means $\frac{90}{100}$ or .90, 100% must mean $\frac{100}{100}$ or 1.00. Therefore, 100% of anything is the *whole* of it or *all* of it. When we speak of 100% production, we usually mean the amount of material that would be produced in a given time if the machine were running continuously without stopping for cleaning, oiling, doffing, etc.

FINDING THE PERCENT

Base.   4 is what percent of 5? This question really means: What number multiplied by 5 will give 4? We can find this number by using equations:

The unknown number $\times$ 5 = 4.   Dividing both sides by 5.

The unknown number $= \frac{4}{5} = .80$

Hence, 4 is 80% of 5. And, of course, 5 is 100% of 5. 5 is the base. The base in any percentage problem is always the number that is 100%. Hence, we see that *to find what percent any number is of the base we divide the number by the base.*

EXAMPLE: 100% *production for a card running a certain weight and grade sliver is* 550 *pounds per day. What percent production is obtained when the card produces* 522 *pounds?*

Base is 550.

```
          .9490
550) 522.000
     495 0
      27 00
      22 00
       5 000
       4 950
         500
```

Answer: 94.9% production.

NOTE: The decimal in the 3rd place in the quotient is $\frac{9}{1000}$. But $\frac{9}{1000}$ is $\frac{9}{10}$ of $\frac{1}{100}$ which means that it is .9 of 1 percent.

5. 100% production for a picker running 16-ounce lap is 16,560 pounds for 40 hours. What is its percent of production if it delivers 14,860 pounds in 40 hours?

6. A two delivery drawing frame produced in 40 hours 8858 pounds of 65-grain sliver. Each delivery of this frame, if it could run continuously for 10 hours, would produce 1476 pounds. What percent of production was obtained?

Decimal Fractions of Percent.   We have seen that 1% = .01. What is the meaning of .1%? .1% must mean $\frac{1}{10}$ of 1%. Hence .1% = .1 × 1% = .1 × :01 = .001.

EXAMPLE: *Express .03% as a plain decimal.*

.03% = .03 × .01 = .0003   **Answer:**   .0003.

7. Last week the percent of production for the drawing frames was 80%. The week before last its percent of production was 79.5%. How much did the percent of production increase?

8. For the week ending April 9th the drawing frame production was 80.5%. During the week ending April 16th, the production was 79.7%. What was the decrease in percent of production?

In figuring percentage it is necessary that you first select the proper base.

EXAMPLE: *During the week ending April 9th, the pickers of a certain plant produced 234,000 pounds. 100% production for this weight of lap is 260,000 pounds. The week ending April 16th, the pickers produced 238,000 pounds. How much did production increase?*

234,000 ÷ 260,000 = .90 = 90%. 238,000 ÷ 260,000 = .915 = 91.5%. Hence, increase in *percent of production* = 91.5% − 90% = 1.5%.

We might also obtain the same result with less work as follows: Increase in pounds = 238,000 − 234,000 = 4,000. 4,000 ÷ 260,000 = .015 = 1.5%.

Increase in *production,* based upon the first week's production, was 4,000 ÷ 234,000 = .017 = 1.7%. Be sure you select the proper base for the result desired.

9. 100% production for the frames of a certain spinning room running on number $11\frac{1}{2}$ warp yarn is 42,000 pounds per week. During the week ending December 2nd it produced 37,800 pounds. The following week it produced 38,010 pounds. (a) What was the increase in percent of production? (b) What was the increase in production?

10. In 6 days 380 looms wove 114,912 yards of cloth. What percent did the looms weave if 52.5 yards per loom per day is 100% production? *Hint:* Use cancellation.

11. A loom supposed to run 160 picks per minute, on account of the belt being slack, is running 152 picks per minute. What percent of production is it losing?

12. A tying-in machine tying 250 knots a minute tied 60 warps, 2125 knots each, in 10 hours. What percent of the time was the machine stopped? *Hint:* Use cancellation.

13. If 5844 pounds of cotton are used to manufacture 5113.5 pounds of first-quality cloth, what percent went into waste and seconds?

14. In one year a plant used 6,768,600 pounds of cotton and manufactured 5,922,525 pounds of first-quality cloth. What percent of the cotton went into waste and seconds?

15. In weaving a certain style of cloth it was found that a 63-yard

beam of warp from the slasher made a 60-yard roll of cloth. What was the percent of contraction of the warp based on the original length of warp?

16. In weaving a certain style of fabric which is 46 inches wide, the width of the warp in the reed is $49\frac{1}{4}$ inches. What is the percent of contraction in the filling?

FINDING THE BASE

EXAMPLE: *The carding room report of a certain plant for one week shows* 82,500 *pounds of a certain number of roving. This is stated as* 90.5% *production. What is* 100% *production?*

$$90.5\% = 82,500. \quad \therefore 1\% = \frac{82,500}{90.5}.$$

$$\therefore 100\% = \overset{20}{\cancel{100}} \times \frac{82,500}{\underset{18.1}{\cancel{90}.5}} = 91,160. \quad \textbf{Answer:}\quad 91,160 \text{ pounds.}$$

But this same result could have been obtained more quickly as follows: From the preceding we see that $100\% = \dfrac{100 \times 82,500}{90.5}$. Dividing both numerator and denominator by 100: $100\% = \dfrac{82,500}{.905}$. Hence, we would set this problem down as follows:

$$
\begin{array}{r}
91\ 160. \\
90.5\% = .905 \qquad .905)\overline{82,500.000.}
\end{array}
$$

Dividing as in ordinary long division.

EXAMPLE: *The pay for a certain style cloth was increased* 10%. *The pay is now* $27\frac{1}{2}$ *cents per cut. What was the pay per cut before it was increased?*

$$110\% = 27.5$$

Following the same reasoning as in the previous example, we divide as follows:

$$
\begin{array}{r}
25. \\
1.10.)\overline{27.50.} \\
\underline{22\ 0} \\
5\ 50
\end{array}
$$

Answer: 25 cents.

17. How many pounds of fiber will be required to manufacture 126,000 pounds of lap if .24% of the fiber is removed in going through the pickers?

18. If cotton loses 5% in carding, how many pounds of lap will be required to make 5187 pounds of card sliver?

19. If a loom is stopped 15% of the time and weaves 42.2 yards of fabric in a day, how many yards would it weave if it did not stop?

20. A certain loom beam contains 165 pounds of sized warp yarn. 8% was added to the original weight of the yarn by the slasher. How much unsized warp yarn does the beam contain?

21. 3 yards of sized warp yarn from a sample of cloth weigh 2.14 grains. If 7% of size has been added to the warp, what is the number of the yarn?

22. What must be the length of warp from the slasher to make a 60-yard cut of cloth if the warp contracts $6\frac{1}{2}\%$ in weaving?

23. What must be the width of warp in the reed if the cloth is to be 46 inches wide and the contraction in filling of this style of cloth is 6%?

MISCELLANEOUS PROBLEMS

24. The supplies for section 1 for 1 month cost $58.52. The supplies for section 2 for the same month cost $63.05. Both sections had the same number of looms on the same goods. What percent higher was the cost of supplies for section 2 than for section 1?

25. A weekly cloth room report is as follows: first-quality cloth, 450,832 yards; second-quality cloth, 23,728 yards. What percent of the cloth was second quality?

26. In one week a plant manufactured 473,714 yards of cloth. 4% of it was seconds. $1\frac{1}{2}\%$ was shorts and the remainder was first quality. How many yards of each quality were manufactured?

27. One kind of sizing compound contains 39 percent water, 34 percent tallow, 9 percent starch, 17 percent crude glycerine and one percent ash. How many pounds of each are required to make a batch of 2550 pounds of compound?

28. A cut of cloth whose weight is 22 pounds contains 8.8 pounds of filling. Find the percent of warp in the cloth.

29. 1080 bales of cotton were stored in a warehouse which caught fire. The insurance company estimated that 15% was destroyed by fire. How many bales were saved?

30. In a weave room there are 840 looms, 35% of them making sheeting, 40% making drills and the remainder of them making sateens. How many looms are there on each style?

31. If there are 80 employees in a weave room and 15% of them are loom fixers, how many loom fixers are there in the room?

32. In weaving a certain style sheeting it was found that the contraction was 6% in length. How many yards of this style of cloth will 63.6 yards of warp make?

33. Since getting an increase of 9% a fixer's wages average $28.80 a day. How much was he earning before the increase?

34. If 4% of the cloth made on a loom in one week was second quality and the first-quality cloth made was 640 yards, how many yards were made on the loom?

Chapter XVII

MEASURES OF WEIGHT, LENGTH, TIME, & VOLUME

The following tables contain most of the units of measure needed for textile calculations. It will be helpful to commit these to memory and become familiar with methods of converting units between the various measuring systems. Note: See the chapter on lap, sliver, roving and single yarn calculations.

Tables of Weights and Measures

Length:

1 millimeter (mm) = .03937 inches (in.) or (")
1 centimeter (cm) = .3937 inches
1 inch = 2.54 centimeters
12 inches = 1 foot (ft.) or (')
36 inches = 1 yard (yd.)
39.37 inches = 1 meter (m)
3 feet = 1 yard
120 yards = 1 skein
840 yards = 1 hank (cotton system)
5280 feet = 1 mile

Area:

144 square inches (sq. in.) = 1 square foot (sq. ft.)
9 square feet = 1 square yard
27 cubic feet = 1 cubic yard

Weight:

7000 grains (grs.) = 1 pound (lb.) (#)
16 ounces (oz.) or (ozs.) = 1 pound
453.6 grams (gms.) or (g) = 1 pound
437.5 grains = 1 ounce
28.35 grams = 1 ounce
15.432 grains = 1 gram
2000 pounds = 1 ton

Liquid:

$$1 \text{ gallon (gal.)} = 4 \text{ quarts (qts.)}$$
$$1 \text{ gallon} = 3785.33 \text{ cubic centimeters (cc)}$$
$$1 \text{ quart} = 2 \text{ pints (pts.)}$$
$$1 \text{ quart} = 946.33 \text{ cc}$$
$$1 \text{ pint} = 16 \text{ ounces}$$
$$1 \text{ pint} = 473.17 \text{ cc}$$
$$1 \text{ ounce} = 29.57 \text{ cc}$$

Time:

$$60 \text{ seconds} = 1 \text{ minute (min.)}$$
$$60 \text{ minutes} = 1 \text{ hour (hr.)}$$
$$24 \text{ hours} = 1 \text{ day}$$
$$7 \text{ days} = 1 \text{ week}$$
$$365 \text{ days} = 1 \text{ year}$$

PROBLEMS:

1. How many grains in an ounce?
2. How many skeins in a cotton hank?
3. How many minutes in 10 hours?

EXAMPLE: *How shall we measure .8 of a yard with a yard stick?*

There are 36 inches in one yard. $.8 \times 36$ in. $= 28.8$ in. A foot rule or a yard stick is divided into $\frac{1}{2}'', \frac{1}{4}'', \frac{1}{8}''$ and $\frac{1}{16}''$ spaces and sometimes into $\frac{1}{32}''$ spaces.

$$.8 \text{ in.} = .8 \times \frac{16}{16} \text{ in.} = \frac{12.8 \text{ in.}}{16} \text{ or practically } \frac{13}{16} \text{ in.}$$

$$\therefore .8 \text{ yd.} = 28.8 \text{ in.} = 28\frac{13}{16} \text{ in. approximately.}$$

4. Reduce 63.7 yards to yards, inches and sixteenths of an inch.
5. Reduce 58.85 yards to yards, inches and eighths of an inch.
6. Reduce 18.36 hours to hours and minutes.
7. Reduce 25.7 lbs. to pounds and ounces.
8. Reduce 210 yards to inches.
9. Reduce 44 oz. to grains.
10. Reduce 11 hanks to yards.

EXAMPLE: *Reduce 2 lbs. 6 oz. to pounds.*

$$2 \text{ lbs. } 6 \text{ oz.} = 2\frac{6}{16} \text{ lbs.} = 2\frac{3}{8} \text{ lbs.} = 2.375 \text{ lbs.}$$

11. Reduce 2 hrs. 33 min. to hours.

12. Reduce 10 yards 24 inches to yards.
13. Reduce 9 lbs. 7 oz. to pounds.

EXAMPLE: *Reduce 153 minutes to hours and minutes.*

$$2\frac{33}{60}$$ 153 minutes $= 2\frac{33}{60}$ hours $= 2$ hrs. 33 min.
$$60\overline{)153}$$
$$\underline{120}$$
$$33$$

14. Reduce 44 ounces to pounds and ounces.
15. Reduce 276 inches to yards and inches.
16. Reduce 305 minutes to hours and minutes.
17. Reduce 52,500 grains to pounds.
18. Reduce 64,750 grains to pounds.
19. Reduce 7840 yards to hanks.
20. Reduce 468,720 inches to hanks.

Compound Addition.   Such quantities as 2 lbs. 3 oz. are *compound quantities* because they are made up of more than one kind of unit. The following will make clear the method of adding compound quantities.

EXAMPLE: *What is the total weight of three picker laps if they weigh as follows: 68 lbs. 9 oz., 69 lbs. 1 oz., 68 lbs. 11 oz., and 68 lbs. 12 oz.?*

```
  68 lbs.   9 oz.
  69        1
  68       11
  68       12
 273       33 oz. = 2 lbs. 1 oz.
   2 lbs.   1 oz.
 275 lbs.   1 oz.    Answer:  275 lbs. 1 oz.
```

Compound Subtraction.

EXAMPLE: *From a cut of cloth 122 yds. 27 in. long, a piece 8 yds. 33 in. long had to be cut. How much remained?*

```
 121      36
 122 yds. 27 in.
          63
 − 8      33
 113 yds. 30 in.    Answer:  113 yds. 30 in.
```

Compound Multiplication.

EXAMPLE: *How many yards in a case of cloth containing 21 pieces, 40 yds. 29 in. long?*

$$16\frac{33}{36}$$

40 yds.	29 in.	$36\overline{)609}$
21	21	36
40	29	249
80	58	216
840 yds.	609 in.	33
16 yds. 33 in.		
856 yds. 33 in.		

Answer: 856 yds. 33 in.

Compound Division.

EXAMPLE: *The rear roll of a slasher requires about 4 yards of slasher cloth to cover it. We have a roll of slasher cloth containing 15 yds. 34 in. How many pieces can we cut from this roll and exactly how long will each piece be?*

We see that there is almost enough to make four 4-yd. pieces. We shall divide it into 4 pieces.

$$3\frac{3}{4}\text{ yds. } 8\frac{2}{4}\text{ in.}$$
$$4\overline{)15\text{ yds. }34\text{ in.}} \qquad \frac{3}{4}\text{ yd.} = \frac{3}{4} \times 36\text{ in.} = 27\text{ in.}$$

$$\therefore 3\frac{3}{4}\text{ yds.} = 3\text{ yds. }27\text{ in.}$$

$$\therefore 8\frac{2}{4}\text{ in.} = \frac{8\frac{1}{2}\text{ in.}}{3\text{ yds. }35\frac{1}{2}\text{ in.}}$$

Answer: Each piece 3 yds. $35\frac{1}{2}$ in. long.

21. A waste test report for 4 pickers is as follows: 146 lbs. 8 oz., 140 lbs. 4 oz., 152 lbs. 12 oz., 130 lbs. 8 oz. Find the total waste for the 4 pickers.

22. The waste report for nine slashers for the day is as follows: 2 lbs. 4 oz., 3 lbs., 2 lbs. 11 oz., 4 lbs. 1 oz., 2 lbs. 14 oz., 5 lbs. 1 oz., 3 lbs. 13 oz., 4 lbs. 9 oz., 6 lbs. 2 oz. Find the total pounds for the day.

23. To clothe the cylinder of a certain card 275′ 9″ of 2″ clothing filleting is required. To clothe the cylinder of another card 307′ 8″ of the same filleting is required. How much 2″ filleting will be required for the cylinders of both cards?

24. The gross weight of a case of cloth is 462 lbs. 11 oz. The empty case and ties weigh 7 lbs. 14 oz. How many lbs. of cloth are in the case?

25. A mechanic started a job at 7:45 A.M., and finished at 11:10 A.M. How long did the job take?

26. From a cloth roll 121 yds. 20 in. long a piece 10 yds. 24 in. had to be cut. How much cloth was left in the piece?

27. Find the number of feet of pipe necessary to make 24 humidifier drain pipes if each drain pipe is to be 10′ 1″ long.

28. How many pounds of yarn in 540 cones if each cone weighs 3 lbs. 3 oz.?

29. How many yards of slasher cloth will be required to cover the rear and front rolls of 4 slashers if the rear rolls each require 3 yds. 27 in. of 16-oz. slasher cloth and the front rolls each require 4 yds. 30 in. of 12-oz. slasher cloth?

30. A space 29′ 6″ long is to contain 8 bobbin bins. How long will each bin be?

CIRCULAR MEASURE

If we hold a piece of chalk against the face of a moving pulley the chalk will mark a circle on the pulley. The center of the circle will be at the center of the shaft on which the pulley runs. The distance from any point on the circle through the center of the circle to the chalk mark on the opposite side of the pulley is the *diameter* of the circle. The *length* of the chalk mark on the face of the pulley is the *circumference* of the circle. The drawing to the left makes this clear. The *radius* is the distance from the center to the circumference. Hence, the radius is half of the diameter.

Finding the Circumference. If you should take a steel tape measure and measure very accurately the diameter and the circumference of a pulley, you would find that the circumference is a little more than 3 times the diameter.

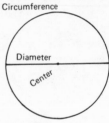

Figure 1

In all our calculations we shall consider that:

$$circumference = 3.1416 \times diameter$$

This is sufficiently accurate for our work. We shall use the abbreviations (cir.) or (circum.) for circumference and (dia.) for diameter. We will use these terms repeatedly.

> EXAMPLE: *What is the circumference of a pulley whose diameter is 36″?*
>
> 3.1416 × 36 = 113.098   **Answer:**   113.098 inches.

31. What is the circumference of a front roll on a spinning frame if its diameter is 1″?

32. What is the circumference of the calender roll of a card if the roll is 2″ in diameter?

Revolutions. The word *revolution* means one complete turn. If you should take hold of a pulley and turn it until your hand is back in the exact spot it was when you started to turn the pulley, the pulley has made one revolution.

33. The front roll of a certain roving frame is $1\frac{1}{4}''$ in diameter. How many inches of roving does it deliver in a minute if during the minute the roll makes 200 revolutions?

34. If the calender roll of a picker is 9" in diameter, how many yards of lap will the picker deliver in a minute if the calender roll makes $7\frac{1}{4}$ revolutions in one minute?

Finding the Diameter. Since the cir. = 3.1416 × dia. we can divide both sides of the equation by 3.1416 and obtain the following equation:

$$\text{diameter} = \frac{\text{circumference}}{3.1416}$$

35. The circumference of a pulley is $23\frac{9}{16}$ inches. What is the diameter?

36. What is the diameter of a slasher cylinder, if the circumference is 15 ft. $8\frac{1}{2}$ in.?

37. (a) Find the diameter of a pulley whose circumference is 18 ft. $10\frac{3}{4}$ in.

(b) If the circumference of a shaft is $7\frac{27}{32}$ in., what is the diameter?

38. A pattern maker is required to draw a circle for a pulley 2' 9" in circumference. What radius should he use?

SQUARE OR AREA MEASURE

Thus far we have discussed measures of length, weight and time. Now we come to measures of *surface* or *area*. The *length* of the *square* in figure 2 is 1 inch. The *width* of the *square* is also 1 inch. How much surface or area does it have? Any figure that is 1 inch long and 1 inch wide is said to have an area of 1 *square inch*.

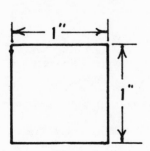

Figure 2

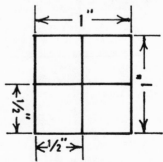

Figure 3

Suppose we should divide this square into 4 equal but smaller squares as shown in figure 3. We see at once that the length and width of each of these little squares is $\frac{1}{2}$ inch. How much area does each of the little squares have? Since the large square has 1 square inch of area, each small square must have $\frac{1}{4}$ of a square inch of area.

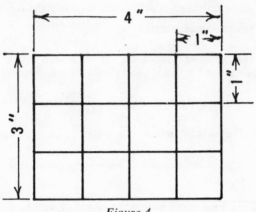

Figure 4

Now let us consider figure 4, which is 4″ long and 3″ wide and divided into squares 1″ long and 1″ wide. The lower row contains four squares, and since the figure is 3″ wide, the whole object contains 3 × 4 squares = 12 squares. To prove this we can count the squares. We find that there are 12 squares. Hence, the number of square inches in any figure that has four square corners = number of inches in its length × number of inches in its width. We also see that this is true of the little squares in figure 3. We said that each little square has an area of $\frac{1}{4}$ of a square inch. The length and width of each square is $\frac{1}{2}$ of an inch. Now multiply $\frac{1}{2} \times \frac{1}{2}$ and we get $\frac{1}{4}$. A figure with four square corners is called a *rectangle*. A square is a rectangle with its width equal to its length. Hence,

the area of any rectangle = width × length.

A square with a length of 1 inch is said to be 1 *inch square*. A square with a length of 2 inches is said to be 2 *inches square*. A surface 2 *inches* square has 4 square inches of area. Be sure you understand the distinction between inches square and square inches.

39. How many square inches in a sample of cloth 3 inches square?

40. How many square inches in a sample of cloth 4 inches square?

41. How many square inches in a sample of cloth 9 inches square?

42. Back in chapter XIII we discussed powers of numbers. Why is the second power of a number called the square of the number?

43. How many square inches in a sample of cloth 10 inches square?

44. How many square inches in a sample of cloth 12 inches square?

45. What is the area of a sample of cloth 27″ wide and 12″ long?

A square with a length of 1 foot has an area of 1 square foot and is said to be 1 foot square. A square with a length of 1 yard has an area of 1 square yard and is said to be 1 yard square.

46. How many square inches in a square foot?

47. How many square inches in a square yard?

EXAMPLE: *How many square inches in a 1-yard piece of cloth that is 40″ wide?*

Length = 1 yd. = 36″. Width = 40″. Square inches = 40 × 36 = 1440.

48. How many square inches in a 1-yard length of cloth that is $48\frac{1}{2}$ inches wide?

49. How many square inches of cloth in a piece of cloth that is 16.5 inches long and 11 inches wide?

50. How many samples of cloth 4″ wide and 5″ long can be cut from a yard of cloth that is 40″ wide?

51. How many square feet are there in one square yard?

52. Find the square feet of floor space in a supply room 72 ft. 6 in. long and 27 feet wide. *Hint:* Reduce the inches to fractions of feet.

The supply room in the preceding problem would be spoken of as: 72′ 6″ by 27′ or 27′ by 72′ 6″. Instead of the word "by," the dimensions are often written: 27′ × 72′ 6″.

In the following problems, disregard the amount of metal needed for seams or laps:

53. Find the number of square feet of copper that will be required to cover a mixing platform 4′ 8″ × 2′ 6″.

54. How many square inches of sheet iron will be required to make a quill can without a top of the following dimensions: bottom 8″ × 12″, depth 24″. *Hint:* First find the areas of the sides and bottom. Then add to find total area.

55. How many square feet of sheet copper will be required to line the bottom, ends and sides of a size box, whose inside dimensions are 66″ long × 28″ wide × 12″ deep?

56. Find the number of square inches of sheet metal that will be required to make a quill can $12\frac{1}{2}″ \times 8\frac{1}{2}″ \times 24\frac{1}{2}″$ high, with a bottom, but no top.

57. How many square feet of sheet iron will be required to line a filling chute 22″ × 22″ × 38′ high?

58. A certain card is 63 inches wide and 10′ $3\frac{1''}{2}$ long. How many square feet of floor space does it require?

Areas of Circles. The area of a circle is equal to 3.1416 times the diameter squared divided by 4. Thus:

$$area\ of\ a\ circle = 3.1416 \times \frac{dia.^2}{4}$$

59. From the preceding, prove that:

area of a circle = .7854 × dia.²

EXAMPLE: *Find the area of a circle 2′ 6″ in diameter.*

2′ 6″ = 30″.   30² = 30 × 30 = 900.   .7854 × dia.² =
.7854 × 900 = 706.86.
Area of circle = 706.86 square inches.

60. How many square inches of copper will be required to make a head for a slasher flue 14 inches in diameter?

61. (a) What is the area of one head of a slasher cylinder, if the diameter is 3 ft.?

(b) What is the total pressure on the head of a slasher cylinder when the pressure is 10 pounds per square inch?

62. How many square feet of copper will be needed to line the head of a size kettle whose diameter is 48 inches?

CUBIC OR VOLUME MEASURE

The object shown in figure 5 is a *cube.* All of its sides are squares. Any figure with its sides made of squares is a cube. The sides of the cube in figure 5 are 1 inch squares. Hence, the cube in figure 5 is 1″ long, 1″ wide and 1″ high (or deep). A cube 1″ long, 1″ wide and 1″ high is said to have a *volume* of 1 *cubic inch.* Other names for volume are *cubic capacity, capacity, cubic contents,* or *contents.* If the sides of this cube were made of tin, it would hold 1 cubic inch of water.

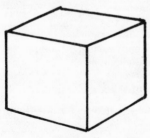

Figure 5

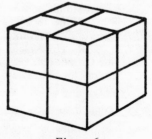

Figure 6

Now consider this same cube with divisions run through it as shown in figure 6, cutting the edges at their middle points. These divisions make eight smaller cubes, each having a length, width and height of $\frac{1}{2}$ of an inch. What is the volume of each of the smaller cubes? Their volume must be, of course, $\frac{1}{8}$ of a cubic inch.

Now consider the object shown in figure 7. This object is 2 inches wide or thick, 3 inches long and 4 inches high or deep and has square corners. Its sides are rectangles. Such an object is called a *prism*.

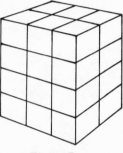

A cube is a prism, with all its sides equal. We see that it is divided into 1-inch cubes. The area of the bottom of the object = 2×3 square inches = 6 square inches. So there must be 6 cubes on the bottom layer. And since the object is 4 inches high, there are 4 layers of cubes. Therefore, there must be 4×6 cubes in the object, or 24 cubes. Therefore, the volume of the object is 24 cubic inches. From this we conclude that to find the volume of a prism, we multiply the area of the bottom or base by the height. This is also true of the

Figure 7

little cubes in figure 6. We found the volume of the little cubes to be $\frac{1}{8}$ of a cubic inch. The area of one side is $\frac{1}{2} \times \frac{1}{2}$ square inches. The height is $\frac{1}{2}$ of an inch. $\frac{1}{2} \times \frac{1}{2} \times \frac{1}{2} = \frac{1}{8}$.

Hence,

volume of any prism = area of base × height.

It makes no difference which surface of a prism we consider as the base.

EXAMPLE: *What is the volume of a prism* $\frac{3''}{4} \times 4\frac{1''}{2} \times 5''$?

$$\frac{3}{4} \times 4\frac{1}{2} \times 5 = \frac{3}{4} \times \frac{9}{2} \times 5 = \frac{135}{8} = 16.875$$

Answer: 16.875 cubic inches.

63. How many cubic inches are contained in a tank 1' 6" long × 1' wide × 6" deep?

A gallon contains 231 cubic inches.

A *cubic foot* is a volume equal to the volume of a prism all of whose edges are 1 foot long.

64. How many cubic inches in 1 cubic foot?

65. How many gallons would be contained in a prism 6" × 7" × 11"?

66. How many gallons in a cubic foot?

67. How many gallons of size will be required to fill a size box whose inside dimensions are as follows: length, $5\frac{1}{2}$ ft.; width, $2\frac{1}{2}$ ft.; and depth, $10\frac{1}{2}$ in.?

68. The size boxes on slashers are generally kept $\frac{1}{2}$ full. How many gallons of size will be required to fill 9 size boxes $\frac{1}{2}$ full, the boxes being 66″ × 28″ × 12″ deep (inside measure)?

69. How many cubic feet of a box car 34 ft. long, 8 ft. wide and 7 ft. high, will be left empty if 200 cases of cloth, each case 36 in. high, 22 in. wide and 18 in. thick, are placed in it?

A cubic foot of water weighs $62\frac{1}{2}$ pounds.

70. A tank is 8 ft. long, 6 ft. wide and $3\frac{1}{2}$ ft. deep. How many pounds of water will it hold?

71. What is the capacity in cubic feet of a humidifier tank $16\frac{1}{2}$ feet long, 8 feet 9 inches wide and 2 feet 10 inches deep?

72. It is desired to make a water tank for a humidifier that will hold 1000 gallons. But on account of other things in the way, the tank can be but 77 inches long and 55 inches wide. What will be the required depth?

AREAS AND VOLUMES OF CYLINDERS

Figure 8 represents a *cylinder*. As will be seen from figure 8, the ends (or bases) of a cylinder are circles of the same diameter. It is also evident that if the side of a cylinder were laid out flat, it would make a rectangle whose height would be the height of the cylinder and whose width would be the circumference of a circle, since the circumference of a circle = 3.1416 × the diameter:

area of the side of a cylinder
= circum. × height
area of the side of a cylinder
= 3.1416 × dia. × height

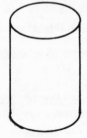

Figure 8

73. How many square feet of tin would be required to make a slasher ventilator flue 15 inches in diameter and 14 feet long?

74. Find the number of square feet of copper that would be required to line the sides and bottom of a cylindrical size kettle 48 × 48 inches (inside dimensions)?

75. The heads of a slasher cylinder are made of cast iron and the drum part is sheet copper. How many square feet of sheet copper would be required to make a cylinder drum 5' 6" long whose heads are 3' in diameter?

We have seen that the volume of a prism is equal to the area of its base times its height. We would expect the same to be true of a cylinder. Hence,

volume of a cylinder = .7854 × dia.² × height.

EXAMPLE: *What is the volume of a cylinder with a diameter of 2" and a height of 10"?*

.7854 × 4 × 10 = 31.416   **Answer:**   31.416 cubic inches.

76. How many gallons of size will be required to fill a cylindrical size kettle 36" in dia. × 36" high?

77. How many pounds of starch will be needed to fill a 48" × 48" (cylindrical) kettle with cooked size, if one gallon of size contains 12 ounces of starch?

78. How many gallons of size will fill a circular storage kettle 6 ft. 5 in. in diameter and 6 ft. deep?

Chapter XVIII

SQUARE ROOTS

SQUARE ROOTS OF PERFECT SQUARES

$2 \times 2 = 4$; $3 \times 3 = 9$; $4 \times 4 = 16$. The *square root* of 4 is 2; the square root of 9 is 3; the square root of 16 is 4. That is, the square root of a given number is a number which when multiplied by itself will produce the given number. Many necessary textile calculations involve square root. The sign $(\sqrt{})$ means "the square root of." Thus, $\sqrt{4} = 2$; $\sqrt{9} = 3$; $\sqrt{16} = 4$.

PROBLEMS. **Find the value of:**

1. $\sqrt{25}$ 3. $\sqrt{49}$ 5. $\sqrt{81}$ 7. $\sqrt{121}$

2. $\sqrt{36}$ 4. $\sqrt{64}$ 6. $\sqrt{100}$ 8. $\sqrt{144}$

Experiments and tests have shown that for ordinary warp yarn the number of twists per inch should be $4.75 \times$ square root of the number of the yarn. For ordinary filling the twists per inch should be $3.25 \times$ square root of the number of the yarn. For roving the twists per inch are usually equal to $1.2 \times$ square root of the number of the roving.

Find the proper twists per inch of:

9. Number 9 filling   12. Number 25 filling

10. Number 16 warp   13. Number 4 roving

11. Number 25 warp   14. Number 1 roving

EXAMPLE: *Find the square root of* $2\frac{1}{4}$.

$$2\frac{1}{4} = \frac{9}{4}. \quad \therefore \sqrt{2\frac{1}{4}} = \sqrt{\frac{9}{4}}. \quad \frac{9}{4} = \frac{3}{2} \times \frac{3}{2}. \quad \therefore \sqrt{\frac{9}{4}} = \frac{3}{2} = 1\frac{1}{2}.$$

$$\therefore \sqrt{2\frac{1}{4}} = 1\frac{1}{2}.$$

Find the value of:

15. $\sqrt{1\frac{7}{9}}$ 17. $\sqrt{1}$ 19. $\sqrt{\frac{4}{9}}$ 21. $\sqrt{\frac{1}{4}}$

16. $\sqrt{1\frac{9}{16}}$ **18.** $\sqrt{\frac{9}{16}}$ **20.** $\sqrt{\frac{9}{25}}$ **22.** $\sqrt{\frac{1}{16}}$

EXAMPLE: *Find the value of* $\sqrt{.04}$.

$\sqrt{.04} = \sqrt{.2 \times .2} = .2$. Or looking at the problem another way,

$$\sqrt{.04} = \sqrt{\frac{4}{100}} = \sqrt{\frac{2}{10} \times \frac{2}{10}} = \frac{2}{10} = .2.$$

Find the value of:

23. $\sqrt{.01}$ **24.** $\sqrt{.09}$ **25.** $\sqrt{.16}$ **26.** $\sqrt{.81}$
                     27. $\sqrt{1.00}$

By studying your answers to the preceding problems answer the following:

28. Is the square root of a given number that is greater than one, greater or less than the given number?

29. Is the square root of a given number that is less than one, greater or less than the given number?

30. Prove that the square root of a fraction equals the square root of the numerator divided by the square root of the denominator.

Square Root by Factoring.   Consider the number 36. $\sqrt{36} = 6$. We also see that $\sqrt{36} = \sqrt{4 \times 9} = \sqrt{4} \times \sqrt{9} = 2 \times 3 = 6$. That is, the *square root of a product is equal to the product of the square roots of the factors.*

$$
\begin{array}{r}
2)\underline{36} \\
2)\underline{18} \\
3)\underline{9} \\
3
\end{array}
$$

Now let us factor 36 into its prime factors. The prime factors are two 2's and two 3's. The prime factors of 6 are one 2 and one 3. That is, the square root of a given number contains as factors half the number of each of the given number's prime factors.

$$
\begin{array}{r}
2)\underline{144} \\
2)\underline{72} \\
2)\underline{36} \\
2)\underline{18} \\
3)\underline{9} \\
3
\end{array}
$$

Now consider the number 144. The prime factors of 144 are four 2's and two 3's. Therefore, $\sqrt{144}$ must contain as factors two 2's and one 3. That is, $\sqrt{144} = 2 \times 2 \times 3 = 12$.

By factoring find the square roots of:

31. 225   **32.** 256   **33.** 441   **34.** 1225   **35.** 11,025

The preceding problems might have been solved by the following method: Suppose we wish to find the square root of 2209.

22′ 09   Set down the number and starting at the right and moving toward the left, separate it into *periods* of two digits each.

$\overline{22′ 09}$ Cover the number with a bar.

      4
  ‾‾‾‾‾
  22′ 09

Find the largest square root in the first period and set it over the first period. The largest square root contained in 22 is 4. Thus, 4 is the first digit of the square root.

      4
  ‾‾‾‾‾
  22′ 09
  16
  ‾‾‾‾‾
) 6 09

Square the 4 which gives 16 and set the 16 under the 22. Subtract the 16 from the 22. Set the difference under a division bar and bring down the 09.

      4
  ‾‾‾‾‾
  22′ 09
  16
  ‾‾‾‾‾
8) 6 09

Double the 4 which makes 8. Set the 8 two spaces to the left of the division bar.

      4 7
  ‾‾‾‾‾
  22′ 09
  16
  ‾‾‾‾‾
87) 6 09

Divide the 8 into 60, the first two digits of 609. It goes 7 times. Put the 7 after the 4 and the 8.

      4 7
  ‾‾‾‾‾
  22 09
  16
  ‾‾‾‾‾
87) 6 09
   6 09
  ‾‾‾‾‾
        0

Multiply the 87 by the 7 and set the product under the 609. $87 \times 7 = 609$.

Draw a bar and subtract. The remainder is 0. Hence, the $\sqrt{2209} = 47$. Proof: $47 \times 47 = 2209$.

SQUARE ROOT OF ANY NUMBER

All of our preceding discussion has considered only *perfect squares,* that is, numbers whose square roots can be found exactly. Now suppose we wish to find the square root of 924.157.

      3   0.
  ‾‾‾‾‾‾‾‾‾
  9′ 24. 15′ 7
  9
  ‾‾‾‾‾‾‾‾
60) 0 24
    00
  ‾‾‾‾‾‾‾
    24 15

We separate the number into periods starting at the decimal point and moving both ways and then proceed as before. Six goes into 02 0 times. Multiply the 60 by the 0. Set down the product, 00; subtract and bring down the next period.

      3   0. 3
  ‾‾‾‾‾‾‾‾‾‾‾
  9′ 24. 15′ 7
  9
  ‾‾‾‾‾‾‾‾
60) 0 24
    00
  ‾‾‾‾‾‾‾
603)   24 15
      18 09
  ‾‾‾‾‾‾‾‾‾
      6 067

Double the part of the square root already obtained. This gives 60. Divide the 60 into 241. It goes 4 times. But if we try to multiply 604 by 4 we obtain 2416 which will not subtract from 2415. Therefore, we put down 3. Put down 1809, the product of 3×603. Subtract and bring down the next period.

```
  3   0.  3  9        Double the part of the square root already found.
  9' 24. 15' 7     This gives 606. Divide 606 into 6067, which gives 10.
  9                 The largest number, however, that we put down is 9. Set
60) 0  24           down the 9 as before. 9 × 6069 = 54,621.
      00               Therefore, the approximate square root of 924.157
603)  24  15       is 30.39.
      18  09          Proof: 30.39 × 30.39 = 923.5521.
6069)  6  06  7
       5  46  2
          60  5
```

If we wish to obtain the approximate square root quite accurately we can annex periods of 0's to the number. Suppose we wish to obtain the $\sqrt{5}$ carried to 3 decimal places:

```
  2.  2   3   6
  5. 00' 00' 00
  4
42) 1  00
    84
443)  16  00
      13  29
4466)  2  71  00
       2  67  96
          3  04
```

∴ $\sqrt{5}$ = 2.236.
Proof: 2.236 × 2.236 = 4.9999696.

By one of the preceding methods find the twists per inch required by the following numbers of yarn and roving. Use the shortest method suitable for each problem. Carry approximate square roots to four decimal places and twists per inch to two decimal places.

36. .6 roving
37. 6 roving
38. .55 roving
39. 55 warp yarn
40. 10.5 filling yarn
41. 30.56 filling yarn

Interpolation of Tables.   Suppose we wish to find from the table the square root of 40.76. The table gives the square root of 40 and the square root of 41. From these two square roots, we can roughly approximate the square root of 40.76. This is called *interpolation*. We reason as follows:

```
  41.00    40.76   √41 = 6.4031
- 40.00  - 40.00  - √40 = 6.3246
   1.00      .76         .0785
```

Square Root Tables

Number	Square Root	Number	Square Root	Number	Square Root
.25	.500	.68	.825	1.22	1.105
.26	.510	.69	.831	1.24	1.114
.27	.520	.70	.837	1.26	1.122
.28	.529	.71	.843	1.28	1.131
.29	.539	.72	.849	1.30	1.140
.30	.548	.73	.854	1.32	1.149
.31	.557	.74	.860	1.34	1.158
.32	.566	.75	.866	1.36	1.166
.33	.574	.76	.872	1.38	1.175
.34	.583	.77	.874	1.40	1.183
.35	.592	.78	.883	1.42	1.192
.36	.600	.79	.889	1.44	1.200
.37	.608	.80	.894	1.46	1.208
.38	.616	.81	.900	1.48	1.217
.39	.624	.82	.906	1.50	1.225
.40	.632	.83	.911	1.52	1.233
.41	.640	.84	.917	1.54	1.241
.42	.648	.85	.922	1.56	1.249
.43	.655	.86	.927	1.58	1.257
.44	.663	.87	.933	1.60	1.265
.45	.671	.88	.938	1.62	1.273
.46	.678	.89	.943	1.64	1.281
.47	.686	.90	.949	1.66	1.288
.48	.693	.91	.954	1.68	1.296
.49	.700	.92	.959	1.70	1.304
.50	.707	.93	.964	1.72	1.311
.51	.714	.94	.970	1.74	1.319
.52	.721	.95	.975	1.76	1.327
.53	.728	.96	.980	1.78	1.334
.54	.735	.97	.985	1.80	1.342
.55	.742	.98	.990	1.82	1.349
.56	.748	.99	.995	1.84	1.356
.57	.755	1.00	1.000	1.86	1.364
.58	.762	1.02	1.010	1.88	1.371
.59	.768	1.04	1.020	1.90	1.378
.60	.775	1.06	1.030	1.92	1.386
.61	.781	1.08	1.039	1.94	1.393
.62	.787	1.10	1.049	1.96	1.400
.63	.794	1.12	1.058	1.98	1.407
.64	.800	1.14	1.068	2.00	1.414
.65	.806	1.16	1.077	2.02	1.421
.66	.812	1.18	1.086	2.04	1.428
.67	.819	1.20	1.095	2.06	1.435

Number	Square Root	Number	Square Root	Number	Square Root
2.08	1.442	2.94	1.715	7.00	2.646
2.10	1.449	2.96	1.721	7.10	2.665
2.12	1.456	2.98	1.726	7.20	2.683
2.14	1.463	3.00	1.732	7.30	2.702
2.16	1.470	3.10	1.761	7.40	2.720
2.18	1.476	3.20	1.789	7.50	2.739
2.20	1.483	3.30	1.817	7.60	2.757
2.22	1.490	3.40	1.844	7.70	2.775
2.24	1.497	3.50	1.871	7.80	2.793
2.26	1.503	3.60	1.897	7.90	2.811
2.28	1.510	3.70	1.924	8.00	2.828
2.30	1.517	3.80	1.949	8.10	2.846
2.32	1.523	3.90	1.975	8.20	2.864
2.34	1.530	4.00	2.000	8.30	2.881
2.36	1.536	4.10	2.025	8.40	2.898
2.38	1.543	4.20	2.049	8.50	2.915
2.40	1.549	4.30	2.074	8.60	2.933
2.42	1.556	4.40	2.098	8.70	2.950
2.44	1.562	4.50	2.121	8.80	2.966
2.46	1.568	4.60	2.145	8.90	2.983
2.48	1.575	4.70	2.168	9.00	3.000
2.50	1.581	4.80	2.191	9.10	3.017
2.52	1.587	4.90	2.214	9.20	3.033
2.54	1.594	5.00	2.236	9.30	3.050
2.56	1.600	5.10	2.258	9.40	3.066
2.58	1.606	5.20	2.280	9.50	3.082
2.60	1.612	5.30	2.302	9.60	3.098
2.62	1.619	5.40	2.324	9.70	3.114
2.64	1.625	5.50	2.345	9.80	3.130
2.66	1.631	5.60	2.366	9.90	3.146
2.68	1.637	5.70	2.387	10.00	3.162
2.70	1.643	5.80	2.408	11.00	3.3166
2.72	1.649	5.90	2.420	12.00	3.4641
2.74	1.655	6.00	2.449	13.00	3.6056
2.76	1.661	6.10	2.470	14.00	3.7417
2.78	1.667	6.20	2.490	15.00	3.8730
2.80	1.673	6.30	2.510	16.00	4.0000
2.82	1.679	6.40	2.530	17.00	4.1231
2.84	1.685	6.50	2.550	18.00	4.2426
2.86	1.691	6.60	2.569	19.00	4.3589
2.88	1.697	6.70	2.588	20.00	4.4721
2.90	1.703	6.80	2.606	21.00	4.5826
2.92	1.709	6.90	2.627	22.00	4.6904

Number	Square Root	Number	Square Root	Number	Square Root
23.00	4.7958	66	8.1240	109	10.4403
24.00	4.8990	67	8.1854	110	10.4881
25.00	5.0000	68	8.2462	111	10.5357
26.00	5.0990	69	8.3066	112	10.5830
27.00	5.1962	70	8.3666	113	10.6301
28.00	5.2915	71	8.4261	114	10.6771
29.00	5.3852	72	8.4853	115	10.7238
30.00	5.4772	73	8.5440	116	10.7703
31.00	5.5678	74	8.6023	117	10.8167
32	5.6569	75	8.6603	118	10.8628
33	5.7446	76	8.7178	119	10.9087
34	5.8310	77	8.7750	120	10.9544
35	5.9161	78	8.8318	121	11.0000
36	6.0000	79	8.8882	122	11.0453
37	6.0828	80	8.9443	123	11.0905
38	6.1644	81	9.0000	124	11.1355
39	6.2450	82	9.0554	125	11.1803
40	6.3246	83	9.1104	126	11.2250
41	6.4031	84	9.1652	127	11.2694
42	6.4807	85	9.2195	128	11.3137
43	6.5574	86	9.2736	129	11.3578
44	6.6332	87	9.3274	130	11.4018
45	6.7082	88	9.3808	131	11.4455
46	6.7823	89	9.4340	132	11.4891
47	6.8557	90	9.4868	133	11.5326
48	6.9282	91	9.5394	134	11.5758
49	7.0000	92	9.5917	135	11.6190
50	7.0711	93	9.6437	136	11.6619
51	7.1414	94	9.6954	137	11.7047
52	7.2111	95	9.7468	138	11.7473
53	7.2801	96	9.7980	139	11.7898
54	7.3485	97	9.8489	140	11.8322
55	7.4162	98	9.8995	141	11.8743
56	7.4833	99	9.9499	142	11.9164
57	7.5498	100	10.0000	143	11.9583
58	7.6158	101	10.0499	144	12.0000
59	7.6811	102	10.0995	145	12.0416
60	7.7460	103	10.1489	146	12.0830
61	7.8102	104	10.1980	147	12.1244
62	7.8740	105	10.2470	148	12.1655
63	7.9373	106	10.2956	149	12.2066
64	8.0000	107	10.3441	150	12.2474
65	8.0623	108	10.3923		

Since the difference between 40.76 and 40.00 is .76 of the difference between 41.00 and 40.00, the difference between $\sqrt{40.76}$ and $\sqrt{40.00}$ will be .76 of the difference between $\sqrt{41.00}$ and $\sqrt{40.00}$.

$.76 \times .0785 = .0597$ 6.3246
                                          .0597
                                         ‾‾‾‾‾‾
                                   6.3843 $\therefore$ Interpolated $\sqrt{40.76} = 6.3843$

This reasoning, however, is not mathematically true and will give only an approximately correct result when the two numbers between which we interpolate are close together, such as 40 and 41.

Interpolate the square roots of the following numbers:

42. 16.25   **43.** 18.50   **44.** 20.75   **45.** 31.83
46. 42.93

Multiplying or Dividing by 10.   Suppose we wish to find the square root of .15:

$.15 = \dfrac{15}{100} . \therefore \sqrt{.15} = \sqrt{\dfrac{15}{100}} = \dfrac{\sqrt{15}}{\sqrt{100}} = \dfrac{\sqrt{15}}{10}$. The table shows that $\sqrt{15} = 3.8730. \therefore \dfrac{\sqrt{15}}{10}$ .38730. $\therefore \sqrt{.15} = .38730.$ Suppose we wish to find the square root of 180. $\sqrt{180} = \sqrt{100 \times 1.8} = 10 \times \sqrt{1.8}.$ The table shows that $\sqrt{1.8} = 1.342. \therefore \sqrt{180} = 13.42.$

Find the square root of:

47. .20   **48.** .18   **49.** 156   **50.** 1.43

Chapter XIX

RATIOS
&
PROPORTIONS

PROPORTION CONSIDERED AS A FRACTIONAL EQUATION

Suppose we have a sample of cloth 3″ square which weighs 7 grains and we wish to find the weight of a 1-yard length of this cloth 60″ wide. We can reason this way: The square inches of the 3″ square sample must be contained in the square inches of the 1-yard length just as many times as the grains of the sample are contained in the grains of the 1-yard length. That is to say, the square inches of the 1-yard length divided by the square inches of the sample = the grains of the 1-yard length divided by the grains of the sample. Putting this statement in the form of fractions we have:

(a) $$\frac{square\ inches\ of\ 1\text{-}yard\ length}{square\ inches\ of\ sample} = \frac{grains\ of\ 1\text{-}yard\ length}{grains\ of\ sample}$$

$$square\ inches\ of\ 1\text{-}yard\ length = 36 \times 60 = 2160$$
$$square\ inches\ of\ sample = \ \ 3 \times \ \ 3 = \ \ \ \ \ 9$$
$$grains\ of\ sample = \ \ 7$$

Substituting these numbers in equation (a) we obtain the following:

(b) $\dfrac{2160}{9} = \dfrac{grains\ of\ 1\text{-}yard\ length}{7}$. We remember from chapter XVI

that we can multiply and divide and add to and subtract from both sides of an equation with the same number and still keep the equation true.

Multiplying both sides by 7 and then canceling we obtain the following equation:

(c) $$\frac{\overset{240}{\cancel{2160}} \times 7}{\cancel{9}} = \frac{\cancel{7} \times grains\ of\ 1\text{-}yard\ length}{\cancel{7}}$$

This simplified gives us:

(d) 1680 = grains of 1-yard length. ∴ Weight of 1 yard = 1680 grains.

Ratio and Proportion. Equations (a), (b), and (c) are *proportions*. Both sides of equations (a), (b) and (c) are *ratios*. A ratio, therefore, is a fraction. A proportion is, therefore, an equation showing that one ratio is equal to another ratio. Looking at equations (a) and (b) we see that the ratio on the left side compares, or expresses the relationship of, the *area* of 1 yard of cloth to the *area* of a 3″ square piece of the same kind of cloth; while the ratio on the right compares, or expresses the relationship of, the *weight* of one yard of the same cloth to the *weight* of a 3″ square piece of the same cloth. And the proportion (or equation) expresses the fact that the relation of the *area* of the yard to the *area* of the 3″ square is exactly the same as the relation of the *weight* of the yard to the *weight* of the 3″ square.

Solving a problem, therefore, by *ratio and proportion* consists, first in reasoning out in your mind the relationships existing between the quantities given and asked for in the problem; second, in setting these relationships on paper in the form of a proportion; third, in reducing and simplifying the proportion.

Short Cuts in Simplifying Proportions.   Suppose we have the following proportion:

(1) $\dfrac{A \times B}{C \times D} = \dfrac{a \times b}{c \times d}$

Let us see into how many forms we can rearrange this equation without changing its truth. Multiplying both sides by $C \times D \times c \times d$ we obtain:

$$\frac{A \times B \times C \times D \times c \times d}{C \times D} = \frac{a \times b \times C \times D \times c \times d}{c \times d}$$

Canceling we obtain:

(2) $A \times B \times c \times d = a \times b \times C \times D$

Here we see that the product of the left numerator and right denominator always equals the product of the right numerator and left denominator. Dividing both sides of (2) by $A \times B \times a \times b$ we obtain:

$$\frac{A \times B \times c \times d}{A \times B \times a \times b} = \frac{a \times b \times C \times D}{A \times B \times a \times b}$$

Canceling we obtain:

$$\frac{c \times d}{a \times b} = \frac{C \times D}{A \times B}$$

Reversing sides we have:

(3) $\dfrac{C \times D}{A \times B} = \dfrac{c \times d}{a \times b}$

Here we see that the original proportion can be inverted and still be true. Multiplying both sides of (1) by C × D we obtain:

$$\frac{A \times B \times C \times D}{C \times D} = \frac{a \times b \times C \times D}{c \times d}$$

Canceling we obtain:

(4) $A \times B = \dfrac{a \times b \times C \times D}{c \times d}$

Here we see that the left numerator equals the product of the right numerator and the left denominator divided by the right denominator.

PROBLEMS. By means similar to those used in working out equations (2), (3) and (4) prove that:

1. (5) $C \times D = \dfrac{c \times d \times A \times B}{a \times b}$

2. (6) $a \times b = \dfrac{A \times B \times c \times d}{C \times D}$

3. (7) $c \times d = \dfrac{C \times D \times a \times b}{A \times B}$

4. (8) $A = \dfrac{a \times b \times C \times D}{B \times c \times d}$

5. (9) $B = \dfrac{a \times b \times C \times D}{A \times c \times d}$

6. (10) $a = \dfrac{A \times B \times c \times d}{b \times C \times D}$

7. (11) $b = \dfrac{A \times B \times c \times d}{a \times C \times D}$

8. (12) $C = \dfrac{c \times d \times A \times B}{D \times a \times b}$

9. (13) $D = \dfrac{c \times d \times A \times B}{C \times a \times b}$

10. (14) $c = \dfrac{C \times D \times a \times b}{d \times A \times B}$

11. (15) $d = \dfrac{C \times D \times a \times b}{c \times A \times B}$

EXAMPLE: *If 12 cards produced 40,425 lbs. of 60-grain sliver in 1 week, how many pounds of the same sliver will 15 cards produce in a week?*

We see at once that the ratio of 12 cards to 15 cards must be the same as the ratio of 40,425 lbs. to the pounds that 15 cards will produce.

Let p stand for the pounds that 15 cards will produce, $\therefore \frac{12}{15} = \frac{40,425}{p}$. In this equation we see that p corresponds in position to $c \times d$ in equation (1). Hence, from the short cut shown by equation (7) in problem 3 preceding we see that $p = \frac{15 \times 40,425}{12} = 50,531\frac{1}{4}$.

Answer: $50,531\frac{1}{4}$ lbs.

12. If 24 drawing frame deliveries produce 10,464 lbs. of 65-grain sliver in one day, how much will 40 deliveries, delivering at the same rate, produce of the same sliver in one day?

13. 304 spindles delivered 2772.48 hanks of number 3.00 roving in 8 hours, how many hanks of the same roving will 256 spindles deliver in 8 hours?

14. In 75 hours 1360 spindles have produced 10,098 lbs. of number 16 warp yarn for a certain order. How much should these same spindles produce at this rate in the next 35 hours?

15. If 1372 spindles are required to make filling for 98 looms, how many spindles will be required to make filling for 420 looms on the same style of cloth?

PROPORTION CONSIDERED AS A METHOD OF REASONING

Meaning of Direct Proportion.   Let us again consider the problem at the beginning of this chapter: If a sample of cloth 3″ square weighs 7 grains, what will be the weight of the 1-yard length? We see at once that doubling the square inches in the 1-yard length would double the grains in the 1-yard length. In other words, the square inches are *directly proportional* to the grains. This meaning of *direct proportion* can also be illustrated from equation *(a)*; for we see that since the ratios are equal, if the denominators remain the same, any increase in the numerator on one side must bring about an increase in the numerator of the other side. Now this brings us to the real meaning of ratio and proportion. Ratio and proportion is more than merely an equation between two fractions. It is a *method of reasoning* or *of seeing mathematical relationships* that will quicken your insight into all calculations.

Elements of a Proportion.   In the few ratio and proportion problems which we have studied thus far there has been *one unknown* quantity which you were required to find from the *three known* quantities which were given in each problem. Hence, in every proportion there are four quantities, which we may call the *elements* of the proportion.

How to Reason.   Let us again consider the problem at the beginning of this chapter. There are four elements of the problem: two of the elements are areas; two are weights. We have seen that a ratio expresses the relationship between two elements of the same kind; that is, a ratio compares area with area, weight with weight, length of time with length of time, etc. Very well, put the first element that you see down on paper. In this problem it is "3 inch square" or 9 square inches.

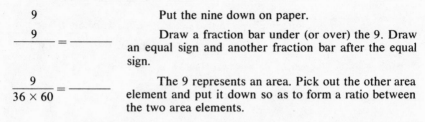

9   Put the nine down on paper.

$\dfrac{9}{} = \dfrac{}{}$ Draw a fraction bar under (or over) the 9. Draw an equal sign and another fraction bar after the equal sign.

$\dfrac{9}{36 \times 60} = \dfrac{}{}$ The 9 represents an area. Pick out the other area element and put it down so as to form a ratio between the two area elements.

Then pick out the remaining known element. In this case it is 7 grains. Then reason out whether or not the 7 grains is directly proportional to the area of the sample. That is, would increasing the area of the sample increase the weight of the sample at the same rate? It would. Therefore, the 7 and the 9 are directly proportional.

$\dfrac{9}{36 \times 60} = \dfrac{7}{}$ Therefore, put the 7 on the right side of the proportion in line with the 9.

The unknown element must go in the remaining blank space forming a ratio between itself and the element on the opposite side of the fraction bar from itself. Let u stand for the unknown element.

$\dfrac{9}{36 \times 60} = \dfrac{7}{u}$ Put the u in its proper place. Solve for u. That is, find the value of u by one of the short cuts.

$u = \dfrac{7 \times \overset{4}{\cancel{36}} \times 60}{\cancel{9}}$ Now since 7 stands for grains and forms a ratio with u, u *must* stand for grains. Therefore, a yard of this cloth weighs 1680 grains. Be sure you understand the last bit of reasoning.

$u = 1680$

Meaning of Inverse Proportions.   Let us consider this problem: A certain plain cloth 58″ wide contains 5 yds. to a pound. If this cloth is made 60″ wide, how many yards will there be to the pound?

58   As a starter we set down the first element we come to, which is 58, which stands for width.

$\dfrac{58}{60} = \dfrac{}{}$ Pick out the other width element and form a ratio between it and the first width element.

Then pick out the remaining known element. It is "5 yards to the pound." Now then, is the number of yards to a pound of cloth directly proportional to the width of the cloth? No, because the *greater* the width of the cloth the heavier a yard will be, and, hence, the *fewer* the yards to the pound. For instance, if the width of the cloth were *doubled* the yards to the pound would be *halved*. Therefore, we say that width and yards to the pound are *inversely proportional*. That is, increasing the width from 58″ to 60″ makes the yards per pound less than 5. *u*, the unknown element, represents the "yards to the pound" of the 60″ width and must form a ratio with the 5. But *u*, as we have just reasoned, must be less than 5. Since the ratio on the right must equal the ratio on the left, and since the left numerator is less than the left denominator, the right numerator must be less than the right denominator. Hence, *u* must be the numerator and 5 the denominator of the right side.

$$\frac{58}{60} = \frac{u}{5}$$ Put *u* and 5 in their proper places.

$$u = \frac{5 \times 58}{60}$$ Solve for *u*, using one of the short cuts.

$$u = 4.83$$ This must mean that the 60″ width of cloth contains 4.83 yards to a pound.

PROBLEMS: Some of the following problems involve inverse proportion. The others involve direct proportion. You must first reason out whether the problem involves direct or inverse proportion.

16. A picker is delivering 48-yard rolls of 13-oz. lap. We wish to change to 12-oz. lap. How many yards shall we put in the rolls of lap in order that the rolls of 12-oz. lap shall weigh the same as the rolls of 13-oz. lap?

17. The spinning frames making number 40 filling produced 12,560 lbs. in one week, which was 88% production. How many pounds of this number per week must these frames produce to obtain 90% production?

18. During one week 960 roving frame spindles produced 33,264 hanks of number 10 roving which was 92.8% production. The next week these same spindles produced 33,148 hanks of number 10 roving. What was their percent of production for this week?

19. A spinner trainee running 24 sides makes $80.33 in 5 days. How much will she make when she can run 30 sides?

20. 12,000 spindles produced in 90 hours half of the filling yarn required for a certain order. How long will it require 9000 spindles to produce the remaining half of the order?

21. If 20 looms will weave 4880 yards of cloth in a week, how many yards will 76 looms weave?

22. If 24 looms will weave the cloth for a certain order in 72 hours, how many hours will be required for 36 looms to weave the same amount and kind of cloth for another order?

23. A weaver trainee makes 90 dollars a week running 20 looms, how much will she make when she becomes efficient enough to run 24 looms?

24. If a loom will make 51 yards of cloth, 48 picks to the inch, in 8 hours, how many yards of cloth, 60 picks per inch, will it make in 8 hours?

25. A loom on a test ran $9\frac{1}{2}$ hours and wove $43\frac{7}{10}$ yards, how many yards will it weave in 55 hours?

26. A certain weaver on a certain style of cloth runs 20 looms and earns on the average $100.00 per week of 40 hours. How long would it take him to earn this same amount if he could run 22 looms?

27. A certain style of cloth 64″ wide is being made with 2880 warp ends; it is desired to make this cloth 70 inches wide with the same amount of warp ends per inch in the cloth. How many warp ends will be required?

28. A drill 60″ wide and containing 1.25 yards per pound is being made, but it is desired to make this cloth 64″ wide, changing the width and weight only. What will be the yards per pound?

Proportions of More Than Four Elements.   Suppose we wish to solve the following problem by proportion: A 58-yard cut of cloth 60 inches wide weighs 24 lbs. What will be the weight of a 60-yard cut of this same cloth made 72 inches wide?

Let w stand for the weight of a 60-yard cut of cloth 72″ wide. We reason that w is directly proportional to the length of the cut.

$\dfrac{w}{} = \dfrac{60}{}$ Therefore, set w down as one numerator and 60 as the other numerator, since they are directly proportional. Is w directly proportional to any other element? Yes, it is directly proportional to the width of the cloth.

$\dfrac{w}{} = \dfrac{60 \times 72}{}$ Set 72 down as a factor beside 60.

$\dfrac{w}{24} = \dfrac{60 \times 72}{}$ Put 24 under w, since 24 and w are the same kind of elements.

$\dfrac{w}{24} = \dfrac{60 \times 72}{58 \times 60}$ And since 24 is directly proportional to 58×60, for the same reason that w is directly proportional to 60×72, set 58×60 down in line with 24.

$w = \dfrac{60 \times 72 \times 24}{58 \times 60}$ Solve for w.

$w = 29.79$ Therefore, a 60-yard cut 72″ wide will weigh 29.79 lbs.

29. If a weaver is paid $90.00 for running 95% of a job for 36 hours, how much can she make in 40 hours running 100% of a job?

30. An order is received for 142,560 lbs. of a certain number of yarn. In 12 days 4320 spindles produce 15,552 lbs. of the order. How many spindles must be put on this yarn to produce the balance of the order in 90 days?

31. If a 65-yard cut of cloth 72″ wide weighs 50 lbs., what should be the weight of a $63\frac{1}{2}$-yard cut of the same cloth made $70\frac{1}{2}''$ wide?

Chapter XX

MECHANICAL CALCULATIONS

CONVENTIONAL POWER TRAINS

Two-Pulley and Belt Trains. Referring to figure 1 and your study of circular measure, *surface speed, SS,* of a pulley is the *surface distance, SD,* measured in number of any 1 linear unit, that a point on its rim moves because of its number of *revolutions, rev,* during any 1 ("per") time unit.

    1. Find the SD of A if the dia. of A is 3′ and A makes (a) 1 (b) 5 rev.

    2. Find the SD of B if its dia. is 20″ and it runs (a) 10 (b) 60 rev.

    3. From the foregoing show that

$$(1)\ \frac{\text{surface speed}}{\text{of a pulley}} = \frac{\text{surface distance of the pulley in number}}{\text{of any linear units during 1 time unit}} =$$

$$\pi \times \frac{\text{diameter of the pulley}}{\text{in the same linear unit}} \times \frac{\text{revolutions of the pulley during}}{\text{1 of (per) the same time unit.}}$$

Hereafter in this book such expressions as "the rev of A," "the dia. of the pulley," "the dia. of A," or "SS of B" may be abbreviated "rev A," "dia. pulley," "dia. A," or "SS B."

    In a train such as fig. 1 the driver pulley transmits the power to the belt and the driven pulley. A pulley is known by its dia.

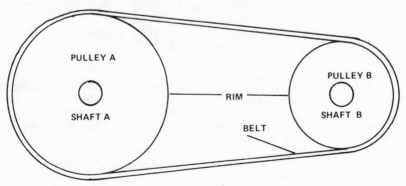

Figure 1

4. In fig. 1 if A is the driver, dia. A is 30″, and rev. A is 50 what (a) by formula (1) ∴ is SD A; (b) ∴ must be SD driven pulley if there is no slippage; (c) ∴ must be rev. 6″ driven pulley; and (d) is the ratio of $\dfrac{\text{rev. driven pulley}}{\text{rev. driver pulley}}$?

5. If B is an 8″ driver and the 25″ driven pulley must make 36 rev. what must be (a) SD driven pulley; (b) SD driver pulley; (c) rev. driver; and (d) the ratio of $\dfrac{\text{rev. driver pulley}}{\text{rev. driven pulley}}$.

6. The shaft of B makes 112 rev., A is 28″, and its shaft makes 40 rev. in the same time. (a) What is SD driver or driven pulley? (b) What is cir. B? (c) What is $\dfrac{\text{SD B}}{\text{cir. B}}$. Why? (d) What is dia. B? Prove it. (e) What is the ratio of $\dfrac{\text{dia. A}}{\text{dia. B}}$? (f) What is the ratio of $\dfrac{\text{dia. B}}{\text{dia. A}}$?

7. From the preceding three problems select the correct word or words within each set of the following parentheses: In a power train of two pulleys and a belt the revolutions of the one are (a) (directly, inversely) proportional to its own diameter and (b) (directly, inversely) proportional to the diameter of the other; and to calculate revolutions and diameters it (c) (is, is not) necessary to distinguish between driver and driven.

8. From the preceding problems derive

(2) $\dfrac{\text{revolutions of the one pulley}}{\text{revolutions of the other pulley}} = \dfrac{\text{diameter of the other pulley}}{\text{diameter of the one pulley}}$,

(3) $\dfrac{\text{revolutions of}}{\text{the one pulley}} = \dfrac{\text{revolutions of the other pulley} \times \text{diameter of the other pulley}}{\text{diameter of the one pulley}}$, and

(4) $\dfrac{\text{diameter of}}{\text{the one pulley}} = \dfrac{\text{diameter of the other pulley} \times \text{revolutions of the other pulley}}{\text{revolutions of the one pulley}}$.

9. The 6″ pulley on the motor of a cleaning and blending feeder runs 1200 rev. in 1 min. and drives a 12″ pulley on the apron. How many rev. does the apron pulley make in 1 minute?

10. The same motor in the preceding problem must run the blender pulley 450 rev. in a min. What must be the size of the blender pulley?

RPM, IPM, FPM, and YPM.   In textile machinery calculations the most frequent unit of time for measuring *speed* of rotation and surface distance is the minute. Hence the following expressions of speed are frequent: *revolution or revolutions per minute,* both abbreviated *RPM,* meaning any fraction or multiple of 1 revolution in 1 minute; *inch or inches per minute, IPM; foot or feet per minute, FPM;* and *yards per minute, YPM.*

From here on in this book, unless otherwise indicated, surface distance, circumferences, diameters, and radiuses are understood as in inches.

11. The 18″ doffer driven pulley of a picker is run by a belt from the doffer driver pulley which is available in whole inch sizes 3″ to 8″. The driver pulley makes 800 RPM. Find the size of the driver that must be used to give the driven pulley as near as possible to the following speeds and then find the IPM and FPM of the belt and the RPM of the driven pulley that that pulley will give: (a) 125 RPM (b) 235 RPM and (c) 350 RPM.

12. The feed pulley of a picker, available in whole in. 4″ to 15″, runs 1250 RPM and by belt drives the 24″ calender drive shaft pulley. If the calender drive shaft must make as near as possible to the following RPM what feed pulley must be put and what IPM, FPM, and RPM calender drive shaft will this make: (a) 200 (b) 340 (c) 510 and (d) 700.

Effective Diameters.

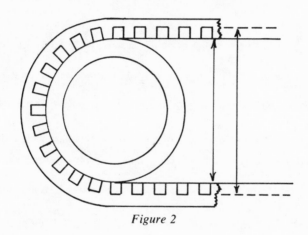

Figure 2

13. (a) Why is the inside of thick leather belts running on small pulleys wrinkled and the outside stretched; and the inside of some thick composition belts on small smooth pulleys, as in fig. 2, made with cross grooves? (b) Show that

(5) *effective dia.* of pulley = dia. of pulley + thickness of belt.

14. On a spinning frame an 8″ spindle driver pulley making 1250 RPM through a tape $\frac{1}{16}$″ thick drives the $1\frac{1}{16}$″ spindle whorl. By ignoring tape thickness what is the + or − error in (a) RPM spindle (b) % of true RPM spindle?

15. The feed pulley of a picker making 1250 RPM and through a belt $\frac{1}{4}$″ thick driving the 24″ calender drive shaft pulley is changed from 4″ to 15″ (a) By ignoring belt thickness with which of these 2 driver pulleys is the error greater and by what (b) RPM (c) % of true RPM?

Crossed Belts, Revolving Surfaces in Contact, and Signs of Direction.

16. If the belt in fig. 1 is crossed so that it runs between the upper surface of A and the lower surface of B or A and B are brought in contact without a belt select the correct word or words within each set of the following parentheses: (a) One pulley runs in a direction the (same as, opposite to) the other pulley. (b) If one is considered as running forward the other must be considered as running (forward, backward). (c) If one is considered as running in a *positive* or plus, +, direction the other must run in a (positive, *negative* or minus, −,) direction.

As one views a pulley or other revolving part if the surface at the upper portion of one's view moves toward one's right hand, that is, as one looks at a clock, the direction is *right hand, RH,* or *clockwise;* if opposite, the direction is *left hand, LH,* or *counterclockwise.* Occasionally when necessary to distinguish between directions usually RH is + and LH −.

17. As you look at the 18″ card cylinder pulley, which by a crossed belt drives the $6\frac{1}{2}''$ licker-in pulley, it makes 225 RPM RH. (a) What is the licker-in RPM? The $3\frac{3}{4}''$ pulley at the other end of the licker-in by a crossed belt $\frac{1}{4}''$ thick drives the 18″ doffer pulley. (b) What is RPM doffer?

18. The outside dia. of the yarn tube onto which the winder packages the yarn is $1\frac{5}{16}''$. The package revolves by pressured contact with the drum of $7\frac{1}{2}''$ dia. and making 850 RPM RH. The full package is 9″ dia. What is (a) IPM yarn (b) hanks per hr. of a 40-drum winder not allowing for stops (c) RPM bare tube and (d) RPM full package?

Two-Gear, Sprocket and Chain, Gear and Rack, and Gear and Track Trains. A gear's *pitch circle* has its center at the gear's center and its *pitch circumference, p. cir.,* as in fig. 3, running through the contact points of the

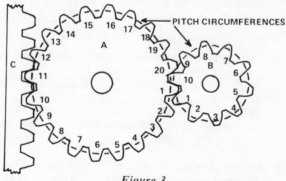

Figure 3

gear's teeth with the teeth of any other gear or *rack* or *track,* such as C, with which the gear *meshes.* The *circumferential pitch, cir. p.,* is the distance along the p. cir. between corresponding points of two adjacent teeth. The *pitch diameter, p. dia.,* is the diameter of the pitch circle.

19. For any gear as in fig. 3 from the foregoing prove that:

(6) pitch circumference $= \pi \times$ pitch diameter $= 2 \times \pi \times$ pitch radius,

(7) pitch circumference $=$ number of teeth $\times$ circumferential pitch,

(8) circumferential pitch $= \dfrac{\text{pitch circumference}}{\text{number of teeth}}$, and

(9) number of teeth $= \dfrac{\text{pitch circumference}}{\text{circumference pitch}}$.

20. From fig. 3 show that

$$(10) \quad \begin{array}{c} \text{circumferential pitch} \\ \text{of the one gear,} \\ \text{rack, or track} \end{array} = \begin{array}{c} \text{circumferential pitch} \\ \text{of the other gear,} \\ \text{rack, or track meshed} \\ \text{to it,} \end{array}$$

and   (11)

$$\begin{array}{c} \text{surface distance along} \\ \text{straight line of rack} \\ \text{or along pitch circumference} \\ \text{of one gear meshed} \\ \text{with the rack of another gear} \end{array} = \begin{array}{c} \text{revolutions} \\ \text{of one of} \\ \text{the gears} \end{array} \times \begin{array}{c} \text{teeth of} \\ \text{the same} \\ \text{gear} \end{array} \times \begin{array}{c} \text{circumferential} \\ \text{pitch.} \end{array}$$

Henceforth in this book "teeth" may mean "number of teeth"; and the name, initials, or other designation of a gear may mean its number of teeth. As with pulleys, if in a train of two meshing gears one is considered the driver the other must be the driven.

21. In fig. 3 if from the point of contact of tooth 1 of A with tooth 10 of B to the corresponding point of tooth is 2″ what is: (a) p. cir. A? Why? (b) cir. p. A? Why? (c) cir. p. B? (d) p. cir. B? Why? (e) p. dia. B? Why?

22. A 34-tooth gear must be ordered so that it will drive a 60-tooth gear that is 5″ between the contact points of opposite teeth. What cir. p. must be ordered?

23. From formula (11) prove: In fig. 3 that rev. A $\times$ A $\times$ cir. p. $=$ $-$rev. B $\times$ B $\times$ cir. p. or $-$rev. A $\times$ A $\times$ cir. p. $=$ rev. B $\times$ B $\times$ cir. p. and in either case $\therefore \dfrac{\text{rev. A}}{\text{rev. B}} = -\dfrac{B}{A}$. and $\therefore$ that

$$(12) \quad \dfrac{\text{revolutions of the one gear}}{\text{revolutions of the other gear}} = -\dfrac{\text{teeth of the other gear}}{\text{teeth of the one gear.}}$$

24. In fig. 3, reasoning from common sense observation, if tooth 1 of A is about to drive tooth 1 of B what tooth of B will it be about to

drive when A has made (a) $\frac{1}{4}$ (b) $\frac{1}{2}$ (c) $\frac{3}{4}$ and (d) 1 rev. From this prove

that rev. $B = -\dfrac{\text{rev. A} \times A}{B}$ and $\therefore \dfrac{\text{rev. B}}{\text{rev. A}} = -\dfrac{A}{B}$.

25. A 13-tooth loom motor gear making 1755 RPM LH as you stand facing the motor and the breast beam drives a 171-tooth crank shaft. Find RPM crank shaft.

26. In a two-sprocket and chain train if the sprockets are A and B show that: (a) rev. A and rev. B are of the same sign. Why? (b) cir. p. A = cir. p. B. Why? (c) rev. A $\times$ p. cir. A = rev. B $\times$ p. cir. B. Why? (d) $\therefore$
$\dfrac{\text{rev. A}}{\text{rev. B}} = \dfrac{\text{p. cir. B}}{\text{p. cir. A}}$. Why? (e) $\therefore \dfrac{\text{rev. A}}{\text{rev. B}} = \dfrac{B \times \text{cir. p. B}}{A \times \text{cir. p. A}} = \dfrac{B}{A}$. Why? (f) $\therefore$

$$(13)\quad \frac{\begin{array}{c}\text{revolutions}\\ \text{of the one sprocket}\end{array}}{\begin{array}{c}\text{revolutions}\\ \text{of the other sprocket}\end{array}} = \frac{\text{teeth of the other sprocket}}{\text{teeth of the one sprocket}}.$$

27. The 14-tooth wind-down motor sprocket of a roving frame runs 3450 RPM RH and drives the 26-tooth sprocket on the wind-down shaft. Find RPM driven sprocket.

The surface distance of a point on a machine part, especially the straight-line distance oscillating across the direction of the stock, is often called *traverse*. Thus, in fig. 3 if C is a rack it *traverses* relative to the center of A and if C is a track the center of A traverses relative to C.

28. From formula (11) prove that

$$(14)\quad \begin{array}{c}\text{traverse of rack}\\ \text{relative to gear cen-}\\ \text{ter or of gear center}\\ \text{to track}\end{array} = \begin{array}{c}\text{revolutions}\\ \text{of}\\ \text{gear}\end{array} \times \begin{array}{c}\text{teeth}\\ \text{in}\\ \text{gear}\end{array} \times \begin{array}{c}\text{circumferential}\\ \text{pitch.}\end{array}$$

29. The cone rack of a roving frame has 32 teeth per foot and is driven by a 16-tooth gear which is now making 3 rev. for 40 layers wound onto the bobbin. How far does the cone rack move for each layer?

30. If the 16-tooth .5238″ − cir. p. gear driving the lift rack of a roving frame makes 3 RPM during the winding of the first layer what is IPM lift rack?

Screw and Worm and Worm Gear Trains. A screw may be single threaded or, as in fig. 4, multiple threaded. The *pitch* is the surface distance parallel to the axis of the screw between adjacent corresponding points of a single thread or of multiple threads. If a screw is threaded into a nut or other part and either of them revolves while the other does not, the traverse during 1 rev. is the *lead*. If facing the end of the screw at which power is designed to be applied, its clockwise revolution would traverse that end and the part threaded to the screw toward each other, the threads are RH and, if necessary to calculate their hand, their sign is +.

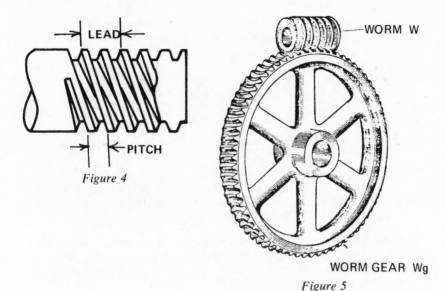

Figure 4

WORM W

WORM GEAR Wg

Figure 5

31. (a) Show that lead = threads × pitch. As to the screw in fig. 4: (b) at which end would power be applied? Why? (c) What is its hand and sign? Why?

32. Remembering that revolutions in the same direction are of the same sign and revolutions opposite must be of opposite signs, for a screw and part threaded to it, whether one revolves while the other does not or both revolve, derive

$$(15) \quad \text{traverse} = \left(\begin{array}{c} \text{revolutions} \\ \text{of the screw} \end{array} - \begin{array}{c} \text{revolutions of the} \\ \text{part threaded to it} \end{array} \right) \times \text{lead.}$$

33. On a certain roving frame the single-thread builder screw has .1667 pitch. Facing its upper end, its upper end is threaded RH to the upper jaw and its lower end LH to the lower jaw. The jaws do not revolve. While the bobbins are winding, the builder screw makes 8 rev. LH. What is the sign of the (a) rev. screw (b) upper thread (c) upper lead (d) lower thread (e) lower lead. Relative to the upper end of the screw what is the traverse of the (f) upper jaw (g) lower jaw? (h) Do the jaws approach or recede from each other? Why?

34. On another kind of roving frame each bobbin is threaded to its .5″-lead RH bobbin screw driven at its lower end. If during resetting the frame the bobbins do not revolve and the bobbin screws make 27.6 RPM RH (a) What is IPM bobbin (b) does bobbin traverse up or down? What is IPM bobbin and in which direction if during the winding of (c) one layer the bobbin screw makes 1472 RPM LH while the bobbin makes 1406 RPM LH (d) the next layer the bobbin screw makes 1339 RPM LH while the bobbin makes 1396 RPM LH?

In a train such as in fig. 5 the *worm*, W, is a screw with pitch equal to the cir. p. of the *worm gear*, with lead, and may be single or multiple threaded either RH or LH.

35. In fig. 5 show why: rev. Wg $= \dfrac{\text{traverse W}}{\text{p. cir. Wg}} =$

$$\dfrac{\text{rev. W} \times \text{threads} \times \text{cir. p. Wg}}{\text{Wg} \times \text{cir. p. Wg}} = \dfrac{\text{rev. W} \times \text{threads}}{\text{Wg}} \text{ and}$$

(16) $\dfrac{\text{revolutions of worm gear}}{\text{revolutions of worm}} = \dfrac{\text{threads in worm}}{\text{teeth in worm gear}}.$

36. On a certain picker if the RPM of the triple threaded top cone worm at this instant is 468 what is the RPM of its 78-tooth worm gear?

37. If the double take-up worm on a certain loom runs 90 RPM find the RPM of its 30-tooth worm gear.

Multiple Shaft, Pulley, and Gear Trains.   Parts which move or act as one are integral. Thus in fig. 6 roll A and gear B, gears D and E and pulley I, gear G and roll H, and pulleys J and K are integral. A gear such as C or F which conveys power by its teeth only is a carrier, intermediate, or idler.

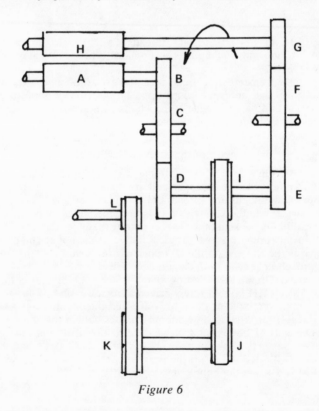

Figure 6

38. By formula (12) show why:

(a) $\dfrac{\text{rev. A}}{\text{rev. C}} = \dfrac{C}{B}$, (b) $\dfrac{\text{rev. C}}{\text{rev. D}} = \dfrac{D}{C}$, (c) $\dfrac{\text{rev. E}}{\text{rev. F}} = \dfrac{F}{E}$, and (d) $\dfrac{\text{rev. F}}{\text{rev. H}} = \dfrac{G}{F}$.

By multiplying the left sides of equations (a), (b), (c), and (d) together

and the right sides together obtain (e) $\dfrac{\text{rev. A} \times \text{rev. C} \times \text{rev. E} \times \text{rev. F}}{\text{rev. C} \times \text{rev. D} \times \text{rev. F} \times \text{rev. H}} =$

$\dfrac{C \times D \times F \times G}{B \times C \times E \times F}$. Noting the integral gears and by cancelling on both sides of equation (e) prove that

(17) $\dfrac{\text{rev. A}}{\text{rev. H}} = \dfrac{D \times G}{B \times E}$,

(18) rev. $A = \dfrac{\text{rev. H} \times D \times G}{B \times E}$,

(19) rev. $H = \dfrac{\text{rev. A} \times B \times E}{D \times G}$,

(20) $B = \dfrac{\text{rev. A} \times D \times G}{\text{rev. A} \times E}$,

(21) $D = \dfrac{\text{rev. A} \times B \times E}{\text{rev. H} \times G}$,

(22) $E = \dfrac{\text{rev. H} \times D \times G}{\text{rev. A} \times B}$,

(23) $G = \dfrac{\text{rev. A} \times B \times E}{\text{rev. H} \times D}$.

39. By formulas (2) and (12) and reasoning as in the preceding problem prove that

(24) $\dfrac{\text{rev. A}}{\text{rev. L}} = \dfrac{D \times \text{dia. J} \times \text{dia. L}}{B \times \text{dia. I} \times \text{dia. K}}$,

(25) rev. $A = \dfrac{\text{rev. L} \times D \times \text{dia. J} \times \text{dia. L}}{B \times \text{dia. I} \times \text{dia. K}}$,

(26) rev. $L = \dfrac{\text{rev. A} \times B \times \text{dia. I} \times \text{dia. K}}{D \times \text{dia. J} \times \text{dia. L}}$,

(27) $D = \dfrac{\text{rev. A} \times B \times \text{dia. I} \times \text{dia. K}}{\text{rev. L} \times \text{dia. J} \times \text{dia. L}}$,

(28) dia. $J = \dfrac{\text{rev. A} \times B \times \text{dia. I} \times \text{dia. K}}{\text{rev. L} \times D \times \text{dia. L}}$,

(29) dia. $K = \dfrac{\text{rev. L} \times D \times \text{dia. J} \times \text{dia. L}}{\text{rev. A} \times B \times \text{dia. I}}$.

By studying formulas (17) *to* (29) *find the answer to the following two problems:*

40. What effect does a carrier gear have upon the (a) revolutions, (b) RPM (c) IPM of any other member of the train? (d) Why?

41. Select the correct word within each set of the following parentheses: In any train: If one member is, or is temporarily classified as, a driver or driven the other member next before or after must be classified as the (a) (one, other). The ratio of the revolution of one member to the revolution of any other member equals the ratio of the product of the teeth or diameter of every intervening member of the (b) (one, other) classification to the product of the teeth or diameter of every intervening member of the (c) (one, other) classification. The revolutions of a member classified as a driven equal the product of the revolutions of any (d) (driven, driver) and the teeth or diameter of every intervening (e) (driven, driver) divided by the product of the teeth or diameter of every intervening (f) (driven, driver). The revolutions of a member classified as a driven are (g) (directly, inversely) proportional to the revolutions of any (h) (driven, driver) and the teeth or diameter of any intervening (i) (driven, driver) and (j) (directly, inversely) proportional to teeth or diameter of any intervening (k) (driven, driver).

42. In fig. 6 by applying formula (1) to rolls and to formula (17)

show that $= \dfrac{\dfrac{SD\ A}{dia.\ A \times \pi}}{\dfrac{SD\ H}{dia.\ H \times \pi}} = \dfrac{D \times G}{B \times E}$ and $\therefore$ derive

(30) $\dfrac{\text{surface distance of A}}{\text{surface distance of H}} = \dfrac{dia.\ A \times D \times G}{dia.\ H \times B \times E}$ or

$$\frac{IPM\ A}{IPM\ H} = \frac{dia.\ A \times D \times G}{dia.\ H \times B \times E}.$$

As you will study in Part Two, (30) is the most used basic formula in the carding and spinning departments.

43. Derive an equation expressing (a) rev. H to rev. L, (b) RPM H, (c) IPM H.

In fig. 6 *dia. A is* 6″, *H* 5″, *I* 12″, *L* 6″, *RPM L is* 100; *B has* 24 *teeth and G* 30. *Use the easiest formulas, equations, or principles developed in the preceding six problems to answer the following nine problems:*

44. What is the ratio SD A to SD H if D has 36 teeth and E has (a) 24 (b) 30 teeth?

45. Find the ratio IPM A to IPM H if E has 27 teeth and D has (a) 33 (b) 39 teeth?

46. Determine the IPM A if D has 36 teeth, J is 8″, and K is (a) 12″ (b) 11″.

47. What is IPM A if D has 36 teeth, K is 13″, and J is (a) 7″ (b) 9″?

48. Find IPM H if E has 24 teeth, J is 8″, and K is (a) 12″ (b) 11″.

Change Pulleys and Gears and Constants. Changeable train members (such as E, D, J, and K are considered to be in the preceding five problems) are change gears and *change pulleys.*

49. As in a preceding problem, let us in this problem consider E the only change gear in the train in formula (30). Prove that

$$\frac{SD\ A}{SD\ H} \times E = \frac{dia.\ A \times D \times G}{dia.\ H \times B} = 54;$$ ∴ that regardless of how much SD A, SD H, and E change the **product** of the ratio of SD A to SD H and E never changes and ∴ is a constant; i.e., (a) constant = ratio × change gear = 54; ∴ that (b) ratio = $\dfrac{constant}{change\ gear}$; and ∴ that (c) $\dfrac{change}{gear} = \dfrac{constant}{ratio}$.

EXAMPLE: *What ratio of SD A to SD H is given if E has* (a) 18 (b) 24 (c) 27 *teeth?*

By equations (a) and (b): (a) ratio $= \dfrac{54}{18} = 3$ (b) ratio $= \dfrac{54}{24}$ (c) ratio $= \dfrac{54}{27} = 2$.

EXAMPLE: *How many teeth in E are needed to give a ratio of SD A to SD H of* (a) 1.5 (b) 4.5 (c) 6?

By equations (a) and (c): (a) $E = \dfrac{54}{1.5} = 36$ (b) $E = \dfrac{54}{4.5} = 12$ (c) $E = \dfrac{54}{6} = 9.$

50. Considering D the only change gear and E has 24 teeth prove that

$$\frac{\dfrac{SD\ A}{SD\ H}}{D} = \frac{dia.\ A \times G}{dia.\ H \times B \times E} = \frac{1}{16} ;$$ ∴ that the *quotient of the ratio of* SD A to SD H by D is the constant; i.e., (a) constant $= \dfrac{ratio}{change\ gear} = \dfrac{1}{16}$; ∴ that (b) ratio = constant × change gear; and ∴ (c) change gear $= \dfrac{ratio}{constant}$. (d) What ratio of SD A to SD H is given if D has (d) 20 (e) 28 teeth? How many teeth are needed to give a ratio of SD A to SD H of (f) 1.5 (g) 2.25.

51. Select the correct word in each set of the following parentheses: In the ratio of the speed of a driven to a driver if the change member is a driver the constant is the (a) (product, quotient) of the ratio by the change member; if a driven the constant is the (b) (product, quotient) of ratio by the change gear.

52. If E has 24 teeth, dia. J is 8″, and K the only change pulley, by the easiest equation which you already have derived find: (a) a constant for calculating IPM H and dia. K; IPM H if dia. K is (b) 15″ (c) 20″; dia. K if IPM H must be (d) 359 (e) 314.

LEVERS

Power, Response, Arms, and Distances.   Lever power trains are of three classes, as in figs. 7, 8, and 9. Each class has a *fulcrum,* i.e., the common center of the circle along which the *power* is applied to the lever and of the circle along which the *response* is applied by the lever. The *power arm* and the *response arm* are the radiuses of the foregoing circles and the *power distance* and the *response distance* are the lengths simultaneously moved along the circumference of these circles. Thus a first class lever is mathematically the same as two pulleys, rolls, or gears integral through a shaft between the two; the fulcrum, the power and response arms, and distance being, respectively, the shaft center, the diameters or pitch diameters, and surface distances along the circumferences or pitch circumferences.

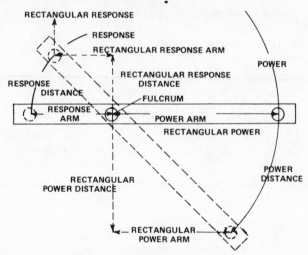

Figure 7.   First Class Lever

Basic Formulas.   By simple interesting experiments with a yardstick, spring balance, and scale weights you can confirm, as Archimedes 2000 years ago formulated, these ratios and proportions:

$$(31)\ \frac{\text{power}}{\text{response}} = \frac{\text{response arm}}{\text{power arm}} \qquad (32)\ \frac{\text{power}}{\text{response}} = \frac{\text{response distance}}{\text{power distance}}.$$

53. From either (a) formulas (31) and (32) or (b) formula (1) and the mathematical identity between two pulleys, two rolls, or two gears integral through a connection derive

$$(33)\ \frac{\text{surface (circular) response distance}}{\text{surface (circular) power distance}} = \frac{\text{(radial) response arm}}{\text{(radial) power arm}}.$$

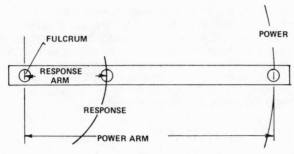

Figure 8.   Second Class Lever

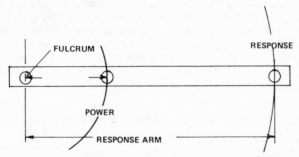

Figure 9.   Third Class Lever

or

$$\frac{\text{rectangular response distance}}{\text{rectangular power distance}} = \frac{\text{rectangular response arm}}{\text{rectangular power arm}}.$$

54. When is $\dfrac{\text{rectangular response distance}}{\text{circular response distance}}$ (a) least and least (b) greatest and most nearly = 1?

55. A square-hole wrench, $\dfrac{3''}{4}$ corner to corner of hole, $7\dfrac{1}{2}''$ hole center to handle pivot center snugly fits a valve stem. What is the (a) fulcrum (b) power arm length (c) response arm length (d) lever class (e) pressure at hole corner if a man pushes $2\dfrac{1}{2}$ lbs. on the handle?

56. The level length of a crow bar from its lip bearing up a machine to its bearing on the floor is about 2″ and to the center of the foot of a 200-lb. fixer bearing his full weight down upon the otherwise free crowbar is about 42″. About what is the (a) power arm length (b) fulcrum (c) up lift on machine (d) fixer's drop to lift machine $\dfrac{1''}{32}$?

57. A driven gear of 25″ p. dia. is integral through a shaft with a driver gear of 10″ p. dia. (a) what class of lever is this? Why? (b) If SD driven gear is 2″, what is SD driver?

58. On the builder of a spinning frame it is 14″ from the center line of the fulcrum shaft along the builder arm to the center line of the pitman roll which follows the contour of the builder cam. At its extreme adjustment the center line of the lifter cable stud is 2″ still farther along the arm beyond the center of the pitman roll. (a) What class of lever is the builder arm? Why? (b) If the difference between the maximum and minimum radiuses, i.e., the *throw,* of the cam is 5.8″ what is the SD of the center of the lifter cable stud?

EPICYCLIC GEAR TRAINS

Internal-Ring One-Size Planet Spur Gear Compounds and Differentials. An epicyclic gear train has at least one gear running on another gear as a track. Fig. 10a is of such a train as if it were transparent and we could see the *planet gear, pg,* running upon both the *sun gear, sg,* and the internal *ring gear, rg,* as tracks. Fig. 10b is of a side section of fig. 10a along the center line of the *center shaft, cs,* and the *planet stud, ps.* For the present let us consider that the *disc, d,* rg, and sg are free to turn upon cs. Always ps and d are integral and pg is free to revolve on ps. Thus the *planet center, pc,* is the center of both ps and pg.

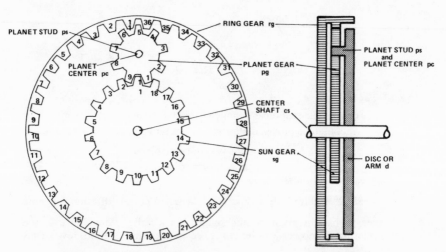

Figure 10a. Face Section of an Epicyclic Internal-Ring One-Size-Planet Spur Gear Train

Figure 10b. Side Section of Figure 10a

59. Prove: From figs. 10a and c that (a) rad. pc = p. rad. rg − p. rad. pg and that (b) rad. pc = p. rad. sg + p. rad. pg. By adding the left sides and right sides of equations (a) and (b) that (c) 2 × rad. pc = p. rad. rg + p. rad. sg. By multiplying both sides of equation (c) by 2 × π and from formulas (10) and (11) that

$$(34) \ \text{cir. pc} = \frac{\text{rg} \times \text{cir. p. pg} + \text{sg} \times \text{cir. p. pg}}{2} = \frac{\text{cir. p. pg} \times (\text{rg} + \text{sg})}{2}.$$

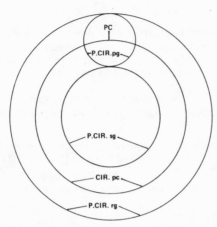

Figure 10c. Circumferences of Figure 10a

In the following three problems assume in figs. 10a and c that rg revolves and sg is stationary and acts as a track for pg:

60. Why is pg a lever? (a) Where is the power applied to pg? (b) Where is its fulcrum? (c) What is its power arm? (d) Where is its response applied? (e) What is its response arm? (f) What is its class?

61. If rev. rg is + what is the sign of: (a) rev. pg? Why? (b) rev. pc? Why? (c) rev. d? Why? If rev. rg is − what is the sign of (d) rev. pg? Why? (e) rev. pc? Why? (f) rev. d? Why?

62. Show: That (a) rev. d = rev. pc = $\dfrac{\text{SD pc}}{\text{cir. pc}}$. Why? From formula

(33) that (b) SD pc = $\dfrac{\text{SD rg} \times \text{p. rad. pg}}{\text{p. dia. pg}} = \dfrac{\text{SD rg}}{2}$. Why? By substituting the value of SD pc from equation (b) into equation (a) that

$$(35) \ \text{rev. d} = \frac{\text{SD rg}}{2 \times \text{cir. pc}}.$$

In the following three problems assume in figs. 10a and c that sg revolves while rg is stationary and acts as a track for pg:

63. (a) Where is the fulcrum of pg? (b) What is its power arm? (c) What is its response arm? (d) What is its class?

64. If rev. sg is + what is the sign of: (a) rev. pg? Why? (b) rev. pc.? Why? (c) rev. d? Why? If rev. sg is − what is the sign of: (d) rev. pg? Why? (e) rev. pc? Why? (f) rev. d? Why?

65. Show: that (a) rev. d = rev. pc = $\dfrac{\text{SD pc}}{\text{cir. pc}}$. Why? From formula

(33) that (b) SD pc $= \dfrac{\text{sg} \times \text{p. rad. pg}}{\text{p. dia. pg}} = \dfrac{\text{SD sg}}{2}$. Why? From equations

(a) and (b) that (36) rev. d $= \dfrac{\text{SD sg}}{2 \times \text{cir. pc}}$.

66. Select the correct word or words within each set of the following parentheses: The sign of rev. d responding to rev. rg is always (a) (opposite to, the same as) the sign of rev. rg and to rev. sg is always (b) (the same as, opposite to) the sign of rev. sg.

In the following problem and three examples assume in fig. 10a and c that simultaneously rg and sg may revolve and act as tracks for pg:

67. Show: From equations (35) and (36) and the preceding problem that (a) rev. d $= \dfrac{\text{SD rg}}{2 \times \text{cir. pc}} + \dfrac{\text{SD sg}}{2 \times \text{cir. pc}} = \dfrac{\text{SD rg} + \text{SD sg}}{2 \times \text{cir. pc}}$. Why? From equations (a) and (34) and formula (11) that

(b) rev. d $= \dfrac{\text{rev. rg} \times \text{rg} \times \text{cir. p. pg} + \text{rev. sg} \times \text{sg} \times \text{cir. p. pg}}{2 \times \dfrac{\text{cir. p. pg} \times (\text{rg} + \text{sg})}{2}} =$

$\dfrac{\text{rev. rg} \times \text{rg} + \text{rev. sg} \times \text{sg}}{\text{rg} + \text{sg}}$ and $\therefore$ in such a train as in fig. 10a and c that

(37) $\dfrac{\text{revolutions}}{\text{of disc}} = \dfrac{\dfrac{\text{revolutions}}{\text{of ring gear}} \times \dfrac{\text{ring}}{\text{gear}} + \dfrac{\text{revolutions}}{\text{of sun gear}} \times \dfrac{\text{sun}}{\text{gear}}}{\text{ring gear} + \text{sun gear}}$.

EXAMPLE: *If rev. rg = 1 and rev. sg = 1 find rev. d.*

By formula (37):   rev. d $= \dfrac{1 \times 36 + 1 \times 18}{36 + 18} = 1$.

EXAMPLE: *If rg makes 1 rev. counterclockwise and sg 1 rev. clockwise what rev. does d make?*

By formula (37):   rev. d $= \dfrac{-1 \times 36 + 1 \times 18}{36 + 18} = \dfrac{-18}{54} = -\dfrac{1}{3}$.

Answer: $\dfrac{1}{3}$ rev. counterclockwise.

EXAMPLE: *If rg makes 100 RPM forward and d 50 RPM backward, what is RPM sg?*

By formula (37): $-50 = \dfrac{100 \times 36 + \text{RPM sg} \times 18}{36 + 18}$.

$\therefore -50 \times 54 = 3600 + \text{RPM sg} \times 18$.

$\therefore -\text{RPM sg} \times 18 = 2700 + 3600$. $\therefore -\text{RPM sg} = \dfrac{6300}{18}$. $\therefore$ RPM

sg $= -350$.

Answer: 350 RPM backward.

68. In figs. 10a find (a) $\dfrac{\text{RPM d}}{\text{RPM sg}}$ if rg is held stationary while sg
runs 100 RPM (b) $\dfrac{\text{RPM rg}}{\text{RPM sg}}$ if d is held stationary while rg runs 100 RPM
backward.

69. Which of the preceding examples and problems shows that
the epicyclic train in fig. 10a can be a (a) *compound* to add or subtract
one power or speed to or from another (b) *differential* to separate one
power or speed into two (c) reducer (d) multipler?

Figs. 11, 12, and 13 are of some of the many internal rings spur gear
compounds, differentials, reducers, or multiplers, the chief difference between
which is in which part is integral with cs. For balance and reduced wear there
may be several equal planet gears.

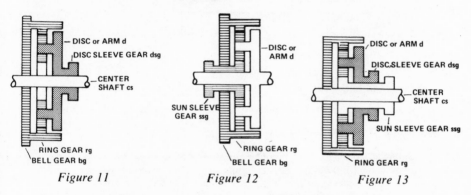

Figure 11   Figure 12   Figure 13

70. The 84-tooth internal rg of the epicyclic draft train of a spinning frame is integral with the frame while the 28-tooth sg is integral
with the front roll. What (a) fig. does this train correspond to (b) is
$\dfrac{\text{rev. front roll}}{\text{rev. dsg}}$?

71. The 78-tooth internal rg of a roving frame's one-size spur gear
compound is integral with cs and runs a constant 276 RPM. At the start
of a set (i.e., bobbin winding) the 26-tooth sg runs 100 RPM and at the
end 25 RPM in the same direction. What (a) fig. does this correspond to
(b) is RPM dsg: RPM cs at start of set (c) is RPM dsg: RPM rg at end
of set (d) is change in RPM dsg?

72. An intermediate roving frame's single-planet spur geat compound has an 80-tooth internal rg integral with cs running 440 RPM
while in the same direction 26-tooth sg varies from 216 RPM at the start
of a set to 54 at the close. Find (a) the fig. to which this compound corresponds (b) RPM dsg: RPM cs at start (c) RPM dsg: RPM cs at end
(d) by how many RPM does dsg change.

73. The lead screw single planet spur gear compound of a certain
roving frame has an 84-tooth internal rg integral with cs and a 28-tooth

sg. At various times in a set (b) cs runs 362 RPM and sg 54 in the same direction (c) cs and sg run same speed but sg reversed (d) cs runs 337 RPM in the same direction and sg 42 reversed. Find (a) the fig. to which this compound corresponds and RPM dsg in (b) (c) and (d).

Internal Ring One-Size Planet Bevel Gear Multipliers.   Until recent years bevel gear compounds were common on roving frames and bevel gear differentials were common on wide sheeting looms. A common epicyclic bevel gear train today is in the yarn reel represented in fig. 14. Your understanding of other epicyclic bevel gear trains that may be in your plant as well as of the yarn reel will be enhanced by studying fig. 14 and formula (37).

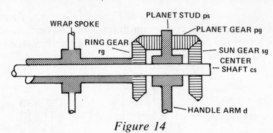

Figure 14

74. In the yarn reel cs, sg, and the reel frame are integral and wrap winds $1\frac{1}{2}$ yds. at each revolution. Calculate (a) rev. d: rev. wrap (b) rev. handle required to wind 120 yds.

External-Ring Two-Size Planet Spur Gear Reducer.   Until recent years roving frames with two-size-planet spur and bevel gear compounds were common. Your understanding of such that may be in your plant will be enhanced by deriving the formula for figs. 15a and b and applying it to a reducer on a recently developed roving frame.

The following seven problems refer to figs. 15a and b:

75. Show: That (a) rad. pc = p. rad. rg + p. rad. rpg = p. rad. sg + p. rad. spg.

That ∴, multiplying the sides of equation (a) by $2 \times \pi$ and from formulas (6), (7), and (11),

(38) cir. pc = cir. p. rg × (rg + rpg) and

(39) cir. p. rg $= \dfrac{\text{cir. p. sg} \times (\text{sg} + \text{spg})}{(\text{rg} + \text{rpg})}$

76. If rg revolves while sg is stationary: What is the (a) power arm (b) response arm (c) class of lever (d) sign of rev. pc if rev. rg is + (e) sign of rev. pc if rev. rg is − ? (f) From formula (33) prove that

(40) rev. d $= \dfrac{\text{SD rg} \times \text{p. rad. spg}}{\text{cir. pc} \times (\text{p. rad. rg} - \text{p. rad. sg})}.$

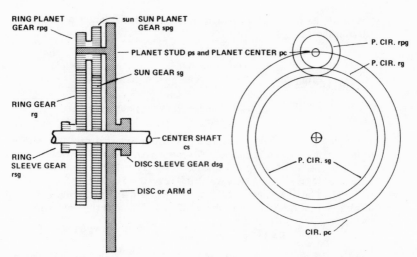

Figure 15a. Side Section of an Epicyclic External-Ring Two-Size-Planet Spur Gear Reducer

Figure 15b. Circumferences of Figure 15a

77. If sg revolves while sg is stationary: What is the (a) power arm (b) response arm (c) class of lever (d) sign of rev. pc if rev. sg is + (e) sign of rev. pc if rev. sg is −? (f) From formula (33) prove that

$$(41) \quad \text{rev. d} = -\frac{\text{SD sg} \times \text{p. rad. rpg}}{\text{cir. pc} \times (\text{p. rad. rg} - \text{p. rad. sg})}.$$

78. Select the correct word or words in each set of the following parentheses: It makes (a) (no, a) difference which of the two gears meshing with the planet gears is considered rg or sg. The sign of rev. d is always (b) (the same as, opposite to) the sign of revolution of the gear with the larger p. rad. and (c) (the same as, opposite to) that of the gear with the smaller p. rad.

79. If rg and sg revolve simultaneously prove: From the preceding problem and equation (40) and (41) that (a)

$$\text{rev. d} = \frac{\text{SD rg} \times \text{p. rad. spg} - \text{SD sg} \times \text{p. rad. rpg}}{\text{cir. pc} \times (\text{p. rad. rg} - \text{p. rad. sg})}.$$

Multiplying numerator and denominator of the right side of equation (a) by $2 \times \pi$, then from formulas (6) and (7) that (b) rev. d =

$$\frac{\text{rev. rg} \times \text{rg} \times \text{cir. p. rg} \times \text{spg} \times \text{cir. p. sg} - \text{rev. sg} \times \text{sg} \times \text{cir. p. sg} \times \text{rpg} \times \text{cir. p. rg}}{\text{cir. pc} \times (\text{rg} \times \text{cir. p. rg} - \text{sg} \times \text{cir. p. sg})}$$

Substituting into the denominator of the right side of equation (b) the value of cir. pc from equation (38) and the value of cir. p. rg from equation (39), simplify ng the denominator, and cancelling cir. p. rg and cir. p. sg from numerator and denominator that for an external ring spur gear train as in fig. 15 in which the gear with the larger p. rad. is considered the ring gear

$$(42)\ \frac{\begin{array}{c}\text{revolutions}\\\text{of}\\\text{ring gear}\end{array} \times \begin{array}{c}\text{ring}\\\text{gear}\end{array} \times \begin{array}{c}\text{planet}\\\text{gear}\end{array} - \begin{array}{c}\text{rev.}\\\text{of}\\\text{sun gear}\end{array} \times \begin{array}{c}\text{sun}\\\text{gear}\end{array} \times \begin{array}{c}\text{ring}\\\text{planet}\\\text{gear}\end{array}}{\begin{array}{c}\text{ring}\\\text{gear}\end{array} \times \text{planet} - \begin{array}{c}\text{sun}\\\text{gear}\end{array} \times \text{planet gear}}.$$

80. A spur gear train has a 100-tooth external rg, 100-tooth external sg, a 49-tooth rpg, and a 50-tooth spg, find rev. d while (a) rev. rg = 1 ahead and rev. sg = 1 ahead (b) rev. rg = 1 ahead and rev. sg = 1 backward (c) rev. rg = 1 backward and rev. sg = 1 ahead.

81. The lay speed reducer of a certain roving frame has a 30-tooth external rg, a 28-tooth external sg, a 15-tooth rpg, and a 15-tooth spg. What is (a) $\dfrac{\text{RPM d}}{\text{RPM sg}}$ and (b) RPM sg when between sets rg is stationary and d runs 1857.7 RPM and (c) $\dfrac{\text{RPM sg}}{\text{RPM rg}}$ when during sets d is stationary.

Part Two

Chapter I

LAP, SLIVER, ROVING, & SINGLE YARN CALCULATIONS

SIZING SYSTEMS

Standard Length and Standard Weight of Each Sizing System. As you will note in Table 1 each sizing system has a standard length and standard weight. Hence, every lap, sliver, roving and yarn calculation involves: (1) *a standard length, std ln,* (2) *standard lengths, std lns,* (3) *length* (4) *a standard weight, std wt,* (5) *standard weights, std wts,* and (6) *weight.* Suppose we have 3360 yds. of roving or yarn and that it weighs 2 lbs. From Table 1 we see that on the cotton system its std lns $= \dfrac{3360}{840} = 4$ and its std wts $= \dfrac{2}{1} = 2$. That is

(1) standard lengths $= \dfrac{\text{length}}{\text{standard length}}$

(2) standard weights $= \dfrac{\text{weight}}{\text{standard weight}}$

From Table 1 and formulas (1) and (2) find the (a) std lns (b) std wts if the sizing system and the length weights are as in the following 14 problems:

    1. Ctn 840 yds. weigh 1 lb.
    2. Ctn 1680 yds. weigh 2 lbs.
    3. Ctn 2100 yds. weigh 8 oz.
    4. Ctn 2730 yds. weigh 4 oz.
    5. Ctn 420 yds. weigh 3500 grs.
    6. Ctn 120 yds. weigh 350 grs.
    7. Wsd 560 yds. of yarn weigh 700 grs.
    8. Wsd 80 yds. of yarn weigh 70 grs.
    9. Run 1600 yds. weigh 500 grs.
    10. Run 200 yds. weigh 140 grs.
    11. Cut 90 yds. weigh 35 grs.
    12. Met 500 mtr. weigh 250 gm.
    13. Den 900 mtr. weigh 10 gm.
    14. Tex 2000 mtr. weigh 200 gm.

Table 1.   Lap, Sliver, Roving, and Yarn Sizing Systems

Systems	Standard		Designation for Size of Lap (l) Sliver (s) Roving (r) Yarn (y)
	Length	Weight	
Indirect systems			
cotton, ctn	hank, hk 840 yards	1 pound	(r) hank roving, HR
			(y) counts, s
thousand yards per pound, typ	hank, hk 1000 yards	1 pound	(r) hank roving, HR
			(y) counts, s
worsted, wsd.	" " 560	" " "	(r) roving
			(y) counts, s
run	run 1600	" " "	(r) run roving
			(y) counts, s
cut (woolen) and lea (linen)	cut and lea 300	" " "	(r) roving
			(y) counts, s
metric, met	1000 meters	1 kilogram	(r) met roving
			(y) counts, s
Direct systems			
denier, den	9000 meters	1 gram	(y) denier, den
gram textile, grex, grx	10000 "	" "	(y) grx
textile, tex	1000 "	" "	(r) gram roving
			(y) counts, s
dram roving (worsted)	40 yards	1 dram	(r) dram roving
ounce lap, oz. lap	1 yard	1 ounce	(l) ounce lap
grain lap, gr. lap	1 yard	1 grain	(l) grain lap
grain sliver, gr. sl	1 "	1 "	(l) grain sliver

Basic Formula of Indirect Roving and Yarn Sizing Systems.   On any indirect system, ind. sys., as in *Table 1*, the size is the std lns required to weigh 1 std wt.

Find the size of the quantity of roving or yarn on the ind sys in each of the following examples and 8 problems:

EXAMPLE: *840 yds. ctn roving weighs 1 lb.*

Only 1 std ln is required to weigh 1 std wt. The size is 1. Or it is 1 HR.

EXAMPLE: *1680 yds. of ctn roving weigh 2 lbs.*

By formula (1) std lns $= \dfrac{1680}{840} = 2$. By formula (2) std wts $= \dfrac{2}{1} = 2$.

Std lns ∴ required to weigh 1 std wt $=\dfrac{2}{2}=1$. It is 1 HR. Or the hank roving is 1.

EXAMPLE: 2100 *yds. of ctn yarn weigh 8 oz.*

By formula (1) std lns $=\dfrac{2100}{840}-2.5$. By formula (2) std wts $\dfrac{8}{16}=$

$\dfrac{1}{2}$. Std lns ∴ required to weigh 1 std wt $= 2 \times 2.5 = 5$. The counts is 5. Or 5's.

15. 2730 yds. of ctn yarn weigh 4 oz.
16. 420 yds. ctn yarn weigh 2625 grs.
17. 560 yds. of wsd yarn weigh 700 grs.
18. 80 yds. of wsd yarn weigh 70 grs.
19. 12 yds. of run roving weigh 100 grs.
20. 200 yds. of run yarn weigh 140 grs.
21. 80 yds. of cut yarn weigh 350 grs.
22. 100000 yds. of met yarn weigh 10 kg.
23. For any quantity of roving or yarn on ind sys show: from the answers to the preceding 3 examples and 10 problems that

(a) ind size $=\dfrac{\text{std lns}}{\text{std wts}}$;

from (a) and formulas (1) and (2) that

(b) ind size $=\dfrac{\dfrac{\text{length}}{\text{std ln}}}{\dfrac{\text{weight}}{\text{std wt}}}=\dfrac{\text{length} \times \text{std wt}}{\text{std ln} \times \text{weight}}$;

from (b) and the std wt always $= 1$; that

(c) ind size $=\dfrac{\text{length} \times 1}{\text{std ln} \times \text{weight}}$;

and from (a) and (c)

(3) indirect size $=\dfrac{\text{standard lengths}}{\text{standard weights}}=\dfrac{\text{length}}{\text{standard length} \times \text{weight}}$.

24. By studying formula (3) select the correct word in the following parentheses: On an indirect system the coarser the roving and yarn the (larger, smaller) the size.

25. Apply the formula (3) to the 8 preceding problems.

Increasing Conversion of Roving and Yarn Sizes and Suggestions for Study.   Increasingly many plants deal with more than one roving and yarn sizing system. Because of the greater number, capacity, and employment of American and British mills on the cotton system there are predictions that other systems may disappear. But because of the increasing processing of filament synthetic fibers, sized mostly like filament silk on the denier system by plants now on indirect systems, and because most continental European plants are on systems, both indirect or direct, with standards in the calculating ease of meters and grams or kilograms, there is advocacy of some universal system with these standards. Two such are the tex system and the metric system with its indirect sizes closely compromising between those of the cotton, worsted, run, and cut systems. Certainly there are increasing occasions for understanding conversion from one system to another.

After the next main section of this chapter "Conversion of Roving and Yarn Sizes" the rest of this book, unless otherwise specified at each exception, is on the cotton system. Hence, the following suggestions:

(1) If your plant is on the cotton system exclusively and likely to remain so, you may see fit to skip the next subsection "Basic formula of direct roving and yarn sizing systems," the next main section, and calculations on other systems in the rest of the book.

(2) If your plant is on a system other than cotton it is necessary for you to study in the next subsection and the next main section everything about the other system and the conversion between, at least, its sizes and those of the cotton system.

Basic Formula of Direct Roving and Yarn Sizing Systems. On any direct system, dir sys as in *Table 1,* the size is the std wts required to weigh 1 std ln.

Find the size of the quantity of roving or yarn on the dir sys in each example and 6 problems following:

EXAMPLE: 9000 *mtr. den weigh* 20 *gm.*

Std wts required to weigh 1 std ln = 20. It is 20 den.

EXAMPLE: 100 *mtr. den weigh* 50 *cg.*

By formula (1) std lns $= \dfrac{100}{9000} = \dfrac{1}{90}$. By formula (2) std wts $=$

$\dfrac{50 \text{ cg.}}{1 \text{ gm}} = \dfrac{50 \text{ cg.}}{100 \text{ cg.}} = .5$. Std wts required to weigh 1 std wt $= 90 \times .5$ or

$\dfrac{.5}{\dfrac{1}{90}} = 45$. It is 45 den.

26. 450 mtr. den weigh 12.5 gm.
27. 500 mtr. grx weigh 15 gm.
28. 10 mtr. tex roving weigh 6 gm.
29. 100 mtr. tex yarn weigh 60 cg.
30. 100000 mtr. tex yarn weigh 1.5 kg.
31. 80 yds. of wsd roving weigh 6 dr.
32. For any quantity of roving or yarn on a dir sys show from the answers to the preceding two examples and 6 problems that

(a) dir size $= \dfrac{\text{std wts}}{\text{std lns}}$;

from (a) and formulas (1) and (2) that

(b) dir size $= \dfrac{\dfrac{\text{weight}}{\text{std wt}}}{\dfrac{\text{length}}{\text{std ln}}} = \dfrac{\text{std ln} \times \text{weight}}{\text{length} \times \text{std wt}}$;

from (b) and the std wt always $= 1$; that

(c) dir size $= \dfrac{\text{std ln} \times \text{weight}}{\text{length}}$;

and from (a) and (c)

(4) direct size $= \dfrac{\text{standard weights}}{\text{standard lengths}} = \dfrac{\text{standard length} \times \text{weight}}{\text{length}}$

33. By studying formula (4) select the correct word in the following parenthesis. On a direct system the coarser the sliver, roving, and yarn the (smaller, larger) the size.

34. Apply formula (4) to the preceding 2 examples and 6 problems.

CONVERSION OF SLIVER, ROVING, AND YARN SIZE

Conversion Between Indirect Sizing Systems.

35. Let us consider that we know the size of roving or yarn on a first indirect system, 1st sys, and must find its size on a second indirect system, 2nd sys. Show from formula (3) that

(a) 1st sys size $= \dfrac{\text{1st sys std lns}}{\text{1st sys std wts}}$

and (b) 2nd sys size $= \dfrac{\text{2nd sys std lns}}{\text{2nd sys std wts}} =$

$\dfrac{\text{1st sys std lns} \times \text{2nd sys std ln}}{\text{1st sys std wts} \times \dfrac{\text{1st sys std ln}}{\text{1st sys std wt}}} = \dfrac{\text{1st sys std lns}}{\text{1st sys std wts}} \times$

$\dfrac{\dfrac{\text{2nd sys std ln}}{\text{2nd sys std wt}}}{}$

$\dfrac{\text{1st sys std ln} \times \text{2nd sys std wt}}{\text{2nd sys std ln} \times \text{1st sys std wt}}$; from (a) and (b) that (c) 2nd sys size $=$

1st sys size $\times \dfrac{\text{1st sys std ln} \times \text{2nd sys std wt}}{\text{2nd sys std ln} \times \text{1st sys std wt}}$ and $\therefore$

(5) $\dfrac{\begin{array}{c}\text{second} \\ \text{indirect} \\ \text{system} \\ \text{size}\end{array}}{} = \dfrac{\begin{array}{c}\text{first} \\ \text{indirect} \\ \text{system} \\ \text{size}\end{array} \times \begin{array}{c}\text{first} \\ \text{indirect} \\ \text{system} \\ \text{standard length}\end{array} \times \begin{array}{c}\text{second} \\ \text{indirect} \\ \text{system} \\ \text{standard weight}\end{array}}{\begin{array}{c}\text{second indirect system} \\ \text{standard length}\end{array} \times \begin{array}{c}\text{first indirect} \\ \text{system standard weight}\end{array}}$

In the following 3 examples and 6 problems convert to the 2nd sys the size on the 1st sys:

EXAMPLE: 10s *ctn to wsd.*

By formula (5): wsd size $= \dfrac{10 \times 840(\text{yds.}) \times 1(\text{lb.})}{560(\text{yds.}) \times 1(\text{lb.})} = 15.$

EXAMPLE: 10s *wsd to ctn.*

By formula (5): ctn size $= \dfrac{10 \times 560(\text{yds.}) \times 1(\text{lb.})}{840(\text{yds.}) \times 1(\text{lb.})} = 6.67.$

EXAMPLE: 10s *ctn to met.*

By formula (5): met size $= \dfrac{10 \times 840\text{(yds.)} \times 1\text{(kg.)}}{1000\text{(mtr.)} \times 1\text{(lb.)}} =$

$\dfrac{10 \times 840 \times .9144\text{(mtr.)} \times 1\text{(kg.)}}{1000\text{(mtr.)} \times .4536\text{(kg.)}} = 16.9.$

36. .8 HR ctn to wsd.   **39.** 2 run roving to ctn.
37. 18s wsd to ctn.   **40.** 30s cut to met.
38. 40s ctn to run.   **41.** 100s met to run.

Conversion Between Direct Sizing Systems.

42. By reasoning corresponding to that in deriving formula (5), from formula (4) derive (6) $\dfrac{\text{second direct}}{\text{system size}} =$

$$\frac{\dfrac{\text{first direct}}{\text{system size}} \times \dfrac{\text{first direct system}}{\text{standard weight}} \times \dfrac{\text{second direct system}}{\text{standard length}}}{\dfrac{\text{second direct system}}{\text{standard weight}} \times \dfrac{\text{first direct system}}{\text{standard length}}}.$$

In the following 3 examples and 5 problems convert to the 2nd sys the size on the 1st sys:

EXAMPLE: 500 *den to the tex sys.*

By formula (6): tex size $= \dfrac{500 \times 1\text{(gm.)} \times 1000\text{(mtr.)}}{1\text{(gm.)} \times 9000\text{(mtr.)}} = 55.6.$

EXAMPLE: 50s *tex to the den sys.*

By formula (6): den size $= \dfrac{50 \times 1\text{(gm.)} \times 9000\text{(mtr.)}}{1\text{(gm.)} \times 1000\text{(mtr.)}} = 450.$

EXAMPLE: 4 *dram roving to the tex system.*

By formula (6): tex size $= \dfrac{4 \times 1\text{(dram)} \times 1000\text{(mtr.)}}{1\text{(gm.)} \times 40\text{(yds.)}} =$

$\dfrac{4 \times 1 \times 1.77\text{(gm.)} \times 1000\text{(mtr.)}}{1\text{(gm.)} \times 40 \times .9144\text{(mtr.)}} = 194.$

43. 150 den to the grex sys.
44. 200 grex to the den sys.
45. 400 den to the tex sys.
46. 45 tex to den sys.
47. 200 gram roving tex to dram roving wsd.

Conversion Between an Indirect and a Direct Sizing System.

48. Let us consider that we know the size of roving or yarn on an indirect sys and must find its size on a dir sys. Show from formula (3) that $\text{ind sys size} = \dfrac{\text{ind sys std lns}}{\text{ind sys std wts}}$ and $\therefore$ (a) $\dfrac{1}{\text{ind sys size}} =$

$\dfrac{1}{\dfrac{\text{ind sys std lns}}{\text{ind sys std wts}}} = \dfrac{\text{ind sys std wts}}{\text{ind sys std lns}}$; from formula (4) that (b) dir sys size =

$\dfrac{\text{dir sys std wts}}{\text{dir sys std lns}} = \dfrac{\text{ind sys std wts} \times \dfrac{\text{ind sys std wt}}{\text{dir sys std wt}}}{\text{ind sys std lns} \times \dfrac{\text{ind sys std ln}}{\text{dir sys std ln}}} = \dfrac{\text{ind sys std wts}}{\text{ind sys std lns}} \times$

$\dfrac{\text{ind sys std wt} \times \text{dir sys std ln}}{\text{dir sys std wt} \times \text{ind sys std ln}}$; from (a) and (b) that (c) $\dfrac{\text{dir sys}}{\text{size}} =$

$\dfrac{1}{\text{ind sys size}} \times \dfrac{\text{ind sys std wt} \times \text{dir sys std ln}}{\text{dir sys std wt} \times \text{ind sys std ln}}$; $\therefore$ that (7) $\dfrac{\text{direct}}{\text{system}} = \dfrac{}{\text{size}}$

$\dfrac{\dfrac{\text{indirect system}}{\text{standard weight}} \times \dfrac{\text{direct system}}{\text{standard length}}}{\dfrac{\text{indirect}}{\text{system size}} \times \dfrac{\text{direct system}}{\text{standard weight}} \times \dfrac{\text{indirect system}}{\text{standard length}}}$; and $\therefore$ (8) $\dfrac{\text{indirect}}{\text{system}} = \dfrac{}{\text{size}}$

$\dfrac{\dfrac{\text{indirect system}}{\text{standard weight}} \times \dfrac{\text{direct system}}{\text{standard length}}}{\dfrac{\text{direct}}{\text{system size}} \times \dfrac{\text{direct system}}{\text{standard weight}} \times \dfrac{\text{indirect system}}{\text{standard length}}}$.

Convert as indicated in the following 2 examples and 6 problems:

EXAMPLE: 10s *ctn to tex.*

By formula (7): $\dfrac{\text{tex}}{\text{size}} = \dfrac{1(\text{lb.}) \times 1000(\text{mtr.})}{10 \times 1(\text{gm.}) \times 840(\text{yds.})}$

$= \dfrac{1 \times 453.6(\text{gm.}) \times 1000(\text{mtr.})}{10 \times 1(\text{gm.}) \times 840 \times .9144(\text{mtr.})} = 59.1.$

EXAMPLE: 3 *dram roving wsd to wsd counts.*

By formula (8) $\dfrac{\text{wsd}}{\text{counts}} = \dfrac{1(\text{lb.}) \times 40(\text{yds.})}{3 \times 1(\text{dram}) \times 560(\text{yds.})}$

$= \dfrac{1 \times 256(\text{drams}) \times 40(\text{yds.})}{3 \times 1(\text{dram}) \times 560(\text{yds.})} = 6.10.$

49. 100 ctn to den.   **52.** 75s wsd to tex.
50. 300 den to ctn.   **53.** 160s met to tex.
51. 3.5 dram roving to met.   **54.** 1.5 HR ctn to tex.

Sliver, Roving, and Yarn Size Conversion Constants. A *conversion constant* saves calculating labor in converting repeatedly to a given roving and yarn sizing system from another given sliver, roving, and yarn sizing system.

55. Show from formula (5) that (a) $\dfrac{\text{2nd ind sys size}}{\text{1st ind sys size}} =$

Table 2. Sliver, Roving, and Yarn Size Conversion Constants
Carried to 4 Significant Digits

from the roving and yarn sizing systems below calculate with the conversion constants as shown below:

| To convert to | | | | | | | | | |
cotton size	typ size	worsted size	run size	cut or lea size	metric size	denier size	grex size	tex size	dram roving size
	.8400 × cotton size	1.500 × cotton size	.5250 × cotton size	2.800 × cotton size	1.693 × cotton size	5315 ÷ cotton size	5905 ÷ cotton size	590.5 ÷ cotton size	12.19 ÷ cotton size
1.190 × typ size		1.786 × typ size	.6250 × typ size	3.333 × typ size	2.016 × typ size	4464 ÷ typ size	4961 ÷ typ size	496.1 ÷ typ size	10.24 ÷ typ size
.6667 × worsted size	.5600 × worsted size		.3500 × worsted size	1.867 × worsted size	1.129 × worsted size	7972 ÷ worsted size	8858 ÷ worsted size	885.8 ÷ worsted size	18.29 ÷ worsted size
1.905 × run size	1.600 × run size	2.857 × run size		5.333 × run size	3.225 × run size	2790 ÷ run size	3100 ÷ run size	310.0 ÷ run size	6.400 ÷ run size

cut or lea	metric	denier	grex	tex	dram roving	grain sliver
34.13 ÷ cut or lea size	20.64 ÷ metric size	.002294 × denier size	.002064 × grex size	.02064 × tex size		1.463 × grain sliver
1654 ÷ cut or lea size	1000 ÷ metric size	.1111 × denier size	.1000 × grex size		48.44 × dram roving size	7.087 × grain sliver
16540 ÷ cut or lea size	10000 ÷ metric size	1.111 × denier size		10.00 × tex size	484.4 × dram roving size	70.87 × grain sliver
14880 ÷ cut or lea size	9000 ÷ metric size		.9000 × grex size	9.000 × tex size	436.0 × dram roving size	63.78 × grain sliver
.6048 × cut or lea size		9000 ÷ denier size	10000 ÷ grex size	1000 ÷ tex size	20.64 ÷ dram roving size	14.11 ÷ grain sliver
	1.654 × metric size	14880 ÷ denier size	16540 ÷ grex size	1654 ÷ tex size	34.13 ÷ dram roving size	23.33 ÷ grain sliver
1.875 × cut or lea size	.3101 × metric size	2790 ÷ denier size	3100 ÷ grex size	310.0 ÷ tex size	6.400 ÷ dram roving size	4.375 ÷ grain sliver
.5357 × cut or lea size	.8859 × metric size	7972 ÷ denier size	8858 ÷ grex size	885.8 ÷ tex size	18.29 ÷ dram roving size	12.50 ÷ grain sliver
.3000 × cut or lea size	.4961 × metric size	4464 ÷ denier size	4961 ÷ grex size	496.1 ÷ tex size	10.24 ÷ dram roving size	7.000 ÷ grain sliver
.3571 × cut or lea size	.5906 × metric size	5315 ÷ denier size	5905 ÷ grex size	590.5 ÷ tex size	12.19 ÷ dram roving size	8.333 ÷ grain sliver

$\dfrac{\text{1st ind sys std ln} \times \text{2nd ind sys std wt}}{\text{2nd ind sys std ln} \times \text{1st ind sys std wt}}$; $\therefore$ that, so long as we convert from the same 1st ind sys to the same 2nd ind sys, regardless of the sizes, $\dfrac{\text{2nd ind sys size}}{\text{1st ind sys size}} = $ always the fixed right side of (a). This fixed right side of (a) is the *conversion constant to the second indirect system*. Show $\therefore$ that (9)

(9) $\dfrac{\begin{array}{c}\text{conversion}\\ \text{constant to the}\\ \text{second indirect}\\ \text{system}\end{array}}{} = \dfrac{\dfrac{\text{first indirect system}}{\text{standard length}} \times \dfrac{\text{second indirect system}}{\text{standard weight}}}{\dfrac{\text{second indirect system}}{\text{standard length}} \times \dfrac{\text{first indirect system}}{\text{standard weight}}}$ and

(10) $\dfrac{\text{second indirect}}{\text{system size}} = \dfrac{\text{first indirect}}{\text{system size}} \times \dfrac{\text{conversion constant to the}}{\text{second indirect system.}}$

56. By reasoning corresponding to that in deriving formulas (9) and (10), from formula (6) derive

(11) $\dfrac{\begin{array}{c}\text{conversion}\\ \text{constant to the}\\ \text{second direct}\\ \text{system}\end{array}}{} = \dfrac{\dfrac{\text{first direct system}}{\text{standard weight}} \times \dfrac{\text{second direct system}}{\text{standard length}}}{\dfrac{\text{second direct system}}{\text{standard weight}} \times \dfrac{\text{first direct system}}{\text{standard length}}}$ and

(12) $\dfrac{\text{second direct}}{\text{system size}} = \dfrac{\text{first direct}}{\text{system size}} \times \dfrac{\text{conversion constant to the}}{\text{second direct system.}}$

57. By reasoning corresponding to that in deriving formulas (9) and (10), from formulas (7) and (8) derive

(13) $\dfrac{\begin{array}{c}\text{conversion}\\ \text{constant between}\\ \text{indirect and}\\ \text{direct systems}\end{array}}{} = \dfrac{\dfrac{\text{indirect system}}{\text{standard weight}} \times \dfrac{\text{direct system}}{\text{standard length}}}{\dfrac{\text{direct system}}{\text{standard weight}} \times \dfrac{\text{indirect system}}{\text{standard length}}}$ and

(14) $\dfrac{\begin{array}{c}\text{indirect}\\ \text{or direct}\\ \text{system size}\end{array}}{} = \dfrac{\dfrac{\text{conversion constant between}}{\text{indirect and direct systems}}}{\text{the other system size}}$.

58. From formulas (9), (11), or (13) prove whichever conversion constants in Table 2 are or likely will be needed in your plant:

Convert as required in the following 3 examples and 6 problems:

EXAMPLE: 30s *ctn to met.*

By Table 2: met size $= 1.693 \times 30 = 50.8$.

EXAMPLE: .5 *HR ctn to tex.*

By Table 2: tex size $= \dfrac{590.5}{.5} = 1181$.

EXAMPLE: 100s *tex to ctn.*

By Table 2: ctn size $= \dfrac{590.5}{100} = 5.91$.

59. 30s met to ctn.   **62.** 500 den to tex.
60. 3.2 dram roving to wsd.   **63.** 20s run to lea.
61. 60s wsd to den.   **64.** 24s cut to tex.

SIZE, WEIGHT, LENGTH, AND ENDS OF VARIOUS QUANTITIES OF LAP, SLIVER, ROVING, AND YARN

Sizing from Length and Weight of Single Ends of Sliver, Roving, and Yarn. From this point on this book, unless it specifies otherwise at each exception, is on the cotton sizing system.

65. From formula (3) and Table 1 prove that (15) cotton size =

$$\frac{yards}{840 \times pounds}, \therefore HR \text{ or counts} = \frac{yards}{840 \times \frac{grains}{7000}}, \text{ and } \therefore (16) \quad \frac{hank}{roving} \text{ or counts} =$$

$$\frac{7000 \times yards}{840 \times grains} = \frac{8\frac{1}{3} \times yards}{grains} = \frac{25 \times yards}{3 \times grains} = \frac{100 \times yards}{120 \times grains} = \frac{200 \times yards}{24 \times grains}$$
$$= \frac{1000 \times yards}{120 \times grains} = \frac{4000 \times yards}{480 \times grains}.$$

In the following 2 examples and 8 problems find by the easiest formula or part of formula the roving or yarn if:

EXAMPLE: 2100 *yds. of roving weigh* $2\frac{1}{2}$ *lbs.*

By formula (15): $HR = \dfrac{2100}{840 \times 2.5} = 1$. It is 1 HR.

EXAMPLE: 3 *yds. of yarn weigh .4 gr.*

By formula (16): counts $= \dfrac{8\frac{1}{3} \times 3}{.4} = 62.5$. It is 62.5's.

66. 840 yds. of roving weigh 5 lbs.

67. 1260 yds. of roving weigh $1\frac{1}{4}$ lbs.

68. 2 hks. of roving weigh 2 lbs. 3 oz.

69. 8 yds. of sliver weigh 8 oz.

70. 1 yd. of sliver weighs 70 grs.

71. 105 yds. of roving weigh 350 grs.

72. 1 yd. 18 in. of yarn weigh 2.5 grs.

73. 60 yds. of yarn weigh 50 grs.

EXAMPLE: *What is the met counts if 33 yds. weigh 12.5 grs.?*

By Table 2 and formula (16): met counts $= \dfrac{1.693 \times 25 \times 33}{3 \times 12.5} =$ 37.2.

74. What is wsd counts if 10.5 yds. weigh 5 grs.?

75. If 42 yds. weigh 14 grs. what is the cut counts?

Sizing roving and yarn at the reel and balance.

76. By formula (16) prove that if 100 is divided by the grain weight of 12 yds., or 200 by that of 24 yds., or 1000 by that of 120 yds; or 4000 by that of 480 yds. the quotient is the HR or counts. It is the usual practice to weigh 12 yds. of heavier roving, 24 yds. of lighter roving, and 120 yds. of yarn. The roving reel provides for 1 bobbin, i.e., 1 end. The yarn reel provides for 4 bobbins, i.e., 4 ends or 480 yds. and thus more accuracy, especially for finer yarns. Show that in usual sizing practice (17) hank roving $= \dfrac{100}{\text{grain weight of 12 yards}} = \dfrac{200}{\text{grain weight of 24 yards}}$ and (18) counts $= \dfrac{1000}{\text{grain weight of 120 yards}} = \dfrac{4000}{\text{grain weight of 480 yards}}$.

With a minimum of written calculating tell the HR or counts in the following 4 problems if:

77. 12 yds. weigh (a) 500 (b) 400 (c) 250 (d) 200 (e) 125 (f) 100 grs.

78. 24 yds. weigh (a) 160 (b) 133.3 (c) 114.2 (d) 100 (e) 80 (f) 50 grs.

79. 120 yds. weigh (a) 250 (b) 200 (c) 125 (d) 100 (e) 80 (f) 50 grs.

80. 480 yds. weigh (a) 400 (b) 320 (c) 250 (d) 200 (e) 100 (f) 40 grs.

What is the roving or yarn size in the following 8 problems:

81. Typ roving if 12 yds. weigh 100 grs.?

82. Wsd yarn if 120 yds. weigh 35 grs.?

83. Run yarn if 120 yds. weigh 62.5 grs.?

84. Lea counts if 480 yds. weigh 84.4 grs.?

85. Met counts if 480 yds. weigh 160.8 grs.?

86. Den if 480 yds. weigh 40 grs.

87. Grx if 480 yds. weigh 33.3 grs.

88. Tex roving if 12 yds. weigh 125.4 grs.

89. As assigned by your instructor reel, weigh, and calculate the sizes of roving and yarn used or made in your mill.

Finding the Size, Length, Weight, and Ends of Roving and Yarn in Various Forms. Many circumstances arise that make necessary the calculation of one of these missing or essential data about roving and yarn in various packages and other forms.

90. From formulas (15) and (16) prove that (19) size $= \dfrac{\text{ends} \times \text{yards per end}}{840 \times \text{pounds}} = \dfrac{8\frac{1}{3} \times \text{ends} \times \text{yards per end}}{\text{grains}} = \dfrac{25 \times \text{ends} \times \text{yards per end}}{3 \times \text{grains}}$.

Find the size or average size from the other data in the following example and 6 problems:

EXAMPLE: 270 *yarn ends from cloth each* $3\frac{1}{4}''$ *long weigh* 4.2 *grs.*

By formula (19): size $= \dfrac{25 \times 270 \times \dfrac{3.25}{36}}{3 \times 4.2} = 48.4.$

Answer: 48.4s.

91. 315 yarn ends from cloth each $3\frac{3}{16}''$ long weigh 5.4 grs.

92. 208 yarn ends from cloth each $4\frac{1}{4}''$ long weigh 11.3 grs.

93. 434 yarn ends each 13500 yds. long on section beam weigh 303 lbs.

94. 454 yarn ends each 22000 yds. long on a section beam weigh 531 lbs.

95. 2624 warp ends each 2265 yds. long on a loom beam weigh 347 lbs. including 12.6% of sizing compound which has been added to the yarn by the slasher.

96. 2718 warp ends each 1200 yds. long on a loom beam weigh 450 lbs. including 12.5% of sizing compound which has been added to the yarn by the slasher.

97. From formula (19) derive (20) $\dfrac{\text{yards}}{\text{per end}} = \dfrac{840 \times \text{size} \times \text{pounds}}{\text{ends}} = \dfrac{\text{size} \times \text{grains}}{8\frac{1}{3} \times \text{ends}} = \dfrac{3 \times \text{size} \times \text{grains}}{25 \times \text{ends}}.$

How many yds. in each end on the package in the following examples and problems:

EXAMPLE: *Quill of* 9.70s *weighs* 532 *grs. net?*

By formula (20): yds. per end $= \dfrac{3 \times 9.7 \times 532}{25 \times 1} = 619.$

EXAMPLE: *Section beam of* 393 *ends of* 14.2s *weighs* 428 *lbs. net?*

By formula (20): yds. per end $= \dfrac{840 \times 14.2 \times 428}{393} = 12990.$

98. Bobbin of 1.60 HR weighs 5.7 lbs. net?

99. Bobbin of 1.50 wsd roving weighs $7\frac{3}{4}$ lbs.?

100. Bobbin of 5.00s run weighs 24 oz. net?

101. Quill of 3.04s weighs 560 grs. net?

102. Warp bobbin of 105.0s weighs 10.20 oz. net?

103. Cheese of 26.0s weighs 2.87 lbs. net?

104. Cone of 8.10s weighs 6 lb. 5 oz. net?

105. Twister creel beam of 293 ends of 16.0s weighs 723 lbs. full and 200 lbs. empty?

106. Section beam of 434 ends of 23.5s weighs 225 lbs. net?

107. From formula (19) derive (21) pounds $= \dfrac{\text{ends} \times \text{yards per end}}{840 \times \text{size}}$

and (22) grains $= \dfrac{8\frac{1}{3} \times \text{ends} \times \text{yards per end}}{\text{size}} = \dfrac{25 \times \text{ends} \times \text{yards per end}}{3 \times \text{size}}$.

What are the net lbs. of yarn in the following 5 problems.

108. Section beam of 410 ends of 17.25s 10500 yds. long?

109. Section beam of 436 ends of 26.0s 26000 yds. long?

110. Loom beam of 2480 ends of 17.25s 2115 yds. long?

111. Loom beam of 5672 ends of 26.0s 1645 yds. long?

112. 9.00s warp that has contracted 8% in weaving into 1 yd. of duck 29″ wide with 76 ends of warp per inch of width?

113. From formula (19) derive (23) ends $= \dfrac{840 \times \text{size} \times \text{pounds}}{\text{yards per end}} =$

$\dfrac{\text{size} \times \text{grains}}{8\frac{1}{3} \times \text{yards per end}} = \dfrac{.12 \times \text{size} \times \text{grains}}{\text{yards per end}}$.

How many ends are on or must be put on the beams in the following 4 problems:

114. Section beam of 334 lbs. net of 9.00s and 8000 yds. per end?

115. Section beam of 540 lbs. net of 22.0s and 22000 yds. per end?

116. After deducting the calculated weight of sizing compound that has been added, a loom beam of 34.5s and 1760 yds. per end ought to weigh 492 lbs. net?

117. A loom beam of 1240 yds. per end of 22.0s with 19% of sizing added weighs 513 lbs.

Finding the Ounce Lap, Grain Sliver, Grain Lap, Yards, Hanks, and Pounds in Cans, Rolls, and Other Forms.

118. From Table 1 show that: oz. lap $= \dfrac{\text{ozs.}}{\text{yds.}}$ and $\therefore$ (24) $\dfrac{\text{ounce}}{\text{lap}} = \dfrac{16 \times \text{pounds}}{\text{yards}}$, (25) yards $= \dfrac{16 \times \text{pounds}}{\text{ounce lap}}$, and (26) pounds $= \dfrac{\text{ounce lap} \times \text{yards}}{16}$.

119. What is the oz. lap if a (a) 16-yd. sheet weighs 16 lbs. (b) a 10-lb. sheet is 11 yds. 2 in. long (c) a full 80-yd. 9-in. roll weighs 79 lbs. 7 ozs.?

120. What ought to be the (a) yds. in an 80-lb. roll of 14.8 oz. lap (b) weight of a 69-yd. roll 16.6 oz. lap?

121. From Table 1 show that: gr. sl or gr. lap $= \dfrac{\text{grs.}}{\text{yds.}}$ and $\therefore$ (27)

$$\frac{\text{grain sliver}}{\text{or grain lap}} = \frac{\text{grains}}{\text{yards}} = \frac{\text{pounds}}{.12 \times \text{hanks}}, (28)\ \text{yards} = \frac{\text{grains}}{\text{grain sliver or grain lap}}$$

$$= \frac{7000 \times \text{pounds}}{\text{grain sliver or grain lap}}, (29)\ \text{hanks} = \frac{\text{pounds}}{.12 \times \text{grain sliver or grain lap}},$$

and (30) pounds $= .12 \times$ hanks $\times$ grain sliver or grain lap.

122. What is the (a) gr. sl if 10 yds. weigh 645 grs. (b) gr. lap if a 12-yd. sheet weighs 15 oz?

123. How many (a) yds. in a can holding 41 lbs. 4 oz. of 60 gr. sl (b) yds. in a 26 lb. 9 oz. roll of 950 gr. lap (c) hks. of 56.6-gr. sl ought be run into a can that holds 43 lbs. 8 ozs.?

124. How many lbs. of (a) 60-gr. sl in a can filled by 8.3 hks. (b) 58-gr. lap in a roll containing 3.9 hks. (c) 55.2-gr. sl per hr. from a machine running 329.1 hks. in 8 hrs.?

125. As assigned by your instructor solve practical problems that involve finding and using the oz. lap, gr. sl, gr. lap, HR, counts, ends, yds., hks., ozs., grs., and lbs. of the stock as run in your plant.

Chapter II

PLY YARN CALCULATIONS

Equivalent Counts of Yarn Plied of Ends of Equal Counts. Such a *ply yarn* is designated by the counts and number of ends of the single yarn composing it. Thus if 2 ends of single 10s are plied (i.e., twisted together) the ply yarn is called "2-ply 10s" or "10s 2 ply" and written "2/10s" or "10s/2." It is often necessary to find the *equivalent counts* of ply yarn (i.e., the counts of a single yarn of the same standard lengths per standard weight).

EXAMPLE: *Find the equivalent counts of 2/40s.*

From formula (3), Chap. I: 40s means that: 40 standard lengths (i.e., 40 hks.) weigh 1 standard weight (i.e., 1 lb.); $\therefore$ 1 std ln weighs $\frac{1}{40}$ lb.; 1 std ln of 2/40s weighs $\frac{1}{40}$ lb. $+ \frac{1}{40}$ lb. And $\therefore$ from formula (3),

Chap. I: ind size (i.e., equivalent counts) of $2/40\text{s} = \dfrac{1}{\dfrac{1}{40}+\dfrac{1}{40}} = \dfrac{1}{\dfrac{2}{40}} =$

$\dfrac{40}{2} = 20.$

1. From the preceding example derive:

$$(1) \quad \frac{\text{equivalent counts of yarn}}{\text{plied of ends of equal counts}} = \frac{\text{counts of 1 end}}{\text{ends}}.$$

Calculate, without writing if possible, the equivalent counts in the following 12 problems:

2. 2/10s	**6.** 3/60s	**10.** 6/120s
3. 20s/2	**7.** 48s/3	**11.** 13.5s/3
4. 2/35s	**8.** 4/60s	**12.** 4/55.6s
5. 21s/3	**9.** 70s/5	**13.** 64.5s/5

Equivalent Counts of Yarn Plied of Ply Ends of Equal Counts. If 4 ends of 20s/6 are plied the resulting ply yarn is usually written "20s/6/4." Such a ply yarn is often known as *cord* or *cable*.

EXAMPLE: *Find the equivalent counts of 20s/6/4.*

From formula (1): equivalent counts of 20s/6 = $\dfrac{20}{6}$ and $\therefore$.

equivalent counts of 20s/6/4 = $\dfrac{\dfrac{20}{6}}{4} = \dfrac{20}{6 \times 4} = .833$.

Twisting—as will be studied with the roving, spinning, and twisting frames—causes contraction in length of yarn.

14. Select the correct word in each of the following parentheses: more contraction results from (a) (higher, lower) counts, (b) (fewer, more) ends, and (c) (less, more) twists per inch; and $\therefore$ *actual equivalent counts* is (d) (lower, higher) than the *calculated equivalent counts* from formula (1). Why?

Sometimes if the calculated equivalent counts differ enough from the actual as to make the calculated impractical the actual hanks or yard per pound might be specified.

Calculate the equivalent counts in the following 4 problems:

15. 20s/4/3   **16.** 22s/4/3   **17.** 23s/5/3   **18.** 24s/8/3

Equivalent Counts of Yarn Plied of Single or Ply Ends of Different Counts. If 10s, 2/50s, and 3/60s are plied the resulting ply yarn might be written "10s 2/50s 3/60s" and be known as *novelty* yarn.

EXAMPLE: *Calculate the equivalent counts of* 10s 2/50s 2/50s 3/60s.

By formula (1): equivalent counts of 2/50s = 25 and 3/60s = 20.
By formula (3), Chap. I: 1 hk of 10s weighs $\dfrac{1}{10}$ lb., 1 hk of 25s weighs $\dfrac{1}{25}$ lb., 1 hk of 20s weighs $\dfrac{1}{20}$ lb., and $\therefore$ the equivalent counts of 10s 2/50s 3/60s =

$$\dfrac{1}{\dfrac{1}{10} + \dfrac{1}{25} + \dfrac{1}{20}} = \dfrac{1}{\dfrac{10}{100} + \dfrac{4}{100} + \dfrac{5}{100}} = \dfrac{1}{\dfrac{19}{100}} = 5.26 \text{ or } =$$

$$\dfrac{1}{.1 + .04 + .05} = \dfrac{1}{.19} = 5.26.$$

By the easiest method calculate the equivalent counts in each of the following 4 problems:

19. 10s 20s 30s   **21.** 2/40s 3/60s
20. 25s 30s 35s   **22.** 2/32s 40.5s 50s 60s

Counts to Ply with Known Counts to Give a Required Equivalent Counts.

EXAMPLE: *Find the counts to ply with* 24s *to give the equivalent of* 14s.

Let uc stand for the unknown counts to be found. As in Chap. XV,

Part One and the preceding example show that: $\dfrac{1}{\dfrac{1}{uc} + \dfrac{1}{24}} = 14,\ \therefore$

$\dfrac{1}{\dfrac{24 + uc}{24 \times uc}} = 14,\ \therefore\ \dfrac{24 \times uc}{24 + uc} = 14,\ \therefore\ 24 \times uc = 14 \times 24 + 14 \times uc,\ \therefore$ sub-

tracting $14 \times uc$ from each side $24 \times uc - 14 \times uc = 14 \times 24,\ \therefore (24 - 14)$

$\times uc = 14 \times 24,$ and $\therefore\ uc = \dfrac{14 \times 24}{24 - 14} = 33.6$

23. From the preceding example derive:

(2) $\dfrac{\text{counts to ply with}}{\text{known counts}} = \dfrac{\dfrac{\text{known}}{\text{counts}} \times \dfrac{\text{required equivalent}}{\text{ply counts}}}{\dfrac{\text{known}}{\text{counts}} - \dfrac{\text{required equivalent}}{\text{ply counts}}}$

Calculate the counts to ply with the known counts to give the re-
quired ply counts in each of the following 8 problems:

24. 20 10	**27.** 4/100s 20	**30.** 2/42.5s 10.6
25. 120 60	**28.** 60 25	**31.** 3/57.5 8.7
26. 2/30s 10	**29.** 30.6 11.8	

Chapter III

ACTUAL DRAFT CALCULATIONS

Basic formulas. The following abbreviations mean the same as in Chapter I: std ln, std lns, ln, std wt, std wts, and wt. The std ln for lap and sliver at the comber is 1 yd. and the std wt is 1 gr. If a comber from 8 ends of lap fed in, each 3 yds. long and weighing 2700 grs. delivers 2 ends of sliver, each 120 yds. long and weighing 7440 grs; the *doublings, db.,* = 8; the std wts of 1 std ln of 1 end fed $= \dfrac{2700}{3}$ gr.; the *deliveries, dv,* = 2; the std wts of 1 std ln of 1 end delivered $= \dfrac{7440}{120}$ grs.; and the *actual draft, ad,* $= \dfrac{8 \times \dfrac{2700}{3} \text{ gr.}}{2 \times \dfrac{7440}{120} \text{ grs.}} =$

$\dfrac{8 \times 900}{2 \times 62}$ or $\dfrac{8 \times 2700 \times 120}{2 \times 7440 \times 2} = \dfrac{21600 \times 120}{14880 \times 2} = 62.$

1. From the foregoing equation show that

(1) $\dfrac{\text{actual}}{\text{draft}} = \dfrac{\text{doublings} \times \text{standard weights of 1 standard length of 1 end fed}}{\text{deliveries} \times \text{standard weights of 1 standard length of 1 end delivered}}$

or (2) $\dfrac{\text{actual}}{\text{draft}} = \dfrac{\text{weight fed} \times \text{standard lengths of 1 end delivered}}{\text{weight delivered} \times \text{standard lengths of 1 end fed}}.$

Find the ad if the stock fed is drafted into the stock delivered in the following 7 problems and example:

2. 12 laps, each 1000 grs. per yd., into 2 slivers each 48 grs. per yd.

3. 24 slivers, each 82.4 grs. per yd., into 8 slivers, each 61.8 grs. per yd.

4. 48 slivers, each 80.8 grs. per yd., into 8 slivers, each 64.8 grs. per yd.

5. 1 lap, 16.4 oz. per yd., into 1 card sliver, 82 grs. per yd.

EXAMPLE: *1 yd. of lap, weighing 15.5 oz. into 10 yds. of sliver weighing 678 grs.*

By formula (2): $ad = \dfrac{15.5 \text{ oz.} \times 10 \text{ yds.}}{678 \text{ grs.} \times 1 \text{ yd.}} = \dfrac{15.5 \times 437.5 \times 10}{678} =$ 100.

6. 3 yds. of lap weighing $2\frac{1}{2}$ lbs. into 9 yds. of sliver weighing 1000 grs.

7. 2 mtrs. of lap weighing 1.2 kg. into 144 mtrs. of sliver weighing 800 grams.

Relation of Actual to Mechanical Draft Formulas. *Mechanical draft, md,* is the ratio of the surface distance in a given time (i.e., surface speed, SS) of whatever roll is taken as the *delivery roll, dv roll,* to the surface distance in the given time of whatever roll is taken as the *feed roll, fd roll.* That is

(3) mechanical draft $= \dfrac{\text{surface distance of delivery roll in given time}}{\text{surface distance of feed roll in given time}} =$

$\dfrac{\text{surface speed of delivery roll}}{\text{surface speed of feed roll}}$.

8. Select the correct sign in each of the following parentheses: If stock slips on dv roll std lns of 1 end delivered in the given time (a) ($> = <$) SS dv roll. Why? If stock contracts upon leaving dv roll std lns of 1 end delivered in the given time (b) ($> = <$) SS dv roll. Why? If stock is lost between fd roll and dv roll, wt del (c) ($> = <$) wt fed.

9. From the foregoing: expressing such slip as the *percent of slip,* % s, and such contraction as the *percent of contraction,* % c, of the std lns of 1 end that otherwise would be delivered show that (a) std lns of 1 end delivered in the given time $= (1 - .01 \times \% \text{ s}) \times (1 - .01 \times \% \text{ c}) \times$ SS dv roll; expressing such stock loss as the *percent of weight loss,* % wl, similarly show that (b) wt delivered in the given time $= (1 - .01 \times \% \text{ wl}) \times$ wt fed; show that (c) std lns of 1 end fed in the given time = SS fd roll; ∴ substituting from equations (a), (b), and (c) into formula (2) show that

(d) $ad = \dfrac{\text{wt fed} \times (1 - .01 \times \% \text{ s}) \times (1 - .01 \times \% \text{ c}) \times \text{SS dv roll}}{(1 - .01 \times \% \text{ wl}) \times \text{wt fed} \times \text{SS fd roll}}$

$= \dfrac{(1 - .01 \times \% \text{ s}) \times (1 - .01 \times \% \text{ c})}{1 - .01 \times \% \text{ wl}} \times \dfrac{\text{SS dv roll}}{\text{SS fd roll}}$; ∴ substituting from formula (3) into equation (d) derive

(4) $\dfrac{\text{actual}}{\text{draft}} = \dfrac{(1 - .01 \times \% \text{ of slip}) \times (1 - .01 \times \% \text{ of contraction}) \times \text{mechanical draft}}{1 - .01 \times \% \text{ of weight loss}}$

and ∴

(5) $\dfrac{\text{mechanical}}{\text{draft}} = \dfrac{(1 - .01 \times \% \text{ of weight loss}) \times \text{actual draft}}{(1 - .01 \times \% \text{ of slip}) \times (1 - .01 \times \% \text{ of contraction})}$.

10. From formula (4) select the correct sign in the parentheses:

If stock does not slip, contract, and is not lost ad (> = <) md of 1 end fed and delivered. Why?

What md is required in the following example and 3 problems if:

EXAMPLE: *At a card, single lap,* 16.8 *oz. per yd., is fed and single sliver,* 84 *grs. per yd., is del with 5% waste and no slip or contraction.*

By formula (1): ad $= \dfrac{1 \times 16.8 \times 437.5}{1 \times 84} = 87.50.$ By formula

(5) md $= \dfrac{87.5 \times (1 - .01 \times 5)}{(1 - .01 \times 0) \times (1 - .01 \times 0)} = \dfrac{87.5 \times .95}{1 \times 1} = 83.13.$

11. 20 slivers, each 65.5 grs. per yd., into 2 slivers, each 60 grs. per yd. with .5% waste and no slip or contraction?

12. 20 slivers, each 60.5 grs. per yd. into 1 lap, 1200 grs. per yd. with no waste and 1% combined slip and contraction?

13. 8 laps, averaging 1160 grs. each, into 2 slivers, each 58 grs. per yd. with 9.5% weight and no slip or contraction.

14. 1 sliver, 60.0 grs. per yd., into 1 end of .70 HR with 1.5% contraction after leaving delivery roll and no slip or weight loss?

Formulas (3), (4), and (5) and their few preceding applications are in this chapter only to clarify the relation of actual to mechanical draft and thereby to clarify further the meaning of actual draft. The subsequent chapters on machine calculations in the carding and spinning departments further apply formulas (3), (4), and (5).

Actual Draft at Each Process. The rest of this chapter deals only with the applications of formula (1) at each process.

15. The cotton card usually draws 1 picker lap, designated by weight in ounces of 1 yd. of length or *ounce lap, oz. lap,* into 1 sliver designated by its weight in grains of 1 yd. or *grain sliver, gr. sl.* From formula (1) derive

(6) $\dfrac{\text{actual}}{\text{card draft}} = \dfrac{\text{ounce lap} \times 437.5}{\text{grain sliver}}$

Find the ad in the following 3 problems:

16. 16 oz. lap, 64 gr. sl.
17. Oz. lap 19.5, gr. sl. 58.5.
18. 15 oz. lap, 53 gr. sl.
19. The drawing frame, draw box, gill box or pin drafter draws multiple gr. slivers into single or multiple gr. slivers. Sometimes on the worsted system sliver fed is called *tow* and delivered *top.* On some drawing machines doublings and deliveries are grouped into heads.

Derive (7) $\dfrac{\text{actual}}{\substack{\text{drawing} \\ \text{machine} \\ \text{draft}}} = \dfrac{\dfrac{\text{doublings}}{\text{per machine}} \times \dfrac{\text{grain sliver}}{\text{fed}}}{\dfrac{\text{deliveries}}{\text{per machine}} \times \dfrac{\text{grain sliver}}{\text{delivered}}} =$

$$\frac{\dfrac{\text{doublings}}{\text{per head}} \times \dfrac{\text{grain sliver}}{\text{fed}}}{\dfrac{\text{deliveries}}{\text{per head}} \times \dfrac{\text{grain sliver}}{\text{delivered}}} =$$

$$\frac{\text{doublings per delivery} \times \text{grain sliver fed}}{\text{grain sliver delivered}}.$$

What is the ad in the following 3 problems if:

20. A frame draws 64 68-gr. slivers into 8 62-gr. slivers?

21. A head drafts 10 53-gr. slivers into 1 44-gr. slivers?

22. A pin drafting frame draws 12 ends of 250-gr. tow (sliver) into 1 end of 300-gr. top (sliver).

23. The sliver lapper draws multiple gr. slivers into 1 *grain lap, gr. lap.* Derive

$$(8) \quad \frac{\text{actual sliver}}{\text{lapper draft}} = \frac{\text{doublings} \times \text{grain sliver}}{\text{grain lap}}.$$

24. What is the ad if 20 44-gr. slivers are drawn into 850 gr. lap?

25. What is the ad if 20 52-gr. slivers are drawn into 1000 gr. lap?

26. What is the ad if 8 250-gr. worsted slivers are drafted into 1925 gr. lap?

27. The comber draws single or multiple gr. laps into single or multiple gr. slivers. Derive

$$(9) \quad \frac{\text{actual}}{\text{comber draft}} = \frac{\text{laps} \times \text{grain lap}}{\text{slivers} \times \text{grain sliver}}.$$

Find the ad in the following 3 problems:

28. A 6-head worsted comber at each head draws an 1800 gr. lap into a 50 gr. sliver.

29. An 8-head comber draws 8 900-gr. laps into 1 75-gr. sliver.

30. A 12-head comber draws 12 850-gr. laps into 2 60 gr. slivers.

31. Where the stock goes through successive roving frames the first is the slubber which draws 1 sliver into 1 roving and changes the designation of the stock from grain sliver to an indirect size as discussed in Chap. I. From formula (3), Chap. I show that

(a) $\dfrac{\text{std wts}}{\text{std lns}} = \dfrac{1}{\text{ind size}}$, $\therefore$ (b) std wts per std ln $= \dfrac{1}{\text{ind size}}$, $\therefore$, sub-

stituting from (b) into formula (1), (c) ad $= \dfrac{1 \times \dfrac{\text{grs. per yd. fed}}{7000} \times \text{std ln}}{1 \times \dfrac{1}{\text{ind size}}} =$

$\dfrac{\text{gr. sl} \times \text{std ln} \times \text{ind size}}{7000}$, and $\therefore$

$$(10) \quad \frac{\text{cotton}}{\text{actual}} = \frac{840 \times \dfrac{\text{grain}}{\text{sliver}} \times \dfrac{\text{hank}}{\text{roving}}}{7000} = .12 \times \frac{\text{grain}}{\text{sliver}} \times \frac{\text{hank}}{\text{roving}}, \text{ and}$$

     slubber
     draft

$$(11) \quad \frac{\text{worsted}}{\text{actual}} = \frac{560 \times \dfrac{\text{grain}}{\text{top}} \times \dfrac{\text{worsted}}{\text{counts}}}{7000} = .08 \times \frac{\text{grain}}{\text{top}} \times \frac{\text{worsted}}{\text{counts}}.$$

32. A succeeding roving frame draws single or multiple rovings into 1 roving. Derive

$$(12) \quad \frac{\text{actual succeeding}}{\text{roving frame draft}} = \frac{\text{doublings} \times \text{hank roving delivered}}{\text{hank roving fed}} =$$

$$\frac{\text{doublings} \times \text{worsted counts delivered}}{\text{worsted counts fed}}.$$

Find the ad in the following 4 problems:

33. 60-gr. sliver into .70 HR.
34. 62.5 gr. sliver into 1.25 HR.
35. 1.60 HR from 60-gr. sliver.
36. 72.5-gr. sliver into 1.5 wsd.
37. 2.10 wsd from 63 gr. top.
38. 3.2 HR from 2 1.10 HR.

39. The spinning frame draws single or multiple rovings—delivered by the roving frame on the ctn system or sliver delivered by the card, drawing frame or pin drafter on other systems (such as wsd, woolen)—into single yarn designated by a sizing system, usually indirect, as in Chap. I. By the same reasoning as in deriving formulas (10) to (12) derive

$$(13) \quad \frac{\text{cotton actual}}{\text{spinning frame}} = .12 \times \text{doublings} \times \frac{\text{grain}}{\text{sliver}} \times \text{counts} =$$

$$\frac{\text{doublings} \times \text{counts}}{\text{hank roving}},$$

$$(14) \quad \frac{\text{worsted actual}}{\text{spinning frame}} = .08 \times \text{doublings} \times \frac{\text{grain}}{\text{sliver}} \times \text{counts} =$$

$$\frac{\text{doublings} \times \text{counts delivered}}{\text{counts fed}},$$

$$(15) \quad \frac{\text{woolen actual}}{\text{spinning frame}} = \frac{\text{doublings} \times \text{run counts}}{\text{run roving}} =$$

$$\frac{\text{doublings} \times \text{cut counts}}{\text{cut roving}}.$$

Find the spinning frame ad in the following 11 problems:

40. 16.50s from single .80 HR.
41. Single 1.65 HR into 120.0s.
42. Double 2.10 HR into 75.50s.
43. Single 125-gr. sl into 2.25s ctn.
44. 1.75s ctn from double 100.0-gr. sl.

45. 40.00s wsd from double 4.50s.
46. 3.25s wsd from single 70.0-gr. sl.
47. Single 2.75 run into 5.90s run.
48. 3.10s run from single 1.40 run.
49. 65.50s cut from single 37.00 cut.
50. 64.00 wsd from single 10.00 dram roving.

Finding the Weight Fed and Weight Delivered. The peculiarities of the stock fed, the specifications for the stock delivered, or, as is discussed in Chap. VI to XII, the range or precision of the md of the machine may determine the ad and the weight or size that is required to be fed or that will be delivered.

What is the weight or indirect size that is required to be fed or that will be delivered in the following example and 31 problems:

EXAMPLE: 85.0-*gr. sliver and* 95 *card ad?*

Rearranging formula (6): oz. lap $= \dfrac{ad \times gr.\ sl}{437.5} = \dfrac{95 \times 85}{437.5} = 18.5.$

51. Card ad 87.5 and 75.5-gr. sl?
52. 55-gr. sl and card ad 135?
53. Card ad 140 and 16.0-oz. lap?
54. 17.5-oz. lap and card ad 112?
55. Drawing frame ad 12, 2 44-gr. sl del, and 20 fed?
56. 16 slivers fed, 2 60-gr. slivers del, and drawing frame ad 8.50?
57. Actual draft 12.0 32 72-gr. slivers fed and 4 delivered?
58. 2 ends of top delivered, 6 400-gr. tow ends fed, and gill box ad 8?
59. Sliver lapper ad 1.035, gr. lap 920, and 20 doublings?
60. Sliver lapper ad 1.040 and 8 240-gr. tops fed?
61. Worsted comber ad 28.40 and 1 60-gr. sliver from each lap?
62. 12-head comber ad 92.50 and 2 58.2-gr. slivers?
63. 8-head comber ad 92.5, 920.0 gr. lap, and 2 deliveries?
64. Slubber ad 6.050 and .68 HR?
65. HR 1.25 and slubber ad 12.50?
66. Slubber ad 10.50 and .955s wsd?
67. Gr. sl 60 and slubber ad 8.28?
68. Gr. top 75 slubber ad 10.20?
69. Succeeding roving frame ad 2.515 2 doublings, and HR 2.15 del?
70. Two .850 HR fed ad 7.250?
71. Spinning frame ad 42.50, single roving, and counts 25.50?
72. 16.50s, double HR, and spinning frame ad 34.50?
73. 120.0s, single HR, and spinning frame ad 75.00?
74. Double .650 HR and 32.60 ad?
75. 45.00s wsd, ad 18.00, and single roving?
76. Single dram roving 6.10 and ad 12.00?
77. Single run roving, ad 2.350, and 15.00s run?

78. Double cut roving, ad 1.750, and 1.25s cut?
79. Single 3.00 cut roving and ad 2.450?
80. Single 70.0-gr. sl and ctn spinning frame ad 16.80?
81. 4.25 wsd from single sliver and spinning frame ad 24.14?
82. As assigned by your instructor solve problems from your mill involving actual drafts and weights fed and delivered.

Chapter IV

LAY & TWIST CALCULATIONS

Lay Calculations and Roving And Yarn Diameters.

1. Select the correct word in each of the following parentheses: If no pressure or tension acts upon roving or yarn the number of ends of the same roving or of the same yarn that lie — "lay" in earlier accepted English — evenly in parallel contact in 1 inch, i.e., *ends per inch, epi,* or in 1 centimeter, i.e., *ends per centimeter, epc,* is (a) (directly, inversely) proportional to the dia. of an end. The epi = dia. in inches (b) (multiplied, divided) (c) (into, by) 1. Why? The epc = dia. in centimeters (d) (multiplied, divided) (e) (by, into) 1. Why? The epi is the (f) (product, reciprocal) of the dia. in ins. of the end.

Calculations of epi and epc and ∴ of diameters of ends are *lay calculations.*

Basic Diameter and Lay Formulas of Indirect Yard and Pound Sizing Systems.

2. Using the meanings and their abbreviations of Chap. I show that: (a) inches in an end = 36 × std ln × std lns; from formula (3), Chap. I (b) std lns = lbs. × ind size; substituting from (b) into (a) ∴ (c) ins. in an end = 36 × std ln × lbs. × ind size; from your study of cubic measures and from (c) ∴ (d) cu. ins. in an end = .7854 × dia.^{2} × 36 × std ln × lbs. × ind size; dividing both sides of (d) by cu. ins. in an end and reversing sides ∴ (e) $1 = \dfrac{.7854 \times \text{dia}^2 \times 36 \times \text{std ln} \times \text{lbs.} \times \text{ind size}}{\text{cu. ins. in an end}}$; from (e) ∴

(f) $\dfrac{\text{lbs.}}{\text{cu. ins. in an end}} = \dfrac{1}{.7854 \times \text{dia.}^2 \times 36 \times \text{std ln} \times \text{ind size}}$; since $\dfrac{\text{lbs.}}{\text{cu. ins. in an end}}$ means lbs. per cu. in. and from (f) ∴ (g) dia.$^2 = \dfrac{1}{.7854 \times 36 \times \text{std ln} \times \text{lbs. per cu. in.} \times \text{ind size}}$; from your study of square roots of equations, products, and fractions and from (g) ∴

$$\frac{\text{diameter}}{\text{of an end}} = \frac{1}{\sqrt{.7854 \times 36 \times \underset{\text{length}}{\text{standard}} \times \underset{\substack{\text{per} \\ \text{cubic} \\ \text{inch}}}{\text{pounds}} \times \sqrt{\text{indirect}}}}$$

and $\therefore$

(2) $\dfrac{\text{ends per}}{\text{inch}} = \sqrt{.7854 \times 36 \times \underset{\text{length}}{\text{standard}} \times \underset{\text{cubic inch}}{\text{pounds per}}} \times \sqrt{\underset{\text{size}}{\text{indirect}}}$

Lay, Coil, and Layer Multiples of Indirect Yard and Pound Sizing Systems. In formulas (1) and (2) the

(3) $\begin{array}{c}\text{lay multiple of} \\ \text{indirect yard} \\ \text{and pound sizing} \\ \text{system}\end{array} = \sqrt{.7854 \times 36 \times \underset{\text{length}}{\text{standard}} \times \underset{\text{cubic inch.}}{\text{pounds per}}}$

3. Show that $\therefore$

(4) diameter of an end in inches $= \dfrac{1}{\text{lay multiple} \times \sqrt{\text{indirect size}}}$

and (5) $\dfrac{\text{ends per}}{\text{inch}} = \text{lay multiple} \times \sqrt{\text{indirect size}}$

Table 1. Approximate Pounds Per Cubic Inch

Fiber	Roving	Soft Yarn	Hard Yarn
Cotton and staple rayon	.0139	.0270	.0355
Woolen, worsted, and staple acetate	.0122	.0238	.0312
Staple nylon	.0105	.0205	.0268
Staple Dacron	.0127	.0248	.0326
Filament rayon			.0483
Filament nylon			.0330
Filament Dacron			.0402

EXAMPLE: *Find the approximate lay multiple on the ctn system of cotton roving.*

By Table 1, Chap. I, formula (3) and Table 1:

lay multiple $= \sqrt{.7854 \times 36 \times 840 \times .0139} = \sqrt{330.1} = 18.2$

4. Similarly prove the approximate lay multiple of each such end in Table 2 and any other end as is run in your mill.

Table 2.   Approximate Lay Multiples on Indirect Yard
and Pound Sizing Systems

Fiber	Sizing System	Roving	Soft Yarn	Hard Yarn
Cotton	Cotton	18.2	25.3	29.0
Staple rayon	"	18.2	25.3	29.0
Staple dacron	"	17.4	24.3	27.8
Worsted	worsted	13.9	19.4	22.2
Staple dacron	"	14.2	19.8	22.7
Woolen	run	23.5	32.8	37.6
Filament rayon	cotton			33.9
Filament nylon	"			28.0
Filament dacron	"			30.9

Calculate the approximate (a) *dia. in ins.* and (b) *epi of the end on the sizing system in the example and* 6 *problems following:*

EXAMPLE: 1.60 *HR ctn cotton.*

(a) By formula (4) and the lay multiple from Table 2:

$$\text{dia. in ins.} = \frac{1}{18.2 \times \sqrt{1.60}} = \frac{1}{18.2 \times 1.265} = \frac{1}{23.02} = .0434.$$

(b) By formula (5): epi $= 18.2 \times 1.265 = 23.0$

5. 25.0s ctn hard cotton.
6. 110s ctn soft cotton.
7. 36.0s ctn soft staple rayon.
8. 48.0s wsd hard worsted.
9. 9.60s run hard woolen.
10. 90.0s wsd hard filament dacron.

However, on a bobbin of roving, depending on fuzziness and space between the ends lengthwise of the bobbin, the *coils per inch, cpi,* are less than by formula (5); and, depending on tension also, the *layers per inch, lpi,* through the bobbin are more than by formula (5). Roving *coil multiples, cm,* from less than $\frac{1}{2}$ to about $\frac{2}{3}$ of the lay multiples calculated by formula (3); and roving *layer multiples, lm,* from about $1\frac{1}{2}$ to 3 × the lay multiples calculated by formula (3) may be found in mill practice. Yarn in loosely knitted and woven fabrics may be as in formula (5); but in closely woven cloth may be squeezed and beaten flat.

Diameter and Lay Formulas and Lay Multiples of the Indirect Metric Sizing System.   Here the units are centimeters, *cms,* cubic centimeters, *ccs,* and kilograms, **kgs.**

11. Similar to your derivation of formulas (3) to (5) derive

(6) $\dfrac{\text{indirect metric}}{\text{lay multiple}} = \sqrt{.7854 \times 100 \times 1000 \times \text{kilograms per}}$, cubic centimeter

(7) $\dfrac{\text{diameter of an end}}{\text{in centimeters}} = \dfrac{1}{\dfrac{\text{indirect metric}}{\text{lay multiple}} \times \sqrt{\dfrac{\text{indirect metric}}{\text{size}}}}$, and

(8) $\dfrac{\text{ends per}}{\text{centimeter}} = \text{indirect metric lay multiple} \times \sqrt{\text{indirect metric}}$ size.

12. From your study of cubic measure prove that

(9) $\dfrac{\text{kilograms per}}{\text{cubic centimeter}} = \dfrac{\text{pounds per cubic inch}}{36.13}$

Calculate the approximate (a) *dia. in cms. and* (b) *epc of the end in the following example and 3 problems.*

EXAMPLE: *.95 met roving cotton.*

By formula (9) and Table 1: kgs. per cu. cm. $= \dfrac{.0139}{36.13}$. By formula

(6) lay multiple $= \sqrt{78540 \times \dfrac{.0139}{36.13}} = \sqrt{30.2} = 5.50$. (a) By formula

(7) dia. $= \dfrac{1}{5.50 \times \sqrt{.95}} = \dfrac{1}{5.50 \times .975} = \dfrac{1}{5.363} = .1865$. (b) By formula (8):

epc $= 5.4$.

13. 169s met soft cotton.
14. 67.5s met hard worsted.
15. 140s met hard filament nylon.

Diameter and Lay Formulas and Lay Multiples of Direct Meter and Gram Sizing Systems.

16. Similar to your derivation of formulas (6), (7), (8), and (9), but from formula (4), Chap. I derive

(10) $\begin{array}{l}\text{lay multiple of direct} \\ \text{meter and gram sizing} \\ \quad\quad\text{system}\end{array} = \sqrt{.7854 \times 100 \times \text{standard} \times \text{grams}}$, length per cubic centimeter

(11) $\begin{array}{l}\text{diameter of an} \\ \text{end in} \\ \text{centimeters}\end{array} = \dfrac{\sqrt{\text{direct meter and gram size}}}{\begin{array}{c}\text{lay multiple of direct meter and gram} \\ \text{system}\end{array}}$,

(12) $\dfrac{\text{ends per}}{\text{centimeter}} = \dfrac{\text{lay multiple of direct meter and gram system}}{\sqrt{\text{direct meter and gram size}}}$, and

(13)   grams per $= \dfrac{1000 \times \text{pounds per cubic inch}}{36.13}$
        cubic centimeter

$= \begin{array}{l} 27.68 \times \text{pound per} \\ \quad \text{cubic inch.} \end{array}$

Calculate the approximate (a) *lay multiple* (b) *dia. in cms. and* (c) *epc of the end in the following example and 6 problems:*

EXAMPLE: 53.2 *den hard filament nylon.*

By formula (13) and Table 1: grams per cc. = 27.68 × .0330 = .9134.

(a) By Table 1, Chap. I and formula (10):

lay multiple = $\sqrt{.7854 \times 100 \times 9000 \times .9134}$ = $\sqrt{645646}$ = 804.

(b) By formula (11):

dia. in cms. = $\sqrt{\dfrac{53.2}{804}} = \dfrac{7.29}{804}$ = .006967.

(c) By formula (12):

epc $= \dfrac{804}{7.29}$ = 110.

17. 280 den hard filament nylon.
18. 12.0s tex hard filament dacron.
19. 492 tex roving cotton.
20. 5.37s tex soft cotton.
21. 20.0s tex hard worsted.
22. 59.0s tex soft woolen.

Twist Calculations and Roving and Yarn Diameters.

23. Select the correct word in each set of the following parentheses: Considering strength and evenness, other conditions being the same, the number of complete twists that need to be and can be inserted in 1 inch of end, i.e., *twist per inch, tpi,* or 1 centimeter of end, i.e., *twist per centimeter, tpc,* is (a) (directly, inversely) proportional to the dia. of the end. Why? Therefore, tpi and tpc are (b) (directly, inversely) proportional to the $\sqrt{\text{indirect size}}$ and (c) (directly, inversely) proportional to the $\sqrt{\text{direct size}}$. By formula number cite the proof of each of your answers. Therefore, tpi and tpc must equal some number (d) (multiplied, divided) by the $\sqrt{\text{indirect size}}$ and some number (e) (multiplied, divided) by $\sqrt{\text{direct size}}$.

Twist Multiples and Twist Formulas.   The number referred to in the preceding sentence is the *twist multiple, tm.*

24. From the foregoing derive

(14) twist per inch or centimeter $=$ indirect twist $\times \sqrt{\dfrac{\text{indirect}}{\text{size}}}$ and
     on indirect sizing systems   multiple

(15)   twist per centimeter on $= \dfrac{\text{direct twist multiple}}{\sqrt{\text{direct metric size}}}$
direct metric sizing systems

25. From formula (14) derive

(16) $\dfrac{\text{twist}}{\text{per inch}} = \dfrac{\text{cotton system}}{\text{twist multiple}} \times \sqrt{\dfrac{\text{cotton system hank roving}}{\text{or counts}}}$

Depending upon many conditions, such ctn system twist multiples as in Table 3 may be found in mill practice.

Table 3.   Cotton Sizing Twist Multiples

	Variations	Common Standards
Roving	.70 to 1.60	1.20 to 1.50
Single yarn	2.50 to 5.50	
hosiery yarn		2.75 to 3.65
sewing thread yarn		3.00 to 3.50
filling yarn		3.25 to 3.50
warp yarn		4.50 to 4.75
Ply yarn	3.00 to 6.00	

Find the tpi of the cotton system end in each of the following 15 *problems:*

26. .25 HR 1.10 tm.   34. 30.0s 3.25 tm.
27. .50 HR 1.25 tm.   35. 33.5s 4.50 tm.
28. 1.75 HR 1.35 tm.   36. 55.0s 4.75 tm.
29. 4.00 HR 1.50 tm.   37. 110.0s 3.40 tm.
30. 2.00s 4.75 tm.   38. 17.5s/2 5.00 tm.
31. 3.00s 2.74 tm.   39. 60.0s/3 3.25 tm.
32. 15.0s 3.12 tm.   40. 120s/6 5.00 tm.
33. 24.0s 3.48 tm.

Twist Multiple Conversion Factors. With the possibility of having to convert roving and yarn sizes between sizing systems is the possibility of having to convert twist multiples between sizing. Hence, the convenience of *twist multiple conversion factors.*

EXAMPLE: *Find the tm conversion factors to convert between tms on the ctn and tex systems.*

From your study of measures: 1 in. = 2.540 cms. From formulas (14) and (15): $\text{tpi} = \text{ctn tm} \times \sqrt{\text{ctn size}}$ and $\text{tpc} = \dfrac{\text{tex tm}}{\sqrt{\text{tex size}}}$.

Since on both systems the twists in any given length must be equal; $\therefore$, $\text{ctn tm} \times \sqrt{\text{ctn size}} = 2.540 \times \dfrac{\text{tex tm}}{\sqrt{\text{tex size}}}$; and $\therefore$, $\text{tex tm} = \dfrac{\text{ctn tm} \times \sqrt{\text{ctn size}} \times \sqrt{\text{tex size}}}{2.540}$. From Table 2, Chap. I and your

Table 4.   Twist Multiple-Conversion Factors Carried to
Four Significant Digits

		To convert to a				
cotton	worsted	run	cut or lea	metric	denier	tex

sizing system twist multiple
from an equivalent twist multiple on a sizing system below
multiply with the twist multiple conversion factor as shown below:

cotton	worsted	run	cut or lea	metric	denier	tex
	ctn tm ×.8165	ctn tm × 1.380	ctn tm ×.5976	ctn tm ×.3026	ctn tm × 28.70	ctn tm ×9.567
wsd tm × 1.225		wsd tm ×.1690	wsd tm ×.7319	wsd tm ×.3705	wsd tm × 35.15	wsd tm × 11.72
run tm ×.7245	run tm ×.5916		run tm ×.4330	run tm ×.2192	run tm × 20.80	run tm × 6.932
cut or lea tm ×.5976	cut or lea tm × 1.366	cut or lea tm × 2.309		cut or lea tm ×.5062	cut or lea tm × 48.02	cut or lea tm × 16.01
met tm × 3.305	met tm ×.3705	met tm × 4.561	met tm × 1.975		met tm × 94.87	met tm × 31.62
den tm ×.03484	den tm ×.02844	den tm ×.04809	den tm ×.02082	den tm ×.01054		den tm ×.3333
tex tm ×.1045	tex tm ×.08534	tex tm ×.1443	tex tm ×.06246	tex tm ×.03162	tex tm × 3.000	

study of square root: ∴, $\text{tex tm} = \dfrac{\text{ctn tm} \times \sqrt{\text{ctn size}} \times \text{tex size}}{2.540} =$

$\dfrac{\text{ctn tm} \times \sqrt{\text{ctn size} \times \dfrac{590.5}{\text{ctn size}}}}{2.540} = \dfrac{\text{ctn tm} \times \sqrt{590.5}}{2.540} = \text{ctn tm} \times 9.567$ and

$\text{ctn tm} = \dfrac{\text{tex tm}}{9.567} = \text{tex tm} \times .1045.$

41. By reasoning equivalent to that in the preceding example
prove whichever tm conversion factors in Table 2 or others are or
likely to be needed in your plant.

Calculate from the twist specifications given the (a) *equivalent
twist specifications, including the* (b) *tpi or tpc, whichever is the ap-*

*propriate equivalent, on the system indicated in the following example
and problems:*

EXAMPLE: 75 *HR ctn* 1.20 *tm on the met system.*

By Table 2, Chap. I:

met size = 1.693 × .75 = 1.27.

By Table 4:

met tm = 1.20 × .3026 = .363.

(a) 1.27 met roving .363 tm. By formula (14):

(b) tpc = .363 × $\sqrt{1.27}$ = .41.

42. 110s ctn 3.25 tm on the tex system.
43. 133 den 158 tm on the wsd system.
44. 16.0s run 6.25 tm on the tex system.

Chapter V

CLOTH CALCULATIONS

Construction. All cloth is made according to certain specifications called the construction of the cloth. Here is the complete construction of a certain kind of plain cloth.

40″ 2.90 48 × 48 15s warp 15.5s filling 48 selvage ends.

This construction means that the cloth is 40″ wide between selvages; there are 2.90 yards in a pound; there are 48 warp ends per inch in the body of the cloth; there are 48 picks of filling per inch; the warp yarn is 15s; the filling yarn is 15.5s and that there are 48 ends in both selvages—or 24 ends in each selvage. The warp ends per inch are always given immediately before the picks per inch. The warp ends per inch are often referred to as ends per inch or as the sley.

Picks per inch are referred to as the picks. The above construction would be read like this: "40–2.90–48 × 48 15s warp 15.5s filling." When the sley and the picks are equal the term "square" is used. Thus the above cloth might be referred to as "48 square." The complete specifications are not always sent to the plant. Often a sample is all that is available. Many heavy fabrics are known by the ounces per yard instead of yards per pound.

Finding the Weight of Cloth from Construction.

EXAMPLE: What is the weight of 1 yard of 36″ 4.50 48 × 52?

Weight of 4.5 yds. = 1 lb. Weight of 1 yd. $= \dfrac{1 \text{ lb.}}{4.5} = .222$ lbs. = 3.55 oz. = 1553.1 grs.

PROBLEMS:

1. Find the weight in ounces of one yard of 31″ 3.00 44 × 40 sheeting.

2. How many pounds would be in 7 yds. of 8-oz. denim?

3. If $7\frac{1}{2}$ yards of a certain style cloth weigh one pound, how many grains are there in one yard?

4. If an 80-yd. length of worsted suiting weighs 60 pounds, what is the weight in ounces per yard?

5. Find the weight in grains of $\frac{1}{8}$ yds. of moleskin cloth if 1.65 yds. weigh one pound.

6. If 3 pieces of cotton bedspread each 80 yards long weigh a total of 264 lbs., what is the weight in ounces per yard?

7. If a $4\frac{1}{2}$-yd. sheeting is baled 10 pieces to the bale, 110 yds. to each piece, what will be the weight of 100 bales, allowing $\frac{5}{9}$ lb. per bale for burlap and ties?

Finding Yards Per Pound from Samples.

EXAMPLE: *A sample of fabric 3 inches square weighs 15 grains. Find the yards per pound if the cloth is to be made 30 inches wide.*

The sample contains $3'' \times 3'' = 9$ square inches. One yard of fabric would contain $30'' \times 36'' = 30 \times 36$ square inches. But 9 sq. in. weighs 15 grs. $15 \text{ grs.} = \frac{15}{7000 \text{ lbs.}}$ $\therefore$ By proportion:

$$\frac{30 \times 36}{9} = \frac{\text{weight (in pounds) of 1 yd.}}{\dfrac{15}{7000}} \cdot \therefore \text{ the weight in pounds of}$$

$$1 \text{ yd.} = \frac{15 \times 30 \times 36}{9 \times 7000} \cdot \therefore \text{ the yds. in 1 lb.} = \frac{9 \times 7000}{15 \times 30 \times 36} = 3.89.$$

8. From the preceding example work out the following formula:

$$(1) \text{ yds. per lb.} = \frac{\text{square inches in sample} \times 7000}{\text{weight (in grains) of sample} \times \text{cloth width} \times 36}$$

9. If a sample 4 inches square weighs 41 grains, find the number of yards 30 inches wide required to make 1 pound.

10. A sample of sheeting 3 inches square weighs 15 grains. Find the yards per pound if woven 74 inches wide.

11. A $4'' \times 4''$ sample weighs 20 grains. Find the number of yards required to make a pound if the cloth is 36 inches wide.

12. A rayon sample is $4''$ square and weighs 16 grains. How many yards will weigh 1 pound if made 54 inches wide?

13. A sample of moleskin one inch square weighs 3.4 grains. It is desired to make the cloth $34\frac{1}{2}$ inches wide. Find the number of yards per pound.

14. A sample of worsted suiting is $2'' \times 2''$ and weighs 4 grains. What will be the yards per pound if the cloth is 48 inches wide?

Finding the Number of Ends in the Width of the Cloth.

EXAMPLE: *How many warp ends in 36″ 3.00 48 × 52 if 16 extra ends are added for selvages?*

$48 \times 36 + 16 = 1744$.   **Answer:**   total ends $= 1744$.

15. How many warp ends will be required to make $90''$ 2.75 44×40 sheeting with 20 ends for selvages?

16. If a fabric is to be $31\frac{1}{4}$ inches wide, 72 warp ends per inch with no selvage, how many warp ends will be required?

17. A gingham pattern calls for 8 ends of blue, 4 ends of red and 8 ends of white in one repeat. What will be the total ends in the body of the cloth if there are 84 repeats of the pattern each $\frac{1}{2}$ inch wide?

18. A striped seersucker has 10 red ends and 10 white ends to each repeat. A repeat is $\frac{5''}{16}$ in width. If the cloth is 40 inches wide between the selvages, how many warp ends are in the body?

19. In a certain worsted tropical suiting the warp ends in a $\frac{1''}{4}$ repeat are arranged as follows: 1 blue, 3 brown, 1 black, 5 brown, 1 black, 1 brown. If there are 12 ends in each $\frac{1''}{4}$ selvage and the total width of the fabric is $46''$, how many total warp ends will be needed?

Finding the Ends Per Dent and Total Dents Required.   A dent is the opening between adjacent wires in the reed. Reeds are numbered according to the number of dents per inch or according to the total number of dents in a given length. Consider a reed containing 890 dents in a length of 40 inches. The number of this reed might be expressed in any one of the following ways:

(a) It is a 22.25-dent reed $\left(\frac{890}{40} = 22.25\right)$; or a 22.25's reed; or the reed has 22.25 dents per inch; or the reed counts are 22.25's.

(b) It is an 890–40 reed; or 890 dents are spread on 40 inches.

A reed should always be the same length as the reed slot in the loom lay, regardless of the number of dents used on the width of the cloth woven.

EXAMPLE: *If there are 1748 ends in the warp including the selvages; 16 ends in the selvages; the selvages drawn 4 per dent and the balance of the warp 2 per dent, what is the total number of dents required?*

$1748 - 16 = 1732$ ends in the body of the warp.

$\frac{1732}{2} = 866$ dents in the body of the cloth.

$\frac{16}{4} = 4$ dents in selvages; $866 + 4 = 870$ dents required.

20. How many dents will be required to draw a 2142 end warp with no selvage 3 ends per dent?

21. Find the number of dents needed to weave a cloth containing 3648 ends including 28 selvage ends all drawn 4 ends per dent.

22. How many dents are required to draw 36" 3.25 48 × 44; warp drawn 2 ends per dent; 32 selvage ends drawn 4 ends per dent?

23. One repeat of a certain pattern contains 24 ends of plain weave drawn 4 per dent and 20 ends of sateen weave drawn 5 per dent. If there are 16 ends in each selvage drawn 4 per dent, how many total dents will be required? There are 104 repeats in the width of the cloth.

Finding the Percent of Contraction of Filling. The warp is spread out in the reed. After they interlace with the filling the warp ends are drawn together. The difference between the width at reed and the width of the cloth is the amount of contraction of the filling. The amount of contraction depends upon the manner in which the warp and filling interlace, the tension on the warp in the loom and the differences between the warp yarn counts and the filling yarn counts. The contraction in filling is usually expressed as a percent.

EXAMPLE: *What is the percent of contraction of filling if the width at reed is 50 inches and the width of the cloth is 47 inches?*

$$50'' - 47'' = 3''; \frac{3}{50} = .06; \text{Contraction is 6\%.}$$

From this example prove the following formula.

(2) % filling contraction $= \dfrac{\text{width at reed} - \text{cloth width}}{\text{width at reed}} \times 100.$

24. The width at reed is 50" and the cloth width is $46\frac{3''}{4}$. What is the percent of filling contraction?

25. The cloth is $69\frac{1''}{4}$ wide and the width at reed is 75". What is the percent of filling contraction?

26. If the width at reed is $53\frac{1''}{2}$ and there is $6\frac{1}{2}\%$ contraction of the filling, how wide is the cloth?

27. How many inches wide is the warp at the reed if the filling contraction is 8% and the cloth is 40" wide?

Finding the Dents Per Inch Required and the Total Dents in the Reed.

EXAMPLE: *Find the dents per inch required in the reed to make sheeting with 48 ends per inch in the cloth if the ends are drawn 2 per dent and the filling contraction is $7\frac{1}{2}\%$.*

$\dfrac{48}{2} = 24.$ ∴ 48 ends occupy 24 dents. $100\% - 7\frac{1}{2}\% = 92.5\%.$

∴ there are 92.5% of 24 dents in one inch.

.925 × 24 dents = 22.20 dents. ∴ 22.20 dents per inch required.

28. How many dents per inch will be required in a reed to make sateen containing 110 ends per inch in the cloth reeded 5 ends per dent if the contraction in width is 5%?

29. Find the number of dents in a reed $40\frac{1}{4}''$ long required to make 30" 88 × 56 twills, reeded 4 ends to the dent, the contraction in width being 5%?

30. It is desired to make cloth $38\frac{1}{2}''$ 44 × 40, reeded one end per dent. The contraction in width is $8\frac{1}{2}\%$. Find the number of dents per inch required in the reed.

31. Find the number of dents in a reed $44\frac{1}{4}''$ long required to make 38" 96 × 64 drills, reeded 3 per dent if the contraction is $3\frac{1}{2}\%$.

32. If one repeat of the pattern in problem 23 is $\frac{1}{2}''$ wide and the contraction is $6\frac{1}{2}\%$, what will be the dents per inch in the reed?

Finding the Width of the Warp at the Reed.

EXAMPLE: *Find the total width at reed of* 38" 44 × 40 *reeded 2 per dent with* 24 *selvage ends reeded* 4 *per dent if the contraction in width is* 5%.

Width (in inches) of body of cloth at reed $= \dfrac{38}{.95} = 40$.

Dents per inch $= 22 \times .95 = 20.9$. Dents occupied by selvage $= 6$.

∴ width (in inches) of selvages at reed $= \dfrac{6}{20.9} = .29$ or $.3$.

∴ total width at reed $= 40.3$ inches.

33. Find the width at reed of 30" 88 × 56 with 16 extra selvage ends all reeded 4 per dent, allowing $5\frac{3}{4}\%$ for contraction.

34. Find the width at reed of 72" 64 square reeded 2 per dent with 16 extra selvage ends reeded 4 per dent, allowing $6\frac{1}{2}\%$ for contraction.

35. Find the width at reed of 44" 108 × 56 with no selvages, allowing 5% for contraction.

36. Find the width at reed of 36" 48 × 52 with no selvages, allowing 4% for contraction.

Finding the Weight of Filling in Fabric.   It is evident that each pick of filling in the fabric before contraction takes place is exactly the width at the reed of the fabric including the selvages. Hence, calculations to find the weight of filling in fabric must be based upon the total width at reed.

EXAMPLE: *Find the weight of* 20s *filling in* 1 *yard of* 38″ 44 × 40 *reeded* 2 *ends per dent with* 24 *selvage ends reeded* 4 *per dent if the contraction in width is* 5%.

Width at reed including selvages $= \dfrac{38}{.95} + .3 = 40.3''$.

∴ One pick of filling is 40.3″. There are 40 × 40.3 inches of filling in one inch of fabric. There are 40 × 40.3 × 36 inches of filling in one yard of fabric. There are $\dfrac{40 \times 40.3 \times 36}{36}$ yards of filling in one yard of fabric. There are $\dfrac{40 \times 40.3 \times 36}{36 \times 840}$ hanks of filling in one yard of fabric. From formula (21), Chapter 1, Part Two, we know that: pounds of yarn $= \dfrac{\text{hanks of yarn}}{\text{counts}}$; therefore, there are $\dfrac{40 \times 40.3 \times 36}{36 \times 840 \times 20}$ pounds of filling in one yard. By cancellation we find that $\dfrac{40 \times 40.3}{840 \times 20} = .096$ pounds of filling in one yard of fabric. If the weight in grains were required, from the preceding work we see that: weight in grains $= \dfrac{40 \times 40.3 \times 7000}{840 \times 20} =$ 671.7. From this example work out the following formulas:

(3) $\dfrac{\text{lbs. of filling}}{\text{in fabric}} = \dfrac{\text{yds. of fabric} \times \text{width at reed} \times \text{ppi}}{840 \times \text{counts of filling}}$

Note: For yarns made from fibers other than cotton, use the appropriate standard hank length or convert to cotton counts.

(4) $\dfrac{\text{grains of filling}}{\text{in fabric}} = \dfrac{25 \times \text{yds. of fabric} \times \text{width at reed} \times \text{ppi}}{3 \times \text{counts of filling}}$

37. Find the weight in grains of 24s filling in one yard of 36″ 64 square reeded 2 per dent with 16 extra selvage ends reeded 4 per dent, allowing 6% contraction.

38. What is the weight in grains of 45s worsted filling in one yard 30″ 48 × 54 reeded 2 per dent with 24 extra ends in each selvage reeded 4 per dent allowing 7% for contraction in width?

39. Find the weight in grains of 177 denier nylon filling in one yard of 30″ 88 × 60 with 16 extra selvage ends all reeded 4 per dent, allowing 4% contraction.

40. How many pounds of 23s cotton filling would there be in 60 yards of 34″ 3.00 110 × 56 sateen with no selvages if the filling contraction is 6%?

41. How many pounds of 30s worsted filling will be needed to make 60 yards of 30″ 5.00 48 × 48 with no selvages if the filling contraction is 6%?

42. The width of a cotton filling spot fabric is 32″ at the reed. In a one-inch pattern there are 16 blue picks, 16 grey picks and 4 white extra filling picks. How many pounds each of (a) 80/2 blue, (b) 80/2 grey, and (c) 13/1 white filling will be needed to make 200 yards of cloth?

Finding the Percent of Contraction of Warp.   The length of the warp from the slasher is always greater than the length of the woven cloth. The amount of contraction of the warp is affected by the amount of interlacing, the diameter of the warp and the filling, and the tension on the warp on the loom.

EXAMPLE: *How many yards of warp will be required to make one yard of cloth containing 1744 ends if the contraction in length of warp is 5%?*

100% − 5% = 95%; 1744 × 1 yd. = 1744 yds. of contracted warp in 1 yd. of cloth. Therefore, the yards of warp in 1 yd. of cloth $= \dfrac{1744}{.95}$ = 1835.79 yards.

43. An end of warp yarn is picked out of a piece of cloth exactly 3″ long. The yarn, after being smoothed out evenly, measures $3\frac{1}{4}$ inches. What is the percent of warp contraction?

44. Find the number of yards of warp yarn in 3 yards of 63″ 3.00 44 × 40 sheeting, 16 extra ends for selvage, if the contraction in length is $4\frac{1}{4}\%$.

45. How many yards of warp yarn are in one pound of 30″ 2.50 72 × 60, no selvages, allowing $4\frac{1}{2}\%$ for contraction?

46. Find the total number of yards of warp in one pound of 36″ 4.70 48 × 52 with 16 ends for selvages, allowing $5\frac{3}{4}\%$ for contraction in length.

47. How many yards of cloth can be woven from a 2150-yard warp if the contraction in length is $6\frac{1}{4}\%$?

48. If a roll of sheeting measures 130 yds. in length, what was the length of the warp if the contraction is $6\frac{1}{2}\%$?

Finding the Weight of Warp in Cloth.   To find the total weight of warp in a given length of cloth, we must first find the weight of the length of warp which when contracted will make the given length of cloth. Then to the weight of this length of yarn we must add whatever weight of sizing compound has been added to the yarn.

EXAMPLE: *What is the weight of the warp in one yard of cloth 40″ wide with 40 ends of 20s cotton warp yarn per inch plus 16 extra ends for selvages, if the contraction of the warp is 6% and 11% of sizing has been added to the warp?*

Number of yards of contracted warp yarn in one yard of cloth = $40 \times 40 + 16 = 1616$. $100\% - 6\% = 94\% = .94$. Number of yards of uncontracted warp in one yard of cloth $= \dfrac{1616}{.94}$. Hence, hanks of warp

in cloth $= \dfrac{\dfrac{1616}{.94}}{840} = \dfrac{1616}{94 \times 840}$. From formula (21), Chapter 1, Part Two: lbs.

of unsized warp $= \dfrac{\dfrac{1616}{.94 \times 840}}{20} = \dfrac{1616}{.94 \times 840 \times 20} \cdot 100\% + 11\% = 111\% =$

1.11. $\therefore$ pounds of warp with sizing in 1 yd. of cloth $= \dfrac{1616 \times 1.11}{.94 \times 840 \times 20} =$

$.1135$. $\therefore$ grains of warp with sizing in 1 yd. of cloth $= \dfrac{1616 \times 1.11 \times 7000}{.94 \times 840 \times 20} =$

795.11.

From the preceding example work out the following formulas:

$$(5)\ \begin{array}{c}\text{pounds of sized} \\ \text{warp in cloth}\end{array} = \dfrac{\begin{array}{c}\text{yds. of} \\ \text{cloth}\end{array} \times \begin{array}{c}\text{number of} \\ \text{ends}\end{array} \times (100\% + \% \text{ size})}{(100\% - \% \text{ contraction}) \times 840 \times \text{counts}}$$

$$(6)\ \begin{array}{c}\text{grains of sized} \\ \text{warp in cloth}\end{array} = \dfrac{\begin{array}{c}\text{yds. of} \\ \text{cloth}\end{array} \times \begin{array}{c}\text{number of} \\ \text{ends}\end{array} \times (100\% + \% \text{ size}) \times 7000}{(100\% - \% \text{ contraction}) \times 840 \times \text{counts}}$$

49. Find the weight in pounds of the warp in 5 yards of 30″ 2.50 71×60 made with $11\frac{1}{2}$s warp, no selvages, allowing $5\frac{1}{2}\%$ for contraction and $10\frac{1}{2}\%$ for size.

50. How many grains of warp are there in 1 yard of 34″ cloth, 64 ends of $11\frac{1}{2}$s warp per inch, allowing 6% for contraction and 12% for size, 16 extra ends for selvages?

51. Find the weight in pounds of the warp in 60 yards of $38\frac{1}{2}″$ 2.85 96×64 jeans, no extra selvage ends, number 23 warp, allowing 4% for contraction and 13% for size.

Finding the Desired Information from Given Cloth Specifications. The specifications for a cloth to be made by the plant often give only a minimum amount of information. Sometimes the only information given is the width and a small sample of cloth. From the specifications given, however, all the rest of the essential information must be found. The problems in this chapter up to this point have covered the basic cloth calculations. With a command of these basic calculations and by rearranging some of the formulas you have learned, the following problems can be solved.

The plant receives orders to make a certain fabric. From the following specifications all the necessary information must be found: "Width 40 in. as per attached sample." A careful examination under the pick glass reveals the following: sley, 48; picks, 48; ends in each selvage, 24; body of warp drawn 2 per dent - selvages, 4 per dent. A sample trimmed exactly 3 inches square weighs 15 grains. The sample is then picked apart and this additional information is found. The sample is a plain weave fabric. The filling weighs 7.26 grains and the sized warp weighs 7.74 grains. It is observed that these two weights check exactly with the weight of the sample. The uncontracted warp is $3\frac{1}{4}''$ long and the uncontracted filling is $3\frac{3}{8}''$ long.

52. What is the percent of filling contraction?
53. What is the percent of warp contraction?
54. How many total ends will be required to make the cloth?
55. How many dents per inch in the reed?
56. What is the overall width of the warp at the reed?
57. Assuming that the warp contains about 11% of size, calculate the warp yarn counts.
58. What is the filling yarn counts?

An order is received by a plant to make some cloth. It will be a fancy weave of all cotton, 45" wide. Analysis of a sample reveals the following data: sley, 84; picks, 68; ends in each selvage, 20; body of warp drawn 2 per dent – selvages 4 per dent. A 3-inch square swatch weighs 13.88 grains. When it is picked apart it is discovered that there are 80 ends of white warp, then 4 ends of blue warp in each repeat. The filling weighs 6.87 grains and the sized warp weighs 6.91 grains. The uncontracted warp is $3\frac{1}{5}''$ long and the uncontracted filling is $3\frac{1}{4}''$ long.

59. What is the percent of warp contraction?
60. What is the percent of filling contraction?
61. How many total ends of white warp are required to make the fabric? (The selvage is white)
62. How many blue warp ends are required if the 4 blue ends which would be near the edge of the cloth are omitted so the fabric would have 80 ends of white warp next to each selvage?
63. How many dents per inch in the reed?
64. What is the overall width of the warp at the reed?
65. If the warp contains 11% size, what is the count of warp yarn?
66. What is the filling yarn count?

A salesman sent an exact 2-inch square of cloth to a plant and requested 500 yards of the same construction. The fabric was to be 40" wide with 12 selvage ends on each side drawn 4 per dent. The body was drawn 3 per dent. Examination of the sample revealed: sley, 90; picks, 72. The 2 × 2 swatch weighed 5.42 grains. Analysis showed the filling weighed 2.22 grains and the warp weighed 3.20 grains. The uncontracted warp measured 2.13 inches and the uncontracted filling measured 2.20 inches. The fabric was a plain weave, the warp was cotton and the filling was nylon.

67. What is the warp contraction?
68. What is the filling contraction?
69. How many total warp ends are required?
70. What is the warp yarn count if the sample contained 8 percent size?
71. What is the filling count in denier size?
72. How many pounds of nylon will be required to run the order allowing 3% waste?

A sample of unsized plaid cloth is sent to a plant by a company salesman who has an order for 1000 yards, 48″ wide. Analysis of the sample reveals: sley, 30; picks, 30; (both sley and picks contain 10 black ends, 10 red ends, 10 black, 10 red, etc.). There is a total of 16 selvage ends, 8 red and 8 black. Body ends are drawn one per dent and selvage ends 2 per dent. A 3 × 3 swatch of the *worsted* material weighs 24.28 grains. When separated, the filling weighs 12.22 grains and the warp weighs 12.06 grains. The uncontracted warp is $3\frac{7}{16}''$ long and the filling is $3\frac{1}{2}''$ long.

73. What is the warp contraction?
74. What is the filling contraction?
75. What are the dents per inch in the reed?
76. What is the worsted system filling count?
77. What is the worsted system warp count?
78. How many pounds of black warp yarn will be used to manufacture the order?
79. How many pounds of red warp yarn will be used?
80. Calculate the total pounds of filling, both red and black, that will be used in the 1000 yards.

Chapter VI

STATISTICAL QUALITY CONTROL CALCULATIONS

Purpose. The competitive economic system within which the usual textile plant must operate dictates that the quality each employee produces is one of the most important factors in the plant's success and that of its employees. Therefore, in your study of textile mathematics, familiarity with the terms, procedures, and calculations involved in controlling quality is quite important. The purpose of this chapter is not to cover broadly and deeply all the facets of this subject but to enable you to adequately cope with the quality control reports you receive.

It is the responsibility of the quality control laboratory, however named, in the usual plant to measure and report the quality. How well the laboratory thus measures and reports is of utmost importance; but no more so than production personnel understanding the reports and any corrective action they must take.

Variation, Mean, Median, and Mode. Variation exists between measurements of corresponding dimensions of objects . . . even those considered identical. Statistical quality control measures variation to keep it within acceptable limits. Within a given *test* (i.e., a completed series of original observations, measurements, or *values*) each value is often indicated by an *x* (abbreviation for "example"). Each x is often numbered in *consecutive order* from 1 up; thus: X1, X2, X3, etc. The total number of Xs is designated by *n*.

1. If in a test of n consecutive measurements the first is x1 what is the final measurement?

Σ (the Greek capital letter Sigma corresponding to our capital S) means and usually is read "sum of." Thus Σx means sum of all the xs in a test.

2. From the foregoing show that

(1) $\Sigma x = x1 + x2 + x3 + \cdots xn.$

We will begin to understand the variation of the xs in a test if we have a measure of a *central tendency* of the xs. One central tendency with which we are already familiar is the **average**. In statistical mathematics a bar over a quantity indicates the average of the quantities expressed by that symbol. Thus x̄ indicates the average or arithmetic **mean** of the xs in a test or group.

3. From the foregoing prove that

(2) mean, $\bar{x} = \dfrac{x1 + x2 + x3 + \cdots xn}{n} = \dfrac{\Sigma x}{n}$.

If the xs are arranged in their ascending or descending *value order* another central tendency is the *median*, i.e., the middle value above and below which are an equal number of other x values. If n is an even number the median is the mean of the 2 middle values. The remaining central tendency is the *mode*, i.e., the x value that repeats with the greatest *frequency, F.*

Find the n, Σx, $\bar{x}$, *median, and mode of the tests in the following examples and 3 problems:*

EXAMPLE: *Test 1: Grain weights of 1-yd. lengths of 59-gr. sliver from 1 card:* x1 63, x2 59, x3 59, x4 60, x5 57, x6 59, x7 59, x8 65, x9 59, x10 60.

By definition: n = 10. By formula (1): Σx = 600 grs. By formula (2): $\bar{x} = \dfrac{600 \text{ grs.}}{10} = 60$ grs. In value order: x5 57, x2 59, x3 59, x6 59, x7 59, x9 59, x4 60, x10 60, x1 63, x8 65. By definition: since n is even, median $= \dfrac{(59 + 59) \text{ grs.}}{2} = 59$ grs.

By definition: mode = 59 grs.

4. *Test 2 of the lb. weight of 1 lap from each picker:* 72.0, 73.5, 71.5, 72.0, 72.0, 72.5, 73.0, 72.0.
5. *Test 3 of the yds. per lb. of a certain cloth construction from the first roll doffed from each loom involved:* 1.67, 1.67, 1.64, 1.67, 1.66, 1.69, 1.67, 1.65, 1.67, 1.67.
6. *Test 4 to locate the cause of excessive weight variation and substandard quality in cloth was concluded when the % of size in each warp sample from 1 slasher was found to be:* 11.4, 12.0, 12.2, 14.0, 18.2, 18.0, 24.0, 20.1, 21.0, and 12.0.

Range and Percent of Variation.   The difference between the *highest, Hi,* and *lowest, Lo,* values of xs is the *range, r,* which is a meaningful measure of extreme variation, especially if expressed as a *percent of variation, % v,* i.e., as a percentage of a central tendency such as $\bar{x}$.

7. From the foregoing derive

(3)   percent of variation, $\% v = \dfrac{100 \times \text{range}}{\text{mean}} = \dfrac{100 \times (\text{Hi} - \text{Lo})}{\text{mean}}$

8. For Tests 1, 2, 3 and 4, find (a) r (b) $\% v$.

Let us consider how much thus far we have advanced the precision of our measurement of variation. It seems sensible to believe that the nearer $\bar{x}$, median, and mode agree the more they lend credibility to each other, ∴ to a more pronounced central tendency and less variation than they otherwise might. For instance, we sensed that variation in Test 3, with 3 central tendencies agreeing, is some less than in Test 1, with median and mode agreeing but not quite with $\bar{x}$. Then formula (3) tells us that variation in Test 3 is much less than in Test 1, by what percent, and that % v is a far more precise measure.

Normal Distribution, Curves, and Deviation. To visualize variation of values in a test a variation or distribution "curve" (i.e., a line or continuous series of lines) is "plotted" (i.e., drawn). To interpret distribution curves we ought to know some relevant facts of *normal distribution* which have been evolving and accepted over the last two centuries from experiments and tests each with so many values and frequencies that each n has the same practical result as if it were infinite. To visualize normal distribution suppose Fig. 1 deals with a test with a tremendous number (n) of values (xs) and that on the horizontal line marked "each value" in ascending value order from left to right we place a dot, the distance between successive dots proportional to the difference of values they represent. The left and right ends ∴ represent Lo and Hi, respectively. Perpendicularly to each value line above each value dot at a distance proportional to its frequency (F) place its value – frequency dot. If enough xs have been observed, if every x and F has been measured, counted, and entered with identical accuracy, low or high; between Lo and Hi through each successive value – frequency dot plot a *normal distribution curve.*

Whether a normal distribution curve is tall or squat depends upon the ratio of the distance we choose to represent a unit of frequency to the distance we choose to represent a unit of value. But the first phenomenon we note here is every normal distribution curve is perfectly *symmetrical.* If a distribution curve is not symmetrical, it and distribution is said to be *skewed* and often whether to left or right.

From the foregoing answer the following 3 problems:

9. If a distribution is normal what is the relation of $\bar{x}$ to the (a) median and why (b) mode and why?

10. Let us take the *deviation, D,* between $\bar{x}$ and every x value $< \bar{x}$ as −; and every D between $\bar{x}$ and every x value $> \bar{x}$ as +. If distribution is normal what does $\Sigma(D \times F)$ equal?

11. With the preceding signs, in which direction is distribution, i.e., variation, skewed if $\Sigma(D \times F)$ is (a) − (b) +?

12. *Test 5.* Tensile strength of skeins of 26.0s warp yarn:

lb.	59	60	61	62	63	64	65	66	67	68	69	70	71	72	73
frequency	3	2	1	5	11	10	14	12	15	8	5	6	4	2	2

(a) Plot a distribution curve using the same distance $\left(\text{say } \dfrac{1''}{4}\right)$ for the difference between successive values as for an F of 1. Merely by sight of the shape write your guess: is distribution (a) normal (b) skewed and in which direction? Find (c) n (d) $\bar{x}$ (e) % v (f). $\Sigma (D \times F)$ using the preceding + and − signs (g) compare (b) with (f).

Standard Deviation. Since deviation of values from the mean in normal distribution is thus an unvarying relationship, the measurement unit of average deviation in normal distribution ∴ becomes and is called the *standard deviation,* σ (Greek small s read "sigma") for measuring average deviation in every test.

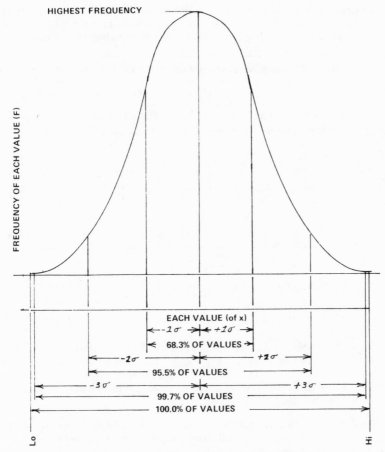

HIGHEST FREQUENCY

FREQUENCY OF EACH VALUE (F)

EACH VALUE (of x)

← -1σ → ← +1σ →

← 68.3% OF VALUES →

← -2σ → ← +2σ →

95.5% OF VALUES

← -3σ → ← +3σ →

99.7% OF VALUES

100.0% OF VALUES

Lo   Hi

Figure 1.   A Normal Distribution Curve

Much of statistical mathematics is reasoning by trial and error experimentation, i.e., *empirically,* rather than as in the other chapters of this book.

One largely empirical but precise formula, called "sum of squares," evolved through years of experimental research, in which the letters have their previous meanings, is

$$(4) \quad \text{standard deviation } \sigma = \sqrt{\frac{\Sigma(D \times F)^2 - \dfrac{[\Sigma(D \times F)]^2}{n}}{n - 1}}$$

Note: if n > 25 use n instead of n − 1.

EXAMPLE: *Find σ in Test 1.*

In Table 1 under x list xs in value order; under D the deviation of each x value from the mean; under F the frequency of each x value; under D × F the product of each deviation by its frequency and these products added, as in previous problems to find $\Sigma(D \times F)$, and then $[\Sigma(D \times F)]^2$, the "square of the sum"; and under $(D \times F)^2$ the square of each $D \times F$ and these squares added to $\Sigma(D \times F)^2$, the "sum of squares."'

Table 1.   Preparation of Data from Test 1 for Formula (4)

X	D	F	D × F	(D × F)²
Grs./Yd.	Deviation from the Mean	Frequency	Deviation × Frequency	(Deviation × Frequency)²
57	−3	1	−3	9
59	−1	5	−5	25
60	0	2	0	0
63	3	1	3	9
65	5	1	5	25

$$\Sigma(D \times F) = 0 \qquad \Sigma(D \times F)^2 = 68.$$

$$\text{By formula (4): } \sigma = \sqrt{\dfrac{68 - \dfrac{0}{10}\text{ grs.}}{10 - 1}} = \sqrt{\dfrac{68}{9}}\text{ grs.} = 2.75\text{ grs.}$$

Using formula (4) and previous answers find σ in the following 5 problems.

13. Under normal distribution. Hints: The previously found value of $\Sigma(D \times F)$. In Fig. 1 deviations to right − deviation to left.

14. *Test 2.*   **15.** *Test 3.*   **16.** *Test 5.*

17. *Test 6.* Grs./yd. of each 1-yd. length of finishing sliver: 48, 50, 53, 50, 50, 50, 51, 52, 48, 47, 51, and 50.

Standard Deviation Estimated.   Often if a *standard deviation estimated*, σe, is sufficiently accurate the following empirical formula with Table 2, together called "average range," is used

(5) $\begin{array}{l}\text{standard}\\ \text{deviation}\\ \text{estimated, } \sigma e\end{array} = \dfrac{\Sigma \text{ range of each equal subgroup of values}}{\text{subgroups} \times \text{subgroup size factor}}$

Note: $\sigma e2$, $\sigma e3$, $\sigma e4$, etc. indicate the subgroup size used.

Table 2 with Formula 5

Subgroup Size	Subgroup Size Factor	Subgroup Size	Subgroup Size Factor	Subgroup Size	Subgroup Size Factor
2	1.128	7	2.704	12	3.258
3	1.693	8	2.847	13	3.336
4	2.059	9	2.970	14	3.407
5	2.326	10	3.078	15	3.472
6	2.534	11	3.173	16	3.532

EXAMPLE: *Find* (a) σe *for test 6 and* (b) *its difference from* σ.

(a) In consecutive order if the x values are in 3 subgroups ∴ each equal subgroup size = 4; the r of each subgroup = (53 − 48), (52 − 50), and (51 − 47) respectively; by Table 2 this subgroup size factor = 2.059; and by formula

(5) $\sigma e4 = \dfrac{(53-48)+(52-50)+(51-47)}{3 \times 2.059} = \dfrac{11}{6.177} = 1.78$ grs./yd.

(b) By a previous problem and (a): (1.95 − 1.78) grs./yd. = .17 grs./yd.

Find the (a) σe *indicated* (b) *difference between the* σ *from previous answers and* σe *in the following 4 problems:*

18. *Test 1* $\sigma e5$.
19. *Test 2* $\sigma e4$.
20. *Test 3* $\sigma e5$.
21. *Test 6* $\sigma e4$.
22. *Test 7.* Lbs./in. tensile strength of a 9-oz. denim in consecutive order: warpwise 155, 157, 155, 152, 159, 153, 154, 154, 157, 156, 155, 156, 155, 155, 156; fillingwise: 45, 39, 48, 40, 45, 47, 41, 46, 45, 45, 43, 46, 45, 41, 45. Find σ and $\sigma e5$ (a) warpwise (b) fillingwise.

Coefficient of Variation. While σ is the precise measure for comparison between: (a) average deviation of x from the $\bar{x}$ in any test and average deviation from the ideal mean of normal distribution (b) ∴ average deviation in tests of identical values, σ expressed as a percent of its mean, called *coefficient of variation*, CV, is the precise universal measure of variation. In textile manufacturing quality control CV seems the most frequently cited statistic.

23. From the foregoing derive

(6) coefficient variation, $\text{CV} = \dfrac{100 \times \text{standard deviation}}{\text{mean}}$

Note: CVe 2, CVe 3, etc. indicates aσe and the subgroup size.

From previous answers find the (a) *CV and* (b) *CVe designated in the following 8 problems:*

24. Normal distribution and the ideal CV and CVe.
25. *Test 1* CVe5.   **26.** *Test 2* CVe4. **27.** *Test 3* CVe5.
28. *Test 5* (a) only.   **29.** *Test 6* CVe4.   **30.** *Test 7* warp CVe5.
31. *Test 7* filling CVe5.

Thus in the CV and CVe we now can calculate more precisely (a) to compare the quality of one kind of production with other kinds (b) to confirm and prove convincingly our impression of the quality of our production if correct (c) to correct our impression and to begin to correct our production if both are amiss.

Normal Distribution, Standard Deviations, and Percents. The next phenomena of normal distribution to be noted in Fig. 1 are: (a) If we control the x values that deviate in each direction from the normal mean of our total production by: (a) only 1 σ we control only 68.3% of production (b) 2 σ's we control 95.5% (c) 3 σ's we control 99.7%.

32. If of 1000 values we mass produce we control those that deviate from the normal mean of their total production by the following σ's how many are likely to escape control (a) 2 (b) 3?

Standard Error of the Mean. But what is the probable error of the $\bar{x}$ of any test calculated from an n that is feasible under practical conditions as a measure of the normal mean of the practically infinite n of any size, style, or design that we mass produce? The answer begins in calculating the error of the $\bar{x}$ per standard deviation in each direction from the normal mean, called the *standard error of the mean,* $\sigma\bar{x}$.

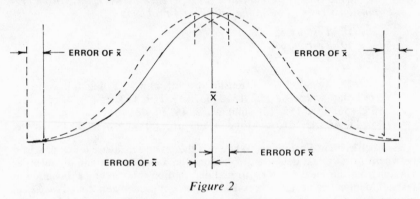

Figure 2

33. As visualized in Fig. 2 whatever may be the error of $\bar{x}$ in each direction from whatever may be the normal mean show that

(7) normal mean lies between $\bar{x}$ − error of $\bar{x}$ and $\bar{x}$ + error of $\bar{x}$.

The long established empirical formula for the error of $\bar{x}$ per σ is

(8) $\quad$ standard error $\quad$ = $\dfrac{\text{standard deviation}}{\sqrt{n-1}}$
$\qquad$ of the mean, $\sigma\bar{x}$

Notes: (1) If n > 25 use n instead of n − 1. (2) If the test is composed of a series of identical subtests and n and $\sigma\bar{x}$ are of each subtest, use σ of the series over-all. (3) $\sigma\bar{x}e2$, $\sigma\bar{x}e3$, etc., indicate a σe and the subgroup size used.

34. From formula (8) and the meaning of $\sigma\bar{x}$ show that

(9) error of $\bar{x}$ in each direction = σ's controlled × $\sigma\bar{x}$ or $\sigma\bar{x}e$.

From previous answers find the (a) $\bar{x}$ or $\bar{x}e$ (b) error of $\bar{x}$ in each direction for the percent of total production controlled in the following example and 8 problems:

EXAMPLE: *Test 1 $\sigma\bar{x}$ 97.7%.*

From previous answer: $\sigma = 2.75$ grs. (a) By formula (8): $\sigma\bar{x} =$

$\dfrac{2.75 \text{ grs.}}{\sqrt{10-1}} = .917$ grs. (b) From Fig. 1 and previous discussion control of 97.7% of total production requires 3 σ's controlled. By formula (9):

∴ error of $\bar{x} = 3 \times .917$ grs. $= 2.75$ grs.

35. *Test 1* $\sigma\bar{x}e5$ 95.5%.   **36.** *Test 2* $\sigma\bar{x}99.7\%$
37. *Test 2* $\sigma\bar{x}e4$ 95.5%.   **38.** *Test 3* $\sigma\bar{x}99.7\%$.
39. *Test 5* $\sigma\bar{x}99.7\%$.   **40.** *Test 6* $\sigma\bar{x}99.7\%$.
41. *Test 7* warp $\sigma\bar{x}e5$ 99.7%   **42.** *Test 7* filling $\sigma\bar{x}e5$ 99.7%.

Normal Mean and Control Limits.   From our study thus far of normal distribution emerges one of the more specific aims of statistical quality control: To reduce at least 2 σ's and preferably 3 σ's from the normal mean of what otherwise would be the normal distribution of total production to as close as possible to the normal mean.

43. To approach the foregoing aim prove from formulas (7) and (9) that production must be kept within the

(10) lower control limit, LCL $= \bar{x} - \dfrac{\text{error}}{\text{of } \bar{x}} = \bar{x} - \sigma$'s controlled $\times \sigma\bar{x}$ or $\sigma\bar{x}e$

and

(11) upper control limit, UCL $= \bar{x} + \dfrac{\text{error}}{\text{of } \bar{x}} = x + \sigma$'s controlled $\times \sigma\bar{x}$ or $\sigma\bar{x}e$.

What ought to be the (a) LCL (b) UCL to prevent 99.7% of total production from exceeding the CV or CVe previously calculated for the following 3 problems:

44. *Test 2* CV.   **45.** *Test 3* CV   **46.** *Test 7* warp CVe5
47. *Test 8.* On each of 30 consecutive days 10 bobbins of 20s/1 were sized by the formula (18), Chap. (1). Of the 300 weighings the $\bar{x}$ and σ over-all were 51 and 1.25 grs. which met the plant's standards. Find the (a) CV (b) daily $\sigma\bar{x}$ by formula (8) note (2) and to control 99.7% of total production and in grs. and counts the (c) LCL (d) UCL.

Find the (a) LCL (b) UCL which will confine variation of 99.7% of total production to as near as possible to its normal mean as a preliminary to studying still further reducing the CV or CVe indicated in the following 3 problems:

48. *Test 5* CV   **49.** *Test 7* fillingwise CVe5.
50. *Test 9.* On consecutive days on 23s filling ends down per 1000 spindle-hours were reported as follows: 14.5, 9.0, 11.0, 11.5, 14.5, 17.0, 13.0, 14.0, 14.5, 10.0, 12.5, 14.0. CVe4.

Control Charts.   Control charts, such as Fig. 3 started upon completion of Test 8, make easier for production personnel constantly to know whether production is within control limits and promptly when correction is needed. Each day a dot was placed at the level of the daily mean gr. weight of the 10 bobbins tested. The correction made on Saturday brought spinning back into control.

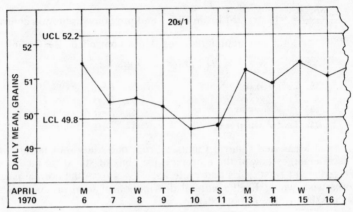

Figure 3.   A Control Chart

51. Using previous answers plot a preliminary control chart from Test 9.

52. As assigned by your instructor plot a control chart for a process with which you are acquainted in your plant.

Size of Test Samples, Sensitive Lengths, and Actual Draft. While there are calculations for finding the n to assure that a test is a reliable sample of the total production, using n − 1 in formulas (4) and (8) enables us to use as small an n as seems practically reasonable. But since in many textile tests length is the value that must be measured first and the other value (such as weight) is proportional to it, lengths in a test to be *sensitive*, i.e., comparable to each other, must contain the identical quantity of the other value.

53. If we measure, cut, and weigh with equal care (a) 12-yd. lengths of sliver and (b) the same number of 1-yd. lengths of the identical sliver; which lengths probably will show the larger CV in grs. per yd. and why? (c) Are these sensitive lengths?

54. From the foregoing and formula (2), Chap. III, since weight delivered = weight fed, prove that

(12) sensitive length delivered = actual draft × sensitive length fed.

What is the sensitive length delivered and its form with the actual draft and sensitive length fed in the following 4 problems:

55. 1 yd. of lap at a card with 130 ad?
56. 1 yd. of sliver at a sliver lapper with 1.04 ad?
57. 8 yds. of lap at a comber with 96 ad?
58. 1 yd. of sliver at a slubber with 5.8 ad?
59. 12 yds. of roving at a spinning frame with (a) 10 (b) 20 ad?

Variation, Over-all, Within, and Between. In textile statistical quality control we are concerned with: *variation over-all* (indicated by *o* added to the name or abbreviation of a measure of variation) such as that measured from bobbins of yarn from each side of each spinning frame on a given count. It is the most important since it is the variation which contributes most to variation of the final product. *Variation within* (similarly indicated by *w*) such as measured from consecutive yds. within one delivery of a drawing frame. It is the next most important. *Variation between* (similarly indicated by *b*) such as measured between the products of frames or deliveries. Of course, CVw and CVb are the contributors to CVo.

60. *Test 10.* In consecutive order, one yard of sliver from each of 12 finisher drawing deliveries weighs as follows: 55, 54, 57, 54, 56, 53, 53, 55, 55, 57, 56, and 55 grs. What is the (a) sensitive length? (b) CVe4? (c) Is this variation over-all, within, or between?

61. *Test 11.* 4 bobbins are randomly taken from each frame on the same count. 4 skeins from each bobbin are sized by formula (18) Chapt. (1) and consecutively are marked x1, x2, x3, x4 and with the frame number. The gr. weights are:

Frame Number	1	2	18	7	11	12	19	3	6	9
x1	52	49	50	52	47	48	52	53	51	49
x2	52	50	50	49	49	48	50	50	53	48
x3	50	50	48	51	50	51	50	50	50	47
x4	51	49	51	48	47	50	51	50	53	48

Write a table with 1 column for xs; 1 for each frame number; 1 after frame 11 headed r5o indicating the range for each x of the 5 preceding frames over-all; after frame 9 a similar r5o column; 1 line below x4, a line for the Σx for each frame; and 1 line below Σx 1 line for the r4w. Find and enter the (a) Σx and r4w for each bobbin of each frame (b) r5o for each x of the first 5 frames (c) r5o for each x of the second 5 frames. Find the (d) Σr4w (e) σe4w (f) $\bar{x}$ (g) CVe4w, (h) Σr5o (i) σe5o (j) CVe5o.

Expected Coefficient of Variation Within.   In seeking to locate the cause of excessive variation of the deliveries of a textile process discussions are common, sometimes argumentative, in the absence of confirmation or refutation by statistical testing, as to whether the excessive variation may lie in a previous process. The statistical testing is approached through the empirical formula.

(13)   expected coefficient of variation within of the delivering process, ECVw $= \dfrac{\text{coefficient of variation overall of the feeding process}}{\sqrt{\text{doublings fed}}}$

What may be the ECVw of the process in the following 3 problems:

62. Combing delivering 1 sliver fed by 6 laps from sliver lapper with a 3.25 CVo?

63. A sliver lapper delivering 1 lap fed by 20 slivers from breaker drawing with a 2.25 CVo?

64. Breaker drawing head delivering 10 slivers from cards with a 5.23 CVo?

65. *Test 12.* Breaker drawing is fed directly to the finished drawing frames 8 ends per head and for the past six months has given over-all a 1.28-grs./yd. σ and the standard 56-grs./yd. $\bar{x}$ for 99% and better of total production. On this basis the LCL and UCL are set and the standard grs./yd. maintained. Find for the breaker drawing the (a) CVo (b) $\sigma\bar{x}$ (c) error of the $\bar{x}$ (d) LCL (e) UCL and for the finisher drawing (f) ECVw.

66. Recently the CVo of our breaker drawing, which experience has shown should not exceed 2.00 has been too high. Our problem is to locate the cause. Our standard for the 8 sliver doublings from our 24 cards fed to each of the 8 heads of our 4 drawing frames is 60 grs./yd. and for the 8 drawing frame slivers is 56 grs./yd. Our steps are to determine the:

(1) CVew of the cards for evidence as to whether the cause may be in the cards (2) CVeo of the cards to find by formula (13) the ECVew of the drawing frames (3) the CVew of the drawing frames. What will be indicated for the drawing frames if between their ECVew and CVew there is a (a) wide difference (b) close agreement?

Test 13. As in Test 11 4 1-yd. lengths from every third card are weighed. The grs./yd. are:

Card Number	3	6	9	12	15	18	21	24
x1	61	59	54	57	64	59	56	60
x2	57	59	56	61	62	57	54	62
x3	59	60	52	57	65	57	56	61
x4	60	62	50	58	60	53	58	57

Make a table similar to that in Test 11. Find and enter the (c) Σx and r4w for each card (d) r4o for each x of the first 4 cards (e) r4o for each x of the second 4 cards. Find for the cards (f) Σr4w (g) σe4w (h) $\bar{x}$ (i) CVe4w (j) Σr4o (k) σe4o (l) CVe4o and for the drawing frames (m) ECVew (n) sensitive length.

Test 14. Accordingly from each of the 8 drawing deliveries 3 1-yd. lengths are weighed. The grs./yd. are

Frame Number	1		2		3		4	
Delivery	left	right	left	right	left	right	left	right
x1	57	56	54	54	55	56	54	54
x2	55	55	55	56	52	54	53	56
x3	55	55	54	56	54	53	57	55

As in Test 11 make a table omitting the ro columns. Find and enter the (o) Σx and r3w for each delivery. Find (p) Σr3w (q) σe3w (r) $\bar{x}$ (s) CVe3w

67. Analyzing the foregoing calculations of Tests 13 and 14: (a) On the drawing frames with the ECVew as the base what is the % difference between it and the CVew? (b) Are the drawing frames ∴ a likely location of the excess variation? (c) Of the 8 cards which 2 ought to be studied first and why? Of these 2 cards what is the (d) σe4w (e) $\bar{x}$ (f) CVe4w (g) with the CVe4w of the 8 cards as a base what is the % difference between it and (f)? (h) If the CVe4w of these 2 cards is changed appreciably for better or worse with a change of lap what, in addition, ought to be studied for the location of the excess variation and why?

Chapter VII

PICKER CALCULATIONS

POWER TRAINS AND EVENER MECHANISMS

Sections and Power Trains. Pickers may be of one or more sections. The stock is fed to the *breaker section* and delivered by the *finisher section*. Between them may be an *intermediate section*. Or the functions of the breaker and finisher sections may be combined in a one-section picker. Each section contains a beater or equivalent mechanism to open up or clean the stock or both. Each section has a power source and train independent of another section. Thus in the two-section two-beater one-process picker in Fig. 1 power is delivered from one motor to the breaker beater pulley and from another to the finisher beater pulley.

    1. In Fig. 1 through which beater pulley is transmitted the power to the (a) feed roll (b) blending reserve doffer (c) evener roll (d) top and bottom cones (e) bottom calender roll and (f) lap rolls?

Evener Mechanisms. Immediately above the evener roll a row, as long as the evener roll, of evener pedals, each pedal about $2\frac{1}{2}''$ long, presses down on the stock passing over the evener roll. Each pedal is free to move up and down depending on the variation in thickness of the stock passing beneath that pedal. Through a series of saddles and levers a multiple of the average variation in thickness is transmitted to the cone belt shifter and cone belt.

    2. Select the correct word in the following parentheses: If the average variation in thickness of stock moves the belt to the larger end of the bottom cone (more, less) stock is fed to the finisher beater and section. Why?

DRAFT

Basic Formulas.

    3. Why on a one-process picker as in Fig. 1 is actual draft not calculated and only the mechanical draft, *md*, of the finisher section is

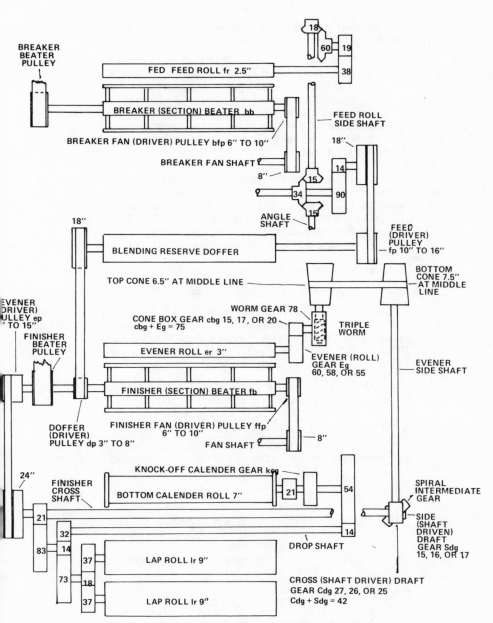

Figure 1.   Power and Draft Trains of a Two-Beater One-Process Picker

calculated? Hence show that formula (3), Chapter III becomes for Fig. 1

(1) $\dfrac{\text{mechanical}}{\text{draft}} = \dfrac{\text{surface speed of lap roll}}{\text{surface speed of evener roll}}$.

In the following 4 problems select the correct word in each set of parentheses giving your reasons:

4. If the RPM of the (a) er is decreased md is (decreased, increased); (b) 1r is increased the md is (decreased, increased).

5. (a) If md is increased the oz. lap is (increased, decreased); and ∴ (b) md is (directly, inversely) proportional to oz. lap.

6. Shifting the belt to the smaller end of the top cone (a) (increases, decreases) md and (b) (increases, decreases) the oz. lap.

7. Why is the middle line of the cone belt normally run at the middle line of each cone?

The calender rolls and the *lap pin* onto which the lap rolls wind the lap, may so compress the lap and the lap may be so thick that the lap may behave like a thick belt and, as studied in Chap. (**XX**), Part One, may make the effective diameter of each 1r greater than its outside diameter. The lap pin forcing the lap into the flutes of each 1r may further add to the effective dia. 1r. The effective dia. 1r minus dia. 1r is expressed as *percent of diameter*, *% of dia.*, *% dia.*

8. From your study of percent show that

(2) effective dia. of lap roll = dia. of lap roll $\times (1 + .01 \times \%$ of dia.$)$

9. What is the effective dia. 1r in Fig. 1 if % dia. is (a) 3 (b) 4 (c) 6?

10. For Fig. 1 from formula (2) and your study of power trains in formula (30), Chapter (**XX**), Part One show that: (a) SS er =
$$\frac{\text{RPM } 1r \times 37 \times 73 \times 83 \times \text{cdg} \times 7.5'' \times 3 \times \text{cbg} \times \pi \times 3''}{18 \times 14 \times 21 \times \text{Sdg} \times 6.5'' \times 78 \times \text{Eg}}$$

(b) SS 1r = RPM 1r $\times \pi \times 9'' \times (1 + .01 \times \%$ dia.); substituting from equations (a) and (b) into formula (1) ∴ (c) md =
$$\frac{\text{RPM } 1r \times \pi \times 9'' \times (1 + .01 \times \% \text{ dia.})}{\dfrac{\text{RPM } 1r \times 37 \times 73 \times 83 \times \text{cdg} \times 7.5'' \times 3 \times \text{cbg} \times \pi \times 3''}{18 \times 14 \times 21 \times \text{Sdg} \times 6.5'' \times 78 \times \text{Eg}}} ;$$
and simplifying and cancelling on the right side of equation (c) ∴

(3) $\dfrac{\text{mechanical}}{\text{draft}}$

$$= \frac{18 \times 14 \times 21 \times \underset{\substack{\text{side draft} \\ \text{gear}}}{\text{gear}} \times 6.5 \times 78 \times \underset{\substack{\text{evener} \\ \text{box} \\ \text{gear}}}{\text{gear}} \times 9 \times (1 + .01 \times \% \text{ dia.})}{37 \times 73 \times 83 \times \underset{\substack{\text{cross} \\ \text{draft} \\ \text{gear}}}{\text{cross}} \times 7.5 \times 3 \times \underset{\substack{\text{cone} \\ \text{box} \\ \text{gear}}}{\text{cone}} \times 3}$$

By formula (3) find the md of Fig. 1 under the conditions in the 2 following problems:

11. Cdg 27, Sdg 15, cbg 20, Eg 55, and % dia. 4.

12. Cdg 26, Sdg 16, cbg 17, Eg 58, and % dia. 5.

Draft Constants.   As in your study of constants in Chapt. (XX), Part One, the use of a draft constant, dc, is a labor saver in such draft problems as the preceding.

13. Multiplying both sides of formula (3) by cdg and cbg and dividing both sides by Sdg, Eg, and $(1 + .01 \times \% \text{ dia.})$ prove that

$$\text{(a)} \quad \frac{md \times cdg \times cbg}{Sdg \times eg \times (1 + .01 \times \% \text{ dia.})} = \frac{18 \times 14 \times 21 \times 6.5 \times 78 \times 9}{37 \times 73 \times 83 \times 7.5 \times 3 \times 3}$$

and ∴ regardless of how md, cdg, cbg, Sdg, Eg, and % dia. may change the left sides of equation (a) always = a constant.

The right side of equation (a) in the preceding problem is the draft constant. That is, for Fig. 1

$$\text{(4)} \quad \frac{\text{draft}}{\text{constant}} = \frac{18 \times 14 \times 21 \times 6.5 \times 78 \times 9}{37 \times 73 \times 83 \times 7.5 \times 3 \times 3}$$

14. From equation (a) in the preceding problem and formula (4) prove that for Fig. 1

$$\text{(5)} \quad \frac{\text{mechanical}}{\text{draft}} = \frac{\dfrac{\text{draft}}{\text{constant}} \times \dfrac{\text{side}}{\text{draft}} \times \dfrac{\text{evener}}{\text{gear}} \times (1 + .01 \times \% \text{ dia.})}{\text{cross draft gear} \times \text{cone box gear}}$$

15. By formula (4) calculate dc of Fig. 1.

Calculate md of Fig. 1 with % dia. of 6 and the gears in the following example and 4 problems:

EXAMPLE: *cdg* 27, *Sdg* 15, *cbg* 20, *and Eg* 55.

By formula 5 and dc found in the preceding problem:

$$md = \frac{1.60 \times 15 \times 55 \times (1 + .01 \times 6)}{27 \times 20} = 2.59.$$

16. Cdg 25 Sdg 17, cbg 20, and Eg 55.
17. Cdg 26 Sdg 16, cbg 17, and Eg 58.
18. Cdg 25 Sdg 17, cbg 17, and Eg 58.
19. Cdg 25, Sdg 17, cbg 15, and Eg 60.
20. Make a diagram of the finisher section of a picker in your plant showing such details as in the finisher section of Fig. 1. With the % of dia. if any, used in your plant, derive all the md and dc formulas and calculate dc and md with the gears or sprockets in use and for the conditions assigned by your instructor.

BEATS PER INCH

Basic Formula.   *Beats per inch, **bpi**,* is the number of times each inch of stock is beaten by the blades of, for instance, the *breaker section beater, **bb**,* in Fig. 1 while the stock is being fed by the *feed roll, **fr**.*

21. Prove that: (a) beats per minute = blades in bb × RPM bb; (b) inches of stock beaten per minute = π × dia. fr × RPM fr; and $\therefore$

$$(6) \text{ beats per inch} = \frac{\text{blades in beater} \times \text{RPM of beater}}{\pi \times \frac{\text{diameter of}}{\text{roll feeding beater}} \times \frac{\text{RPM of roll feeding}}{\text{beater}}}$$

Beaters may have 2 or 3 bar blades or 3 carding blades. Carding blades are considered to have two-thirds the beating capacity of bar blades; in which case bpi from formula (6) is multiplied by $\frac{2}{3}$. In Fig. 1 *breaker bpi, bbpi,* and *finisher bpi, fbpi* are calculated.

Breaker Beats Per Inch and Constants.

22. From Fig. 1 and your study of power trains in Chap. (XX), Part One, prove that:

$$(a) \text{ RPM fr} = \frac{\text{RPM fb} \times \text{dia. dp} \times \text{dia. fp} \times 14 \times 34 \times 18 \times 19}{18 \times 18 \times 90 \times 15 \times 60 \times 38} =$$

$\dfrac{119 \times \text{RPM fb} \times \text{dia. dp} \times \text{dia. fp}}{729000}$; substituting into formula

(6) the value of dia. fr and from equation (a) the value of RPM fr $\therefore$

$$(7) \begin{array}{c}\text{breaker}\\ \text{beats}\\ \text{per inch}\end{array} = \frac{729000 \times \begin{array}{c}\text{blades in}\\ \text{breaker beater}\end{array} \times \text{RPM breaker beater}}{\pi \times 2.5 \times 119 \times \begin{array}{c}\text{RPM}\\ \text{finisher}\\ \text{beater}\end{array} \times \begin{array}{c}\text{dia. doffer}\\ \text{driver}\\ \text{pulley}\end{array} \times \begin{array}{c}\text{dia. feed}\\ \text{driver}\\ \text{pulley}\end{array}}$$

Similar to the draft constant a *breaker beats per inch constant, bbpic* can be a labor saver.

23. For Fig. 1 derive

$$(8) \begin{array}{c}\text{breaker beats per}\\ \text{inch constant}\end{array} = \frac{729000}{\pi \times 2.5 \times 119} \text{ and}$$

$$(9) \begin{array}{c}\text{breaker}\\ \text{beats per}\\ \text{inch}\end{array} = \frac{\begin{array}{c}\text{breaker beats per}\\ \text{inch constant}\end{array} \times \begin{array}{c}\text{blades in}\\ \text{breaker beater}\end{array} \times \begin{array}{c}\text{RPM breaker}\\ \text{beater}\end{array}}{\begin{array}{c}\text{RPM finisher}\\ \text{beater}\end{array} \times \begin{array}{c}\text{dia. doffer}\\ \text{driver}\\ \text{pulley}\end{array} \times \begin{array}{c}\text{dia. feed}\\ \text{driver}\\ \text{pulley}\end{array}}$$

24. Calculate the bbpic of Fig. 1.

Find the bbpi of Fig. 1 under the conditions of the following 6 problems:

	blades in bb	RPM bb	RPM fb	dia. dp	dia. fp
25.	3 bar	700	1250	6 inches	12 inches
26.	3 "	1000	1100	7 "	12 "
27.	2 "	1050	1000	5 "	11 "
28.	2 "	1050	950	5 "	11 "

29.   2 "   1100   950   5 "   10 "
30.   2 "   1200   900   5 "   10 "

31. Suppose you must change bbpi by changing RPM of either or both beaters of Fig. 1 without changing dia. ep or dia. fp. Prove: from formula (9) that (a) new bbpi $= \dfrac{\text{bbpic} \times \text{blades in bb} \times \text{new RPM bb}}{\text{new RPM fb} \times \text{dia. dp} \times \text{dia. fp}}$ and

that (b) old bbpi $= \dfrac{\text{bbpic} \times \text{blades in bb} \times \text{old RPM bb}}{\text{old RPM fb} \times \text{dia. dp} \times \text{dia. fp}}$; dividing the left and right sides of equation (a) by the corresponding side of equation (b) and cancelling $\therefore$ (c) $\dfrac{\text{new bbpi}}{\text{old bbpi}} = \dfrac{\text{new RPM bb} \times \text{old RPM fb}}{\text{old RPM bb} \times \text{new RPM fb}}$; and multiplying both sides of equation (c) by old bbpi;

$$(10)\ \begin{array}{c}\text{new breaker}\\\text{beats per}\\\text{inch}\end{array} = \dfrac{\begin{array}{c}\text{old breaker}\\\text{beats per}\\\text{inch}\end{array} \times \begin{array}{c}\text{new RPM}\\\text{breaker}\\\text{beater}\end{array} \times \begin{array}{c}\text{old RPM}\\\text{finisher}\\\text{beater}\end{array}}{\begin{array}{c}\text{old RPM breaker beater} \times\\\text{new RPM finisher beater}\end{array}}$$

32. In Fig. 1 fb runs 1250 RPM while bb runs 1050 and makes 32.5 bpi. What will be bbpi if (a) RPM fb is changed to 1000 (b) RPM fb and RPM bb are changed to 1000 and 1120 respectively?

33. 43.5 bbpi are delivered by 1000 and 1250 RPM of bb and fb respectively. What will be bbpi if (a) RPM bb is 750 (b) RPM fb is 1000 and RPM bb 900?

34. Suppose you must change bbpi by changing dia. dp or dia. fp or both without changing beater speeds. By reasoning similar to that in deriving formula (10) derive

$$(11)\ \begin{array}{c}\text{new}\\\text{breaker}\\\text{beats per}\\\text{inch}\end{array} = \dfrac{\begin{array}{c}\text{old breaker}\\\text{beats per inch}\end{array} \times \begin{array}{c}\text{old dia.}\\\text{doffer pulley}\end{array} \times \begin{array}{c}\text{old dia.}\\\text{feed pulley}\end{array}}{\text{new dia. doffer pulley} \times \text{new dia. feed pulley}}$$

35. What will be bbpi, now 32.5, if (a) fp, now 12″, is changed to 11″ (b) dp, now 5″ is changed to 6″ (c) fp and dp thus are changed?

36. The present dia. dp, dia. fp, and bbpi are 4″, 12″, and 36.6 respectively. What will be bbpi with (a) fp 14″ (b) dp 5″ (c) fp and dp thus changed?

Finding Pulleys in Changing Breaker Beats Per Inch.

37. (a) If you have to change to a desired or new bbpi without changing beaters or beater speeds what in formula (9) must you change? Why? From formula (11) derive

$$(12)\ \begin{array}{c}\text{new dia.}\\\text{doffer} \times\\\text{pulley}\end{array}\ \begin{array}{c}\text{new dia.}\\\text{feed}\\\text{pulley}\end{array} = \dfrac{\begin{array}{c}\text{old breaker}\\\text{beats}\\\text{per inch}\end{array} \times \begin{array}{c}\text{old dia.}\\\text{doffer}\\\text{pulley}\end{array} \times \begin{array}{c}\text{old dia.}\\\text{feed}\\\text{pulley}\end{array}}{\text{new breaker beats per inch}}$$

What pulleys, available in whole and half-inch sizes within the limits of Fig. 1, are required under the conditions of the following example and 5 problems?:

EXAMPLE: *A 4″ dp and 12″ fp deliver 27.3 bbpi. 20 bbpi are required with the present fp.*

By formula (12): new dia. dp $\times 12'' = \dfrac{27.3 \times 4'' \times 12''}{20}$; dividing

each by 12″ ∴ new dia. dp $= \dfrac{27.3 \times 4''}{20} = 5.46''$.   **Answer:** $5\dfrac{1}{2}''$ dp.

	Present Conditions			Required Conditions		
	dp	*fp*	*bbpi*	*dp*	*fp*	*bbpi*
38.	4″	16″	27	6″		30
39.	5″	14″	30	$7\dfrac{1}{2}''$		36
40.	$6\dfrac{1}{2}''$	12″	32		14″	40
41.	8″	10″	39	$15\dfrac{1}{2}''$		42
42.	3″	10″	55			50

Finisher Beats Per Inch and Constants.

43. As you did for bbpi in Fig. 1, derive for Fig. 1 an equation for fbpi and from this equation derive

(13) finisher beats per inch constant $= \dfrac{24 \times 6.5 \times 78}{\pi \times 3 \times 7.5 \times 3}$ and

(14) finisher beats per inch $= \dfrac{\text{finisher beats per inch constant} \times \text{blades in finisher beater} \times \text{side draft gear} \times \text{evener gear}}{\text{dia. evener pulley} \times \text{cross draft gear} \times \text{cone box gear}}$

44. Calculate the finisher beats per inch constant of Fig. 1.

Find the fbpi with the gear combinations of Fig. 1 under the conditions in the 3 following problems:

	blades in fb	Sdg	Eg	dia. ep	cdg	cbg
45.	3 carding		60	6″	25	
46.	2 bar	15		6″		20
47.	3 carding	16	58	9″		

48. As you did for new bbpi of Fig. 1, derive from formula (14) for Fig. 1.

$$(15)\ \frac{\text{new finisher beats per inch}}{} = \frac{\begin{array}{c}\text{old finisher beats per inch}\end{array} \times \begin{array}{c}\text{new side draft gear}\end{array} \times \begin{array}{c}\text{new evener gear}\end{array} \times \begin{array}{c}\text{old dia. evener pulley}\end{array} \times \begin{array}{c}\text{old cross draft gear}\end{array} \times \begin{array}{c}\text{old cone box gear}\end{array}}{\begin{array}{c}\text{old side draft gear}\end{array} \times \begin{array}{c}\text{old evener gear}\end{array} \times \begin{array}{c}\text{new dia. evener pulley}\end{array} \times \begin{array}{c}\text{new cross draft gear}\end{array} \times \begin{array}{c}\text{new cone box gear}\end{array}}$$

Find the new fbpi for Fig. 1 under the conditions of the following 4 problems:

	\multicolumn{5}{c}{Present Conditions}						\multicolumn{5}{c}{Required Conditions}				
	dia. ep	cdg	cbg	Sdg	Eg	fbpi	dia. ep	cdg	cbg	Sdg	Eg
49.	9″	25	15			34.7	11″	25	15		
50.	9.5″	26	17			25.4	9.5″			15	58
51.	10″			16	55	19.4	$8\frac{1}{2}''$	26	20		
52.	10″			15	55	17.5	12″			16	58

Finding Pulleys in Changing Finisher Beats Per Inch.

53. From formula (15) derive

$$(16)\ \text{new dia. evener pulley} = \frac{\begin{array}{c}\text{old finisher beats per inch}\end{array} \times \begin{array}{c}\text{new side draft gear}\end{array} \times \begin{array}{c}\text{new evener gear}\end{array} \times \begin{array}{c}\text{old dia. evener pulley}\end{array} \times \begin{array}{c}\text{old cross draft gear}\end{array} \times \begin{array}{c}\text{old cone box gear}\end{array}}{\begin{array}{c}\text{old side draft gear}\end{array} \times \begin{array}{c}\text{old eveners gear}\end{array} \times \begin{array}{c}\text{new finisher beats per inch}\end{array} \times \begin{array}{c}\text{new cross draft gear}\end{array} \times \begin{array}{c}\text{new cone box gear}\end{array}}$$

What pulleys, available in whole and half-inch sizes within the limits of Fig. 1, are required under the conditions of the following 3 problems?:

	\multicolumn{5}{c}{Present Conditions}						\multicolumn{5}{c}{Required Conditions}			
	dia. ep	cdg	cbg	Sdg	Eg	fbpi	cdg	cbg	Sdg	Eg	fbpi
54.	6″	27	15			42.5			15	60	35
55.	7″	27	17			31.1			16	58	near as possible to but not over 28
56.	12″			17	55	17.9	26	17			near as possible to but not under 25

Total Beats Per Inch.   Increased attention is given to the *total beats per inch, tbpi,* that assure the necessary cleaning and opening without damaging the fiber.

Thus for Fig. 1

(17) total beats per inch = breaker beats per inch + finisher beats per inch.

57. Find the tbpi of Fig. 1 with a 3-bar bb making 1000 RPM, 3-blade carding fb making 1100 RPM, 7″ dp, 12″ fp, 9″ ep, 26-tooth cdg, and 17-tooth cbg.

58. Fig. 1 gives 31.3 bbpi and 29.2 fbpi with a 5″ dp, 11″ fp, and 6″ ep. What tbpi will it give changing only dp to $5\frac{1}{2}''$, fp to $11\frac{1}{2}''$, and ep to $6\frac{1}{2}''$?

59. Add to the diagram which you have made of the finisher section of a picker in your plant a diagram of the intermediate section, if any, and of the breaker section. Derive formulas for the bpi and pulleys. From the trains and speeds find the breaker, intermediate, finisher, and total bpi, and the bpi and pulleys required for such conditions as assigned by your instructor.

PRODUCTION

Basic Formula.   100 *percent production,* 100% p, of a picker and subsequent carding department and other textile plant machines is based on whatever the standard lengths considered that would pass the delivery roll if it could be run without stopping during the production time considered, i.e., unmodified by the production time that it is stopped for creeling, doffing, and servicing and by whatever production is unsatisfactory. Thus picker 100% p is based on 100 *percent yards,* 100% *yds.*

60. From the foregoing derive

$$(17)\quad 100\% \text{ yards} = \frac{\text{IPM lap roll} \times 60 \times \text{hours}}{36}$$

Often the production time is included in such expressions as 100 *percent yards per hour,* 100% *yds./hr.,* 100 *percent yards per 8 hours,* 100% *yds./8 hrs.* and when converted to pounds, as will be studied in the next subsection, as 100% *lbs./hr.* or 100% *lbs./8 hrs.*

Production Constants.

61. From Fig. 1, your study of power trains in Chapter (20), Part One, and formulas (2) and (17) prove that: (a) 100% yds. = $\dfrac{\text{RPM lr} \times \text{dia. lr} \times (1 + .01 \times \% \text{ dia.}) \times \pi \times 60 \times \text{hrs.}}{36}$; from (a) ∴.

(b) 100% yds. $= \dfrac{\text{RPM fb} \times \text{dia. er} \times 21 \times 14 \times 18}{24 \times 83 \times 73 \times 37} \times$

$\dfrac{9 \times (1 + .01 \times \% \text{ dia.}) \times \pi \times 60 \times \text{hrs.}}{36}$; since lbs. $= \dfrac{\text{yds.} \times \text{oz. lap}}{16}$ $\therefore$

(c) 100% lbs. $= \dfrac{100\% \text{ yds.} \times \text{oz. lap}}{16}$; substituting the value of 100 yds.

from (b) into (c) $\therefore$ (d) 100% lbs. $= \dfrac{21 \times 14 \times 18 \times 9 \times \pi \times 60}{24 \times 83 \times 73 \times 37 \times 36 \times 16} \times$ RPM

fb $\times$ dia. er $\times$ $(1 + .01 \% \text{ dia.}) \times$ hrs. $\times$ oz. lap.

Obviously the fraction on the right side of (d) in the preceding problem is a constant and $\therefore$ no matter how the other quantities in equation (d) may vary, the product of this constant and the variables on the right side always $= 100\%$ lbs. This is the production constant, pc, which, like the draft and beats per inch constants, is a labor saver.

62. From the foregoing for Fig. 1 derive

(18) $\dfrac{\text{production}}{\text{constant}} = \dfrac{21 \times 14 \times 18 \times 9 \times \pi \times 60}{24 \times 83 \times 73 \times 37 \times 36 \times 16}$ and

(19) $\begin{array}{l}100\% \\ \text{pounds}\end{array}$

$= \dfrac{\text{production}}{\text{constant}} \times \begin{array}{c}\text{RPM} \\ \text{finisher} \\ \text{beater}\end{array} \times \begin{array}{c}\text{dia.} \\ \text{evener} \\ \text{pulley}\end{array} \times \left(\begin{array}{c}1 + .01 \\ \times \% \text{ dia.}\end{array}\right) \times \begin{array}{c}\text{ounce} \\ \text{lap}\end{array} \times \text{hours.}$

63. Compute the pc of Fig. 1.

Find the production of Fig. 1 under the conditions of the following example and 3 problems:

EXAMPLE: *100% lbs./hr. of 15 oz. lap with 1075 RPM fb, 8" ep, and 6% dia. lr.*

By the pc from the preceding problem and formula (19):

100% lbs./hr. $= .00290 \times 1075 \times 8 \times (1 + .01 \times 6) \times 15 \times 1 = 396.5.$

64. 100% lbs./8 hrs. of 13 oz. lap with 975 RPM fb, $10\frac{1}{2}''$ ep, and 4.5% dia. lr.

65. 100% lbs./40 hrs. of 14.5 oz. lap with 1030 RPM fb, 11" ep, and 5% dia. lr.

66. 100% lbs. for 2 pickers on 3 40-hr. shifts of 16 oz. lap with 850 RPM fb, $14\frac{1}{2}$ ep, and 5.5% diam. lr.

Percent of Production.   Due to doffing, cleaning, and servicing a picker may produce for less than 100% of the production time. This actual percent of production time that a picker or other machine produces is its *percent of production, % production, % p* or *percent of efficiency, % e.* As will be indicated later, some plants adjust picker % p to take cognizance also of the percent of laps produced that are rejected and rerun through the picker, i.e., the *percent set back or percent reset, % r.*

67. From the foregoing and formula (19) for actual production derive

$$(20)\ \text{pounds} = \frac{\text{production}}{\text{constant}} \times \frac{\text{RPM}}{\text{finisher beater}} \times \frac{\text{dia.}}{\text{evener pulley}} \times \left(\frac{1 + .01}{\times\% \text{ dia.}}\right) \times$$

$$\frac{\text{ounce}}{\text{lap}} \times \text{hours} \times .01 \times \% \text{ production}$$

68. A plant wishes the % p to take cognizance of the 6% of production time the picker is stopped but also of the 4% of the laps produced that must be reset. What is the % p?

Find the production of Fig. 1 that will be fed to the cards under the conditions of the following example and 2 problems:

EXAMPLE: *lbs/hr. of* 16 *oz. lap with* 850 *RPM fb,* 9″ *ep,* 4% *dia. lr,* 5% *stops, and* 6% *r from* 1 *picker.*

% p to cards = 95 × .94 = 89.3.

By formula (20): lbs./hr. = .0029 × 850 × 9 × 1.04 × 16 × 1 × .893 × 1 = 330.

69. lbs./40 hrs. of 14.5 oz. lap with 1080 RPM fb, 7″ ep, 5% dia. lr, 9% stops, and 1% r from 6 pickers.

70. 91.5% lbs./40 hrs. of 13.5 oz. lap with 960 RPM fb, $12\frac{1}{2}''$ ep, 6% dia. lr, and 1% r from 1 picker.

71. How many 68-lb.–15.5 oz. laps at 8% stops and 2% r will 7 pickers similar to Fig. 1 with .0032 pc, 1075 RPM fb. 8″ ep, and 5% dia. lr deliver for the cards in 3 8-hr. shifts?

72. How many hrs. at 2.5% reset and 7.5% stops will 1 picker with a .0030 pc, 1025 RPM fb, 10 ep, and 5.5% dia. lr require to run 125 60-lb.–15-oz. laps?

73. As assigned by your instructor regarding a picker in your plant inquire of what the % p takes cognizance; % stops, % reset, % dia. lr due to flutes expected; determine dia. er and RPM fb; and compute the pc, lbs./hr., and other data.

74. Suppose that from a known or old lbs., oz. lap, and ep and a required or new oz. lap and er you must find the new lbs. Derive: from formula (20).∴

$$(a)\ \frac{\text{new}}{\text{lbs.}} = \text{pc} \times \frac{\text{RPM}}{\text{fb}} \times \frac{\text{dia.}}{\text{new ep}} \times (1 + .01 \times \% \text{ dia. lr}) \times \frac{\text{new}}{\text{oz. lap}} \times$$

$.01 \times \% \text{ p and } (b)\ \dfrac{\text{old}}{\text{lbs.}} = \text{pc} \times \dfrac{\text{RPM}}{\text{fb}} \times \dfrac{\text{dia.}}{\text{old ep}} \times (1 + .01 \times \% \text{ dia. lr}) \times$

$\dfrac{\text{old}}{\text{oz. lap}} \times .01 \times \% \text{ p}$; by dividing each side of equation (a) by the corresponding side of (b) and cancelling

$\therefore$ (c) $\dfrac{\text{new lbs.}}{\text{old lbs.}} = \dfrac{\text{dia. new ep} \times \text{new oz. lap}}{\text{dia. old ep} \times \text{old oz. lap}}$; from (c) $\therefore$ (21) $\dfrac{\text{new}}{\text{pounds}} =$

$\dfrac{\text{old pounds} \times \text{dia. new evener pulley} \times \text{new ounce lap}}{\text{dia. old evener pulley} \times \text{old ounce lap}}$.

75. A picker producing 382 lbs./hr. of 16 oz. lap with an 8″ ep is changed to 14.4 oz. lap and a 7″ ep. What lbs./hr. do you expect?

76. All the pickers with the same 7″ evener pulleys average 56 65-lb. 15-oz. laps each 8 hr. shift. How many 61.5-lb. 16-oz. laps will they average in the same time with 8″ pulleys?

Finding Evener Pulleys and in Changing Pounds.

77. From formula (20) derive:

(22) dia. evener pulley

$$= \dfrac{\text{pounds}}{\dfrac{\text{production}}{\text{constant}} \times \substack{\text{RPM} \\ \text{finisher} \\ \text{beater}} \times (1 + .01 \times \% \text{ dia.}) \times \dfrac{\text{ounce}}{\text{lap}} \times \text{hours} \times \dfrac{.01 \times \%}{\text{production}}}$$

78. (a) What ep in Fig. 1 with 950 RPM fb, 5.5% dia. lr, 8.1% stops will produce as near as possible to 2600 lbs./8 hrs. of 15 oz. lap? (b) What lbs./8 hrs. will this ep produce?

79. (a) With a .0036 pc, 1150 RPM fb, 4% dia. lr what ep is required to produce at 9 3% stops at least and as near as possible to 8 60-lb. 16 oz. laps per hr? (b) How many such laps per hr. does this ep produce?

80. From equation (21) derive:

(23) $\substack{\text{dia. new} \\ \text{evener pulley}}$

$$= \dfrac{\text{new pounds} \times \text{dia. old evener pulley} \times \text{old ounce lap}}{\text{old pounds} \times \text{new ounce lap}}$$

81. With a 6″ ep a picker averages 360.5 lbs./hr. of 14.6 oz. lap. What is the minimum dia. ep for it to run at least 400 lbs./hr. of 15 oz. lap?

82. What (a) minimum ep will derive 9 60-lb. 16-oz. laps per hr. if a $7\frac{1}{2}''$ ep on this picker delivers 8 62.5-lb. 15-oz. laps per hr. (b) lbs./hr. will this ep deliver?

KNOCK-OFF

Basic Formulas.   In Figs. 1 and 2 the *drop shaft* transmits the power to the *knock-off* train and *calender rolls* between which the stock is compressed

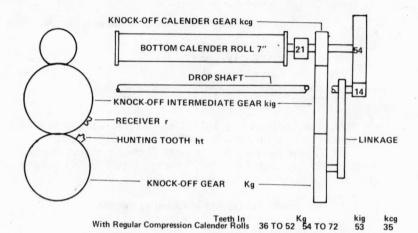

With Regular Compression Calender Rolls	Teeth In	Kg	kig	kcg
With Regular Compression Calender Rolls	36 TO 52	54 TO 72	53	35
" High " " "	" " 60	62 " "	61	27

Figure 2.   Knock-off train of Figure 1

into lap. When the *hunting tooth*, **ht**, on the *knock-off gear*, **Kg**, engages the *receiver*, **r**, on the *knock-off intermediate gear*, **kig**, it pushes Kg out of mesh with kig and, through the linkage, the 14-tooth gear on the drop shaft out of mesh with the 54-tooth gear, and thus stops the calender rolls and separates the lap from the full roll of lap on the lap rolls which continue revolving.

In the following 5 problems consider the revolutions, rev, of lr and the production from one engagement of ht with r to the next.

83. From Figs. 1 and 2 prove

(24) yards $= \dfrac{\pi \times 9 \times (1 + .01 \times \% \text{ dia.}) \times \text{revolutions of lap roll}}{36}$

$= .78540 \times$ revolutions of lap roll $\times (1 + .01 \times \% \text{ dia.})$

84. For ht and r to engage what must always be (a) their position relative to the centers of Kg and kig (b) ∴ the kind of number that expresses the rev kig and rev Kg since the last engagement of ht and r?

85. From Pt. One and Fig. 1 prove that: (a) rev $Kg = \dfrac{\text{rev kig} \times \text{kig}}{Kg}$, since from the preceding problem rev Kg is a whole number and since kig is a prime number ∴ (b) $\dfrac{\text{rev kig}}{Kg} = $ a whole number; since we are considering the least possible number of rev kig and of rev Kg between engagements of ht with r ∴ (c) $\dfrac{\text{rev kig}}{Kg} = 1$; and from (a) and (c) ∴

(25) revolutions of knock-off gear = knock-off intermediate gear.

86. From Figs. 1 and 2 show that:

(a) rev $lr = \dfrac{\text{rev } Kg \times Kg \times 54 \times 32 \times 18}{kcg \times 14 \times 73 \times 37}$; substituting the value of rev Kg from formula (25) into (a) $\therefore$ (b) rev lr $= \dfrac{.82255 \times \text{kig} \times \text{Kg}}{\text{kcg}}$; substituting the value of rev lr from (b) into formula (24) $\therefore$ (c) yds. $= .7854 \times \dfrac{.82255 \times \text{kig} \times \text{Kg}}{\text{kcg}} \times (1 + .01 \times \% \text{ dia.})$ and $\therefore$

(26) yards in
full roll

$$= \dfrac{.64603 \times \genfrac{}{}{0pt}{}{\text{knock-off}}{\text{intermediate gear}} \times \genfrac{}{}{0pt}{}{\text{knock-off}}{\text{gear}} \times (1 + .01 \times \% \text{ dia.})}{\text{knock-off calender gear}}$$

Knock-Off Constants, Gears, and Pounds.   A *knock-off constant, kc,* like the constants you have studied, is a labor saver.

87. From formula (26) show that: (a) $\dfrac{\text{yds. of lap in full roll}}{\text{Kg} \times (1 + .01 \times \% \text{ dia.})} = \dfrac{.6461 \times \text{kig}}{\text{kcg}}$; regardless of how the yds. of lap in a full roll, Kg, or $1 + .01 \times \%$ dia. may change, $\dfrac{\text{yards of lap in full roll}}{\text{Kg}}$ always $=$ a constant; for Figs. 1 and 2 $\therefore$

(27) $\dfrac{\text{knock-off}}{\text{constant}} = \dfrac{.64603 \times \text{knock-off intermediate gear}}{\text{knock-off calender gear}}$;

from equation (a) $\therefore$

(28) yards in full roll = knock-off constant $\times$ knock-off gear $\times$ $(1 + .01 \times \%$ dia.)

(29) pounds in
full roll

$$= \dfrac{\dfrac{\text{knock-off}}{\text{constant}} \times \dfrac{\text{knock-off}}{\text{gear}} \times \dfrac{\text{ounce}}{\text{lap}} \times (1 + .01 \times \% \text{ dia.})}{16}$$

and from formulas (27) and (28)

(30) $\dfrac{\text{knock-off}}{\text{gear}} = \dfrac{\text{yards in full roll}}{\text{knock-off constant} \times (1 + .01 \times \% \text{ dia.})}$

$$= \dfrac{16 \times \text{pounds in full roll}}{\text{knock-off constant} \times \text{ounce lap} \times (1 + .01 \% \text{ dia.})}$$

88. Find the kc of Figs. 1 and 2 with (a) regular (b) high compression calender rolls.

89. In Figs. 1 and 2 with 6% dia. lr what is the range of yds. in a full roll of (a) regular (b) high compression lap?

Find (a) *the teeth in Kg of Figs. 1 and 2 with 6% dia. lr to give as near as possible to but not over the quantity in a full roll and* (b) *the quantity that the Kg in* (a) *gives in the following example and 4 problems:*

EXAMPLE: 60 *yds. of regular compression lap.*

(a) By formula (30): $Kg = \dfrac{60}{.9783 \times 1.06} = 57.9$ ∴ Kg has 57 teeth.

(b) By formula (28): yds. in full roll $= .9783 \times 57 \times 1.06 = 59.11$.

90. 88 yds. of high compression lap.
91. 62 lbs. of regular compression 16 oz. lap.
92. 68 lbs. of regular compression 14.7 oz. lap.
93. 70 lbs. of high compression 15.5 oz. lap.

Finding Knock-Off Gears in Changing Yards or Pounds in Full Roll.

94. Prove: from formula (30) (a) new $Kg = \dfrac{\text{new yds. in full roll}}{kc \times (1 + .01 \times \% \, \text{dia.})}$

and (b) old $Kg = \dfrac{\text{old yds. in full roll}}{kc \times (1 + .01 \times \% \, \text{dia.})}$; dividing each side of equation
(a) by the corresponding side of (b) and cancelling ∴ (c) $\dfrac{\text{new Kg}}{\text{old Kg}} =$
$\dfrac{\text{new yds. in full roll}}{\text{old yds. in full roll}}$; and ∴

(31) $\dfrac{\text{new knock-off gear}}{} = \dfrac{\text{old knock-off gear} \times \text{new yards in full roll}}{\text{old yards in full roll}}$

95. By reasoning similar to that in deriving formula (31) derive

(32) $\dfrac{\text{new knock-off gear}}{} = \dfrac{\dfrac{\text{old knock-off gear}}{} \times \dfrac{\text{new pounds in full roll}}{} \times \dfrac{\text{old ounce lap}}{}}{\text{old pounds in full roll} \times \text{new ounce lap}}$.

Find the teeth in Kg required to give a full roll of lap as close to but not over the required quantity in the following example and 3 problems.

EXAMPLE: *Required 68 yds.; 68-tooth Kg gives 72 yds.*

By formula (31) new $Kg = \dfrac{68 \times 68}{72} = 64.2$; required Kg has 64
teeth.

96. Required 90 yds.; 52-tooth Kg gives 78 yds. 9 in.
97. 64 lbs. of 14.5 oz. lap required; 66-tooth Kg runs 69-lb. 8 oz. full rolls of 16 oz. lap.
98. 44-tooth Kg gives 62.30-lb. full rolls of 15-oz. lap; required the same weight full roll of $14\frac{1}{4}$-oz. lap.
99. As assigned by your instructor derive the kc formula and kc,

calculate the lbs. in a full lap with the Kg in use and compare this with the actual weight; and without the kc of another picker calculate the Kg for changes in full-lap weights and oz. lap.

Doffing, Frequency and Cycle.   *Doffing frequency, dff,* of a picker is the full rolls it produces per hr.; *its doffing cycle, dfc,* the minutes from producing one full roll to the next.

100. Show that

(33) $\dfrac{\text{doffing}}{\text{frequency}} = \dfrac{\text{pounds per hour}}{\text{pounds in full roll}}$ and

(34) $\dfrac{\text{doffing}}{\text{cycle}} = \dfrac{60}{\text{doffing frequency}};$

from formulas (20), (29), and (33) for Figs. 1 and 2 ∴ dff =

$$\frac{\text{pc} \times \text{RPM fb} \times \text{dia. ep} \times (1 + .01 \times \% \text{ dia. lr}) \times \text{oz. lap} \times .01 \times \% \text{ p}}{\dfrac{\text{kc} \times \text{Kg} \times \text{oz. lap} \times (1 + .01 \times \% \text{ dia.})}{16}};$$

and ∴

(35) $\dfrac{\text{doffing}}{\text{frequency}} = \dfrac{16 \times \text{production constant} \times \text{finisher beater} \times \text{evener pulley} \times \dfrac{\text{RPM}}{\text{dia.}} \times .01 \times \% \text{ production}}{\text{knock-off constant} \times \text{knock-off gear}}$

For Figs. 1 and 2 find the (a) *dff and* (b) *dfc under the conditions of the following example and 3 problems:*

EXAMPLE: *92% p of regular compression lap,* 1000 *RPM fb,* 9″ *ep, and 52-tooth Kg.*

(a) By formula (35): dff $= \dfrac{16 \times .00290 \times 1000 \times 9 \times .92}{.9783 \times 52} = 7.55$

(b) By formula (34): dfc $= \dfrac{60}{7.55} = 7.95$ or 8.0 minutes.

101. 90.5% p of regular compression lap, 1075 RPM, 10″ ep and 70-tooth Kg.

102. 91.5% p of high compression lap, 975 RPM, 8″ ep, 72-tooth Kg.

103. 87.6% p of high compression lap, 990 RPM, 15″ ep and 45-tooth Kg.

104. As assigned by your instructor from a picker in your plant gather the data on the right side of equation (35), time the actual dff, calculate the dff, compare the actual and calculated dff, and account for any difference.

Chapter VIII

CARD CALCULATIONS

DRAFT

Basic Total Draft Formulas. The mechanical *total draft, td,* of a typical card such as in Fig. 1 is from the *lap roll, lr,* (which is the actual feed roll) to the *coiler calender roll, ccr.* The draft train from lr to the *calender roll, cr,* is shown as from above; from cr to ccr as from the front.

1. From the foregoing and formula (3), Chap. III derive

$$(1) \quad \frac{\text{total}}{\text{draft}} = \frac{\text{surface speed of coiler calender roll}}{\text{surface speed of lap roll}}$$

In the following 2 problems select the correct word in each set of parentheses:

2. If the speed of: (a) lr is increased td is (increased, decreased); (b) ccr is increased td is (increased, decreased).

3. If td is decreased gr. sl is (a) (decreased, increased) and ∴ td and gr. sl are (b) (directly, inversely) proportional.

4. From the foregoing and your study of power trains in formula (30), Chap. (20), Part One derive

$$(2) \quad \frac{\text{total}}{\text{draft}} = \frac{2 \times \frac{\text{1st}}{\text{lay gear}} \times \frac{\text{3rd}}{\text{lay gear}} \times \frac{\text{5th}}{\text{lay gear}} \times \frac{\text{doffer}}{\text{gear}} \times \frac{\text{side}}{\text{shaft gear}} \times \frac{\text{feed}}{\text{driven gear}} \times \frac{\text{lap}}{\text{gear}}}{\frac{\text{coiler}}{\text{gear}} \times \frac{\text{2nd}}{\text{lay gear}} \times \frac{\text{4th}}{\text{lay gear}} \times \frac{\text{calender}}{\text{shaft gear}} \times 45 \times \frac{\text{draft}}{\text{gear}} \times 17 \times 6}$$

Total Draft Constants, Gears, Ranges, and Control. As with constants previously studied, a *total draft constant, dc,* is a labor saver in calculating from such formulas as (2).

5. Multiplying each side of formula (2) by dg and cancelling on the right prove: (a) $td \times dg = \frac{2 \times flg \times tlg \times filg \times Dfg \times Sg \times Fg \times Lg}{cg \times Slg \times Folg \times Csg \times 45 \times 17 \times 6}$, since in Fig. 1 and Table 1 all quantities on the right side of equation

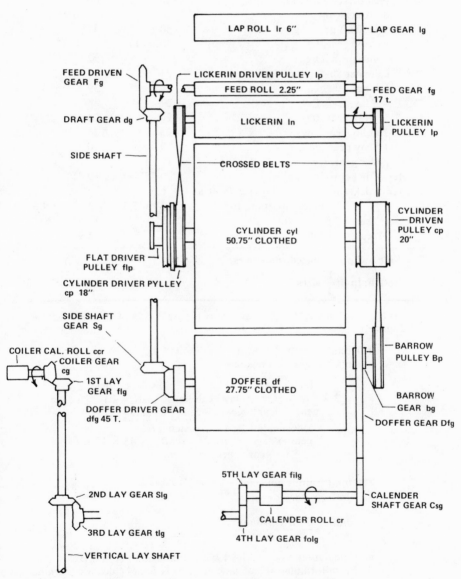

Figure 1.   Power and Draft Trains of a Card

Table 1. Some combinations of Fig. 1

	A	B
teeth in lap gear, Lg	47	48
" " feed driven gear, Fg	120	160
" " draft gear, dg	10 to 32	15 to 40
" " side shaft gear, Sg	40	45
" " barrow gear, bg	20 to 40	13 to 33
" " doffer gear, Dfg	214	192
" " calender shaft gear, Csg	21	25
" " 5th lay gear, filg	24	39
" " 4th lay gear, Folg	27	38
" " 3rd lay gear, tlg	27	24
" " 2nd lay gear, Slg	23	24
" " 1st lay gear, flg	29	30
" " coiler gear, Cg	19	15
diameter of lickerin, ln, clothed	9.75"	10.25"
diameter of lickerin, driven pulley, Lp, (note a)	6.5"	7"
" " " pulley, lp, (note b)	2" to 7.5"	2.75" to 4.5"
" " barrow pulley, Bp	18"	15.5"
" " calender roll, cr	3"	3.9"

Note a: Lp is changed sometimes.

Note b: lp in $\frac{1''}{4}$ sizes.

(a) are constants ∴ (b) td × dg = dc = the right side of equation (a); for Figure 1 ∴.

(3) $\dfrac{\text{total}}{\text{draft}} \times \dfrac{\text{draft}}{\text{gear}} = \dfrac{\text{draft}}{\text{constant}}$

$$= \dfrac{2 \times \substack{\text{1st}\\\text{lay}\\\text{gear}} \times \substack{\text{3rd}\\\text{lay}\\\text{gear}} \times \substack{\text{5th}\\\text{lay}\\\text{gear}} \times \substack{\text{doffer}\\\text{gear}} \times \substack{\text{side}\\\text{shaft}\\\text{gear}} \times \substack{\text{feed}\\\text{driven}\\\text{gear}} \times \substack{\text{lap}\\\text{gear}}}{\substack{\text{coiler}\\\text{gear}} \times \substack{\text{2nd}\\\text{lay}\\\text{gear}} \times \substack{\text{4th}\\\text{lay}\\\text{gear}} \times \substack{\text{calender}\\\text{shaft}\\\text{gear}} \times 45 \times 17 \times 6},$$

(4) $\dfrac{\text{total}}{\text{draft}} = \dfrac{\text{draft constant}}{\text{draft gear}}$, and

(5) $\dfrac{\text{draft}}{\text{gear}} = \dfrac{\text{draft constant}}{\text{total draft}}$

6. Calculate the dc of Fig. 1 with combination A and B.

7. From formula (4) and each dc already found calculate the *total draft range* of Fig. 1 with combination A and B.

8. How fine is total draft control of combination A and B by a 1-tooth change in dg from (a) minimum (b) maximum td?

9. From the foregoing for Fig. 1 select the correct word in the following parentheses: The (a) (smaller, larger) the dg and the (b) (larger, smaller) the dc the finer the td control by a 1-tooth change in the dg.

Find the teeth in dg required in the following 2 problems.

10. On combination A a td of (a) 60 (b) 80 (c) 150.

11. On combination B a td of (a) 75 (b) 120 (c) 225.

12. As assigned by your instructor sketch a diagram similar to Fig. 1 of the draft train of a card in your plant and calculate its total draft constant, range, and fineness of control.

Finding Draft Gears in Changing Total Draft.   It may be convenient to change from a present or old td to a new td without using or knowing the dc.

13. Prove: from formula (3) that (a) new td × new dg = dc and (b) old td × new dg = dc; from equations (a) and (b) that ∴ (c) new td × new dg = old td × old dg; and dividing both sides of equation (c) by new td that ∴

$$(5) \quad \frac{\text{new draft}}{\text{gear}} = \frac{\text{old total draft} \times \text{old draft gear}}{\text{new total draft}}$$

14. If a 30-tooth dg gives 66.6 td what dg ought be tried for 81.5 td?

15. What dg ought to be tried for 125 td if an 18-tooth dg gives 93.6?

16. What dg ought to be tried for as near as possible to but not over 130 td if a 30-tooth dg gives 81.5?

Intermediate Drafts, Formulas, Relation to Total Draft, and Meanings. Calculations involving changeable *intermediate drafts* are sometimes needed in the adjustment of cards and other textile machines and involving all intermediate drafts give an understanding of the action of the machines. The intermediate drafts of the card in Fig. 1 are: *feed tension, ft,* lr to fr; *lickerin draft, ld,* fr to ln; *cylinder draft, cyd,* ln to cyl; *doffer draft, dfd,* cyl to df; *calender tension, ct,* df to cr; and *coiler calender tension, cct,* cr to ccr.

17. From formula (3), Chap. III and Fig. 1 derive

$$(6) \quad \frac{\text{feed}}{\text{tension}} = \frac{2.25 \times \text{lap gear}}{6 \times 17}$$

$$(7) \quad \frac{\text{lickerin}}{\text{draft}} = \frac{\text{dia. lickerin} \times \text{dia. barrow pulley} \times \text{doffer gear} \times \text{side shaft gear} \times \text{feed driven gear}}{\text{dia. lickerin pulley} \times \text{barrow gear} \times 45 \times \text{draft gear} \times 2.25}$$

$$(8) \quad \frac{\text{cylinder}}{\text{draft}} = \frac{50.75 \times \text{dia. lickerin driven pulley}}{18 \times \text{dia. lickerin}}$$

(9) doffer $= \dfrac{27.75 \times \dfrac{\text{barrow}}{\text{gear}} \times \dfrac{\text{dia. lickerin}}{\text{pulley}} \times 18}{\dfrac{\text{doffer}}{\text{gear}} \times \dfrac{\text{dia. barrow}}{\text{pulley}} \times \dfrac{\text{dia. lickerin}}{\text{driven pulley}} \times 50.75}$

(10) calender tension $= \dfrac{\text{dia. calender roll} \times \text{doffer gear}}{27.75 \times \text{calender shaft gear}}$, and

(11) coiler calender tension $= \dfrac{2 \times \dfrac{\text{1st}}{\text{lay gear}} \times \dfrac{\text{3rd}}{\text{lay gear}} \times \dfrac{\text{5th}}{\text{lay gear}}}{\dfrac{\text{coiler}}{\text{gear}} \times \dfrac{\text{2nd}}{\text{lay gear}} \times \dfrac{\text{4th}}{\text{lay gear}} \times \dfrac{\text{dia.}}{\text{calender roll}}}$

18. From formulas (2) and (6) to (11) by calculating prove your selection of the correct word or words in the following parentheses: A total draft equals the (a) (sum, product) of all its intermediate drafts. An intermediate draft equals the total draft (b) (minus, divided by) the (c) (sum, product) of the other intermediate drafts.

As will be studied later, an often used intermediate draft is the *coiler-doffer tension, cdt,* df to ccr.

19. From the preceding problem prove that for Fig. 1

(12) coiler doffer tension $= \dfrac{2 \times \dfrac{\text{1st}}{\text{lay gear}} \times \dfrac{\text{3rd}}{\text{lay gear}} \times \dfrac{\text{5th}}{\text{lay gear}} \times \text{doffer gear}}{\dfrac{\text{coiler}}{\text{gear}} \times \dfrac{\text{2nd lay}}{\text{gear}} \times \dfrac{\text{4th lay}}{\text{gear}} \times 27.75 \times \dfrac{\text{calender}}{\text{shaft gear}}}$

20. Find: (a) ft, cyd, ct, cct, cdt, and the possible ranges of ld and dfd for combination A (b) cdt for combination B.

21. From the preceding problem state the meaning of (a) the dfd or any draft < 1 compared with a draft > 1 (b) the ld or any intermediate draft > the td.

Total and Actual Draft, Waste, Ounce Lap, and Grain Sliver.   In the card, slip and contraction are negligible but the percent of weight loss or *percent of waste, % w,* is appreciable.

22. Prove that: from formula (5), Chap. III and the foregoing (a) $\text{td} = \dfrac{(1 - .01 \times \% \text{ w}) \times \text{ad}}{1 \times 1}$; from formula (6), Chap. III and equation (a)

∴ (b) $\text{td} = (1 - .01 \times \% \text{ w}) \times \dfrac{\text{oz. lap} \times 437.5}{\text{gr. sl}}$; and ∴

(13) total draft $= \dfrac{437.5 \times (1 - .01 \times \% \text{ waste}) \times \text{ounce lap}}{\text{grain sliver}}$

What td is required in the following example and 3 problems.

EXAMPLE: *14.5 oz. lap into 58.6 gr. sl at 6% w?*

By formula (13): $\text{td} = \dfrac{437.5 \times .94 \times 14.5}{58.6} = 101.8$

23. 15.5 oz. lap into 55.5 gr. sl at 5% w?
24. 60.5 gr. sl from 14.8 oz. lap at 7.5% w?
25. At 8.2% w 54.6 gr. sl from 13.8 oz. lap?

Draft Gears and Constants, Waste, Ounce Lap, and Grain Sliver.

26. From formulas (5) and (13) derive:

$$dg = \dfrac{dc}{\dfrac{437.5 \times (1 - .01 \times \% \ w) \times oz. \ lap}{gr. \ sl}} \ ;$$

(14) $\dfrac{draft}{gear} = \dfrac{draft \ constant \times grain \ sliver}{437.5 \times (1 - .01 \times \% \ waste) \times ounce \ lap}$ and

(15) $\dfrac{grain}{sliver} = \dfrac{437.5 \times (1 - .01 \times \% \ waste) \times ounce \ lap \times draft \ gear}{draft \ constant}$

What (a) *dg ought to be tried and* (b) *gr. sl will this dg give in the following example and 4 problems:*

EXAMPLE: *On combination A 14.8 oz. lap must give at least and near as possible to 58.4 gr. sl at 7.2% w?*

(a) by formula (14): $dg = \dfrac{1595.4 \times 58.4}{437.5 \times .928 \times 14.8} = 15.5.$

Answer: 16-tooth.

(b) by formula (15): $gr \ sl = \dfrac{437.5 \times .928 \times 14.8 \times 16}{1595.4} = 60.3$

27. At 6% w combination A from 16 oz. lap must give near as possible to but not over 64 gr. sl?
28. As close as possible to but not over 80 gr. sl must be run from 16 oz. lap on combination B at 7% w?
29. At least and near as possible to 78 gr. sl at 6.7% w on combination B from 13.0 oz. lap?
30. On Fig. 1 with combination A and 15 oz. lap at 5% w what is the difference in gr. sl if dg is changed from (a) 10 to 11 and (b) 32 to 31 teeth?
31. From formula (14) and the preceding problem select the correct word or words in the following parentheses: On a card as in Fig. 1 the dg and gr. sl are (a) (directly, inversely) proportional; and ∴ *the principle* that on any machine with the draft gear and weight per length of product thus proportional the same change or difference in the draft gear anywhere in its range causes a (b) (different, same) change in weight per length of product.

Finding Draft Gears in Changing Waste, Ounce Lap, or Grain Sliver.

32. Substituting the value of td from formula (13) into formula (5), for any card with its dg and gr. sl inversely proportional, derive

(16) new draft gear $=$

$$\frac{(1 - .01 \times \text{old} \atop \% \text{ waste}) \times \text{old ounce} \atop \text{lap} \times \text{old draft} \atop \text{gear} \times \text{new grain} \atop \text{sliver}}{(1 - .01 \times \text{new } \% \text{ waste}) \times {\text{new} \atop \text{ounce} \atop \text{lap}} \times {\text{old grain} \atop \text{sliver}}}$$

and

(17) new grain sliver $=$

$$\frac{(1 - .01 \times \text{new } \% \text{ waste}) \times {\text{new} \atop \text{ounce} \atop \text{lap}} \times {\text{old} \atop \text{grain} \atop \text{sliver}} \times {\text{new} \atop \text{draft} \atop \text{gear}}}{(1 - .01 \times \text{old } \% \text{ waste}) \times {\text{old} \atop \text{ounce} \atop \text{lap}} \times {\text{old} \atop \text{draft} \atop \text{gear}}}$$

What (a) *teeth in dg ought to be tried* (b) *gr. sl will this dg give in the following examples and 7 problems:*

EXAMPLE: *As near as possible to 66 gr sl with the same % w and oz. lap and a 25-tooth dg running 64 gr. sl?*

(a) By formula (16) and cancelling the unchanged quantities on the right side: new dg $= \dfrac{25 \times 66}{64} = 25.7$; 26 is nearer than 25. By the foregoing principle $\therefore$ dg has 26 teeth. By formula (17): new gr sl $= \dfrac{64 \times 26}{25} = 66.6$.

EXAMPLE: *Change from a 28-tooth dg, 6 to 5 % w, 80 to not over 72 gr, sl. and 16 to 15 oz. lap.*

(a) By formula (16): new dg $= \dfrac{.94 \times 16 \times 28 \times 72}{.95 \times 15 \times 80} = 26.6$; $\therefore$ dg has 26 teeth.

(b) By formula (17) new gr sl $= \dfrac{.95 \times 15 \times 80 \times 26}{.94 \times 16 \times 28} = 70.4$.

	Old or Present			New or Required		
dg	% w	oz. lap	gr sl	% w	oz. lap	gr sl near as possible to
33. 14	4.0	15.0	52.5	same	same	57.5
34. 23	4.5	14.3	69.0	"	"	and at least 72.6
35. 29	5.2	13.8	58.0	4.8	"	but not over 54.4
36. 31	6.0	16.2	72.0	same	17.0	68.0
37. 18	5.0	17.1	76.0	6.8	16.2	80.0 but on the heavy side
38. 12	3.8	12.9	48.0	4.9	13.2	52.8 but on the light side
39. 19	7.6	16.8	64.2	5.0	15.4	same

SPEEDS

Cylinder Speed. The RPM of the cylinder is the basic speed of a card, sometimes varying from less than the traditional standard of 165 to around 300.

Lickerin Speeds and Driven Pulleys. Fine adjustment of lickerin speed may be critical in the work of other parts, in cleaning the stock, and on the other hand, in avoiding undue waste. Lp and lp are relatively small.

40. From the foregoing: (a) Why do some plants keep Lp in $\frac{1''}{4}$ dia. variations? (b) Why is the belt on Lp relatively thick? (c) What beside dia. Lp ought to be considered in calculating RPM ln?

41. Derive from the foregoing

(18) $\dfrac{\text{RPM}}{\text{lickerin}} = \dfrac{\text{RPM cylinder} \times (18 + \text{belt thickness})}{\text{dia. lickerin driven pulley} + \text{belt thickness}}$; ∴

dia. Lp + belt thickness = $\dfrac{\text{RPM cyl} \times (18 + \text{belt thickness})}{\text{RPM ln}}$; and ∴

(19) $\dfrac{\text{dia. lickerin}}{\text{driven pulley}} = \dfrac{\text{RPM cylinder} \times (18 + \text{belt thickness})}{\text{RPM lickerin}} - \text{belt}$

thickness.

With $\frac{1''}{4}$ belt thickness and dia. Lp in $\frac{1''}{4}$ variations what (a) dia. Lp ought to be tried and (b) RPM ln will this dia, Lp give in Fig. 1 in the following example and 3 problems:

EXAMPLE: *RPM cyl 165 and RPM ln near as possible to but not over 450?*

(a) By formula (19): dia. LP $= \dfrac{165 \times 18.25}{450} - .25 = 6.4$; dia. Lp $= 6.5''$.

(b) By formula (18): RPM ln $= \dfrac{165 \times 18.25}{6.75} = 446$.

42. RPM cyl 165 and RPM ln near as possible to 425?

43. RPM cyl 200 and RPM ln near as possible to and at least 475?

44. 300 RPM cyl and near as possible to but not over 725 RPM ln?

Flat Speeds and Driver and Driven Pulleys.

45. From your inspection of a card select the correct word in the parentheses and answer the question: The IPM of the flats is approximately but slightly (less, more) than the IPM of what revolving member of the flat train in Fig. 2? Why?

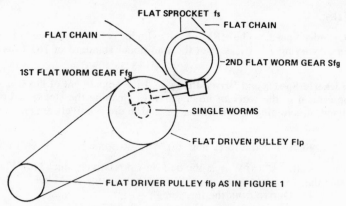

Figure 2.   A Flat Train of Figure 1

46. From the foregoing and Chap. XX, Part One, show that:

$$\text{RPM fs} = \frac{\text{RPM cyl} \times \text{dia. flp} \times 1 \times 1}{\text{dia. Flp} \times \text{Ffg} \times \text{Sfg}} \text{ and approximate}$$

(20) $\dfrac{\text{IPM}}{\text{flats}} = \dfrac{\pi \times \dfrac{\text{dia. flat}}{\text{sprocket}} \times \dfrac{\text{RPM}}{\text{cylinder}} \times \dfrac{\text{dia. flat}}{\text{driver pulley}}}{\dfrac{\text{dia. flat}}{\text{driven pulley}} \times \dfrac{\text{1st flat}}{\text{worm gear}} \times \dfrac{\text{2nd flat}}{\text{worm gear}}}$, ∴

(21) $\begin{matrix}\text{dia. flat}\\\text{driver}\\\text{pulley}\end{matrix} = \dfrac{\dfrac{\text{IPM}}{\text{flats}} \times \dfrac{\text{dia. flat}}{\text{driven pulley}} \times \dfrac{\text{1st flat}}{\text{worm gear}} \times \dfrac{\text{2nd flat}}{\text{worm gear}}}{\pi \times \dfrac{\text{dia. flat}}{\text{sprocket}} \times \dfrac{\text{RPM}}{\text{cylinder}}}$, and

(22) $\begin{matrix}\text{dia. flat}\\\text{driven}\\\text{pulley}\end{matrix} = \dfrac{\pi \times \dfrac{\text{dia. flat}}{\text{sprocket}} \times \dfrac{\text{RPM}}{\text{cylinder}} \times \dfrac{\text{dia. flat}}{\text{driver pulley}}}{\dfrac{\text{IPM}}{\text{flats}} \times \dfrac{\text{1st flat}}{\text{worm gear}} \times \dfrac{\text{2nd flat}}{\text{worm gear}}}$

In Fig. 2 with an 8″ dia. fs what (a) *pulley in* $\dfrac{1''}{2}$ *dia. is needed to give near as possible to the IPM flats* (b) *IPM flats does this pulley give in the following 5 problems:*

	RPM cyl	Ffg	Sfg	dia. flp	dia. Flp	IPM flats
47.	165	15	32		12″	and at least 2.15?
48.	165	15	32		12″	and at least 3.50?
49.	200	16	42	5.5″		" " " 3.60?
50.	250	15	32	5″		but not over 4.25?
51.	325	15	32		16″	but not over 4.50?

Doffer Speeds, Constants, Pulleys, and Barrow Gears. Doffer speed calculations and the labor saving *doffer speed constant, dsc,* are involved in the efficiency of the doffer and in production calculations.

52. Disregarding belt thickness from Fig. 1 and your previous derivations of speed formulas and of constants derive

$$(23) \quad \frac{\text{RPM}}{\text{doffer}} = \frac{\dfrac{\text{RPM}}{\text{cylinder}} \times 18 \times \dfrac{\text{dia. lickerin}}{\text{pulley}} \times \dfrac{\text{barrow}}{\text{gear}}}{\dfrac{\text{dia. lickerin}}{\text{driven pulley}} \times \dfrac{\text{dia. barrow}}{\text{pulley}} \times \dfrac{\text{doffer}}{\text{gear}}}, \; \therefore$$

$$(24) \quad \begin{matrix}\text{doffer}\\ \text{speed}\\ \text{constant}\end{matrix} = \frac{\text{RPM doffer}}{\dfrac{\text{dia. lickerin}}{\text{pulley}} \times \dfrac{\text{barrow}}{\text{gear}}}$$

$$= \frac{\text{RPM cylinder} \times 18}{\dfrac{\text{dia. lickerin}}{\text{driven pulley}} \times \dfrac{\text{dia. barrow}}{\text{pulley}} \times \dfrac{\text{doffer}}{\text{gear}}}, \; \therefore$$

(25) RPM doffer = doffer speed constant × dia. lickerin pulley × barrow gear,

$$(26) \quad \begin{matrix}\text{dia. lickerin}\\ \text{pulley}\end{matrix} = \frac{\text{RPM doffer}}{\text{doffer speed constant} \times \text{barrow gear}}, \text{ and}$$

$$(27) \quad \begin{matrix}\text{barrow}\\ \text{gear}\end{matrix} = \frac{\text{RPM doffer}}{\text{doffer speed constant} \times \text{dia. lickerin pulley}}.$$

From Table 1 find the dsc of Fig. 1 in the following example and 2 problems:

EXAMPLE: *Combination A and 165 RPM cyl.*

By formula (24): $\text{dsc} = \dfrac{165 \times 18}{6.5 \times 18 \times 214} = .119.$

53. Combination A and (a) 200 (b) 250 (c) 300 RPM cyl.
54. Combination B and (a) 165 (b) 200 (c) 250 (d) 300 RPM cyl.
55. At 250 RPM cyl what is the range of RPM df of Fig. 1 with Combination A and B?

For Fig. 1 find (a) *either the lp in* $\dfrac{1''}{4}$ *dia. or the bg to give near as possible to the RPM df* (b) *the RPM df this will give in the following example and* 3 *problems:*

EXAMPLE: *Combination A, 165 RPM cyl, 2″ dia. lp, and 6 RPM df.*

(a) By formula (27) and dsc already found: $\text{bg} = \dfrac{6}{.119 \times 2} = 25.2;$ 25 is nearer than 25.5 to 25.2. (b) By formula (25): RPM df = .119 × 2 × 25 = 5.95.

56. Combination A, 200 RPM cyl, 3″ dia. lp, but not over 11 RPM df.

57. Combination B, 250 RPM cyl, 32-tooth bg, but not over 18 RPM df.

58. Combination B, 300 RPM cyl, 23-tooth bg, and at least 25 RPM df.

59. As assigned by your instructor for a card in your plant derive speed constants and make lickerin, flat, and doffer speed calculations.

LAY

Basic Formula. As in Fig. 3 each revolution of the *tube*, guiding the sliver from the coiler calender roll, and of the *tube gear, Tg,* integral with the tube, lays 1 coil in the cylindrical *can,* temporarily integral with the *turntable, tt,* and the *turntable gear, Ttg.* The circumference of revolution of the outer end of the tube and the cir. of the coils is < the cir. of the can but at one point (i.e., in Fig. 3 nearest the vertical *lay shaft, ls*) is directly above the cir. of the can (as shown by the broken line).

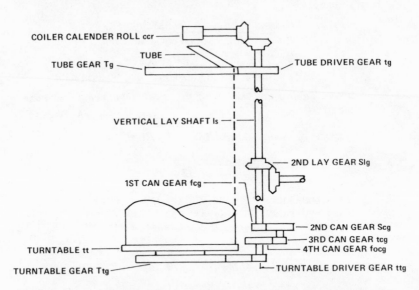

COILER CALENDER ROLL ccr

TUBE

TUBE GEAR Tg

TUBE DRIVER GEAR tg

VERTICAL LAY SHAFT ls

2ND LAY GEAR Slg

1ST CAN GEAR fcg

2ND CAN GEAR Scg
3RD CAN GEAR tcg
4TH CAN GEAR focg

TURNTABLE tt

TURNTABLE GEAR Ttg

TURNTABLE DRIVER GEAR ttg

60. (a) If the can would not revolve, into what form and where would the accumulating coils be laid? (b) If the can also revolves several times slower than the tube, into what form are the coils laid during 1 revolution of the can?

The lay is the number of coils in 1 layer.

61. From the foregoing derive

$$(28) \quad \text{lay} = \frac{\text{revolutions of tube}}{\text{revolutions of can}}.$$

Lays of Spur and Epicyclic Gear Lay Trains.

62. From formula (28) and Chap. (20), Part One, derive

$$\text{lay of Fig. 3} = \cfrac{\text{rev ls} \times \text{tg}}{\cfrac{\text{rev ls} \times \text{fcg} \times \text{tcg} \times \text{ttg}}{\text{Scg} \times \text{Focg} \times \text{Ttg}}} \quad \text{and} \therefore$$

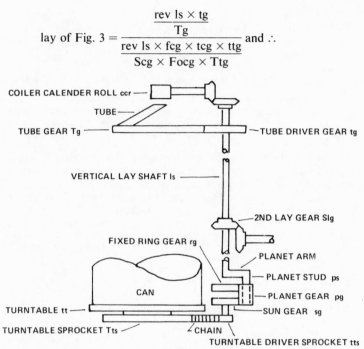

COILER CALENDER ROLL ccr

TUBE

TUBE GEAR Tg — TUBE DRIVER GEAR tg

VERTICAL LAY SHAFT ls

2ND LAY GEAR Slg

FIXED RING GEAR rg

PLANET ARM

PLANET STUD ps

CAN

PLANET GEAR pg

TURNTABLE tt

SUN GEAR sg

TURNTABLE SPROCKET Tts   CHAIN

TURNTABLE DRIVER SPROCKET tts

Figure 4.   An Epicyclic Lay Train of Figure 1

Table 2. Some lay	Figure 3:		Figure 4:				
train combinations	C	D	E	F	G	H	I
tube gear, Tg	126	108	122	142	145	160	120
tube driver gear, tg	42	31	42	41	41	46	44
1st can gear, fcg	12	14					
2nd can gear, Scg	36	50					
3rd can gear, tcg	12	14	.				
4th can gear, Focg	36	50					
turntable driver gear, ttg	9	13					34 (note)
turntable gear, Ttg	60	75					92 "
ring gear, rg			37	43	43	43	43
planet gear, pg			29	34	34	34	34
sun gear, sg			36	42	42	42	42
turntable driver sprocket, tts			21	16	16	16	16
turntable sprocket, Tts			46	49	77	82	26

Note: Combination I has the additional ttg integral with Tts and meshing with the additional Ttg integral with ttg.

$$\text{(29) } \frac{\text{lay of}}{\text{Fig. 3}} = \frac{\text{tube}}{\text{driver gear}} \times \frac{\text{2nd}}{\text{can gear}} \times \frac{\text{4th}}{\text{can gear}} \times \frac{\text{turntable}}{\text{gear}}$$
$$\frac{}{\frac{\text{tube}}{\text{gear}} \times \frac{\text{1st}}{\text{can gear}} \times \frac{\text{3rd}}{\text{can gear}} \times \frac{\text{turntable driver}}{\text{gear}}}$$

63. Calculate the lay of Fig. 3 with combination C and D.

In Fig. 4 the ring gear, rg, is fixed to the housing and cannot revolve; the planet gear, pg, meshes with rg and the sun gear, sg, and can revolve on the planet study, ps; and ps through the planet arm, pa, is integral with ls and revolves with ls.

64. (a) Basically, Fig. 4 is the same as which fig. of an epicyclic train in Chap. (20), Part One? (b) What is the difference between Fig. 4 and the fig. referred to in Chap. (20), Part One?

65. Show: from the foregoing; Fig. 4; formula (42) and the meaning of a revolution with a minus sign in Chap. (20), Part One; and your study of calculating with minus signs in Chap. (20), Part One that (a) rev

$$\text{pa} = \frac{0 \times \text{rg} \times \text{pg} - \text{rev sg} \times \text{sg} \times \text{pg}}{\text{rg} \times \text{pa} - \text{Sg} \times \text{pg}} = \frac{-\text{rev sg} \times \text{sg}}{\text{rg} - \text{sg}} \text{; from Fig. 4 that (b)}$$

$$\text{rev pa} = \frac{-\text{rev tube} \times \text{Tg}}{\text{tg}} \text{ and (c) rev. sg} = \frac{\text{rev can} \times \text{Tts}}{\text{tts}} \text{; substituting}$$

the values of rev pa and rev sg into equation (a) that (d) $\dfrac{-\text{rev tube} \times \text{Tg}}{\text{tg}} =$

$$\frac{\dfrac{-\text{rev can} \times \text{Tts}}{\text{tts}} \times \text{sg}}{\text{rg} - \text{sg}} \text{; simplifying the right side of equation (d) and}$$

multiplying each side by -1 that (e) $\dfrac{\text{rev tube} \times \text{Tg}}{\text{tg}} = \dfrac{\text{rev can} \times \text{Tts} \times \text{sg}}{\text{tts} \times (\text{rg} - \text{sg})}$;

from equation (e) that $\therefore$ (f) $\dfrac{\text{rev tube}}{\text{rev can}} = \dfrac{\text{Tts} \times \text{sg} \times \text{tg}}{\text{tts} \times (\text{rg} - \text{sg}) \times \text{Tg}}$; and from

formula (28) that $\therefore$

$$\text{(30) } \frac{\text{lay of}}{\text{Fig. 4}} = \frac{\text{turntable sprocket} \times \text{sun gear} \times \text{tube driver gear}}{\dfrac{\text{turntable driver}}{\text{sprocket}} \times (\text{ring gear} - \text{sun gear}) \times \text{tube gear}}$$

What is the lay of Fig. 4 with the combinations in the following example and 4 problems:

EXAMPLE: *Combination E?*

By formula (30): lay $= \dfrac{46 \times 36 \times 42}{21 \times (37 - 36) \times 122} = \dfrac{46 \times 36 \times 42}{21 \times 1 \times 122} = 27.1.$

66. F?

67. G?

68. H?

69. I, first adjusting formula (30) to ttg and Ttg?

70. As assigned by your instructor, diagram the lay train of a card in your plant, derive its lay formula, calculate its lay and compare with its actual lay.

PRODUCTION

Meanings and Basic Formulas. Words and their abbreviations in your study of picker production calculations have equivalent meanings with the card.

71. From the foregoing prove: that $\dfrac{100\%}{\text{lbs.}} = \dfrac{\dfrac{\text{IPM}}{\text{ccr}} \times 60 \times \dfrac{\text{gr.}}{\text{sl}} \times \text{hrs.}}{36 \times 7000}$;

and that $\therefore$

$$(31)\quad \frac{100\%}{\text{pounds}} = \frac{\text{IPM coiler calender roll} \times \text{grain sliver} \times \text{hours}}{4200} .$$

72. Show: that (a) $\dfrac{\text{coiler doffer}}{\text{tension, cdt}} = \dfrac{\text{IPM ccr}}{\text{IPM df}} = \dfrac{\text{RPM ccr} \times 2}{\text{RPM df} \times 27.75}$; from

equation (a) that $\therefore$ (b) $\text{RPM ccr} = \dfrac{\text{cdt} \times \text{RPM df} \times 27.75}{2} = 13.875 \times \text{cdt} \times$

RPM df; from formula (31) that (c) $\dfrac{100\%}{\text{lbs.}} = \dfrac{\dfrac{\text{RPM}}{\text{ccr}} \times 2 \times \pi \times \text{gr sl} \times \text{hrs.}}{4200} =$

.00149 $\times$ RPM ccr $\times$ gr sl $\times$ hrs.; substituting the value of RPM ccr from equation (b) into equation (c) that (d) 100% lbs. = .00149 $\times$ 13.875 $\times$ cdt $\times$ RPM df $\times$ gr sl $\times$ hrs.; and that $\therefore$

$$(32)\quad \frac{100\%}{\text{pounds}} = .02076 \times \frac{\text{coiler doffer}}{\text{tension}} \times \frac{\text{RPM}}{\text{doffer}} \times \frac{\text{grain}}{\text{sliver}} \times \text{hours}$$

From the cdt found in a previous problem find 100% lbs./hr. in the following 2 problems:

73. Combination A running 64 gr. sl at 10.8 RPM.
74. Combination B running 60 gr. sl at 17.3 RPM.

Production Constants and Percent of Production.

75. For the same purpose and by the same reasoning as in your study of picker calculations derive

(33) production constant = .02076 $\times$ coiler doffer tension and

$$(34)\quad \frac{100\%}{\text{pounds}} = \frac{\text{production}}{\text{constant}} \times \frac{\text{RPM}}{\text{doffer}} \times \frac{\text{grain}}{\text{sliver}} \times \text{hours}.$$

76. Calculate the pc of combinations A and B.
77. Similarly to your study of picker calculations, from formula (34) derive

(35) pounds = production constant $\times$ RPM doffer $\times$ grain sliver
$\times$ hours $\times$ .01 $\times$ % production and $\therefore$

$$(36)\quad \frac{\text{RPM}}{\text{doffer}} = \frac{\text{pounds}}{\dfrac{\text{production}}{\text{constant}} \times \dfrac{\text{grain}}{\text{sliver}} \times \text{hours} \times .01 \times \text{\% production}}$$

What lbs. will Fig. 1 *produce in the following example and* 3 *problems:*

EXAMPLE: 58 *gr. sl in* 8 *hrs. on combination A at* 15 *RPM df and* 94% *p?*

By formula (35) and a previous problem: lbs. = .02429 × 15 × 58 × 8 × .01 × 94 = 1590.

78. 62.5 gr. sl in 40 hrs. on combination A at 18 RPM df and 95% p?

79. 64.2 gr. sl in 44 hrs. on combination B at 22 RPM df and 94.5% p?

80. 72.8 gr. sl in 3 40-hr. shifts on combination B on 4 cards at 93.5% and 27.5 RPM df?

Production, Cylinder and Doffer Speeds, Barrow Gears, and Lickerin Pulleys.

In Fig. 1 *what* (a) *barrow gear, bg, or lickerin pulley, lp, will give near as possible to the production* (b) *RPM df and production will this bg or lp give in the following example and* 8 *problems:*

EXAMPLE: *At least* 22 *lbs./hr. of* 56 *gr. sl with* 4″ *lp on combination A at* 165 *RPM cyl and* 95% *p?*

(a) By formula (36): RPM df $=\dfrac{22}{.02429 \times 56 \times 1 \times .95}= 17.02.$ By

formula (27) and dsc from a previous example: bg $=\dfrac{17.02}{.119 \times 4}= 35.7; \therefore$

36-tooth bg. (b) By formula (25): RPM df = .119 × 4 × 36 = 17.1. By formula (35): lbs. = .0243 × 17.1 × 56 × 1 × .95 = 22.1

	comb.	production	gr. sl	% p	bg	lp	RPM cyl	cards
81.	A	24 lbs./hr	60	93.5		$3\frac{1}{2}''$	200	1
82.	A	28 lbs./hr.	55.5	94.5		$4\frac{1}{2}''$	250	1
83.	A	3300 lbs./3 8-hr. shifts	62.5	95		$4\frac{3}{4}''$	300	4
84.	A	at least 50 lbs./hr.	70	95	30		300	1
85.	B	18 lbs./hr.	70	95	30		165	1
86.	B	28 lbs./hr.	58.5	93.5	28		200	3
87.	B	3400 lbs./ 24 hrs.	72.6	93		4.5″	250	4
88.	B	18000 lbs./ 120 hrs.	68	93		4.5	300	3

Finding Pounds or Doffer Speed in Changing Either, Grain Sliver, Hours, and % Production.

89. Show: from formula (35) that (a) new lbs. = pc × new RPM df × new gr sl × new hrs. × .01 × new % p and (b) old lbs. = pc × old RPM df × old gr sl × old hrs. × .01 × old % p; dividing each side of equation (a) by the corresponding side of (b), multiplying each side of the result by old lbs., and cancelling on both sides that

$$(37)\quad \frac{\text{new}}{\text{pounds}} = \frac{\substack{\text{old} \\ \text{pounds}} \times \substack{\text{new} \\ \text{RPM} \\ \text{doffer}} \times \substack{\text{new} \\ \text{grain} \\ \text{sliver}} \times \substack{\text{new} \\ \text{hours}} \times \substack{\text{new \%} \\ \text{production}}}{\substack{\text{old} \\ \text{RPM} \\ \text{doffer}} \times \substack{\text{old} \\ \text{grain} \\ \text{sliver}} \times \substack{\text{old} \\ \text{hours}} \times \substack{\text{old \%} \\ \text{production}}}$$

and ∴.

$$(38)\quad \frac{\text{new}}{\text{RPM doffer}} = \frac{\substack{\text{new} \\ \text{pounds}} \times \substack{\text{old} \\ \text{RPM} \\ \text{doffer}} \times \substack{\text{old} \\ \text{grain} \\ \text{sliver}} \times \substack{\text{old} \\ \text{hours}} \times \substack{\text{old \%} \\ \text{production}}}{\substack{\text{old} \\ \text{pounds}} \times \substack{\text{new} \\ \text{grain sliver}} \times \substack{\text{new} \\ \text{hours}} \times \substack{\text{new \%} \\ \text{production}}}$$

EXAMPLE: *What will be the lbs./hr. of 62 gr. sl at 94% p and 20 RPM df if 19 RPM df and 95% p gives 26.8 lbs./hr. of 58 gr. sl?*

By formula (37): new lbs./hr. $= \dfrac{26.8 \times 20 \times 62 \times 1 \times 94}{19 \times 58 \times 1 \times 95} = 29.8$

90. If 14.5 RPM df at 93.5% p yields 196 lbs./8 hrs. of 70 gr. sl what will be the lbs./40 hrs. of 68 gr. sl at 94% p and 15.5 RPM df?

91. If 4 cards at 30 RPM df average 93% p and run 21600 lbs. of 55 gr. sl in 15 8-hr. shifts what will 3 of them run of 62.4 gr. sl at 31 RPM df and 94% p in the same time?

92. If 28 RPM df gives 38.6 lbs./hr. what RPM df will give 41 lbs./hr. of the same gr. sl at the same % p?

93. 30 RPM df at 95.5% p runs 39.4 lbs./hr. of 56.2 gr. sl. What RPM df at 94% p will run 50 lbs./hr. of 72.4 gr. sl?

94. In 3 40-hr. shifts 5 identical cards at 27.5 RPM df and 94.2% p produce 25200 lbs. of 53.5 gr. sl. At what RPM df and 93.5% p will 3 of them produce 20700 lbs. of 56.8 gr sl in 3 44-hr. shifts?

Creeling and Doffing Frequency and Cycle. The *creeling frequency, cf,* of a card is the full laps, i.e., full rolls, fed per hr.; its *creeling cycle, cc,* the minutes from feeding 1 full lap to feeding the next.

95. Show that

$$(39)\quad \text{creeling frequency} = \frac{\text{pounds fed per hour}}{\text{pounds in full lap}} \text{ and}$$

$$(40)\quad \text{creeling cycle} = \frac{60}{\text{creeling frequency}}.$$

96. Show that: (a) lbs. fed per hr. $\times (1 - .01 \times \% \text{ w}) = \text{lbs./hr.}$; $\therefore$

(b) lbs. fed per hr. $= \dfrac{\text{lbs./hr.}}{1 - .01 \times \% \text{ w}}$; from equation (b) and formula (35)

$\therefore$ (c) lbs. fed per hr. $= \dfrac{\text{pc} \times \text{RPM df} \times \text{gr. sl} \times .01 \times \% \text{ p}}{1 - .01 \times \% \text{ w}}$; and substitut-

ing the value of lbs. fed per hr. from equation (c) into formula (39) $\therefore$

$$(41) \quad \begin{array}{c}\text{creeling} \\ \text{frequency}\end{array} = \frac{\begin{array}{c}\text{production} \\ \text{constant}\end{array} \times \begin{array}{c}\text{RPM} \\ \text{doffer}\end{array} \times \begin{array}{c}\text{grain} \\ \text{sliver}\end{array} \times \begin{array}{c}.01 \times \% \text{ p} \\ \text{production}\end{array}}{(1 - .01 \times \% \text{ waste}) \times \text{pounds in full lap}}$$

The *doffing frequency, dff,* of a card is the cans filled per hr.; and its *doffing cycle, dfc,* is the minutes to fill a can.

97. Show that

$$(42) \quad \text{doffing frequency} = \frac{\text{pounds per hour}}{\text{pounds in full can}} \text{ and}$$

$$(43) \quad \text{doffing cycle} = \frac{60}{\text{doffing frequency}}.$$

98. From formulas (42) and (35) show that

$$(44) \quad \begin{array}{c}\text{doffing} \\ \text{frequency}\end{array} = \frac{\begin{array}{c}\text{production} \\ \text{constant}\end{array} \times \begin{array}{c}\text{RPM} \\ \text{doffer}\end{array} \times \begin{array}{c}\text{grain} \\ \text{sliver}\end{array} \times \begin{array}{c}.01 \times \% \\ \text{production}\end{array}}{\text{pounds in full can}}.$$

Find the (a) cf (b) cc (c) dff (d) dfc of the combinations of Fig. 1 under the conditions in the following example and 6 problems:

EXAMPLE: *A, 15.5 RPM df, 60.4 gr. sl, 94.5% p, 4.5% w, 59.2 lbs. in full lap rolls, and 40 lbs. in full cans.*

(a) By formula (41): cf $= \dfrac{.02429 \times 15.5 \times 60.4 \times .945}{.955 \times 59.2} = \dfrac{21.4896}{56.5360}$

$= .380104$; i.e., .380104 of a full roll in 1 hr. (b) By formula (40): cc

$= \dfrac{60}{.380104} = 157.851$; i.e., 157.851 minutes from starting 1 roll to start-

ing the next. (c) From (a) and by formula (44): dff $= \dfrac{21.4896}{40} = .53724$;

i.e., .53724 of a full can in 1 hr. (d) By formula (43): dfc $= \dfrac{60}{.53724}$

$= 111.682$.

		RPM df	gr sl	% p	% w	lbs. in full roll	lbs. in full can
99.	A	16	60	95.5	4.5	60	40
100.	B	18.5	58	95	5	68	40
101.	A	20	62.4	94	6	65	60
102.	B	22.5	60.2	93.6	6.5	60.5	62
103.	A	28.4	62	94	5.5	68	90
104.	B	30	72	93	7	70	90

105. As assigned by your instructor determine the production constant of a card in your plant; calculate the pounds from the doffer speed, gr sl, and % p; calculate the creeling and doffing frequency and cycle; compare all these with actual conditions and account for any differences.

Chapter IX

DRAWING FRAME CALCULATIONS

DRAFT

Rolls. Frequently the term "drafting rolls" does not include the *lifter roll, lr,* if there is such, or the calender roll, cr, and is so used in this book, although lr sometimes and cr oftener draft appreciably.

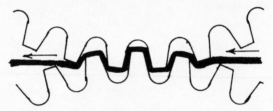

Figure 1. A Metallic Roll Over a Metallic Roll

Drawing frames are variously equipped with drafting rolls, some (a) entirely with cushion top rolls each over a shallowly fluted or smooth bottom roll, (b) entirely with deeply fluted metallic top rolls each meshing with a deeply fluted metallic bottom roll as in Fig. 1, and (c) with one or two backmost rolls as in (a) and the others as in (b). Lifter rolls are usually metallic and smooth. Power is delivered to the bottom rolls and then to the top rolls by contact with the stock.

Calender rolls are smooth or meshing metallic with one receiving power from the other usually through gears. A meshing metallic roll, like a smooth roll, is designated by its outside or *nominal diameter, **nom dia.,*** usually in inches and fractional inches and, like a gear, by its pitch.

1. Select the correct word or words in each set of the following parentheses: meshing metallic rolls, as in Fig. 1, make the draft (a) $(< = >)$ the draft by smooth rolls of the same actual dia. Why? The *effective diameter, **ef dia.,*** of a meshing metallic roll is (b) $(< = >)$ its actual dia. Why? The (c) (deeper, shallower) a metallic roll meshes the larger its ef dia. Why? The thicker the stock the (d) (less, larger) the ef dia. of meshing rolls. Why? Of metallic rolls with the same actual diameters those with the (e) (larger, less) pitch have the greater ef dia. Why?

Basic Total Draft Formulas, Constants, Ranges, Control, and Gears. The mechanical total draft, td, of the frame in Fig. 2 is considered from the *back roll, **br,*** as the feed roll, to the *front roll, **fr,*** as the delivery roll.

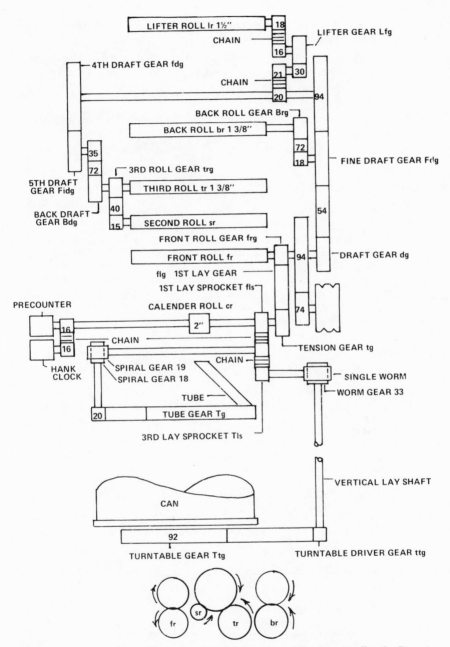

Figure 2.   Draft and Lay Trains and End Elevation of Drafting Rolls of a Drawing Frame with 3 Cushion Rolls Over 4 Metallic Rolls

2. From the foregoing and similarly to your derivations for the picker and card, for Fig. 2 derive

(1) $\dfrac{\text{total}}{\text{draft}} = \dfrac{\text{surface speed of front roll}}{\text{surface speed of back roll}}, \therefore \text{(a) } td = \dfrac{\text{dia. fr} \times \text{Fdg} \times \text{Brg}}{\text{dg} \times 18 \times 1.375};$

since, as shown in Table 1, for each combination dia. fr and Brg are constants, from equation (a) $\therefore$.

(2) draft constant, dc = .04040 × dia. front roll × back roll gear,

(3) total draft = $\dfrac{\text{draft constant} \times \text{fine draft gear}}{\text{draft gear}}$, and

(4) draft gear = $\dfrac{\text{draft constant} \times \text{fine draft gear}}{\text{total draft}}$

3. Find the dc for each combination of Fig. 2.

4. Find the td range for each combination of Fig. 2.

5. For each combination of Fig. 2 how fine is td control by a 1-tooth change in dg from (a) minimum (b) maximum td; and how fine by a 1-tooth change in Fdg from (c) minimum (d) maximum td?

6. From formula (3) select the correct word in each set of parentheses: td is (a) (indirectly, directly) proportional to dg; td is (b) (directly, inversely) proportional to Fdg and $\therefore$ a 1-tooth change from a (c) (larger, smaller) Fdg gives a finer td control.

Table 1. Draft Train Combinations of Fig. 2

	A	B
diameter of 2nd roll, sr	$\dfrac{3''}{4}$	$1''$
diameter of front roll, fr	$1\dfrac{1''}{8}$	$1\dfrac{3''}{8}$
teeth in lifter gear, Lfg	87 to 91	80 to 84
" " fine draft gear, Fdg	85 to	88
" " 4th " " , fdg	82	85
" " 5th " " , Fidg	93	90
" " back draft gear, Bdg	42 to	85
" " draft gear, dg	26 to	64
" " back roll gear, Brg	66	54
" " 3rd roll gear, trg	28	25
" " front roll gear, frg	37	45
" " tension gear, Tng	60 to	68

Find (a) the teeth in the dg and Fdg of Fig. 2 that ought to be tried to give the td and (b) the td these gears will give in the following examples and 3 problems:

EXAMPLE: *Close as possible to but not over 7.41.*

The dg and Fdg ∴ must give 7.41 or < 7.41; ∴ any adjustment needed in td must be upward; and ∴ from (b) and (c) of the preceding problem we must first try the smallest Fdg. By formula (4): $dg = \dfrac{3 \times 85}{7.41} =$ 34.4; and from (a) of the preceding problem ∴ a 35-tooth dg. By formula (3): $td = \dfrac{3 \times 85}{35} = 7.29$. Adjusting upward with an 86- and 87-tooth

Fdg: $td = \dfrac{3 \times 86}{35} = 7.37$ or $= \dfrac{3 \times 87}{35} = 7.46$.   **Answer:**   (a) dg 35 Fdg 86 (b) 7.37.

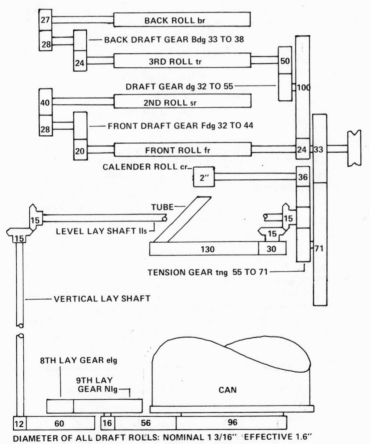

DIAMETER OF ALL DRAFT ROLLS: NOMINAL 1 3/16"   EFFECTIVE 1.6"

Figure 3.   Draft and Lay Trains of a Drawing Frame with 4 Metallic Rolls Over 4 Metallic Rolls

EXAMPLE: *Close as possible to 9.25 td.*

Any adjustment needed in td $\therefore$ may be upward or downward; and $\therefore$ we must first consider the middle sizes of Fdg. By formula (4):

$$dg = \frac{3 \times 86}{9.25} = 27.9 \text{ or } \frac{3 \times 87}{9.25} = 28.2. \text{ By formula (3) td} = \frac{3 \times 86}{27} = 9.56$$

or $\frac{3 \times 86}{28} = 9.21$ or $\frac{3 \times 87}{28} = 9.32$ or $\frac{3 \times 87}{29} = 9.00$.   **Answer:** (a) dg 28 Fdg 86 (b) 9.21.

7. Close as possible to and not over 8.50 td.
8. Not over and close as possible to 5.50 td.
9. At least and near as possible to 7.78 td.
10. Nearest to 4.25.
11. Nearest to 10.0.
12. For the frame in Fig. 3, as you did for Fig. 2, consider the td from the br to fr and derive

(5) draft constant = 8.371,

$$(6) \text{ total draft} = \frac{8.371 \times \text{back draft gear}}{\text{draft gear}}, \text{ and}$$

$$(7) \text{ draft gear} = \frac{8.371 \times \text{back draft gear}}{\text{total draft}}$$

13. What is the td range of Fig. 3?
14. For Fig. 3 how fine is td control by a 1-tooth change in dg from (a) minimum (b) maximum td; and how fine by a 1-tooth change in Bdg from (c) minimum (d) maximum td?

As you did with Fig. 2 find (a) the teeth in the dg and Bdg of Fig. 3 that ought to be tried to give the td and (b) the td these gears will give in the following 3 problems:

15. Near as possible to but not over 9.60 td.
16. At least and near as possible to 7.60 td.
17. Nearest to 6.15 td.
18. For the frame in Fig. 4, for reasons that will later be evident, calculate the td from the lifter roll, lr, to the calender roll, cr, and prove:

$$(a) \quad td = \frac{2 \times 90 \times 39 \times 17 \times 100 \times Tdg \times 50}{Ftng \times 90 \times 19 \times fdg \times dg \times 50 \times 1.375} = \frac{5075.6 \times Tdg}{Ftng \times fdg \times dg};$$

$\therefore$ (b) td $\times$ dg $= \dfrac{5075.6 \times Tdg}{Ftng \times fdg}$; since for each combination in Table 2

all the constants are on the right side of equation (b), for Fig. 4 $\therefore$

$$(8) \text{ draft constant} = \frac{5075.6 \times \text{3rd draft gear}}{\text{4th tension gear} \times \text{1st draft gear}},$$

$$(9) \text{ total draft} = \frac{\text{draft constant}}{\text{draft gear}}, \text{ and}$$

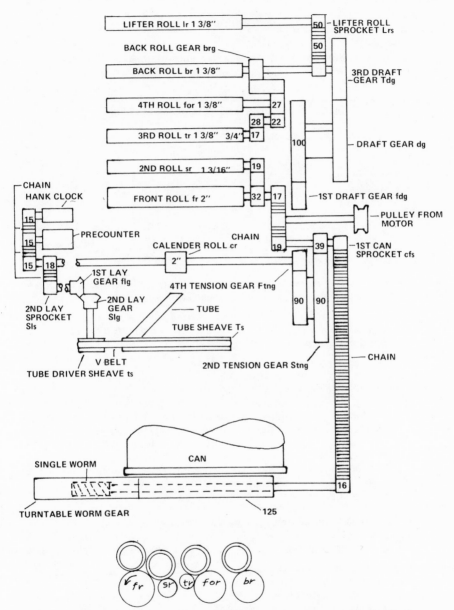

*Figure 4.   Draft and Lay Trains and End Elevation of Drafting Rolls of a Drawing
Frame with 4 Cushion Rolls Over 5 Metallic Rolls*

$$(10)\ \text{draft gear} = \frac{\text{draft constant}}{\text{total draft}}.$$

19. Find the dc of Fig. 4 with combination A, B, C, and D.

20. What is the td range of Fig. 4 with combinations A, B, C, and D.

Table 2.   Some Draft Train Combination of Fig. 4

	A		B	C		D
back roll gear, brg	30		36	40		42
3rd draft gear, Tdg	70		70	70		100
draft gear, dg	48	to	82	39	to	82
1st draft gear, fdg	34		23	23		23
4th tension gear, Ftng	36		36	35		35

Options: If necessary to adjust tensions, Lrs can be changed to 49; Stng to 89; Ftng in combinations A and B to 35, and in C and D to 34.

21. For Fig. 4 with combinations A and D how fine is td control by a 1-tooth change from (a) minimum (b) maximum td?

Find the teeth that ought to be tried in the dg of Fig. 4 with the combination to give (a) the td and (b) the td this dg may give in the following 3 problems:

22. A near as possible to and not over 4.20 td.

23. B at least and close as possible 7.73 td.

24. D nearest to 15.4 td.

25. From the foregoing for Figs. 2, 3, and 4 select the correct word in the following parentheses: The dg is (a) (directly, inversely) proportional to the td. The (b) (smaller, larger) the dc, the (c) (smaller, larger) the dg, and the (d) (smaller, larger) the td the finer the td control by a 1-tooth change in the dg.

26. As assigned by your instructor, sketch the draft train of a drawing frame in your plant and calculate its dc, td range, any dg required, and its fineness of td control.

Finding Draft Gears in Changing Total Drafts.

27. If td of Fig. 2, for instance, is to be changed by changing dg only, from formula (3) show that: $\text{new dg} = \dfrac{\text{dc} \times \text{Fdg}}{\text{new td}}$, $\text{old dg} = \dfrac{\text{dc} \times \text{Fdg}}{\text{old td}}$,

$$\therefore \frac{\text{new dg}}{\text{old dg}} = \frac{\dfrac{\text{dc} \times \text{Fdg}}{\text{new td}}}{\dfrac{\text{dc} \times \text{Fdg}}{\text{old td}}} = \frac{\text{old td}}{\text{new td}}, \therefore$$

$$(11)\ \text{new draft gear} = \frac{\text{old draft gear} \times \text{old total draft}}{\text{new total draft}},$$

and that by equivalent reasoning formula (11) applies to Figs. 3 and 4.

Other gears being satisfactory how many teeth in a dg, inversely proportional to the td, ought to be tried in the following 3 problems:

28. A 50-tooth dg gave 10.50 td and 11.50 td is needed?

29. At least and as near as possible to 9.75 is needed when a 36-tooth dg draws 12.90 td?

30. As near as possible to but not over 6.45 td if 8.75 td is drawn by a 32-tooth dg?

Intermediate Draft Formulas, Constants, Ranges, and Gears. What are considered intermediate drafts of a drawing frame depends upon what is considered the td of that frame, and may be the *lifter tension, lt,* between the *lifter roll, lr* (if any) and the *back roll, br;* the *break* or *back draft, bd,* between the *br* and *4th roll, for* (if any) or *3rd roll, tr;* the *back middle draft, bmd,* between the *for* and *tr;* the *middle draft, mid* (if no *for*) between the *tr* and *2nd roll, sr; front middle draft, fmd* (if any *for*) between the *tr* and *sr;* the *front draft, fd,* between the *sr* and *front roll, fr;* and the *calender tension, ct,* between the *fr* and *calender roll, cr.*

31. For Fig. 2 derive: $lt = \dfrac{1.375 \times 18 \times 94 \times 21 \times Lfg \times 18}{Brg \times Fdg \times 20 \times 30 \times 16 \times 1.5} =$

$\dfrac{61.07 \times Lfg}{Brg \times Fdg}$, ∴ since Brg in each combination of Fig. 2 is constant ∴.

(12) $\dfrac{\text{lifter tension}}{\text{constant, ltc}} = \dfrac{61.07}{\text{back roll gear}}$,

(13) $\dfrac{\text{lifter}}{\text{tension}} = \dfrac{\text{lifter tension constant} \times \text{lifter gear}}{\text{fine draft gear}}$,

(14) $\dfrac{\text{lifter}}{\text{gear}} = \dfrac{\text{lifter tension} \times \text{fine draft gear}}{\text{lifter tension constant}}$,

(15) $\dfrac{\text{back draft}}{\text{constant, bdc}} = \dfrac{.02069 \times \text{4th draft gear} \times \text{back roll gear}}{\text{5th draft gear}}$,

(16) $\dfrac{\text{back}}{\text{draft}} = \dfrac{\text{back draft constant} \times \text{fine draft gear}}{\text{back draft gear}}$,

(17) $\dfrac{\text{back draft}}{\text{gear}} = \dfrac{\text{back draft constant} \times \text{fine draft gear}}{\text{back draft}}$,

(18) $\dfrac{\text{middle}}{\text{draft}} = \dfrac{\text{dia. 2nd roll} \times \text{3rd roll gear}}{20.63}$,

(19) $\dfrac{\text{front draft}}{\text{constant, fdc}} = \dfrac{40.29 \times \text{dia. front roll} \times \text{5th draft gear}}{\text{4th draft gear} \times \text{3rd roll gear} \times \text{dia. 2nd roll}}$,

(20) $\dfrac{\text{front}}{\text{draft}} = \dfrac{\text{front draft constant} \times \text{back draft gear}}{\text{draft gear}}$,

(21) $\dfrac{\text{draft}}{\text{gear}} = \dfrac{\text{front draft constant} \times \text{back draft gear}}{\text{front draft}}$,

(22) $\dfrac{\text{calender tension}}{\text{constant, ctc}} = \dfrac{2 \times \text{front roll gear}}{\text{dia. front roll}}$, and

(23) $\dfrac{\text{calender}}{\text{tension}} = \dfrac{\text{calender tension constant}}{\text{tension gear}}$.

32. Find the tension and intermediate draft constants and ranges and md of each combination of Fig. 2.

33. By calculating with formulas (3), (16), (18), and (20) prove your selection of the correct word or words in the following parentheses: A td = the (a) (sum, product) of all its intermediate drafts. An intermediate draft = the td (b) (minus, divided by) the (c) (sum, product) of the other intermediate drafts.

34. From the foregoing select the correct sign in the parentheses: If lt and ct each appreciably < 1, td calculated from br to fr (a) (< = >) td if calculated from lr to cr. Why? If either lt or ct = 1 and the other appreciably > 1, td from br to fr (b) (< = >) td if from lr to cr. Why? If both lt and ct appreciably > 1, td from br to fr (c) (< = >) td if from lr to cr. Why?

35. Reasoning from the preceding problem what for Fig. 2 with ct at its maximum would be the td if calculated from lr to cr and its % of increase over td calculated by formula (3) at its (a) minimum (b) maximum?

36. For Fig. 3 derive

(24) back draft constant, bdc = .04018,

(25) back draft = .04018 × back draft gear,

(26) back draft gear $= \dfrac{\text{back draft}}{.04018}$,

(27) middle draft $= \dfrac{2917}{\text{front draft gear} \times \text{draft gear}}$,

(28) front draft constant, fdc = .07143,

(29) front draft = .07143 × front draft gear,

(30) front draft gear $= \dfrac{\text{front draft}}{.07143}$, and

(31) calender tension = .01614 × tension gear.

37. For Fig. 3 find the range of bd, mid, fd, and ct.

38. Find the td of Fig. 3 and the % of correction necessary if ct is increased to its maximum when td by formula (6) is at its minimum and cr is (a) smooth (b) meshing metallic with ef dia. = 1.4 × nom dia.

39. For Fig. 4 derive

(32) lifter tension $= \dfrac{\text{lifter roll gear}}{50}$,

(33) back draft = .03704 × back roll gear,

(34) back roll gear = $\dfrac{\text{back draft}}{.03704}$,

(35) $\dfrac{\text{front middle}}{\text{draft constant, fmdc}} = \dfrac{3562 \times \text{3rd draft gear}}{\text{1st draft gear}}$,

(36) $\dfrac{\text{front middle}}{\text{draft}} = \dfrac{\text{front middle draft constant}}{\text{draft gear} \times \text{back roll gear}}$, and

(37) calender tension = $\dfrac{3141}{\text{4th tension gear} \times \text{2nd tension gear}}$.

40. For Fig. 4 find the bmd, fd, and with combinations A, B, C, and D the fmdc.

41. For Fig. 4 find the range of the lt and bd; with combinations A, B, C, and D the range of fmd; and with the options in Table 2 and A and C the range of ct.

42. Reviewing your calculations of and conclusions about the lt and ct of Fig. 2 that <, =, and > 1, why do you think the td of Fig. 4, in contrast to the td of Figs. 2 and 3, is calculated from lr to cr?

Total and Actual Draft, Tensions, Grain Sliver Fed and Delivered.   In drawing frames contraction, slip, and loss of weight are negligible.

43. From the foregoing and formulas (5) and (7), Chap. III show that: When td is calculated between the br and fr and tensions < or practically = 1; or when td is calculated between lr and cr and the tensions are practically = or < 1.

(38) $\dfrac{\text{total}}{\text{draft}} = \dfrac{\text{doublings per delivery} \times \text{grain sliver fed}}{\text{grain sliver delivered}}$ and

when td is calculated between the br and fr and the tensions practically = or appreciably < 1.

(39) $\dfrac{\text{total}}{\text{draft}} = \dfrac{\text{doublings per delivery} \times \text{grain sliver fed}}{\underset{\text{if} > 1}{\text{lifter tension}} \times \underset{\text{if} > 1}{\text{calender tension}} \times \underset{\text{delivered}}{\text{grain sliver}}}$

What td is required in the following examples and 4 problems:

EXAMPLE: *Td between br and fr, lt .92, ct .96, 6 doublings, 82.5 gr. sl fed, 78.25 gr. sl delivered?*

By formula (38): td = $\dfrac{6 \times 82.5}{78.25}$ = 6.326

EXAMPLE: *Td between lr and cr, lt .98, ct 1.04, 10 doublings of 67.5 gr. sl, and 59.4 gr. sl delivered?*

By formula (38): td = $\dfrac{10 \times 67.5}{59.4}$ = 11.36

EXAMPLE: *Td between br and fr, lt .892, ct 1.12, 8 doublings, 56.4 gr. sl fed, and 62.5 gr sl delivered?*

By formula (39): $\text{td} = \dfrac{8 \times 56.4}{1.12 \times 62.5} = 6.446$

44. Td between br and fr, lt .95, ct .95, 12 doublings of 63.7 gr. sl into 56.7 gr. sl?

45. 10 doublings of 73.2 into 61.2 gr. sl, lt .998, ct 1.10, and td from br to fr?

46. 58.5 gr. sl from 8 doublings of 57.3, td between br and fr, no lr, and ct 1.13.

47. 10 doublings of 78.2 gr. sl into 68.8, td from lr to cr, lt 1.00, and ct 1.05.

Grain Sliver Fed and Delivered, Total and Intermediate Drafts, Constants, and Gears.

48. From formulas (4) and (39) for Fig. 2 derive

$$(40) \quad \frac{\text{draft}}{\text{gear}} = \frac{\begin{array}{c}\text{draft}\\\text{constant}\end{array} \times \begin{array}{c}\text{fine}\\\text{draft}\\\text{gear}\end{array} \times \begin{array}{c}\text{lifter}\\\text{tension}\\\text{if} > 1\end{array} \times \begin{array}{c}\text{calender}\\\text{tension}\\\text{if} > 1\end{array} \times \begin{array}{c}\text{grain}\\\text{sliver}\\\text{delivered}\end{array}}{\text{doublings} \times \text{grain sliver fed}}$$

$$(41) \quad \begin{array}{c}\text{grain}\\\text{sliver}\\\text{delivered}\end{array} = \frac{\text{draft gear} \times \text{doublings} \times \text{grain sliver fed}}{\begin{array}{c}\text{draft}\\\text{constant}\end{array} \times \begin{array}{c}\text{fine}\\\text{draft}\\\text{gear}\end{array} \times \begin{array}{c}\text{calender}\\\text{tension}\\\text{if} > 1\end{array} \times \begin{array}{c}\text{lifter}\\\text{tension}\\\text{if} > 1\end{array}}$$

What (a) dg, Fdg, and bdg ought to be tried on Fig. 2 to give near as possible to the gr. sl delivered and bd (b) gr. sl delivered, bd, and fd are these gears expected to yield in the following example and 2 problems:

EXAMPLE: *A with a bd no > 1.25 bd and a 1.08 ct 6 doublings of 64.8 to deliver no heavier than 60.7 gr. sl?*

From a previous problem every lt of A < 1. By formula (41) dg is directly and Fdg is inversely proportional ro gr. sl delivered and ∴ by conditions of the example any adjustment from the result of formula (40) and from the Fdg used in formula (41) must be downward; ∴ the largest Fdg is tried first. By formula (40) and a previous problem: dg =

$\dfrac{3.000 \times 88 \times 1.08 \times 60.7}{6 \times 64.8} = 44.4$; ∴ dg 44. By formula (41): gr. sl

delivered $= \dfrac{44 \times 6 \times 64.8}{3.000 \times 88 \times 1.08} = 60.0$; ∴ try an 87-tooth Fdg: gr. sl

delivered $= \dfrac{44 \times 6 \times 64.8}{3.000 \times 87 \times 1.08} = 60.7$ By formula (17) and a previous problem: $bdg = \dfrac{1.204 \times 87}{1.25} = 83.7; \therefore bdg\ 84; \therefore$ by formula (16): $bd =$

$\dfrac{1.204 \times 87}{84} = 1.25$. By formula (20) and a previous problem: $fd =$

$\dfrac{2.448 \times 84}{44} = 4.67$.

49. A with a 2.00 bd and 1.06 ct to deliver no lighter than 60.6 gr. sl from 8 doublings of 58.2

50. 12 doublings of 58.2 into no lighter than 69.2 gr. sl with B, lt and ct 1.04 each, and a 1.15 bd.

51. From formulas (7) and (39) for Fig. 3 derive

(42) $\dfrac{\text{draft}}{\text{gear}} = \dfrac{8.371 \times \dfrac{\text{back draft}}{\text{gear}} \times \dfrac{\text{calender tension}}{\text{if} > 1} \times \dfrac{\text{grain sliver}}{\text{delivered}}}{\text{doublings} \times \text{grain sliver fed}}$

and

(43) $\dfrac{\text{grain sliver}}{\text{delivered}} = \dfrac{\text{draft gear} \times \text{doublings} \times \text{grain sliver fed}}{8.371 \times \dfrac{\text{back draft}}{\text{gear}} \times \dfrac{\text{calender tension}}{\text{if} > 1}}$

What (a) Bdg, dg, and Fdg ought to be tried of Fig. 3 to give as near as possible to the bd, gr. sl delivered, and fd (b) gr. sl delivered, bd, mid, and fd are these gears expected to give in the following example and 2 problems:

EXAMPLE: *8 doublings of 56.0 into no heavier than 62.0, bd no > 1.40, fd 2.90, and ct 1.05?*

(a) By formula (26): $Bdg = \dfrac{1.40}{.04018} = 34.8; \therefore$ Bdg 34. By formula

(42): $dg = \dfrac{8.371 \times 34 \times 1.05 \times 62.0}{8 \times 56} = 41.4; \therefore$ dg 41. By formula (30):

$Fdg = \dfrac{2.90}{.07143} = 40.6$; by formula (29) a 41-tooth Fdg gives nearer the

required fd. (b) By formula (43): gr. sl delivered $= \dfrac{41 \times 8 \times 56}{8.371 \times 34 \times 1.05}$

$= 61.5$. By formula (25): $bd = .04018 \times 34 = 1.37$. By formula (27):

$mid = \dfrac{2917}{41 \times 41} = 1.73$. By formula (29): $fd = .07143 \times 41 = 2.93$.

52. No lighter than 66.8 from 6 doublings of 72.6 gr. sl, bd no > 1.20, fd 2.75, and ct 1.03?

53. 5 ends of 62.0 gr. sl and 3 of 57.0 into no lighter than 56.0 gr. sl, bd 1.40, fd 3.00, and ct (with meshing metallic cr) 1.24?

54. From formulas (10) and (38) for Fig. 4 derive

(44) $\dfrac{\text{draft}}{\text{gear}} = \dfrac{\text{draft constant} \times \text{grain sliver delivered}}{\text{doublings} \times \text{grain sliver fed}}$ and

(45) $\dfrac{\text{grain sliver}}{\text{delivered}} = \dfrac{\text{draft gear} \times \text{doublings} \times \text{grain sliver fed}}{\text{draft constant}}$

Find the (a) *teeth in the dg and brg that ought to be tried on Fig. 4 to draft near as possible to the gr. sl and bd* (b) *gr. sl, bd, and fmd these gears are expected to draft in the following 4 problems:*

55. Combination A, 6 ends of 64.5 into no heavier than 66.8 gr. sl, and bd no > 1.15.

56. Combination B, no lighter than 65 from 8 doublings of 68.5 gr. sl, and bd 1.50.

57. 10 ends of 72.6 into no heavier than 65.0 gr. sl on combination C with 1.60 bd.

58. 57.8 gr. sl from 5 ends of 62.5 and 3 ends of 64.8 with combination D and 1.45 bd.

59. As assigned by your instructor for a drawing frame in your plant derive formulas of the gr. sliver fed and delivered and gears and apply them to practical problems with the stock being run or to be run.

LAY

Meaning. The same basic considerations and formula involved in the lay of the card are involved in the lay of the drawing frame and the formula for each lay is similarly derived.

Formulas and Lays.

60. From Table 3 derive for Fig. 2

(46) $\text{lay} = \dfrac{3052 \times \text{3rd lay sprocket}}{\text{tube gear} \times \text{turntable driver gear}}$.

61. From Table 3 find the approximate lay range for each diameter of can of Fig. 2.

Table 3.   Lay Train Combinations of Fig. 2

diameter of can	15″	16″	18″	20″
1st lay sprocket, fls	32	29	25	24
3rd lay sprocket, Tls	24, 29, 33, 38	23, 28, 33, 38	26, 30, 33	26, 30
tube gear, Tg	131	129	129	129
Turntable driver gear, ttg	21	19	16	16

Table 4.   Lay Train Combinations of Fig. 3

diameter of can	15″	16″	17″	18″
8th lay gear, elg	17	15	13	11
9th lay gear, Nlg	61	63	65	67

Table 5.   Lay Train Combinations of Fig. 4

diameter of can	15″ or 16″	18″ or 20″
1st can sprocket, fcs	16 or 21	12 or 16
2nd lay sprocket, Sls	20	21
1st lay gear, flg	23	22
2nd lay gear, Slg	23	27
diameter of tube driver sheave, ts	$3\frac{1''}{16}$	$3\frac{1''}{32}$
diameter of tube sheave, Ts	$14\frac{1''}{2}$	$13\frac{3''}{8}$

Options: If necessary to adjust ct, Stng can be changed to 89 and Ftng to 34 or 36.

62. For Fig. 3 derive

$$(47) \quad \text{lay} = \frac{6.923 \times 9\text{th lay gear}}{8\text{th lay gear}}.$$

63. From Table 4 find the approximate lay for each diameter of can of Fig. 3.

64. For Fig. 4 derive

$$(48) \quad \text{lay} = \frac{39 \times 18 \times 16 \times 25 \times \frac{1\text{st lay}}{\text{gear}} \times \frac{\text{dia. tube driver}}{\text{sheave}}}{7 \times \frac{2\text{nd lay}}{\text{sprocket}} \times \frac{2\text{nd lay}}{\text{gear}} \times \frac{\text{dia. tube}}{\text{sheave}} \times \frac{1\text{st can}}{\text{sprocket}}}$$

65. From Table 5 find 2 approximate lays for each diameter of can of Fig. 4.

66. As assigned by your instructor derive the formula for and calculate the lay of a drawing frame in your plant and compare with its actual lay.

WAVE LENGTHS OF DRAFT AND LAY TRAINS

Meaning.   In any machine's draft and lay trains a malfunctioning revolving part—such as a dirty, cutting, worn, or eccentric roll; a broken, worn, or clogged gear or sprocket tooth; an eccentric or clogged sheave; or any other cause of a malfunction—obviously may leave on the machine's finished stock a repeating blemish a repeating distance apart that may be distinctive of the malfunctioning part. The blemishes most frequently and increasingly sought to be corrected are thick and thin places.

A *spectrograph*, if a sample of the finished stock is run through it, traces on a roll of paper a *spectrogram* or wavy line—with a peak at each pronounced thick place—from which can be read the thickness and distance apart of each such place in the finished stock. From the wavy appearance of this line, such a repeating distance apart of any kind repeating blemish that a given revolving part might cause is the *wave length, wl,* of that given part.

67. From the foregoing show that

(49) wave length of a   actual surface distance of the
given part in the = calender roll during 1 revolution of
draft or lay train   the given part.

If the wl of each revolving part is calculated and readily available, when the repeating distance apart of a blemish in the finished stock is read on the spectogram or otherwise measured, the malfunctioning part can be identified more readily.

68. Comparing a pulley pulling a belt, as in formula (5), Chap. (20), Part One, with a roll drawing stock answer the following: (a) What difference does stock thickness make between the SD of a roll drawing it calculated from the dia. of the roll and the actual SD of the roll calculated from its ef dia? (b) What difference does stock thickness make in the draft between two rolls of about equal diameters if stock thickness is about equal at both rolls. (c) What difference does the relatively thick stock at cr and ∴ the relatively greater ef dia. cr compared with the dia. cr have on the actual SD cr during 1 rev of any given part compared with SD cr during that rev.

Basic Wave Length Formulas. For accuracy in calculating wl of the usual range of gr sl delivered a widely accepted authority seems to use $\dfrac{\text{ef dia. cr}}{\text{dia. cr}}$ = 1.019, which ratio is used in the following.

69. Accepting the foregoing ratio prove that (a) actual SD cr = 1.019 × SD cr; ∴ (b) actual ct = 1.019 × ct; from formula (49) (c) if actual ct > 1 wl of part = 1.019 × SD cr during 1 rev part; (d) if actual ct < 1 wl a part = SD fr during 1 rev part. Why?

70. From the foregoing ratio, equations, and formula (49), if actual ct > 1 what is wl cr of (a) any drawing frame (b) Figs. 2 to 4?

71. For Fig. 2 show that: from formula (3), Chap. 111 and previous problems: (a) $\dfrac{\text{SD cr}}{\text{SD lr}}$ = lt > 1 × td × ct > 1; from (a) ∴ (b) SD cr = SD lr × lt > 1 × td × ct > 1 = cir. lr × rev lr × lt > 1 × td × ct > 1; from (b) ∴ (c) SD cr during 1 rev lr = cir. lr × 1 × lt > 1 × td × ct > 1; from formula (49), (c), and a previous problem ∴

(50)   wave length of a   cir.   product of actual tensions if > 1
given roll and parts = of the × and intermediate drafts between
integral with it   roll   the given roll and calender roll.

72. For Fig. 2 show that: from formula (49) and a previous problem

(a) $\dfrac{\text{wl Fdg}}{\text{wl fr}} = \dfrac{\text{actual SD cr during 1 rev Fdg}}{\text{actual SD cr during 1 rev fr}} = \dfrac{1.019 \times \begin{array}{c}\text{SD cr during}\\\text{1 rev Fdg}\end{array}}{1.019 \times \begin{array}{c}\text{SD cr during}\\\text{1 rev fr}\end{array}} =$

$$\frac{\text{cir. cr} \times \text{rev cr during 1 rev Fdg}}{\text{cir. cr} \times \text{rev cr during 1 rev fr}} = \frac{\dfrac{1 \times \text{Fdg} \times \text{frg}}{\text{dg} \times \text{Tng}}}{\dfrac{1 \times \text{frg}}{\text{Tng}}} = \frac{\text{Fdg}}{\text{dg}} \; ; \therefore \text{(b) wl Fdg} =$$

wl fr $\times \dfrac{\text{Fdg}}{\text{dg}}$; by similar reasoning (c) $\dfrac{\text{wl Tg}}{\text{wl cr}} = \dfrac{1.019 \times \dfrac{\text{SD cr during}}{\text{1 rev Tg}}}{1.019 \times \dfrac{\text{SD cr during}}{\text{1 rev cr}}} =$

$$\frac{\text{cir. cr} \times \dfrac{1 \times \text{Tg} \times 18 \times 21}{20 \times 19 \times \text{fls}}}{\text{cir. cr} \times 1} = \frac{.9947 \times \text{Tg}}{\text{fls}} \; ; \text{ and from (b) and (c)} \; \therefore$$

(51)   wave length of a given part   wave length of   speed ratio of
         and parts integral with it = any other part × the other part to
         in draft or lay train   in the train   the given part.

Specific Wave Length Equations and Wave Lengths.   In calculating a wl Table formulas (50) and (51) offer a choice as to what under given conditions seems systematic or to entail less labor. If already knowing the actual tensions > 1 and intermediate drafts one might first by formula (50) find the wl of each roll and the parts that revolve with it; and then by the wl of each such part and formula (51) with the least computing find the wl of every other part.

Derive the equation in inches for the wl of the part and the parts that revolve with it of the combination of Fig. 2 in the following examples and 13 problems:

EXAMPLE I: 80-*tooth gear between Tng and frg of A.*

By a previous example and formula (51): wl 80-tooth gear = wl cr $\times$ $\dfrac{80}{\text{Tng}} = 6.402 \times \dfrac{512.2}{\text{Tng}}$.

EXAMPLE II: *fr of A with a Tng (a)* < 67 *(b)* > 66.

By formula (23) and previous problems: actual ct = $1.019 \times \dfrac{65.78}{\text{Tng}}$;

$\therefore$ actual ct = $1.019 \times \dfrac{65.78}{\text{Tng if} < 67} > 1$ and actual ct = $1.019 \times \dfrac{65.78}{\text{Tng if} > 66} =$

1 or < 1. By formula (50): (a) wl fr = $\pi \times 1.125 \times 1.019 \times \dfrac{65.78}{\text{Tng} < 67}$; $\therefore$

wl fr = $\dfrac{236.9}{\text{Tng} < 67}$; (b) wl fr = $\pi \times 1.125 = 3.53$. Or (simpler in this case

due to example I) by formula (51): (a) wl fr = $\dfrac{512.2}{\text{Tng} < 67} \times \dfrac{37}{80}$; $\therefore$ wl fr =

$\dfrac{236.9}{\text{Tng} < 67}$.

EXAMPLE III: *wl br of A with a Tng < 67.*

By formulas (50), (3), and (23) and 3 previous problems: wl br =

$$\pi \times 1.375 \times td \times 1.019 \times ct = 4.402 \times \frac{3.000 \times Fdg}{dg} \times \frac{65.78}{Tng < 67}; \therefore$$

$$wl\ br = \frac{868.7}{dg \times Tng > 67}.$$

73. $wl\ Fdg\ of\ A = \dfrac{236.9 \times Fdg}{dg \times Tng < 67}$

74. $wl\ Fdg\ of\ A\ with\ Tng > 66 = \dfrac{3.535 \times Fdg}{dg}$

75. $wl\ fdg\ of\ A = \dfrac{22269}{dg \times Tng < 67}$

76. $wl\ fidg\ of\ A = \dfrac{25256}{dg \times Tng < 67}$

77. $wl\ tr\ of\ A = \dfrac{721.6 \times Bdg}{dg \times Tng < 67}$

78. $wl\ sr\ of\ A = \dfrac{386.6 \times Bdg}{dg \times Tng < 67}$

79. 40-tooth gear driving $sr\ of\ A = \dfrac{1031 \times Bdg}{dg \times Tng < 67}$

80. $wl\ fr\ of\ B = \dfrac{288.1}{Tng < 67}$

81. $wl\ sr\ of\ B = \dfrac{491.5 \times Bdg}{dg \times Tng < 67}$

82. $wl\ tr\ of\ B = \dfrac{819.2 \times Bdg}{dg \times Tng < 67}$

83. $wl\ br\ of\ B = \dfrac{864.3 \times Fdg}{dg \times Tng < 67}$

84. $wl\ lr\ of\ B = \dfrac{1066 \times Lfg}{dg \times Tng < 67}$

85. $wl\ Tg\ of\ B = \dfrac{6.366 \times Tg}{fls}$

86. Find the wl dg of combination A, Fig. 2 if Tng has (a) 66 (b) 67 teeth.

87. What is the wl lr of combination B, Fig. 2 with a dg of 42, Lfg of 84, and Tng of (a) 64 (b) 68.

88. For 20″ cans what is the wl Tg of combination B, Fig. 2?

89. As assigned by your instructor derive the wl equations for parts of a drawing frame in your plant and then calculate their wave lengths as the frame is now or about to be set up.

PRODUCTION

Basic Formulas. Drawing frame production calculations use words and abbreviations with meanings equivalent to those you studied with pickers and cards, and introduce others. Wages are usually calculated from hks delivered at cr and recorded on the *hank clock*, i.e., *clock hanks*, **chks.** But production in pounds is usually calculated from hks delivered at fr, i.e., *front roll hanks*, **fhks**, and gr sl delivered at fr.

90. From your previous study of ct select the correct sign or signs in the parentheses: fhks = chks if ct (a) ($< = >$) 1; chks > fhks if ct (b) ($< = >$) 1; gr. sl delivered at cr = grs. per yd. delivered at fr if ct (c) ($< = >$) 1; gr. sl < grs. per yd. delivered at fr if ct (d) ($< = >$) 1.

A drawing frame may have multiple *deliveries, dls,* with corresponding rolls integral.

91. Derive: from the foregoing chks $= \dfrac{\text{cir. cr} \times \text{RPM cr} \times 60 \times \text{hrs.} \times .01 \times \% \text{p}}{36 \times 840}$;

∴ (a) hks $= \dfrac{\text{dls} \times \text{cir. cr} \times \text{RPM cr} \times 60 \times \text{hours} \times .01 \times \% \text{p}}{36 \times 840}$; from for-

mula (3), Chap. III (b) ct $= \dfrac{\text{cir. cr} \times \text{RPM cr}}{\text{cir fr} \times \text{RPM fr}}$; from (a) and (b) ∴

(52) hanks =

$$\frac{\text{deliveries} \times \pi \times \begin{matrix}\text{dia.} \\ \text{front} \\ \text{roll}\end{matrix} \times \begin{matrix}\text{RPM} \\ \text{front} \\ \text{roll}\end{matrix} \times \begin{matrix}\text{calender} \\ \text{tension} \\ \text{if} > 1\end{matrix} \times \text{hours} \times .01 \times \% \text{p}}{504}$$

and from formula (30), Chap. I ∴

(53) pounds =

$$\frac{\text{deliveries} \times \pi \times \begin{matrix}\text{dia.} \\ \text{front} \\ \text{roll}\end{matrix} \times \begin{matrix}\text{RPM} \\ \text{front} \\ \text{roll}\end{matrix} \times \begin{matrix}\text{calender} \\ \text{tension} \\ \text{if} > 1\end{matrix} \times \begin{matrix}\text{grain} \\ \\ \text{sliver}\end{matrix} \times \text{hours} \times .01 \times \% \text{p}}{4200}$$

Find the production in the quantity for the Fig. with the combination and tension gear teeth in the following examples and 3 problems:

EXAMPLE: *In* (a) *hks* (b) *lbs. of 3 frames, 2 dls each, A, Fig. 2, 1350 RPM fr, 67 Tng running 60 gr. sl for 8 hrs. at 75% p.*

By formula (23), a previous problem, and correcting for sliver thickness: ct $= \dfrac{65.78}{67} \times 1.019 = 1.000$. (a) By formula (52): ∴ hks $= \dfrac{3 \times 2 \times 3.1416 \times 1.125 \times 1350 \times 8 \times .75}{504} = 340.8$. (b) By formula (26), Chap. I: ∴ lbs. $= .12 \times 340.8 \times 60 = 2454$.

EXAMPLE: 100% *lbs./hr. for* 1 *dl, Fig.* 3, 2650 *RPM fr,* 65 *tng running* 46 *gr sl.*

By formula (31) and correcting for sliver thickness: ct = .01614 × 65 × 1.019 = 1.069. By formula (53): ∴ 100% lbs./hr. =

$$\frac{3.1416 \times 1.6 \times 2650 \times 1.069 \times 46}{4200} = 156.0.$$

92. (a) 66% hks/40 hrs. (b) 66% lbs./40 hrs. of 9 frames of 2 dls each, Fig. 3, 1430 RPM fr, 66 tng, on 63 gr. sl.

93. 100% lbs./hr., 1 dl, B, Fig. 4, 1400 RPM fr, on 66 gr sl.

94. In (a) hks (b) lbs. of 4 frames, 2 dls each, C, Fig. 4 1260 RPM fr, Stng 34, Ftng 89, on 56 gr. sl for six 8-hr. shifts at 68% p.

Production Constants. Since a constant is intended as a labor saver in calculating with constant quantities, whatever quantities compose (a) production constant, pc, for Figs. 2 to 4 would depend upon the quantities in formulas (52) and (53) that under given plant conditions remain constant long enough to save labor by forming them into a convenient pc.

95. From the foregoing, formulas (30), Chap. I, and (52) show that the usually convenient

$$(54) \text{ production constant} = \frac{\pi \times \dfrac{\text{dia. front}}{\text{roll}} \times \dfrac{\text{RPM front}}{\text{roll}}}{504} = \frac{\text{IPM front roll}}{504}$$

$$= \frac{\text{FPM front roll}}{42} ; \therefore$$

$$(55) \text{ hanks} = \frac{\text{deliveries} \times \dfrac{\text{FPM}}{\text{front}}_{\text{roll}} \times \dfrac{\text{calender}}{\text{tension}}_{\text{if} > 1} \times \text{hours} \times .01 \times \dfrac{\%}{\text{production}}}{42}$$

and

$$(56) \text{ pounds} =$$

$$\frac{\text{deliveries} \times \dfrac{\text{FPM}}{\text{front}}_{\text{roll}} \times \dfrac{\text{calender}}{\text{tension}}_{\text{if} > 1} \times \dfrac{\text{grain}}{\text{sliver}} \times \text{hours} \times \dfrac{.01 \times \%}{\text{production}}}{350}$$

Find the production in the quantity for the Fig. with the combination and tension gear teeth in the following 5 problems:

96. 100%/hr. (a) hks (b) lbs./dl of Fig. 2 with A and 67 Tng on 56 gr. sl at 798.1 FPM fr.

97. 69% lbs./40 hrs. of 3 frames, 4 dls each, of Fig. 2 with B and 62 Tng on 53.2 gr. sl at 600 FPM fr.

98. 68% lbs./80 hrs. of 49.7 gr. sl on 9 frames, 2 dl each, of Fig. 3 with 67 tng at 955 FPM fr.

99. 100% lbs./dl hr. of 63.7 gr. sl at 800 FPM on Fig. 4 with A and (a) 90 Stng and 36 Ftng (b) 89 Stng and 35 Ftng.

100. 70% p (a) hks (b) lbs. of 65 gr. sl for 120 hr. on 9 2-dl Fig. 4 frames with D, 89 Stng and 34 Ftng at 800 FPM fr.

Creeling and Doffing Frequencies and Cycles. For each delivery: the *creeling frequency, cf,* is the full cans fed per hr; the *doffing frequency, dff,* is the full cans delivered per hr.; the *creeling cycle, cc,* is the minutes to empty 1 full can; the *doffing cycle, dfc,* is the minutes to fill 1 can.

101. From the foregoing and formula (56) and since waste is negligible show that

$$(57)\ \text{creeling frequency} = \frac{\text{pounds per hour per delivery}}{\text{pounds per full can fed}}$$

$$= \frac{\underset{\text{roll}}{\text{FPM front}} \times \underset{\text{tension if} > 1}{\text{calender}} \times \underset{\text{delivered}}{\text{grains sliver}} \times \underset{\text{production}}{.01 \times \%}}{350 \times \text{pounds in full can fed}},$$

$$(58)\ \underset{\text{frequency}}{\text{doffing}} = \frac{\text{pounds per hour per delivery}}{\text{pounds in full can delivered}}$$

$$= \frac{\underset{\text{roll}}{\text{FPM front}} \times \underset{\text{if} > 1}{\text{calender tension}} \times \underset{\text{delivered}}{\text{grain sliver}} \times \underset{\text{production}}{.01 \times \%}}{350 \text{ pounds in full can delivered}},$$

$$(59)\ \underset{\text{cycle}}{\text{creeling}} = \frac{60 \times \text{pounds in full can fed} \times \text{cans fed per delivery}}{\text{pounds per hour per delivery}}$$

$$= \frac{60 \times 350 \times \text{pounds in full can fed} \times \text{cans fed per delivery}}{\underset{\text{roll}}{\text{FPM front}} \times \underset{\text{if} > 1}{\text{calender tension}} \times \underset{\text{delivered}}{\text{grain sliver}} \times \underset{\text{production}}{.01 \times \%}},$$

and

$$(60)\ \underset{\text{cycle}}{\text{doffing}} = \frac{60 \times \text{pounds in full can delivered}}{\text{pounds per hour per delivery}}$$

$$= \frac{60 \times 350 \times \text{pounds in full can delivered}}{\underset{\text{roll}}{\text{FPM front}} \times \underset{\text{if} > 1}{\text{calender tension}} \times \underset{\text{delivered}}{\text{grain sliver}} \times \underset{\text{production}}{.01 \times \%}}.$$

Find the cf, dff, cc, and dfc in the following examples and 6 problems:

EXAMPLE: *8 42-lb. cans feed 1 60.8-lb. can at 92.6 lbs./hr.*

By formula (57): cf $= \dfrac{92.6}{42} = 2.20$. By formula (58): dff $= \dfrac{92.6}{60.8} =$

1.52. By formula (59): $cc = \dfrac{60 \times 42 \times 8}{92.6} = 218$. By formula (60): dfc =

$\dfrac{60 \times 60.8}{92.6} = 39.4$.

EXAMPLE: *8 42-lb. cans feed 1 60.8-lb can of 60.2 gr. sl on combination A, Fig. 2 with a 67 Tng at 795 FPM fr and 69% p.*

By formula (23) corrected for thickness: $ct = \dfrac{65.78}{67} \times 1.019 =$

1.000. By formula (57): $cf = \dfrac{780 \times 60.2 \times .69}{350 \times 42} = 2.20$. By formula (58):

$dff = \dfrac{780 \times 60.2 \times .69}{350 \times 60.8} = 1.52$. By formula (59): $cc = \dfrac{60 \times 350 \times 42 \times 8}{780 \times 60.2 \times .69} =$

218. By formula (60): $dfc = \dfrac{60 \times 350 \times 60.8}{780 \times 60.2 \times .69} = 39.4$.

102. *10* 81.7-lb. cans into *1* 59.4-lb. can at 96.6 lbs./dl/hr.

103. *6* 54.3-lb. cans fed per 52.8-lb. can delivered at 114 lbs./dl/hr.

104. *12* 80.8-lb. cans feed *1* 64.2-lb. can of 67.2 gr. sl on combination B, Fig. 2 with a 63 Tng at 696 FPM fr and 65% p.

105. Fig. 3 with a 65 tng feeding *8* 77.3-lb. cans of 56.1 gr. sl into *1* 32.6-lb. can of 60.6 gr. sl at 810 FPM fr and 70% p.

106. Combination A, Fig. 4 running *10* 85-lb. cans into *1* 37.2-lb. can of 60.5 gr. sl at 775 FPM fr and .72% p.

107. *8* 55.5-lb. cans per dl into 46.6-lb. cans of 60.5 gr. sl on combination D, Fig. 4 at 800 FPM fr and 66.6% p.

Chapter X

SLIVER LAPPER CALCULATIONS

DRAFT

Total Draft. The *total mechanical draft, td,* of a sliver lapper as in Figs. 1 and 2 is usually calculated between the *lifter roll, lr,* as the feed roll, and the *back drum, bdm,* as the delivery roll, against which and the *front drum, fdm,* the *lap* is pressed to wind it onto the *lap spool* (not shown).

    1. From the foregoing and Figs. 1 and 2 select the correct sign, word or words in the parentheses: RPM fdm is (a) ($< = >$) bdm. Why? If RPM bdm is + RPM fdm is (b) (+, −). Why? If RPM bdm is constant SS bdm is (c) (constant, variable), SS spool of lap is (d) (variable, constant), dia. spool of lap is (e) (constant, decreasing, increasing) and effective dia. bdm is (f) (variable, constant). Why?

    2. From the foregoing and your study of previous carding department machines derive

$$(1) \quad \text{total draft} = \frac{\text{SS of drums}}{\text{SS of lifter rolls}}.$$

Fig. 1 is designed for 8 or 10 doublings, db, at each lr or a total of 16 to 20 db, and Fig. 2 for 16 to 20 db at the lr of each *area* or a total of 48 to 60 db. On Fig. 2 the stock fed at each area leaves the *table calender rolls, tcr,* of that area as a web with the back area web passing through the middle tcr under the middle area web, the middle and back webs passing through the front tcr under the front web.

Table 1. Draft Train Combinations of Fig. 2

	A	B	C	D
teeth in back roll gear, Bg	51	51	63	63
teeth in back drum driven sprocket, Bds	63	62	63	62

    3. Find the td and dc of Fig. 1.

    4. From Fig. 2, Table 2, and the foregoing description prove

$$td = \frac{18.6875 \times 17 \times 17 \times 42 \times 30 \times 17 \times 65 \times Bg \times 15 \times 24 \times 21}{Bds \times 80 \times 22 \times 20 \times 33 \times 26 \times dg \times 14 \times 26 \times 21 \times 1.375}$$

$$= \frac{179.08 \times Bg}{Bds \times dg}.$$

Draft Constants, Gears, Ranges, and Control.

5. From the preceding problem show that for each area of Fig. 2

(2) draft constant $= \dfrac{179.08 \times \text{back roll gear}}{\text{back drum driven sprocket}}$,

(3) total draft $= \dfrac{\text{draft constant}}{\text{draft gear}}$, and

(4) draft gear $= \dfrac{\text{draft constant}}{\text{total draft}}$

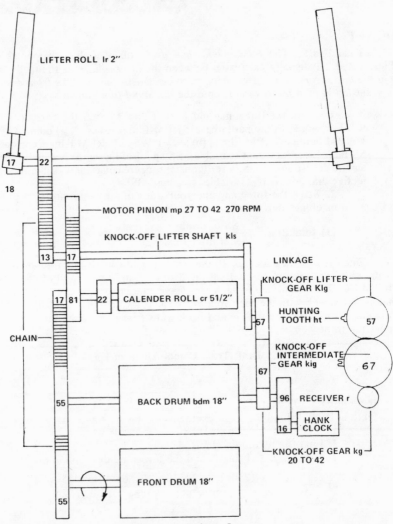

Figure 1.   Sliver Lapper

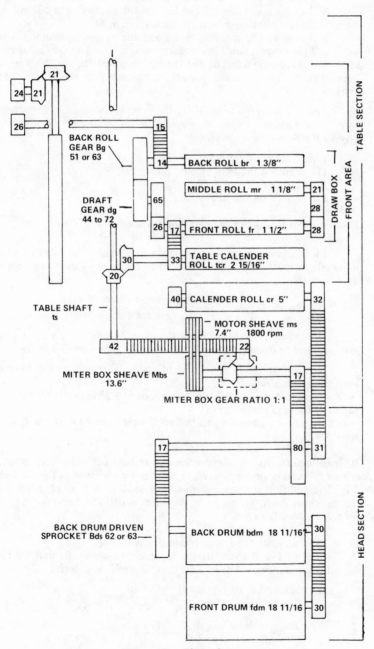

Figure 2.   Sliver Lapper

6. Find the dc of combinations A, B, C, and D of Fig. 2.

7. Find the td range of combinations A, B, C, and D of Fig. 2.

8. For each combination of Fig. 2 how precise is td control by a 1-tooth change from (a) minimum (b) maximum td?

9. From an applicable formula and the preceding problem select for Fig. 2 the correct word in the parentheses: td and dg are (a) (directly, inversely) proportional. The (b) (larger, smaller) the dg the finer the control of td. The (c) (less, greater) the td the finer the control of td. Why?

Find the (a) *teeth in the dg of the combination of Fig. 2 that ought to be tried to give as close as possible to the td and* (b) *td this dg will give in the following 4 problems:*

10. A but not over 2.15.

11. B but on the light side of 2.75.

12. C but not under 3.50.

13. D 4.10 on the heavy side.

Finding Draft Gears in Changing Total Draft.

14. As you proved with previous machines, if the dg and td are inversely proportional and the td must be changed by changing only the dg, prove that

$$(5) \text{ new draft gear} = \frac{\text{old draft gear} \times \text{old total draft}}{\text{new total draft}}$$

How many teeth in the dg of the sliver lapper with its dg inversely proportional to its td ought to be tried in the following 3 problems:

15. A 50-tooth dg gives 2.93 td and as near as possible to and at least 3.45 td is needed?

16. As near as possible to but not over 3.25 is needed where 3.45 td is run by a 53-tooth dg?

17. Close as possible to but no lighter than 4.00 td if a 46-tooth runs 3.92 td?

Intermediate Drafts. *Calender tension, ct,* between the cr and the nearest previous roll and *drum tension, dt,* cr to bdm are common to Figs. 1 and 2; while Fig. 2 in addition at each area has *lifter tension, lt,* lr to br, *back draft, bd,* br to mr, *front draft, fd,* mr to fr, *draw box draft, dbd,* br to fr, and *table calender tension, tct,* fr to tcr.

18. Calculate the intermediate drafts of Fig. 1.

19. For Fig. 2 calculate the (a) intermediate drafts that are fixed for all combinations (b) dt of each combination; and derive

$$(6) \frac{\text{back and draw box draft}}{\text{combinations A and B}} = \frac{139.10}{\text{dg}} \text{ and}$$

$$(7) \frac{\text{back and draw box draft}}{\text{combinations C and D}} = \frac{171.82}{\text{dg}}.$$

20. For Fig. 2 (a) find by formula (7) and your other answers to the preceding problem the product of the intermediate drafts of combination D, and (b) find and explain the difference between your answer to (a) and the td of combination D by formula (3).

21. Find the dbd range of each combination of Fig. 2.

22. If your plant has a sliver lapper and as assigned by your instructor sketch its draft train, derive formulas for its variable total and intermediate drafts and draft gears, if any, and calculate its fixed and variable drafts and draft gears.

Total Draft, Grain Sliver, Grain Lap, and Draft Gears.

23. From the previously described relative position of the web from each area of Fig. 2 and your reasoning about the effect of stock thickness at the drawing frame cr select the correct sign in the parentheses: The back web would be drafted (a) $(<=>)$ and the front web (b) $(<=>)$ the middle web unless the back dg is (c) $(<=>)$ and the front dg is (d) $(<=>)$ the front dg. Why? On any sliver lapper the ad tends to be slightly (e) $(<, >)$ the td. Why?

24. Since sliver lapper contraction, slip, and waste are negligible, with the exception in the preceding problem show that: from formula (5), Chap. III, td = ad; from formula (8), Chap. III, for any sliver lapper ∴.

$$(8)\ \text{total draft} = \frac{\text{doublings} \times \text{grain sliver}}{\text{grain lap}} \ ; \therefore$$

$$(9)\ \text{grain sliver} = \frac{\text{total draft} \times \text{grain lap}}{\text{doublings}} \ ;$$

from formulas (8) and (3) ∴ $\dfrac{\text{db} \times \text{gr. sl}}{\text{gr. lap}} = \dfrac{\text{dc}}{\text{dg}}$; for fig. 2 ∴

$$(10)\ \text{draft gear} = \frac{\text{draft constant} \times \text{grain lap}}{\text{doublings} \times \text{grain sliver}} \ ,$$

$$(11)\ \text{grain lap} = \frac{\text{draft gear} \times \text{doublings} \times \text{grain sliver}}{\text{draft constant}} \ ,$$

and

$$(12)\ \text{grain sliver} = \frac{\text{draft constant} \times \text{grain lap}}{\text{doublings} \times \text{draft gear}}$$

25. Find the td if 16 db of 50 gr. sl must yield 800 gr. lap.

26. What is the td if 900 gr. lap is to be drawn from 58.5 gr. sl doubled 60?

27. On Fig. 1 find the gr. sl required to double (a) 16 to run 1000 gr. lap (b) 20 for 1060 gr. lap.

28. What (a) dg on combination A, Fig. 2 is needed to run 62.4 gr. sl 48 ends up into as close as possible to 960 gr. lap (b) gr. lap will this dg run?

29. On combination B, Fig. 2 find the (a) teeth in dg to draw 63.3

gr. sl 60 ends creeled into as close as possible to but no heavier than 1122 gr. lap (b) gr. lap this dg will draw.

30. What (a) gr. sl is needed on combination D, Fig. 2 to draft as close to but no lighter than 1200 gr. lap from 60 db with a 72-tooth dg (the heaviest available) (b) gr. lap will this gr. sl deliver?

Finding Draft Gears in Changing Grain Sliver, Grain Lap, and Doublings

31. Substituting the value of td from formula (8) derive for any sliver lapper with a changeable dg

$$(13) \quad \frac{\text{new draft gear}}{} = \frac{\text{old draft gear} \times \text{old doublings} \times \text{old grain sliver} \times \text{new grain lap}}{\text{new doublings} \times \text{new grain sliver} \times \text{old grain lap}}.$$

Find the teeth in a dg that ought to be tried in the following example and 3 problems:

EXAMPLE: *950 gr. lap run by a 60-tooth dg; 1000 gr. lap required from the same db of the same gr. sl.*

By formula (13): new dg $= \dfrac{60 \times 1000}{950} = 63$.

32. A 46-tooth dg runs from 48 db of 58-gr. sl; 60 db of 50-gr. sl on the light side to be run into the same gr. lap.

33. With the same db into the same gr. lap 60 gr. sl is to be fed instead of 56.8 with a 66-tooth dg.

34. As close as possible to 1060 gr. lap, any difference being on the heavy side, run from 60 db of 58 gr. sl. The present 900 gr. lap is run from 48 db of 50 gr. sl by a 70-tooth dg.

PRODUCTION

Formulas, FPM of Drum, Hanks, and Pounds. Sliver lapper production calculations use words and abbreviations with meanings equivalent to those you studied with previous carding department machines.

35. Derive formulas for FPM bdm of Figs. 1 and 2.

36. Find the range of FPM bdm of Fig. (a) 1 (b) 2 neglecting belt thickness.

37. For all sliver lappers derive

$$(14) \quad \text{hanks} = \frac{\text{FPM drum} \times \text{hours} \times .01 \times \% \text{ production}}{42}$$

and from formula (30), Chap. 1 and formula (13)

$$(15) \quad \text{pounds} = \frac{\text{FPM drum} \times \text{hours} \times \text{grain lap} \times .01 \times \% \text{ production}}{350}$$

Find the production in hks. and lbs. in the following 4 problems:

38. 850 gr. lap on Fig. 1 with a 28-tooth mp at 82% p for 8 hrs.

39. 6 sliver lappers as in Fig. 1 each with a 40-tooth mp running 920 gr. lap at 87%/120 hrs.

40. 980 gr. lap at 91%/120 hrs. on 6 Fig. 2 sliver lappers each with a (a) 62- (b) 63-tooth Bds.

41. If your plant operates a sliver lapper, as assigned by your instructor solve practical production problems dealing with it.

Knock-Off Constants and Gears; Quantities in Full Rolls.

42. For Figs. 1 and 2 derive: yds. of lap $= \dfrac{\text{rev bdm} \times \pi \times \text{dia. bdm}}{36}$

and ∴

(16) $\dfrac{\text{yards of lap}}{\text{for Fig. 1}} = 1.5708 \times$ revolutions of knock-off gear.

In the following 3 problems review your reasoning in deriving formulas for the picker knock-off and compare with Fig. 1:

43. In Fig. 1 what (a) corresponds to the picker drop shaft (b) moves the linkage?

44. Between successive meshings of ht with r what must be the (a) rev Klg (b) and ∴ rev kg?

45. Substituting the value of rev kg from the preceding problem into formula (16) derive: yds. $= 1.5708 \times \dfrac{67 \times 57}{\text{kg}}$.

(17) yards in full roll $= \dfrac{5998.9}{\text{knock-off gear}}$; ∴

(18) hanks in full roll $= \dfrac{7.1415}{\text{knock-off gear}}$;

and from formula (30), Chap. 1 and formula (17) ∴

(19) pounds in full roll $= \dfrac{.857 \times \text{grain lap}}{\text{knock-off gear}}$; and ∴

(20) $\dfrac{\text{knock-off}}{\text{gear}} = \dfrac{5998.9}{\text{yards in full roll}} = \dfrac{7.1415}{\text{hanks in full roll}}$

$= \dfrac{.857 \times \text{grain lap}}{\text{pounds in full roll}}$.

46. For Fig. 1 what (a) would be called the knock-off constant (b) is the range of yds. (c) hks?

On Fig. 1 find the (a) teeth in kg that ought to be tried to deliver as near as possible to the quantity in a full roll (b) the quantity this kg is expected to deliver in each of the following 4 problems:

47. 250 yds.

48. Quarter hk.

49. 15 lbs. of 450 gr. lap

50. No less than 25 lbs. of 1050 gr. lap.

Creeling and Doffing Frequencies and Cycles. Creeling and doffing words and abbreviations mean the same as in your study of drawing frames, except the doffing units are full rolls of lap.

51. Waste and slip being negligible, by formula (14) derive

(22) $\dfrac{\text{creeling}}{\text{frequency}} = \dfrac{\text{pounds per hour delivered}}{\text{pounds in full can}}$

$= \dfrac{\text{FPM drum} \times \text{grain lap} \times .01 \times \% \text{ production}}{350 \times \text{pounds in full can}}$

(23) $\dfrac{\text{doffing}}{\text{frequency}} = \dfrac{\text{pounds per hour delivered}}{\text{pounds in full roll}}$

$= \dfrac{\text{FPM drum} \times \text{grain lap} \times .01 \times \% \text{ production}}{350 \times \text{pounds in full roll}}$

(24) $\dfrac{\text{creeling}}{\text{cycle}} = \dfrac{60}{\text{creeling frequency}}$

$= \dfrac{60 \times 350 \times \text{pounds in full can}}{\text{FPM drum} \times \text{grain lap} \times .01 \times \% \text{ production}}$; and

(25) $\dfrac{\text{doffing}}{\text{cycle}} = \dfrac{60}{\text{doffing frequency}}$

$= \dfrac{60 \times 350 \times \text{pounds in full roll}}{\text{FPM drum} \times \text{grain lap} \times .01 \times \% \text{ production}}$.

Solve the following examples and 4 problems by the parts of formulas (22) to (25) that involve the least calculating.

EXAMPLE: *For 1 sliver lapper find the* (a) *full cans creeled per hr.* (b) *minutes to empty 1 full can* (c) *full rolls doffed per hr.* (d) *minutes to fill 1 roll with 35 lbs. in full cans, 24 lbs. in full rolls at 375 lbs./hr.*

(a) By formula (22): cf $= \dfrac{375}{35} = 10.7$

(b) By formula (24): cc $= \dfrac{60}{10.7} = 5.61$.

(c) By formula (23): dff $= \dfrac{375}{24} = 15.6$

(d) By formula (25): dfc $= \dfrac{60}{15.6} = 3.85$.

EXAMPLE: *Find the* (a) *full cans emptied per hr.* (b) *full rolls delivered per hr. by 1 sliver lapper with 50 lbs. in full cans, 26-lb. full rolls of 850 gr. lap at 180 FPM and 82% p.*

(a) By formula (22): $cf = \dfrac{180 \times 850 \times .01 \times 82}{350 \times 50} = \dfrac{358.46}{50} = 7.17.$

(b) By formula (23): $df = \dfrac{358.46}{26} = 13.8.$

52. Find the cf, cc, dff, and dfc for 1 machine with 55-lb. full cans and 28-lb. full rolls at 480 lbs./hr.

53. On Fig. 1 with a 40-tooth mp, 60-lb. full cans and 30-lb. full rolls of 1000 gr. lap what is its cf, dff, cc, and dfc at 80% p.

54. On Fig. 2 with a 63-tooth Bds, 60-lb. full cans, and 30-lb. full rolls of 1000 gr. lap what is its cf, dff, cc, and dfc at 90% p.

55. What is the work load in (a) cans creeled (b) rolls doffed per hr. of one tending 6 sliver lappers with 35-lb. full cans, 26-lb. full rolls of 980 gr. lap at 82.5% p. and 190 FPM bdm?

Chapter XI

COMBER CALCULATIONS

NIPS

Meanings. The cycle of a comber from the *nippers* at each *head* seizing a tuft of lap to be combed to seizing the next tuft is a *nip*. Refer to Figs. 1 and 4. A *nip of lap* is the amount of uncombed lap fed by the *feed roll, fr,* from the *lap rolls, lr,* and seized by the nippers at each head during a nip. A *nip of sliver* is the amount of combed sliver released by the nippers, detached by the *detaching rolls, dr,* and taken up by the *pan calender rolls, pcr,* at each head during a nip. A *nip of noils* is the amount of shorter fiber, neps, and trash combed out of a nip of lap by the *needles* of the *cylinder, cy,* and of the *top comb* and brushed out of both by the *brush* on the *brush shaft, brs,* at each head during a nip. A nip of lap, sliver, or noils means also the total amount from all the heads during a nip. Thus, referring to Figs. 2 and 5, a nip of sliver means also the amount delivered by the *coiler calender rolls, ccr,* during a nip into the can or cans. The speed of a comber is rated in *nips per minute, npm.*

Basic Formula. Since the cylinder revolves once during one nip

(1) nips per minute = RPM cylinder

PERCENTS OF SLIVER AND NOILS

Meanings. The *percent of sliver, % sliver or % sl,* and *percent of noils, % no,* mean the weights of, respectively, the sliver and noils delivered expressed as percents of the weight of lap fed during any time or number of nips.

Basic Formulas.

1. Since fiber and trash escaping the sliver and noils is negligible show that during any time or number of nips

(2) weight of lap = weight of sliver + weight of noils ∴

(3) percent of sliver = $\dfrac{100 \times \text{weight of sliver}}{\text{weight of sliver} + \text{weight of noils}}$

and

(4) percent of noils = $\dfrac{100 \times \text{weight of noils}}{\text{weight of sliver} + \text{weight of noils}}$

Usually an authority in a plant, often the laboratory, decides the % sl and % no that should be run. This decision may be based on the strength, evenness, appearance, or other qualities desired in the product. A plant combing raw stock that varies in average staple length from one batch to another or combing less variable stock for varying products may make frequent changes in % sl and % no. Adjusting the comber to obtain the percents desired is often left to the fixer's judgment. Whether the decided percents are being run is determined by calculating, whoever does it.

2. The noils for the staple and goods being run must not exceed 5%. The fixer parts each sliver just under the bite of ccr and each noils on a straight line even with the floor. He runs 30 nips, parts sliver and noils as before, and finds these nips to weigh 976 and 57 grains, respectively. Which way and by what percent must he change the noils?

3. The % no for the long staple and fine counts being run must be 20. 35 nips of sliver, from just after the bite of the pcr, and of noils, from the same head, weigh 146 and 37 grs. respectively. What does this test indicate?

4. As assigned by your instructor, test and calculate % sl and % no being run on a comber and compare with your plant's standard.

DRAFT — TOTAL DRAFT

Determining Total Draft.   Not only is loss of weight from the stock practically all in the noils but slippage and contraction are negligible.

5. Letting *total draft, td,* mean total mechanical draft, show that: from this chapter thus far and formula (5), Chap. III

$$(5)\ \frac{\text{total}}{\text{draft}} = \frac{\text{actual}}{\text{draft}} \times .01 \times \frac{\text{percent}}{\text{of sliver}} = \frac{\text{actual}}{\text{draft}} \times \left(1 - .01 \times \frac{\text{percent}}{\text{of noils}}\right)$$

and substituting from formula (9), Chap. III and formula (5)

$$(6)\ \frac{\text{total}}{\text{draft}} = \frac{\text{laps} \times \frac{\text{grain}}{\text{lap}} \times .01 \times \frac{\text{percent}}{\text{of sliver}}}{\text{slivers} \times \text{grain sliver}}$$

$$= \frac{\text{laps} \times \frac{\text{grain}}{\text{lap}} \times \left(1 - .01 \times \frac{\text{percent of}}{\text{noils}}\right)}{\text{slivers} \times \text{grain sliver}}.$$

Determine the td in the following 4 problems if:

6. Ad is 54 with 88% sl.

7. With 10.5% no ad is 72.5.

8. 6 90-gr. slivers and 90% sl are run from 6 1800-gr. laps.

9. 8 850-gr. laps give 11.5% no and 2 60-gr. slivers.

10. 12 910-gr. laps run 2 65-gr. slivers and 13% no.

Meaning and Basic Formula of Total Draft.   In the meaning of formula (3), Chap. III the td of the comber in Figs. 1 and 2 and of the comber in Figs. 3,

4, and 5 is from the *lap roll, lr,* to the *coiler calender roll, ccr;* and ∴ lr is the feed roll, although another roll is named the *feed roll, fr.*

11. From formula (3), Chap. III and the foregoing show that

$$(7) \frac{\text{total}}{\text{draft}} = \frac{\text{surface speed of coiler calender roll}}{\text{surface speed of lap roll}}.$$

INTERMEDIATE DRAFTS

Meanings. Before further pursuing the study of total draft it is clarifying to study the intermediate drafts that compose it. The intermediate drafts of Figs. 1 and 2 and of Figs. 3 to 5 may be called: *feed tension, ft,* lr to fr; *detaching draft, dd,* fr to dr; *pan tension, pt,* dr to pcr; *table tension, tt,* pcr to fi; *draw box draft, dbd,* fi to cr; and *coiler calender tension, cct,* cr to ccr. But dbd is composed of *back draft, bd,* fi to fo; *back middle draft, bmd,* fo to t; *front middle draft, fmd,* t to s; *front draft, fd,* s to f; and *calender tension, ct,* f to cr.

Tension Limits. In plant practice tensions are seldom calculated. Authorities differ about tensions. One widely respected opinion, which for the sake of definiteness *this chapter* uses unless otherwise specified, seems to recommend tensions of 1.026 *as standard* provided at least a 1-tooth adjustment either way in each tension is left to the fixer's judgment.

Significant Digits. As with carding department machines previously studied carrying drafts and draft constants to 3 significant digits is usually sufficiently accurate. However, in this chapter for later verification *carry draft constants and unchangeable drafts to 5 significant digits.*

Basic Formulas, Intermediate Draft Constants, Ranges, Ratchets, and Gears.

12. From Figs. 1 and 4 and formula (3), Chap. III show that

$$\text{ft} = \frac{\text{SS Fr}}{\text{SS Lr}} = \frac{\pi \times \text{dia. Fr} \times \text{RPM Fr}}{\pi \times \text{dia. Lr} \times \text{RPM Lr}} = \frac{\text{dia. Fr} \times \dfrac{\text{npm}}{\text{Fr}}}{\text{dia. Lr} \times \dfrac{\text{npm}}{\text{Lr}}}$$

$$= \frac{\text{dia. Fr} \times \text{Lr}}{\text{dia. Lr} \times \text{Fr}} ; \therefore$$

(8) $\dfrac{\text{feed tension}}{\text{constant}} = \dfrac{\text{dia. feed roll}}{\text{dia. lap roll}}.$

(9) $\dfrac{\text{feed}}{\text{tension}} = \dfrac{\text{feed tension constant} \times \text{lap ratchet}}{\text{feed ratchet}}$, and

(10) $\dfrac{\text{lap ratchet}}{\text{feed ratchet}} = \dfrac{\text{feed tension}}{\text{feed tension constant}}.$

13. Find the feed tension (a) constant (b) range of Figs. 1 and 2.
14. Find the feed tension (a) constant (b) range of Figs. 3 to 5.
15. What Lr and Fr give most nearly the aforesaid standard ft and

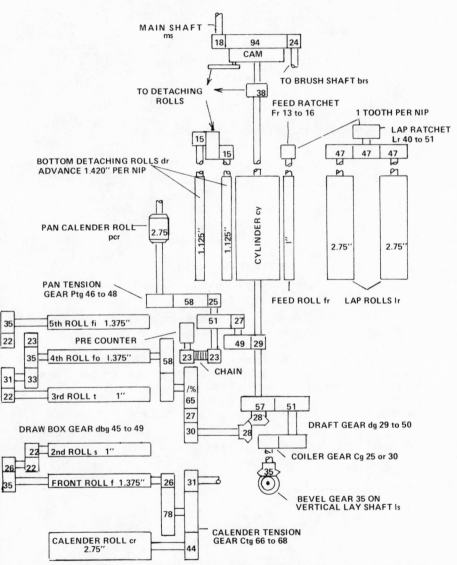

Figure 1. Drive, 8th Head, Draw Box, and Lay Shaft of Single-Side 8-Head Comber for 2 Cans and Which Can Be Rearranged for 1 Can and a Split Sliver

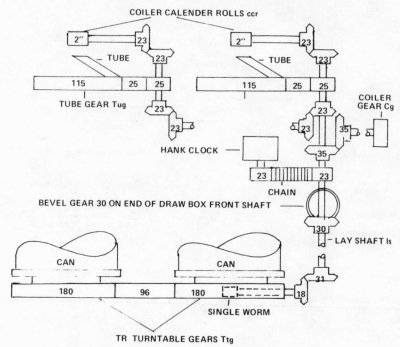

COILER CALENDER ROLLS ccr

TUBE GEAR Tug

HANK CLOCK

COILER GEAR Cg

CHAIN

BEVEL GEAR 30 ON END OF DRAW BOX FRONT SHAFT

LAY SHAFT ls

CAN

CAN

SINGLE WORM

TR TURNTABLE GEARS Ttg

Figure 2.   Two-Can Worm Gear Lay Train of Figure 1

allow at least 1-tooth adjustment of each either way and what ft would
these ratchets give on (a) Fig. 1 and (b) Fig. 4.

The *detaching rolls,* **dr,** by detaching and carrying forward a nip of
stock and returning it combed for piecing it with the next nip make the *net
advance per nip,* **apn,** shown in Figs. 1 and 4.

16. From Figs. 1 and 4 and formula (3), Chap. III show that

$$dd = \frac{SS\ dr}{SS\ fr} = \frac{apn \times npm}{\pi \times dia.\ fr \times RPM\ fr} = \frac{apn \times npm}{\pi \times dia.\ fr \times \dfrac{npm}{Fr}}$$

$$= \frac{apn \times Fr}{\pi \times dia.\ fr},\ \therefore$$

(11) $\dfrac{\text{detaching}}{\text{draft}}\ \text{constant} = \dfrac{\text{advance per nip}}{\pi \times \text{dia. feed roll}},$

(12) $\dfrac{\text{detaching}}{\text{draft}} = \dfrac{\text{detaching}}{\text{draft}}\ \text{constant} \times \dfrac{\text{feed}}{\text{ratchet}},$ and

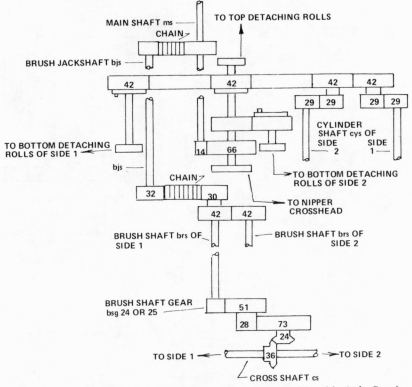

Figure 3.   Drive for Both Sides and up to Cross Shaft of Double-Side Comber

$$(13) \text{ feed ratchet} = \frac{\text{detaching draft}}{\text{detaching draft constant}}.$$

17. Find the dd (a) constant (b) range of Fig. 1.

18. Find the dd (a) constant (b) range of Fig. 4.

19. With the fr that you found would give the aforesaid standard ft what would be the dd of (a) Fig. 1 (b) Fig. 4?

20. Similarly from Figs. 1 and 3 and 4 and formula (1) derive

$$\text{pt Fig. 1} = \frac{\text{SS pcr}}{\text{SS dr}} = \frac{\dfrac{\text{RPM cy} \times 29 \times 27 \times 25 \times 2.75 \times \pi}{49 \times 51 \times \text{ptg}}}{\text{apn} \times \text{npm}}$$

$$= \frac{29 \times 27 \times 25 \times 2.75 \times \pi}{1.42 \times 49 \times 51 \times \text{ptg}} \; ; \; \therefore$$

(14) pan tension constant Fig. 1 = 47.657,

$$(15) \text{ pan tension Fig. 1} = \frac{47.657}{\text{pan tension gear}},$$

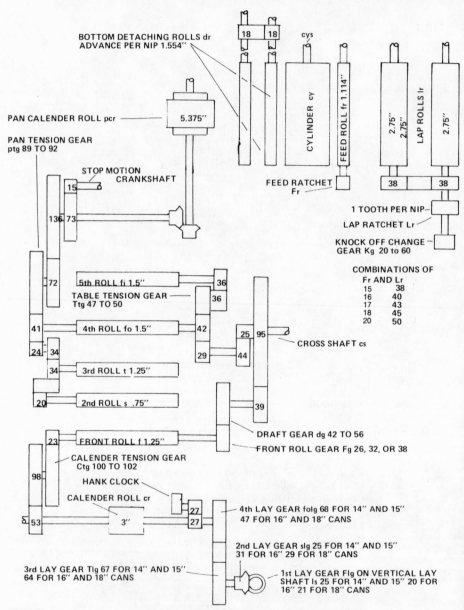

Figure 4.   6th Head, Train from Cross Shaft of Figure 3, Draw Box, and up to Lay Shaft of #1 Side of Double-Side Comber

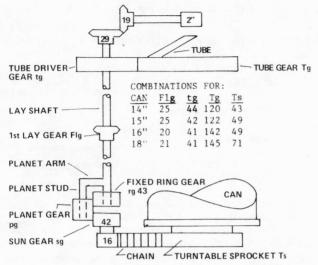

Figure 5.   Epicyclic Lay Train of Figure 4

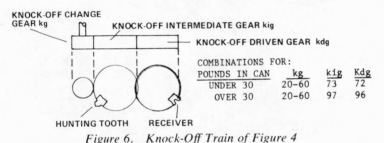

Figure 6.   Knock-Off Train of Figure 4

(16) pan tension gear Fig. 1 $= \dfrac{47.657}{\text{pan tension}}$,

(17) pan tension constant Fig. 4 $= 3.7328$,

(18) pan tension Fig. 4 $= \dfrac{3.7328 \times \text{brush shaft gear}}{\text{pan tension gear}}$, and

(19) pan tension gear Fig. 4 $= \dfrac{3.7328 \times \text{brush shaft gear}}{\text{pan tension}}$.

21. Find the pt range of Fig. 1.

22. Find the pt range of Figs. 3 and 4 with bsg of (a) 24 (b) 25 teeth.

23. What ptg gives most nearly the aforesaid standard pt and allows a 1-tooth adjustment either way and what pt would this ptg give (a) on Fig. 1 and on Fig. 3 with a bsg of (b) 24 (c) 25 teeth?

24. Similarly derive

(20) table tension constant Fig. 1 = .00048586,

(21) table tension Fig. 1 = .00048586 × $\dfrac{\text{pan}}{\text{tension}}$ × $\dfrac{\text{draw}}{\text{box}}$, $\dfrac{}{\text{gear}}$ $\dfrac{}{\text{gear}}$

(22) draw box gear Fig. 1 = $\dfrac{\text{table tension}}{.00048586 \times \text{pan tension gear}}$.

(23) table tension constant Fig. 4 = .53999,

(24) table tension Fig. 4 = $\dfrac{.53999 \times \text{pan tension gear}}{\text{table tension gear}}$, and

(25) table tension gear Fig. 4 = $\dfrac{.53999 \times \text{pan tension gear}}{\text{table tension}}$.

25. Find the tt range of Fig. 1.

26. Find the tt range of Fig. 4.

27. With the gears that you have found would give most nearly the aforesaid standard pt what gear would give most nearly the aforesaid best tt but allowing at least a 1-tooth adjustment either way and what tt would this gear give on (a) Fig. 1 (b) Fig. 4?

28. Similarly derive

(26) draw box draft constant Figs. 1 and 2 = $\dfrac{206.90}{\text{coiler gear}}$,

(27) draw box draft Figs. 1 and 2 = $\dfrac{206.90 \times \text{draft gear}}{\text{coiler gear} \times \text{draw box gear}}$,

(28) draw box draft constant Fig. 4 = 12.574,

(29) draw box draft Fig. 4 = $\dfrac{12.574 \times \dfrac{\text{draft}}{\text{gear}} \times \dfrac{\text{table tension}}{\text{gear}}}{\dfrac{\text{calender tension}}{\text{gear}} \times \dfrac{\text{front roll}}{\text{gear}}}$, and

(30) draft gear Fig. 4 = $\dfrac{\dfrac{\text{draw}}{\text{box draft}} \times \dfrac{\text{calender}}{\text{tension gear}} \times \dfrac{\text{front}}{\text{roll gear}}}{12.574 \times \text{table tension gear}}$.

29. In Figs. 1 and 2 what is the dbd constant and dbd range with the dbg that most nearly gives the aforesaid best tension allowing at least a 1-tooth adjustment either way and a cg of (a) 30 (b) 25 teeth?

30. In Fig. 4 what is the dbd range with the gears that give the aforesaid best tension allowing at least a 1-tooth adjustment either way and a Fg of (a) 38-(b) 32-(c) 26-teeth?

31. (a) Find the back draft of Fig. 1 (b) derive

(31) back draft constant Fig. 4 = .023810

(32) back draft Fig. 4 = .023810 × table tension gear.

(c) With the ttg that gives most nearly the aforesaid best tt what is the bd of Fig. 4?

32. Find the back middle draft of (a) Fig. 1 (b) Fig. 4.

33. Derive

(33) front middle draft constant Figs. 1 and 2 $= \dfrac{11765}{\text{coiler gear}}$, and

(34) $\dfrac{\text{front middle draft}}{\text{Figs. 1 and 2}} = \dfrac{11765 \times \text{draft gear}}{\begin{array}{c}\text{coiler} \\ \text{gear}\end{array} \times \begin{array}{c}\text{draw} \\ \text{box}\end{array} \times \begin{array}{c}\text{calender} \\ \text{tension} \\ \text{gear}\end{array}}$.

34. In Figs. 1 and 2 find the fmd constant and fmd range with the gears that most nearly give the aforesaid best tension and allow at least 1-tooth adjustments and with a cg of (a) 30 (b) 25 teeth.

35. Find the fmd of Fig. 4.

36. (a) Find the fd of Fig. 1 (b) Derive

(35) front draft constant Fig. 4 $= \dfrac{3.5633}{\text{front roll gear}}$ and

(36) front draft Fig. 4 = front draft constant × draft gears.

37. In Fig. 4 find the fd constant and fd range with a Fg of (a) 38 (b) 32 (c) 26 teeth.

38. Derive

(37) calender tension constant Fig. 1 = .015152,

(38) calender tension Fig. 1 = .015152 × calender tension gear,

(39) calender tension constant Fig. 4 = 102.07, and

(40) calender tension Fig. 4 $= \dfrac{102.07}{\text{calender tension gear}}$

39. What ct is given by the Ctg that allows a 1-tooth adjustment either way on (a) Fig. 1 (b) Fig. 4?

40. Find the cct of (a) Figs. 1 and 2 and of Figs. 4 and 5 for (b) 14″ and 15″ (c) 16″ (d) 18″ cans.

TOTAL AND INTERMEDIATE DRAFTS AND GRAIN LAP AND GRAIN SLIVER

Total Draft, Constants, Gears, Ranges, and Control.

41. For the combers in Figs. 1 and 2 and 3 to 5 derive (a) IPM

lr = RPM lr × 2.75 × $\pi = \dfrac{\text{npm} \times 2.75 \times \pi}{\text{Lr}}$; ∴ from (a) and formula (9)

(41) $\dfrac{\text{IPM}}{\text{lap roll}} = \dfrac{8.6394 \times \text{nips per minute} \times \text{feed tension constant}}{\text{feed ratchet} \times \text{feed tension}}$.

42. For Figs. 1 and 2 derive IPM ccr

$= \dfrac{\text{RPM cy} \times 57 \times \text{dg} \times 35 \times 23 \times 2 \times \pi}{51 \times \text{Cg} \times 35 \times 23}$; ∴

(42) IPM coiler calender roll Figs. 1 and 2 $= \dfrac{7.0224 \times \text{nips per minute} \times \text{draft gear}}{\text{coiler gear}}$;

and from formulas (7), (41), and (42) and ftc previously found

$$td = \frac{7.0224 \times \text{npm} \times \text{dg}}{\text{Cg}} \div \frac{8.6394 \times \text{npm} \times .36364}{\text{Fr} \times \text{Ctg}} \text{ ; and } \therefore$$

(43) draft constant Figs. 1 and 2 $= \dfrac{2.2353}{\text{coiler gear}}$;

(44) total draft Figs. 1 and 2 $= \dfrac{\text{draft}}{\text{constant}} \times \dfrac{\text{draft}}{\text{gear}} \times \dfrac{\text{feed}}{\text{ratchet}} \times \dfrac{\text{feed}}{\text{tension}}$; and

(45) draft gear Figs. 1 and 2 $= \dfrac{\text{total draft}}{\text{draft constant} \times \text{feed ratchet} \times \text{feed tension}}$

43. From your study of previous carding department machines select the correct word in the parentheses: A draft is the (sum, product) of its intermediate drafts.

44. As in the preceding problem verify for Figs. 1 and 2 the (a) td with its ft, dd, pt, tt, dbd, and cct (b) dbd with its bd, bmd, fmd, fd, and ct.

45. What is the draft constant and td range of Figs. 1 and 2 with a 16-tooth Fr, 1.16 ft and (a) 30- (b) 25-tooth Cg?

46. For Figs. 1 and 2 how fine is td control by a 1-tooth change from minimum and maximum td with a 16-tooth Fr, 1.16 ft, and (a) 30- (b) 25-tooth Cg?

47. Similarly derive

(46) IPM coiler calender roll Figs. 3 to 5 $= \dfrac{40.077 \times \dfrac{\text{nips per}}{\text{minute}} \times \dfrac{\text{brush}}{\text{shaft}} \times \dfrac{\text{draft}}{\text{gear}} \times \dfrac{\text{4th}}{\text{lay}} \times \dfrac{\text{2nd}}{\text{lay}}}{\dfrac{\text{front}}{\text{roll gear}} \times \dfrac{\text{calender}}{\text{tension}} \times \dfrac{\text{3rd lay}}{\text{gear}} \times \dfrac{\text{1st lay}}{\text{gear}}}$

48. From formulas (7), (41), and (46) and the ftc previously found derive

(47) draft constant Figs. 3 to 5 $= \dfrac{11.452 \times \dfrac{\text{brush shaft}}{\text{gear}} \times \dfrac{\text{4th lay}}{\text{gear}} \times \dfrac{\text{2nd lay}}{\text{gear}}}{\text{3rd lay gear} \times \text{1st lay gear}}$,

(48) total draft Figs. 3 to 5 $= \dfrac{\dfrac{\text{draft}}{\text{constant}} \times \dfrac{\text{draft}}{\text{gear}} \times \dfrac{\text{feed}}{\text{ratchet}} \times \dfrac{\text{feed}}{\text{tension}}}{\text{front roll gear} \times \text{calender tension gear}}$, and

(49) draft gear Figs. 3 to 5 $= \dfrac{\text{total draft} \times \dfrac{\text{front roll}}{\text{gear}} \times \dfrac{\text{calender tension}}{\text{gear}}}{\dfrac{\text{draft}}{\text{constant}} \times \dfrac{\text{feed}}{\text{ratchet}} \times \dfrac{\text{feed}}{\text{tension}}}$

What is the draft constant of Figs. 3 to 5 using a 15-tooth Fr and 1.026 ft as in the following 3 problems:

49. 14″ and 15″ cans and a (a) 24- (b) 25-tooth bsg?
50. 16″ cans and a (a) 24- (b) 25-tooth bsg?
51. 18″ cans and a (a) 24- (b) 25-tooth bsg?

In Figs. 3 to 5 in the following 3 problems cans are 18″, Fr has 15 teeth, Ctg 101, and ft is 1.026.

52. Verify (a) td with ft, dd, pt, tt, dbd, and cct (b) dbd with bd, bmd, fmd, fd, and ct.

53. What is the td range with gear teeth as follows: (a) bsg 24 Fg 38 (b) bsg 24 Fg 32 (c) bsg 24 Fg 26 (d) bsg 25 Fg 38 (e) bsg 25 Fg 32 (f) bsg 25 Fg 26.

54. How fine is td control by a 1-tooth change in dg from minimum and maximum td if bsg has 25 teeth and Fg 32?

Draft Gears, Grain Lap, and Grain Sliver.

55. From Figs. 1 and 2 and formula (6) derive td
$$= \frac{8 \times \text{gr. lap} \times .01 \times \% \text{ sl}}{2 \times \text{gr. sl}}$$

and ∴

$$(50) \quad \frac{\text{total draft}}{\text{Figs. 1 and 2}} = \frac{.04 \times \text{grain lap} \times \text{percent of sliver}}{\text{grain sliver}}$$

In Figs. 1 and 2 with a 16-tooth Fr and 1.16 ft how many teeth in Cg and dg ought to be tried under the conditions in the following example and 2 problems:

EXAMPLE: *800 gr. lap must produce 60-gr. sl and 14% no?*

By formula (50): td $= \dfrac{.04 \times 800 \times 86}{60} = 45.9$. From a previous

problem 45.9 td is seen in the range of a 30-tooth Cg only for which the

dc is seen to be .074510. By formula (45): dg $= \dfrac{45.9}{.0745 \times 16 \times 1.16} = 33.2$.

Answer: Cg 30 dg 33 or 34.

56. 42-gr. sl and 10% no from 850 gr. lap?
57. 1000 gr. lap at 92% sl must give as near as possible to but not lighter than 52 gr. sl?
58. Similarly derive

$$(51) \quad \frac{\text{total draft}}{\text{Figs. 3 to 5}} = \frac{.06 \times \text{grain lap} \times \text{percent of sliver}}{\text{grain sliver}}$$

In Figs. 3 to 5 for 18″ cans if Fr has 15 teeth, Ctg 101, and ft is 1.026 how many teeth in bsg, Fg and dg ought to be tried under the conditions of the following 3 problems:

59. 600 gr. lap must yield 80% of 60 gr. sl?
60. 950 gr. lap must yield 55 gr. sl at 92% sl?
61. At 85% sl 925 gr. lap must give as near as possible to but not heavier than 60 gr. sl?

62. As assigned by your instructor sketch the draft train of a comber in your mill, derive the intermediate and total draft constants and other draft formulas, calculate and verify drafts, calculate the gears required, and compare with those in use.

LAY AND KNOCK-OFF

Lay Formula. Lay means the same as with the card.

63. Calculate the lay of Fig. 2.

64. As with the card in Chap. 8 derive

$$(52) \frac{\text{lay}}{\text{Fig. 5}} = \frac{\text{tube driver gear} \times \text{sun gear} \times \text{turntable sprocket}}{\text{tube gear} \times \text{turntable driver sprocket}}$$

65. Calculate the lay of Fig. 5 for (a) 14″ (b) 15″ (c) 16″ (d) 18″ cans.

66. As assigned by your instructor sketch the lay train of a comber in your mill, calculate its lay and compare with the actual lay.

Knock-Off Formulas and Constants. As with carding department machinery previously studied, some combers such as Fig. 1 may have a precounter which may be set to knock off the power when a given yardage has been delivered by the calender roll, and some combers such as Figs. 4 and 6 may have a hunting-tooth knock off to do this when a given yardage has been fed by the lap rolls.

67. Derive

$$(53) \text{ yards set on precounter} = \frac{7000 \times \text{pounds in full can}}{\text{grain sliver}}.$$

What yds. ought to be set on the precounter to knock off as in the following 4 problems:

68. 30 lbs. of 50 gr. sl?

69. 35 lbs. of 50 gr. sl?

70. 45 lbs. of 60 gr. sl?

71. 54 lbs. of 60 gr. sl?

72. In Figs. 4 and 6: show that (a) rev lr $= \dfrac{\text{rev kig} \times \text{kig}}{\text{kg}}$ and (b) rev Kdg $= \dfrac{\text{rev kig} \times \text{kig}}{\text{Kdg}}$. (c) In what exact position relative to each other ought the meshing hunting teeth be for Kdg and its stud to be pushed back and knock off the power? (d) From one knock off to the next ∴ do kig and Kdg make partial or whole revolutions? (e) Are these revolutions the maximum or minimum possible number or any number? (f) If kig is a prime number, as in Fig. 6, from equation (b) what must rev kig equal if rev Kdg is as in (d) and (e)? From (f) and equation (a) derive (g) rev lr

to fill cans $= \dfrac{\text{Kdg} \times \text{kig}}{\text{kg}}$. From (g) derive (h) lbs. fed to fill the can on each

side $= \dfrac{6 \times \pi \times 2.75 \times \text{Kdg} \times \text{kig} \times \text{gr. lap}}{36 \times 7000 \times \text{kg}}$, (h) lbs. in full can $=$

$\dfrac{6 \times \pi \times 2.75 \times \text{Kdg} \times \text{kig} \times \text{gr. lap} \times .01 \times \% \text{ sl}}{36 \times 7000 \times \text{kg}}$, $\therefore$

(54) knock-off
constant $= .0002057 \times \dfrac{\text{knock-off}}{\text{driven gear}} \times \dfrac{\text{knock-off}}{\text{intermediate gear,}}$
Figs. 4 and 6

(55) . pounds in
full can $= \dfrac{\dfrac{\text{knock-off}}{\text{constant}} \times \dfrac{\text{grain}}{\text{lap}} \times .01 \times \% \text{ sliver}}{\text{knock-off change gear}}$,
Figs. 4 and 6

and

(56) knock-off
change gear $= \dfrac{\dfrac{\text{knock-off}}{\text{constant}} \times \dfrac{\text{grain}}{\text{lap}} \times .01 \times \% \text{ sliver}}{\text{pounds in full can}}$.
Figs. 4 and 6

73. Find the knock-off constant of Figs. 4 and 6 for cans of (a) under (b) over 30 lbs.

On Figs. 4 and 6 what kg ought to be tried for the lbs. in full cans in the following 4 problems:

74. 24 lbs. from 800-gr. lap at 86% sl?
75. 29 lbs. from 825-gr. lap at 91.5% sl?
76. 34 lbs. from 850-gr. lap at 88% sl?
77. 54 lbs. from 900-gr. lap at 83% sl?
78. As assigned by your instructor, if a comber in your plant has a (a) precounter knock-off calculate the yds. for the lbs. in the full can and compare with the yds. set on the precounter (b) hunting knock-off, sketch its train, derive and calculate its constant, calculate its kg for the gr. lap, % sl, and lbs. in full can being run and compare with the kg in use.

PRODUCTION

Meanings. Production; percent of production, % production, % p; 100% lbs; lbs. per hr., lbs./hr; hanks, hks; clock hanks, clhks; production constant, pc; and such terms and abbreviations have the same meaning as with carding department machines previously studied.

Pounds, Grain Lap, Feed Ratchets, and Feed Production Constants.

79. Since practically all the stock fed is delivered as sliver and noils, from formula (41) prove that

$$\text{lbs.} = \frac{8.6394 \times npm \times ftc \times 60 \times hrs. \times gr.\ lap \times laps \times .01 \times \%\ sl \times .01 \times \%\ p}{Fr \times ft \times 36 \times 7000}, \therefore$$

$$(57) \quad \frac{\text{feed production}}{\text{constant}} = .0020570 \times \frac{\text{feed tension}}{\text{constant}} \times laps, \text{ and}$$

(58) pounds =

$$\frac{\genfrac{}{}{0pt}{}{\text{feed}}{\text{production} \times} \genfrac{}{}{0pt}{}{\text{nips}}{\text{per}} \times hours \times \frac{grain}{lap} \times \frac{.01 \times \%}{sliver} \times \frac{.01 \times \%}{production}}{\text{feed ratchet} \times \text{feed tension}}.$$

80. What is the feed pc of (a) Fig. 1 (b) Fig. 4?

What is the production in lbs. in the following 4 problems:

81. 100% lbs./hr. from 800 gr. lap on Fig. 1 with a 1.17 ft and 13-tooth Fr at 10% no and 150 npm?

82. 900 gr. lap on Fig. 1 with a 16-tooth Fr and 1.159 ft for 8 hrs. at 12% no, 150 npm, and 91% p?

83. 94% p for 1 hr. from 800 gr. lap on Fig. 4 with a 15-tooth Fr and 1.026 ft at 88% sl and 140 npm?

84. On Fig. 4 with a 17-tooth Fr and the ft that a 43-tooth Lr gives 850 gr. lap at 140 npm, 95% p, 92% sl for 8 hrs.?

Pounds, Grain Sliver, Gears, and Coiler Production Constants.

85. For Figs. 1 and 2 and both slivers from formula (42) prove that

$$\text{lbs.} = \frac{7.0224 \times npm \times dg \times 60 \times hrs. \times gr.\ sl \times 2 \times .01 \times \%\ p}{Cg \times 36 \times 7000}, \therefore$$

$$(59) \quad \text{coiler production constant Figs. 1 and 2} = \frac{.0033400}{\text{coiler gear}}, \text{ and}$$

(60)

$$\genfrac{}{}{0pt}{}{\text{pounds}}{\text{Figs. 1 \& 2}} = \genfrac{}{}{0pt}{}{\text{coiler}}{\text{production} \times} \genfrac{}{}{0pt}{}{\text{nips}}{\text{per}} \times \frac{\text{draft}}{\text{gear}} \times hours \times \frac{grain}{sliver} \times \frac{.01 \times \%\ p}{\text{production}}$$

86. For Figs. 3 to 5 and both slivers from formula (46) derive:

$$\text{lbs.} = \frac{40.077 \times npm \times bsg \times dg \times folg \times slg \times 60 \times hrs. \times gr.\ sl \times 2 \times .01 \times \%\ p}{Fg \times Ctg \times Tlg \times Flg \times 36 \times 7000}, \therefore$$

$$(61) \quad \genfrac{}{}{0pt}{}{\text{coiler}}{\genfrac{}{}{0pt}{}{\text{production}}{\genfrac{}{}{0pt}{}{\text{constant}}{\text{Figs. 3 to 5}}}} = \frac{.019085 \times \genfrac{}{}{0pt}{}{\text{brush}}{\genfrac{}{}{0pt}{}{\text{shaft}}{\text{gear}}} \times \genfrac{}{}{0pt}{}{\text{4th}}{\genfrac{}{}{0pt}{}{\text{lay}}{\text{gear}}} \times \genfrac{}{}{0pt}{}{\text{2nd}}{\genfrac{}{}{0pt}{}{\text{lay}}{\text{gear}}}}{\text{3rd lay gear} \times \text{1st lay gear}}, \text{ and}$$

(62)

$$\frac{\text{pounds}}{\text{Figs. 3 to 5}} = \frac{\overset{\text{coiler}}{\text{production}} \times \overset{\text{nips}}{\text{per}} \times \frac{\text{draft}}{\text{gear}} \times \text{hours} \times \frac{\text{grain}}{\text{sliver}} \times \frac{.01 \times \% \text{ p}}{\text{production}}}{\text{front roll gear} \times \text{calender tension gear}}$$

87. What is the coiler pc of Figs. 1 and 2 with a (a) 30- (b) 25-tooth Cg?

What is the coiler pc of Figs. 3 to 5 as in the following 3 problems:

88. 15″ cans and a (a) 24- (b) 25-tooth bsg?
89. 16″ cans and a (a) 24- (b) 25-tooth bsg?
90. 18″ cans and a (a) 24- (b) 25-tooth bsg?

What is the production in lbs. under the conditions in the following 4 problems:

91. 95% p for 1 hr. of 50-gr. sl on Figs. 1 and 2 with a 25-tooth Cg and a 29-tooth dg at 150 npm?
92. 60 gr. sl on 6 combers as in Figs. 1 and 2 each with a 30-tooth Cg and 50-tooth dg at 150 npm and 92% p for 120 hrs.?
93. On Figs. 3 to 5 with a bsg of 24 teeth, dg of 42, Fg of 32, and Ctg of 101 running 50 gr. sl into 15″ cans at 140 npm and 92% p for 1 hr?
94. 60 gr. sl into 18″ cans on 4 combers as in Figs. 3 to 5 with a bsg of 25 teeth, dg of 55, Fg of 26, and Ctg of 101 at 92% p and 140 npm for 120 hrs.

Pounds, Clock Hanks, Grain Sliver, and Hank Clock Production Constants. The hank clock registers to $\frac{1}{10}$ hanks the hanks of 1 of the 2 slivers delivered on Figs. 1 and 2 by ccr and on Figs. 3 to 5 by both cr.

95. For Figs. 1 and 2 from the foregoing show that: (a) clhks = $\frac{\text{hks}}{2}$, and ∴ from (a) and formula (30) of Chap. I,

(63) pounds Figs. 1 and 2 = .24 × clock hanks × grain sliver.

96. For Figs. 3 to 5 during 1 minute show: that (a) lbs. = $\frac{\text{RPM ccr} \times 2 \times \pi \times \text{gr. sl} \times 2}{36 \times 7000}$, from the foregoing that (b) clhks = $\frac{\text{RPM cr} \times 3 \times \pi}{36 \times 840}$, from (a) and (b) that (c) $\frac{\text{lbs.}}{\text{clhks}} = \frac{.16 \times \text{RPM ccr} \times \text{gr. sl}}{\text{RPM cr}}$, ∴ from (c) that (d) lbs. = $.16 \times \frac{\text{RPM ccr}}{\text{RPM cr}} \times \text{clhks} \times \text{gr. sl}$, that (e) $\frac{\text{RPM ccr}}{\text{RPM cr}}$ $= \frac{\text{folg} \times \text{slg} \times 29}{\text{Tlg} \times \text{Flg} \times 19}$, from (d) and (e) ∴ lbs. = $.16 \times \frac{\text{folg} \times \text{slg} \times 29}{\text{Tlg} \times \text{Flg} \times 19} \times \text{clhks} \times$ gr. sl, ∴

(64) $\frac{\text{hank clock production}}{\text{constant Figs. 3 to 5}} = \frac{.24421 \times \text{4th lay gear} \times \text{2nd lay gear}}{\text{3rd lay gear} \times \text{1st lay gear}}$

and

$$(65) \text{ pounds Figs. 3 to 5} = \frac{\text{hank clock}}{\text{production constant}} \times \frac{\text{clock}}{\text{hanks}} \times \frac{\text{grain}}{\text{sliver}}.$$

97. For Figs. 3 to 5 find the hank clock pc for (a) 14″ and 15″ (b) 16″ (c) 18″ cans.

What is the production in lbs. on 1 comber for 1 shift according to the hank clock readings in the following 5 problems:

98. 26.8 clhks of 50 gr. sl on Figs 1 and 2?
99. 31.0 clhks of 60 gr. sl on Figs. 1 and 2?
100. 40.3 clhks of 47.6 gr. sl on Figs. 3 to 5 with 15″ cans?
101. 36.2 clhks of 50 gr. sl on Figs. 3 to 5 with 16″ cans?
102. 38.2 clhks of 60 gr. sl on Figs. 3 to 5 with 18″ cans?
103. As assigned by your instructor, derive production constants and formulas for a comber in your plant and apply them to practical production problems.

Chapter XII

ROVING FRAME CALCULATIONS

DRAFT

Basic Total Draft Formula. On every roving frame the speed of the front roll, f, is unchanged by changes in the draft; the back roll, b, is the feed roll; and f is the delivery roll. Hence the mechanical total draft, td, is between b and f.

1. From formula (3), Chap. III derive

$$(1) \text{ total draft} = \frac{\text{surface distance of front roll}}{\text{surface distance of back roll}}$$

Constants, Gears, and Ranges of Independent Total Drafts. Fig. 1 (a) is of the *conventional draft train*. Since between b and f there is only one intervening shaft integral with a driven gear at one end and a driver gear at the other end, the conventional is the minimum train that will allow changing the speed of b relative to the speed of f (i.e., changing td) by changing one convenient total draft gear, dg.

2. For the conventional train with a draft gear as in Fig. 1(a) derive

$$(2) \begin{array}{c} \text{total} \\ \text{draft} \end{array} = \frac{\text{dia. front roll} \times \text{crown gear} \times \text{back roll driven gear}}{\text{dia. back roll} \times \text{front roll driver gear} \times \text{draft gear}}.$$

3. For the same purpose and by similar reasoning as with the carding department machinery which you have studied in previous chapters for the total draft constant, dc, of the conventional train derive:

$$(3) \begin{array}{c} \text{draft} \\ \text{constant} \end{array} = \begin{array}{c} \text{total} \\ \text{draft} \end{array} \times \begin{array}{c} \text{draft} \\ \text{gear} \end{array} = \frac{\frac{\text{dia. front}}{\text{roll}} \times \frac{\text{crown}}{\text{gear}} \times \frac{\text{back roll}}{\text{driven gear}}}{\frac{\text{front roll}}{\text{driver gear}} \times \frac{\text{dia. back}}{\text{roll}}},$$

$$(4) \text{ total draft} = \frac{\text{draft constant}}{\text{draft gear}}, \text{ and}$$

$$(5) \text{ draft gear} = \frac{\text{draft constant}}{\text{total draft}}.$$

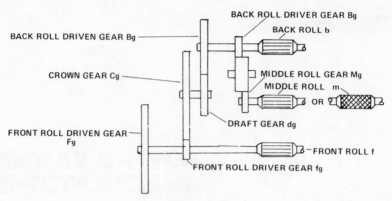

Figure 1,A

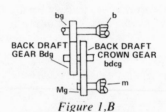

Figure 1,B

Some Draft Train Combinations of Fig. 1

	A	B	C
dia. of front roll, f	$1\frac{1}{8}''$	$1\frac{1}{8}''$	$1\frac{3}{16}''$
dia. of middle roll, m	$1''$	$1.11''$ (note 1)	$1''$
dia. of back roll, b	$1''$	$1''$	$1.44''$ (note 2)
front roll driver gear, fg	41	37	26
crown gear, cg	110	100	123
draft gear, dg	28 to 78	18 to 65	25 to 65
back roll driven gear, Bg	63	82	81
back roll driver gear, bg	27	25	39
back draft gear, Bdg			25 to 56
back draft crown gear, bdcg			52
middle roll gear, Mg	22	23	24

Note 1: includes apron thickness.

Note 2: effective dia. of $1\frac{1}{8}''$ metallic roll.

Find dc for Fig. 1(a) *with the combinations in the following three problems:*

4. A.   5. B.   6. C.

What is the td range of Fig. 1(a) *with the combinations in the following three problems:*

7. A?   8. B?   9. C?

How many teeth in dg ought to be tried for the td and combinations of Fig. 1(a) *in the following two problems:*

10. (a) At least but near as possible to 5.5 with A? (b) What td will this give?

11. (a) Not over and close as possible to 12 with B? (b) What td will result?

12. How fine is the td control by a 1-tooth change in dg from minimum and maximum td on Fig. 1 with combination (a) B (b) C?

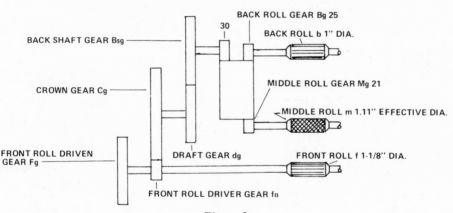

Figure 2

13. For Fig. 2 derive:

$$(6)\quad \frac{\text{draft}}{\text{constant}} = \frac{\text{total}}{\text{draft}} \times \frac{\text{draft}}{\text{gear}} = \frac{1.125 \times \dfrac{\text{crown}}{\text{gear}} \times \dfrac{\text{back shaft}}{\text{driven gear}} \times 25}{\text{front roll driver gear} \times 30}$$

and prove that formulas (4) and (5) are applicable.

Some Draft Train Combinations of Fig. 2		
	A	**B**
front roll driver gear, fg	45	24
crown gear, Cg	120	137
draft gear, dg	14 to 60	25 to 60
back shaft driven gear, Bsg	100	94

Find (a) *dc and* (b) *td range of Fig.* 2 *with the combinations in the following two problems:*

14. A.   **15.** B.

16. For Fig. 3 derive

$$(7) \quad \frac{\text{draft}}{\text{constant}} = \frac{\text{total}}{\text{draft}} \times \frac{\text{draft}}{\text{gear}} = \frac{1.125 \times 41 \times 78 \times \dfrac{\text{second draft}}{\text{constant gear}} \times 32}{36 \times \dfrac{\text{first draft}}{\text{constant gear}} \times 18 \times 1.125}$$

and prove that formulas (4) and (5) are applicable.

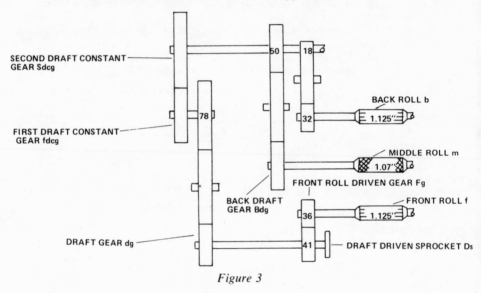

SECOND DRAFT CONSTANT GEAR Sdcg

FIRST DRAFT CONSTANT GEAR fdcg

BACK ROLL b

1.125"

MIDDLE ROLL m

1.07"

FRONT ROLL DRIVEN GEAR Fg

BACK DRAFT GEAR Bdg

FRONT ROLL f

1.125"

DRAFT GEAR dg

DRAFT DRIVEN SPROCKET Ds

Figure 3

Some Draft Train Combinations of Fig. 3

	A	B	C
draft gear, dg, for each combination		30 to 72	
first draft constant gear, fdcg	77	65	25
second draft constant gear, Sdcg	88	100	140
back draft gear, Bdg, for each combination		48 to 77	

Find (a) *dc and* (b) *td range of Fig.* 3 *with the combinations in the following three problems:*

17. A.   **18.** B.   **19.** C.

Basic Intermediate Draft Formulas. The *intermediate drafts, id,* of roving frames are *break or back draft, bd,* between b and the next-to-back roll (i.e., m in Figs. 1, 2, 3, and 4; third roll in Fig. 5) and front draft, fd, between the next-to-back roll and f.

20. In the conventional train in Fig. 1(a): (a) Which two drafts if changed must be changed together? Why? (b) Which intermediate draft is unchangeable? Why? (c) Which intermediate draft is proportional to dg and how? Why?

21. For the conventional train in Fig. 1(a): prove that $bd = \dfrac{bg \times dia.\ m}{Mg \times dia.\ b}$ and $fd = \dfrac{Mg \times Bg \times cg \times dia.\ f}{bg \times dg \times fg \times dia.\ m}$; calculate bd and fd with combination A and a 28-tooth dg; from the foregoing and formula (2) derive

(7) total draft = back draft × front draft,

(8) back draft = $\dfrac{\text{total draft}}{\text{front draft}}$,

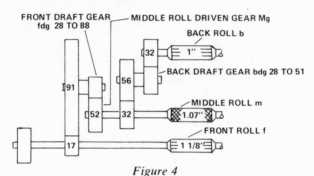

Figure 4

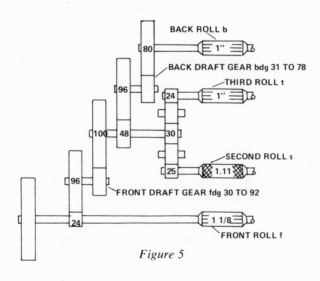

Figure 5

(9) front draft $= \dfrac{\text{total draft}}{\text{back draft}}$; and substituting td from formula (4)

into formulas (8) and (9) derive

(10) back draft $= \dfrac{\text{draft constant}}{\text{front draft} \times \text{draft gear}}$ and

(11) front draft $= \dfrac{\text{draft constant}}{\text{back draft} \times \text{draft gear}}$.

22. By formula (11) find the fd ranges of combinations A and B of Fig. 1(a).

23. For Fig. 2 find (a) bd and by formula (11) the fd range of combination (b) A (c) B.

Constants, Gears, and Ranges of Changeable Independent Back Drafts.

24. For the conventional train of Fig. 1(b) and combination C:

(a) derive bd $= \dfrac{39 \times 52 \times 1}{\text{bdg} \times 24 \times 1.44}$ and fd $= \dfrac{123 \times 81 \times \text{bdg} \times 24 \times 1.1875}{26 \times \text{dg} \times 39 \times 52 \times 1}$

(b) What do these equations and equation (2) prove occurs to td and fd if bd changes? Why? (c) from the foregoing derive

(12) back draft constant = back draft × back draft gear

(13) back draft $= \dfrac{\text{back draft constant}}{\text{back draft gear}}$,

(14) back draft gear $= \dfrac{\text{back draft constant}}{\text{back draft}}$

(d) Prove that formulas (3), (4), (5), and (7) to (11) are true.

25. For the modified conventional train of Fig. 1(b) and combination C find the: (a) bd constant; (b) bd range; (c) corresponding fd range by formula (11); (d) td range from (b) and (c) by formula (7) and check your answer with the td range which you found by formula (4).

26. For Fig. 3 find the (a) bd constant, (b) bd range, and corresponding fd range with combination (c) A, (d) B, and (e) C.

Constant, Gears, and Ranges of Independent Back and Front Drafts and Dependent Total Drafts.

27. For Fig. 4 derive: bd $= \dfrac{1.07 \times 56 \times 32}{32 \times \text{bdg} \times 1}$, fd $= \dfrac{1.125 \times 91 \times 52}{17 \times \text{fdg} \times 1.07}$,

and td $= \dfrac{1.125 \times 91 \times 52 \times 56 \times 32}{17 \times \text{fdg} \times 32 \times \text{bdg} \times 1}$.

28. By studying the equations of Fig. 4 in the preceding problem select the correct word or words within each set of the following parentheses: (a) The bd (can, cannot) be changed (by, without) changing (both, either) fd (and, or) td. Why? (b) The fd (cannot, can) be changed (without, by) changing (either, both) td (or, and) bd. Why? (c) The td (can, cannot) be changed (by, without) changing (either, both) bd (and, or) fd (and, or) both. Why? (d) The id are (dependent upon, independent of) each other and (of, upon) td. Why? (e) The td is (independent of, dependent upon) (one, both) of the id. Why?

29. For Fig. 5 derive: $bd = \dfrac{1 \times 30 \times 96 \times 80}{24 \times 48 \times bdg \times 1}$,

$fd = \dfrac{1.125 \times 96 \times 100 \times 24}{24 \times fdg \times 30 \times 1}$, and $td = \dfrac{1.125 \times 96 \times 100 \times 96 \times 80}{24 \times fdg \times 48 \times bdg \times 1}$.

30. From the three preceding problems for independent intermediate and dependent total drafts as in Figs. 4 and 5: derive

(15) draft constant = total draft × back draft gear × front draft gear,

(16) total draft = $\dfrac{\text{draft constant}}{\text{back draft gear} \times \text{front draft gear}}$ and

(17) back draft gear × front draft gear = $\dfrac{\text{draft constant}}{\text{total draft}}$

prove that formulas (7), (8), (9), (12), (13), and (14) are true: and derive

(18) front draft constant = front draft × front draft gear,

(19) front draft = $\dfrac{\text{front draft constant}}{\text{front draft gear}}$,

(20) front draft gear = $\dfrac{\text{front draft constant}}{\text{front draft}}$, and

(21) draft constant = back draft constant × front draft constant.

Find the bd, fd, and td constants and ranges of the trains in the following two problems:

31. Fig. 4.   **32.** Fig. 5.

Draft Constants, Gears, and Precision.

How precise are the controls by a 1-tooth change from the (a) smallest (b) largest drafts of the trains in the following four problems:

33. Fig. 2 combination A td?
34. Fig. 3 combination A td?
35. Fig. 3 combination C td and bd?
36. Fig. 4 bd, fd, and td?

Find (a) the teeth in the gears that ought to be tried to give as near as possible to the drafts and (b) the expected drafts under the conditions on the trains in the following four problems and example:

37. Fig. 1(b) bd not over 1.25.
38. Fig. 2 combination B, td at least 8.5.
39. Fig. 3 combination C, td at least 27.5, bd not over 2.25.

EXAMPLE: *Fig. 4 td at least 8.00, bd not over 1.40.*

By formula (14) and a previous problem $bdg = \dfrac{59.92}{1.40} = 42.8$; $\therefore$ bdg

must be 43; because if bdg were < 43 bd would be > 1.40. By formula

(16) and the same problem $td = \dfrac{17536}{43 \times fdg} = 8.00$; $\therefore$ $fdg = \dfrac{17536}{43 \times 8.00} =$

50.9; $\therefore$ fdg must be 50 because if fdg were 51 td would be < 8.00; $\therefore$ bd $=$

$\dfrac{59.92}{43} = 1.39$ and $td = \dfrac{17536}{43 \times 50} = 8.16$.   **Answer:**   (a) bdg 43 (b) bd

1.39 (a) fdg 50 (b) td 8.16.

40. Fig. 4 td not over 20, bd not over 2.10.

41. Fig. 5 td 36, bd at least 2.75.

42. From a roving frame in your plant obtain the necessary data; derive the formulas for the total and intermediate draft constants; compute the constants, drafts, gears, ranges, and precision; compare your calculated drafts for the stock being run with the frame's performance; and solve such other problems as are assigned by your instructor.

Finding Gears in Changing Drafts.

43. In changing from a satisfactory present or old draft and draft gear or gears to a required or new draft and draft gear or gears, if the constant remains the same, from the appropriate formulas prove that: (a) in independent total drafts new td $\times$ new dg $=$ old td $\times$ old dg; (b) in independent bd and fd new td $\times$ new bdg $\times$ new fdg $=$ old td $\times$ old bd $\times$ old fd; (c) in any independent id new id $\times$ new idg $=$ old id $\times$ old idg; and $\therefore$.

(22) new   new back   new front
      draft or   draft $\times$ draft $=$
      gear   gear   gear

$\dfrac{\dfrac{\text{old total}}{\text{draft}} \times \dfrac{\text{old draft}}{\text{gear}} \text{ or } \dfrac{\text{old back}}{\text{draft gear}} \times \dfrac{\text{old front}}{\text{draft gear}}}{\text{new total draft}}$ and

(23) $\dfrac{\text{new intermediate}}{\text{draft gear}} =$

$\dfrac{\text{old intermediate draft} \times \text{old intermediate draft gear}}{\text{new intermediate draft}}$

Find the teeth in the gears that ought to be tried to give as near as possible to the drafts required under the conditions in the following example and five problems:

EXAMPLE: *At least* 10.5 *td required.* 27-*tooth dg drafts* 11.8.

By formula (22) new $dg = \dfrac{27 \times 11.8}{10.5} = 30.3$; $\therefore$ 31-tooth dg would

draft 10.5.   **Answer:**   dg $= 30$.

44. Required not over 1.60 bd and 9.50 td. 72-tooth dg and 44-tooth bdg draft 7.50 td and 1.25 bd.

45. 32-tooth dg and 48-tooth bdg give 12.75 td and 1.80 bd. Not over 15.00 td and 2.00 bd needed.

46. 29-tooth fdg and 36-tooth bdg draft 21.60 td and 2.10 bd. Wanted not over 1.80 bd and at least 24.00 td.

47. 16.50 td and no more than 2.25 bd needed. 28-tooth fdg draws 6.50 fd and 32-tooth bdg draws 1.90 bd.

48. As assigned by your instructor, solve by formulas (22) and (23) draft changing problems on the roving frames of your plant.

Contraction, Grain Sliver, Hank Roving, and Draft Constants and Gears. Between the lifter roll and bobbin slip and loss of weight, including trash, is negligible. But between f and the bobbin the stock contracts due to twist. This contraction is expressed as *percent of contraction,* or *%c,* of the length delivered by f.

49. Prove from the foregoing and formula (5), Chap. III that (24)

$$td = \frac{ad}{1 - .01 \times \%c} \text{ ; from formula (10), Chap. III and (24) that for slub-}$$

bers (25) $td = \dfrac{.12 \times gr. \, sl. \times HR}{1 - .01 \times \%c}$; from formula (4) or (16) that (26)

$$\frac{dc}{dg \text{ or } bdg \times fdg} = \frac{.12 \times gr. \, sl. \times HR}{1 - .01 \times \%c} \text{ ; from (26) that (27) dg or bdg or}$$

$$fdg = \frac{dc \times (1 - .01 \times \%c)}{.12 \times gr. \, sl. \times HR} \text{ ; and } \therefore \text{ for slubbers (28) draft gear or back}$$

draft gear × front draft gear = $\dfrac{\text{draft constant} \times (100 - \% \text{ of contraction})}{12 \times \text{grain sliver} \times \text{hank roving}}$

and similarly from formula (11), Chap. III for succeeding frames (29) draft gear or back draft gear × front draft gear =

$$\frac{\text{draft constant} \times \text{hank roving fed} \times (100 - \% \text{ of contraction})}{100 \times \text{doublings} \times \text{hank roving delivered}}$$

Find the teeth in the gears that ought to be tried to draft as required with the contraction on the trains in the following six problems:

50. Fig. 1 combination A. 3%. .55 HR from 80 gr. sl.

51. Fig. 2 combination B. $3\frac{1}{2}$%. 1.35 HR from 65 gr. sl.

52. Fig. 3 combination C. 5%. 60 gr. sl. into 1.60 HR.

53. 75 gr. sl into 2.25 HR at 4% on Fig. 4 with 1.80 bd.

54. Fig. 1 combination C. .50 HR doubled into 1.90 HR. 4.5%.

55. .40 HR doubled into 2.40 HR at 5.5% on Fig. 1 combination C.

Finding Gears in Changing Contraction, Grain Sliver, and Hank Roving.

56. Reasoning similarly to your derivation of formula (22), from formulas (28) and (29) derive for slubbers

(30) new draft gear or new back draft gear × new front draft

$$\text{gear} = \frac{\begin{array}{c}\text{old}\\\text{grain}\\\text{sliver}\end{array} \times \begin{array}{c}\text{old}\\\text{hank}\\\text{roving}\end{array} \times \left(100 - \begin{array}{c}\text{old \% of}\\\text{contraction}\end{array}\right) \times \begin{array}{c}\text{old}\\\text{draft}\\\text{gear}\end{array} \text{ or } \begin{array}{c}\text{old}\\\text{back}\\\text{draft}\\\text{gear}\end{array} \times \begin{array}{c}\text{old}\\\text{front}\\\text{draft}\\\text{gear}\end{array}}{\begin{array}{c}\text{new grain}\\\text{sliver}\end{array} \times \begin{array}{c}\text{new hank}\\\text{roving}\end{array} \times (100 - \text{new \% of contraction})} \text{ and}$$

for succeeding roving frames

(31) new draft gear or new back draft gear × new front draft gear =

$$\frac{\begin{array}{c}\text{old hank}\\\text{roving}\\\text{delivered}\end{array} \times \begin{array}{c}\text{new hank}\\\text{roving}\\\text{fed}\end{array} \times \left(100 - \begin{array}{c}\text{new \% of}\\\text{contraction}\end{array}\right) \times \begin{array}{c}\text{old}\\\text{draft}\\\text{gear}\end{array} \text{ or } \begin{array}{c}\text{old}\\\text{back}\\\text{draft}\\\text{gear}\end{array} \times \begin{array}{c}\text{old}\\\text{front}\\\text{draft}\\\text{gear}\end{array}}{\begin{array}{c}\text{new hank}\\\text{roving delivered}\end{array} \times \begin{array}{c}\text{old hank}\\\text{roving fed}\end{array} \times (100 - \text{old \% of contraction})}$$

Find the teeth in the gears that ought to be tried in the five following problems:

57. A slubber with a 40-tooth dg drafting 62 gr. sl. must be heavied to 65 gr. sl. on the same HR.

58. A frame must be changed from a 48-tooth dg, 50 gr. sl. and .56 HR to 56 gr. sl. and .75 HR at an expected increase in % c from 2.5 to 2.75.

59. A 35-tooth bdg and a 42-tooth fdg run 66 gr. sl. into 1.20 hank at 2.80% c. This must be changed to 63 gr. sl. into 1.40 hank at an increase in bd of 3% at a probable 2.5% c.

60. HR delivered and bd must be maintained although the doubled 1.20 HR fed has lightened to 1.30 with a 42-tooth bdg and 35-tooth fdg.

61. The 72-tooth bdg and 60-tooth fdg have been drawing two .75 HR into 4.00 HR with 2.75% c. But HR fed has heavied to .70 and HR delivered must be heavied to at least and close as possible to 3.50, bd decreased 5%, and tm reduced by an amount that will give 2.25% c.

TWIST

Basic Formula. As in Figs. 6 and 7 the twist train delivers the power from the *main shaft, ms,* to the *flyer, fl,* and through the *twist gear, td,* to the *front roll, f.*

62. Select the correct word in each of the following sets of parentheses: f delivers the stock at (a) (variable, constant) speed to fl which inserts (b) (variable, constant) *twist per inch, tpi.*

63. From the foregoing derive

(32) twist per inch =

$$\frac{\text{RPM flyer}}{\text{IPM front roll}} = \frac{\text{RPM flyer}}{\pi \times \text{dia. front roll} \times \text{RPM front roll}}$$

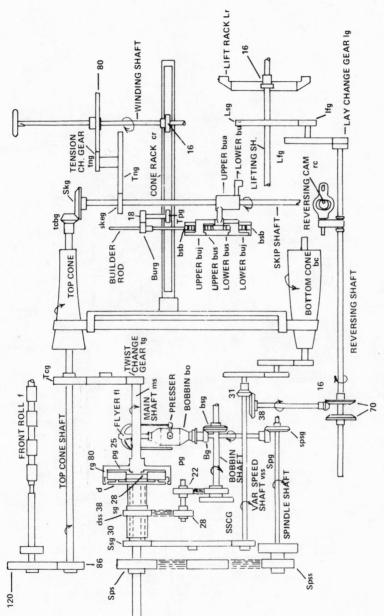

Figure 6. *Twist, Lay, Tension, and Taper Trains of a Cone Roving Frame Viewed from its Back*

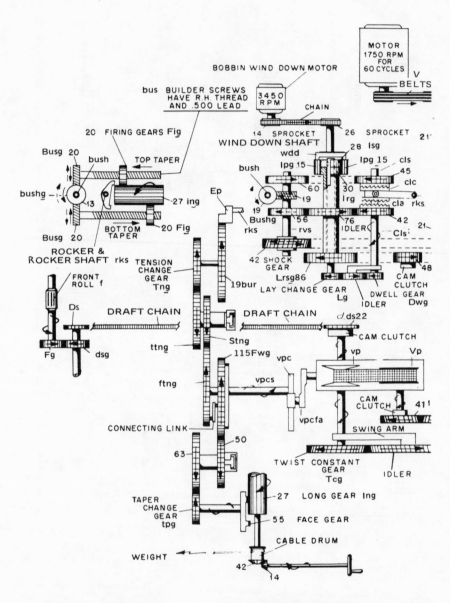

Figure 7.   Twist, Lay, Tension, and Taper Trains of the Variable Pulley

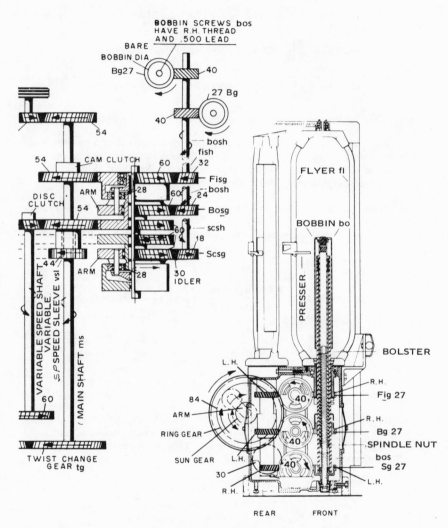

Dashes Between Gears Indicate They Mesh

Roving Frame

Find tpi in the following four problems:

64. Dia. f $1\frac{1}{4}''$ RPM fl 660 RPM f (a) 308 (b) 138.

65. Dia. f $1\frac{1}{8}''$ RPM fl 900 RPM f (a) 214 (b) 147.

66. Dia. f $1\frac{15}{16}''$ RPM fl 1200 RPM f (a) 400 (b) 155.

67. Dia. f $1\frac{1}{8}''$ RPM fl 1800 RPM f (a) 459 (b) 178.

With the largest practical twist multipliers % c is rarely as great as 5.

68. If % c in the preceding problems would reach 5 by how much tpi would your answer to the (a) least (b) most twisted roving be changed? (c) Would this be an increase or decrease? Why? (d) Why is this difference in tpi due to contraction usually ignored?

Twist Per Inch, Constants, Ranges, and Twist Gears of Cone Frames.

69. From your study of power trains show that in Fig. 6

$$(33) \quad RPM\ fl = \frac{RPM\ ms \times sps \times spsg}{Spss \times Spg},$$

$$(34) \quad RPM\ f = \frac{RPM\ ms \times tg \times 86}{Tcg \times 120}, \text{ and substituting the values of}$$

RPM fl and RPM f from equations (33) and (34) into (32) derive

$$(35) \quad \text{twist per inch} = \frac{\dfrac{\text{spindle driver}}{\text{sprocket}} \times \dfrac{\text{spindle shaft}}{\text{driver gear}} \times \dfrac{\text{top cone}}{\text{driven gear}} \times 120}{\pi \times \dfrac{\text{dia. front}}{\text{roll}} \times \dfrac{\text{twist}}{\text{gear}} \times 86 \times \dfrac{\text{spindle shaft}}{\text{driven sprocket}} \times \dfrac{\text{spindle}}{\text{gear}}}$$

It is obvious that if both sides of formula (35) are multiplied by tg and tg cancelled from the right side the right side becomes a constant and ∴ the left side, tpi × tg, equals the same constant. This is the *twist constant, tc,* and is a labor saver like the draft constant.

70. From formula (35) and the foregoing for Fig. 6 derive

$$(36) \quad \frac{\text{twist}}{\text{constant}} = \frac{\text{twist per}}{\text{inch}} \times \frac{\text{twist}}{\text{gear}} =$$

$$\frac{\dfrac{\text{spindle driver}}{\text{sprocket}} \times \dfrac{\text{spindle shaft}}{\text{driver gear}} \times \dfrac{\text{top cone}}{\text{driven gear}} \times 120}{\pi \times \dfrac{\text{dia. front}}{\text{roll}} \times 86 \times \dfrac{\text{spindle shaft}}{\text{driven sprocket}} \times \dfrac{\text{spindle}}{\text{gear}}},$$

$$(37) \quad \text{twist per inch} = \frac{\text{twist constant}}{\text{twist gear}}, \text{ and}$$

$$(38) \quad \text{twist gear} = \frac{\text{twist constant}}{\text{twist per inch}}.$$

Some Twist Train Combinations of Fig. 6

	A	B	C	D
top cone driven gear, Tcg	48	40	62	50
twist gear, tg, range	27 to 60	22 to 38	29 to 47	26 to 38
spindle driver sprocket, sps	42	35	35	35
spindle shaft driven sprocket, Spss	42	35	35	35
Spindle shaft driver gear, spsg	40	45	45	45
spindle gear, Spg	21	22	22	22
diameter of front roll, f	$1\frac{1}{4}''$	$1\frac{1}{4}''$	$1\frac{1}{8}''$	$1\frac{1}{8}''$

Find tc for Fig. 6 with the combinations in the following example and three problems:

EXAMPLE: *Combination A.*

By formula (36) $tc = \dfrac{42 \times 40 \times 48 \times 120}{3.1416 \times 1.25 \times 86 \times 42 \times 21} = 32.49.$

71. B   **72.** C.   **73.** D.

Find the tpi range for Fig. 6 with the combinations in the following example and three problems:

EXAMPLE: *Combination A.*

By formula (37) and the preceding example: $tpi = \dfrac{32.49}{60} = .542$

and $tpi = \dfrac{32.49}{27} = 1.203.$ **Answer:** .542 to 1.203.

74. B.   **75.** C.   **76.** D.

Find the tg that ought to be tried to obtain the correct tpi with the combination of Fig. 6, hank roving, and twist multiplier in the following example and three problems:

EXAMPLE: *Combination A HR .30 twist multiplier 1.20.*

By formula (14) Chap. IV: $tpi = 1.20 \times \sqrt{.30} = .658.$ By formula (38) and the preceding example: $tg = \dfrac{32.49}{.658} = 49.4.$ **Answer:** 49- or 50-tooth.

77. B HR .55 tm 1.25.
78. C HR .95 tm 1.275.
79. D 1.35 HR 1.30 tm.

Twist Per Inch, Constants, Ranges, and Twist Gears of Variable Pulley Frames. In the twist train of Figs. 7 and 8 the 60-tooth *flyer compound gear, flcg,* acts merely as an intermediate between the 54-tooth *main shaft driver gear* and the 32-tooth *flyer shaft driven gear, Flsg.*

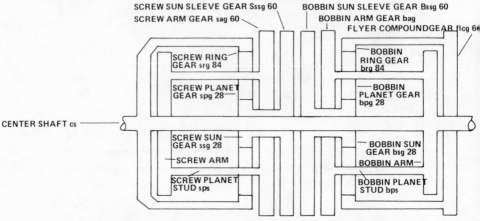

Figure 8.   Tandem Compound of Roving Frame in Figure 7

80. As in deriving formula (36), for the variable pulley frame in Fig. 7 derive

(39) twist constant = twist per inch × twist gear =

$$\frac{54 \times 40 \times \begin{array}{c}\text{twist}\\\text{constant}\\\text{gear}\end{array} \times \begin{array}{c}\text{draft}\\\text{driven}\\\text{sprocket}\end{array} \times \begin{array}{c}\text{front roll}\\\text{driven gear}\end{array}}{\pi \times \begin{array}{c}\text{dia. front}\\\text{roll}\end{array} \times 32 \times 27 \times 22 \times \begin{array}{c}\text{draft shaft}\\\text{driver gear}\end{array}},$$

and prove that formulas (37) and (38) are true.

Some Twist Train Combinations of Fig. 7		
	A	**B**
front roll driven gear, Fg	36	53
draft shaft driver gear, dsg	41	22
draft driven sprocket, Ds	30	19
twist constant gear, Tcg	23, 35, and 49	64 and 70
twist gear, tg	30 to 60	22 to 60
diameter of front roll, f	$1\frac{1''}{8}$	$1\frac{15''}{16}$

Find tc and the tpi ranges for Fig. 7 with the combinations and twist constant gears in the following two problems:

81. A with (a) 23-, (b) 35- and (c) 49-tooth Tcg.
82. B with (a) 64- and (b) 70-tooth Tcg.
83. What tg ought to be tried on Fig. 7 with combination (a) A, a 35-tooth tcg, .80 HR, and a 1.50 tm (b) B, a 64-tooth tcg, 1.40 HR, and a 1.60 tm?

Finding Gears in Changing Twist, Hank, or Multiplier.

84. In changing from a satisfactory present or old tpi and tg to a required or new tpi and tg, if tc remains the same, for Figs. 6 and 7 from formulas (36) and (39) derive

(40) $\dfrac{\text{new twist}}{\text{gear}} = \dfrac{\text{old twist gear} \times \text{old twist per inch}}{\text{new twist per inch}}$ and $\therefore$.

(41) $\dfrac{\text{new twist}}{\text{gear}} = \dfrac{\dfrac{\text{old twist gear} \times \text{old twist}}{\text{multiple} \times \sqrt{\text{old hank roving}}}}{\text{new twist multiplier} \times \sqrt{\text{new hank roving}}.}$

Find the teeth in the tg that ought to be tried in the following problems:

85. A 32-tooth tg inserts 1.25 tpi which must be changed to as close as possible to .75.
86. As near as possible to a third of a turn per inch is needed where a 27-tooth tg now gives a half.
87. HR as close as possible to but no lighter than 1.15 must be changed from a 37-tooth tg satisfactorily twisting 1.35 HR of the same grade and staple.
88. .90 hanks must be changed from a 41-tooth tg and 1.40 to 1.60 tm.
89. A frame must be changed from a 50-tooth tg satisfactorily twisting 1.55 HR with a 1.25 tm to 1.70 HR with a 1.40 tm.
90. From a roving frame in your plant collect the data for and calculate its tc, the tg for the tpi and HR being run, compare these with the frame's actual performance, and solve other twist problems as assigned by your instructor.

LAY

Basic Formula.   The cycle of a roving frame from the start of winding the first *coil* of the first *lay* (i.e., *layer*) onto the empty *bobbin*, *bo*, to the finish of winding the last coil of the last layer on the full bo is a *set*. Each layer is laid by bo traversing up or down.

91. Show that: (a) to lay the maximum layers onto bo any coil of a succeeding layer must be laid in a depression between 2 adjacent coils of the preceding layer and $\therefore$ (b) *coils per inch*, *cpi*, must be constant during a set.

Modern American roving frames are "bobbin led," i.e., IPM bo > IPM fl.

92. If IPM fl would = circular IPM bo what would happen to the roving?

93. Show that: the *presser* of fl pressing the roving as it emerges from fl onto bo constantly keeps (a) cir. fl = cir. bo; (b) IPM of roving wound onto bo = circular IPM bo − IPM fl; (c) IPM of roving wound onto bo = cpi × cir. bo × traversing IPM bo; from (c) and (b) ∴ (d) cpi × cir. bo × traversing IPM bo = circular IPM bo − IPM fl; from (d) ∴

(e) $cpi = \dfrac{\text{circular IPM bo} - \text{IPM fl}}{\text{cir. bo} \times \text{traversing IPM bo}} =$

$$\frac{\text{cir. bo} \times \text{RPM bo} - \text{cir. fl} \times \text{RPM fl}}{\text{cir. bo} \times \text{traversing IPM bo}} ;$$

and from (e) and (a) and cancelling cir. bo ∴

$$(42) \text{ coils per inch} = \frac{\text{RPM bobbin} - \text{RPM flyer}}{\text{traversing IPM bo}} .$$

Coils Per Inch, Lay Constants, Ranges, and Gears of Cone Frames. As in Fig. 6 the modern cone frame has an internal-ring spur-gear compound, as studied in Chap. XX, Part One, with its one or two one-size *planet gears, pg;* its *ring gear, rg,* integral through the *main shaft, ms,* acting as its center shaft, with the *spindle driver sprocket, sps;* its *disc, d,* integral through an outer sleeve with the *disc sleeve sprocket, dss;* and its *sun gear, sg,* integral through an inner sun sleeve with the *sun sleeve gear, Ssg.*

Thus the compound (1) through rg from ms receives a constant RPM; (2) through sg, Ssg, and the *sun sleeve control gear, sscg,* from the *variable speed shaft, vss,* receives an RPM that (as will be studied with the tension train) decreases with each successive layer but is constant during each layer; (3) compounds these two speeds into one speed; and (4) through d, dss, and the bobbin train delivers to bo this compounded RPM that decreases with each successive layer but is constant during each layer.

The bobbin is carried by the bobbin carriage which is integral with the *lift rack, lr.* Thus bo through lr, the *lift rack gear, lrg,* the *lay gear, lr,* and the rest of the lay train receives from vss a traversing IPM that decreases with each successive layer but is constant during each layer.

94. From formula (37), Chap. XX, Part One, prove that in Fig. 6

$RPM\ d = \dfrac{RPM\ rg \times 80 + RPM\ sg \times 28}{80 + 28}$; and if rg (∴ fl) is held stationary

$RPM\ d = \dfrac{RPM\ sg \times 7}{27}$, ∴ $\dfrac{RPM\ d}{RPM\ sg} = \dfrac{7}{27}$, ∴ $\dfrac{7}{27}$, can be substituted for

$\dfrac{sg}{d}$; and ∴

$$(43)\ RPM\ bo - RPM\ fl = \frac{RPM\ vss \times sscg \times 7 \times 38 \times 22 \times bsg}{30 \times 27 \times 28 \times 22 \times Bg}$$

95. For Fig. 6 prove that: from formula (14), Chap. XX, Part One

$$(44)\ \text{IPM Lr} = \frac{\text{RPM vss} \times 31 \times 16 \times \text{lg} \times \text{lfg} \times 16 \times \text{cir. p. lrg}}{38 \times 70 \times \text{Lfg} \times \text{Lsg}} =$$

traversing IPM bo; from equations (42), (43), and (44)

$$\text{cpi} = \frac{\text{sscg} \times 7 \times 38 \times 22 \times \text{bsg} \times 38 \times 70 \times \text{Lfg} \times \text{Lsg}}{30 \times 27 \times 28 \times 22 \times \text{Bg} \times 31 \times 16 \times \text{lg} \times \text{lfg} \times 16 \times \text{cir. p. lrg}};$$

and ∴ reasoning as in your previous similar derivations, for Fig. 6 derive

(45) lay constant = coils per inch × lay gear =

$$\frac{\begin{array}{c}\text{sun sleeve}\\\text{control}\\\text{gear}\end{array} \times 7 \times 38 \times 22 \times \begin{array}{c}\text{bobbin}\\\text{shaft}\\\text{driver}\\\text{gear}\end{array} \times 38 \times 70 \times \begin{array}{c}\text{lift}\\\text{driven}\\\text{gear}\end{array} \times \begin{array}{c}\text{lift}\\\text{shaft}\\\text{driven}\\\text{gear}\end{array}}{30 \times 27 \times 28 \times 22 \times \begin{array}{c}\text{bobbin}\\\text{gear}\end{array} \times 31 \times 16 \times \begin{array}{c}\text{lift}\\\text{driver}\\\text{gear}\end{array} \times 16 \times \begin{array}{c}\text{cir. pitch}\\\text{lift rack}\\\text{gear}\end{array}},$$

$$(46)\ \text{coils per inch} = \frac{\text{lay constant}}{\text{lay gear}}, \text{ and}$$

$$(47)\ \text{lay gear} = \frac{\text{lay constant}}{\text{coils per inch}}$$

Some Lay Train Combinations in Fig. 6

	A	B	C	D
bobbin gear, Bg	21	22	22	22
bobbin shaft driver gear, bsg	40	45	45	45
sun sleeve control gear, sscg	26	23	23	23
lay gear, lg	20 to 45	18 to 32	26 to 44	22 to 33
lift driven gear, Lfg	96	112	112	112
lift driver gear, lfg	18	24	14	18
lift shaft driven gear, Lsg	86	80	90	86
circumferential pitch of lift rack gear, lrg	.5238″	.3925″	.3925″	.3925″

Find the (a) *lay constant, lc, and* (b) *cpi range for Fig. 6 with the combinations in the following four problems:*

96. A.   **97.** B.   **98.** C.   **99.** D.

Find the teeth in lg that ought to be tried to lay as close as possible to the cpi with the conditions and combinations of Fig. 6 in the following example and three problems:

100. Combination A the first 12″ layer must have not over 78 coils.

EXAMPLE: *Combination A coil multiplier 9.3 HR no lighter than .40.*

By formula (5), Chap. IV: cpi = $9.3 \times \sqrt{.40}$. By formula (47) and a preceding problem: td = $\dfrac{170.48}{9.3 \times \sqrt{.40}}$ = 28.9.   **Answer:**   29.

101. B not over HR .50 and cm 9.3.
102. C cm 9.8 HR no heavier than 1.40.
103. D cm not over 9.8 HR no lighter than .65.

Coils Per Inch, Lay Constants, Ranges, and Gears of the Variable Pulley Frame.   The variable pulley roving frame in Figs. 7 and 8 has a *tandum compound* of which one end is the internal-ring spur-gear *bobbin compound,* as studied in Chap. XX, Part One, with its two *bobbin planet gears, bpg;* its *bobbin ring gear, brg,* integral with the *flyer compound gear, flcg;* its two *bobbin arms, ba* (instead of a disc as in a cone frame), integral with its *bobbin arm gear, bag,* and its center shaft, cs; and its *bobbin sun gear, bsg,* integral through a bobbin sun sleeve with its *bobbin sun sleeve gear, Bssg.*

Thus the bobbin compound (1) through brg from flcg receives a constant RPM; (2) through bsg and Bssg from the *variable speed sleeve, vsl* (which is free to revolve upon the *main shaft, ms,* as a stud), receives an RPM that (as will be studied with the tension train) decreases with each successive layer but is constant during each layer; (3) compounds these two speeds into one speed; and (4) through ba, bag, and the bobbin train delivers to bo this compounded RPM that decreases with each layer but is constant during each layer.

104. From formula (37), Chap. XX, Part One, prove that in Figs. 7 and 8 RPM ba = $\dfrac{\text{RPM brg} \times 84 + \text{RPM bsg} \times 28}{84 + 28}$; and if brg ($\therefore$ fl) is held stationary $\dfrac{\text{RPM ba}}{\text{RPM bsg}} = \dfrac{1}{4}$; $\therefore$

(48) $\dfrac{1}{4}$ can be substituted for $\dfrac{bsg}{ba}$; and $\therefore$

(49) RPM bo $-$ RPM fl = $\dfrac{\text{RPM vsl} \times 54 \times 1 \times 60 \times 40}{60 \times 4 \times 24 \times 27}$.

As shown in Figs. 7 and 9 partly in the lay train is the external-ring spur gear *lay wind down compound,* as studied in Chap. XX, Part One, with its two equal *lay planet gears, lpg;* its *lay ring gear, lrg,* integral through a lay ring sleeve with its *lay ring sleeve gear, Lrsg;* its *wind down disc, wdd,* integral with its *wind down driven sprocket, wds;* and its *lay sun gear, lsg,* integral through its *lay center shaft, lcs,* with the *lay gear, lg.* Wdd is stationary during a set; and its action between sets will be studied later.

105. From the foregoing, Fig. 9, and formula (42), Chap. XX, Part One, prove that RPM wdd = $\dfrac{\text{RPM lrg} \times 30 \times 15 - \text{RPM lsg} \times 28 \times 15}{30 \times 15 - 28 \times 15}$; $\therefore$

during a set $0 = \dfrac{\text{RPM lrg} \times 30 - \text{RPM lsg} \times 28}{30 - 28}$; $\therefore \dfrac{\text{RPM lrg}}{\text{RPM lsg}} = \dfrac{28}{30}$,

and $\therefore$

$$(50) \ \frac{\text{lrg}}{\text{lsg}} = \frac{30}{28}.$$

The lay *clutch coller, clc,* is free to slide along the *clutch shaft, cls,* and internally is geared to cls and $\therefore$ revolves with cls. The 45- and 42-tooth gears on cls are free to revolve on cls except during one layer the teeth of clc engage the clutch teeth of the 45-tooth gear, as shown, and during the next layer engage the clutch teeth of the 42-tooth gear. The 76-tooth idler gear uses the lay ring sleeve as a stud and is free to revolve upon it. The *reversing shaft, rvs,* is integral with the shock gear.

106. When clc disengages the 45- or 42-tooth gear and engages the other, what happens to the (a) number of (b) direction of (c) sign before the RPM of the shock gear and the subsequent gears of the lay train?

As shown in Figs. 7 and 8 the shock gear meshes with and drives the *screw sun sleeve gear, Sssg,* which is integral through a screw sun sleeve with the *sun screw gear, ssg,* of the internal-ring spur-gear *screw compound* with its two equal *screw planet gears, spg;* its two *screw arms, sa,* integral with its *screw arm gear, sag;* and its *screw ring gear, srg,* integral through cs with ba of the bobbin compound.

107. Prove the following: From the preceding problem and discussion, Figs. 7 and 8, and equation (50) that considering the direction of ba ($\therefore$ srg) as +, (51) RPM ssg, in the direction of ba =

$+\dfrac{\text{RPM vsl} \times 44 \times 30 \times \text{lg} \times 45 \times 42}{86 \times 28 \times \text{Dwg} \times 60 \times 60} = +\dfrac{\text{RPM vsl} \times \text{lg} \times .288}{\text{Dwg}}$ and in the

opposite direction $-\dfrac{\text{RPM vsl} \times \text{lg} \times .288}{\text{Dwg}}$. From equation (48) that (52)

RPM ba $= \dfrac{\text{RPM vsl} \times 54 \times 1}{60 \times 4} = \text{RPM vsl} \times .225$. From formula (37),

Chap. XX, Part One, equations (51) and (52) that (53) RPM sa when ssg

revolves in same direction as ba $= \dfrac{\text{RPM srg} \times 84 + \text{RPM ssg} \times 28}{84 \times 28} =$

$\dfrac{\text{RPM ba} \times 3 + \text{RPM ssg}}{4} = \dfrac{\text{RPM vsl} \times .675 + \dfrac{\text{RPM vsl} \times \text{lg} \times .288}{\text{Dwg}}}{4} =$

RPM vsl $\times \left(.169 + \dfrac{\text{lg} \times .072}{\text{Dwg}}\right)$ and in opposite direction to ba = RPM

vsl $\times \left(.169 - \dfrac{\text{lg} \times .072}{\text{Dwg}}\right)$. From equation (53), the largest lg having 42

teeth, and the smallest Dwg 56, that (54) maximum RPM sa = +RPM vsl $\times .223$ and minimum RPM sa = +RPM vsl $\times .115$.

108. From the preceding example select the correct word or words within each set of the following parentheses: At the start of each successive layer RPM ba and RPM ssg (a) (increase, decrease) in (b) (direct, inverse) proportion and during each layer (c) (increase, decrease) are constant. Why? During a layer when ssg revolves in the same direction as ba the RPM from ssg (d) (increase, decrease) RPM sa (e) (over, under) the RPM from ba. Why? During the next layer the RPM from ssg (f) (increase, decrease) RPM sa (g) (over, under) the RPM from ba. Why? RPM sa from ssg is always (h) (greater, less) than RPM sa from ba. Why? RPM sa $\therefore$ is (i) (always, alternately) in a direction (j) (the same as, opposite to) RPM ba. Why?

As shown in Fig. 7 the 60-tooth bag of Fig. 8 meshes with the 24-tooth *bobbin shaft driven gear, Bosg,* which is integral through the *bobbin shaft, bosh,* with the *bobbin gear, Bg; Bg* is integral through the *bolster tube* with bo which fits outside of about the upper half of the bolster; inside the bolster is the *spindle* tube of about the same length as the bolster; and inside the spindle is the *bobbin screw, bos,* which is about half the length of the spindle and integral with the *screw gear, Sg.* The spindle is free to traverse vertically within the bolster. But on the inside of the bolster and on the outside of the spindle are vertical keyways in which are short keys that cause the spindle to revolve with the bolster and $\therefore$ with bo. The lower end of the spindle tube is a nut threaded to bos.

109. From the foregoing, the bobbin and screw trains and "hand" of their parts in Fig. 7, and equations (52) and (54) prove that (55) when RPM ssg is at the maximum and in the direction of RPM ba, $\dfrac{\text{RPM bos}}{\text{RPM bo}} =$

$$\dfrac{\dfrac{+\text{RPM vsl} \times .223 \times 60 \times 40}{18 \times 27}}{\dfrac{+\ \text{RPM vsl} \times .225 \times 60 \times 40}{24 \times 27}} = +1.32 \text{ or } +132\%$$ and in the opposite direction to RPM ba, $\dfrac{\text{RPM bos}}{\text{RPM bo}} = +.68$ or $+68\%$.

110. From equation (55) select the correct word or words within each set of the following parentheses: RPM bos is (a) (always, alternately) in the direction (b) (of, opposite to) RPM bo. Why? If $\dfrac{\text{RPM bos}}{\text{RPM bo}}$ = 100%, bo traverses (c) (up, down, none) Why? With a given combination of lg and Dwg, bos is (d) (the same, a different) % (e) (slower, faster) (f) (than, as) bo when ssg and ba revolve in the same direction (g) (as, than) bos is (h) (faster, slower) than bo when ssg and ba revolve in different directions and $\therefore$ bo traverses up and down at (i) (the same, different) IPM. Why?

111. From the preceding problem, formula (15), Chap. XX, Part One, and Fig. 7 prove

$$(56)\ \dfrac{\text{traversing}}{\text{IPM bo}} = \dfrac{\text{RPM vsl} \times 44 \times 30 \times \text{lg} \times 45 \times 42 \times}{86 \times 28 \times \text{Dwg} \times 60 \times 60 \times 4 \times 18 \times 27};$$

and as derived for a cone frame, from equations (42), (49), and (56) for the variable pulley frame in Fig. 7 derive

(57) lay constant = coils per inch × lay gear =

$$\frac{.54 \times 1 \times 60 \times 40 \times 86 \times 28 \times \text{dwell gear} \times 60 \times 60 \times 4 \times 18 \times 27}{60 \times 4 \times 24 \times 27 \times 44 \times 30 \times 45 \times 42 \times 1 \times 60 \times 40 \times .5},$$

and prove that formulas (46) and (47) are true.

Some Lay Train Combinations of Fig. 7			
	A	**B**	**C**
lay gear, lg	18 to 42	18 to 40	18 to 34
dwell gear, Dwg	56	70	79

112. From formula (57) find a factor that can save you labor in finding lc for the combinations of Fig. 7.

Find (a) lc and (b) cpi ranges of Fig. 7 with the combinations in the following three problems:

113. A.   114. B.   115. C.

What number of teeth in lg ought to be tried to obtain the cpi on the combinations of Fig. 7 in the following three problems:

116. A. At least and near as possible to 11.5?

117. B. Not over but as near as possible to 224 coils in a first layer of 14″?

118. C. Close as possible to 10.1 coil multiplier and no lighter than 1.35 hank?

Finding Gears in Changing Coils Per Inch, and Hank.

119. On any frame such as in Figs. 6 and 7 to change from a satisfactory present or old cpi to a new cpi, from formula (47), lc remaining the same, derive

$$(58) \text{ new lay gear} = \frac{\text{old lay gear} \times \text{old coils per inch}}{\text{new coils per inch}}$$

and ∴, cm also remaining the same,

$$(59) \frac{\text{new lay}}{\text{gear}} = \frac{\text{old lay gear} \times \sqrt{\text{old hank}}}{\sqrt{\text{new hank}}}.$$

Find the teeth in lg to lay as required under the satisfactory conditions in the following four problems:

120. At least and as close as possible to 10 cpi if 21 teeth lay 12 cpi.

121. Near as possible to but not over 16.75 cpi if 18 teeth lay 20.5 cpi.

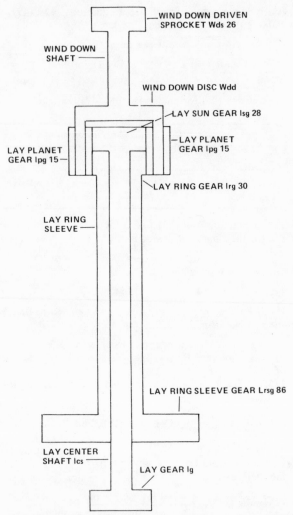

Figure 9. Lay Wind Down Compound of Figure 7

122. No lighter than but as close as possible to .90 HR if 40 teeth lay .80 HR.

123. Close as possible to and heavy as 1.80 hank if 26 teeth lay 1.60 hank.

124. From a frame in your plant ascertain the data for and calculate its lc, cpi range, lg for cpi being run and other cpi and HR as assigned by your instructor.

Lay Wind Down of the Variable Pulley Frame. The action between sets of the lay wind down compound of Fig. 9 and the lay wind down train is studied in the following problems:

125. Calculate from Fig. 9 and formula (42), Chap. XX, Part One, lrg not revolving, (a) $\dfrac{\text{RPM wdd}}{\text{RPM lsg}}$ and (b) $\dfrac{\text{wdd}}{\text{lsg}}$; and from Fig. 8 and formula (37), Chap. XX, Part One, bo not revolving (c) $\dfrac{\text{RPM ssg}}{\text{RPM sa}}$ and (d) $\dfrac{\text{ssg}}{\text{sa}}$.

From the preceding problem derive an equation for the wind down RPM bos and by it calculate the range of wind down (a) RPM bos (b) IPM bo with the lay train combinations in the following three problems:

126. A.   **127.** B.   **128.** C.

TENSION

Basic Formula.

129. Select the correct word in each set of the following parentheses: Other conditions being the same the (a) (more, less) layers in a full bobbin the (b) (less, more) the *tension* in the stock and ∴ tension is (c) (inversely, directly) proportional to *layers per inch, lpi.* From (c) derive the following definition

(60) tension = layers per inch.

Layers Per Inch, Tension Constants, Ranges, and Gears of Cone Frames.

130. From Fig. 6 select the correct word or words in each set of the following parentheses: RPM *top cone* is (a) (constant, variable) during a set. Why? RPM *bottom cone, Bc,* must (b) (be constant, increase, decrease) to start each successive layer and (c) (decrease, be constant, increase) during each layer. Why? The *cone belt* and *cone rack, cr,* must remain in the same position during a (d) (set, layer) and move (e) (toward, away from) the (f) (small, large) end of Bc during a (g) (layer, set).

In Fig. 6 the *skip gear, Skg,* has two toothless skips opposite each other and through the *skip shaft* is integral with the *skip shaft driver gear, sksg,* the *upper builder arm, bua, lower builder arm, bua, reversing cam, rc,* and with a spring not shown. The spring causes Skg to mesh with the *top cone bevel gear, tcbg,* and ∴ causes Skg, sksg, both bua, and rc to make $\frac{1}{2}$ revolution when not restrained by upper bua encountering the *upper builder jaw, buj,* and lower bua encountering the *lower builder jaw, buj.* As shown, such restraint is simultaneous with Skg having made the $\frac{1}{2}$ revolution that leaves tcbg revolving at a skip in Skg.

131. What effect has the $\frac{1}{2}$ revolution of rc upon: (a) The position of cr and the cone belt? How? (b) RPM bo? How? (c) Direction of traverse of Lr? How? (d) Direction of traverse of bo? How? (e) Layers on bo? How?

132. From the preceding problem and formula (14), Chap. XX, Part

One prove that traverse cr for each layer $= \dfrac{\dfrac{1}{2} \times \text{sksg} \times \text{tng} \times 16 \times \text{cir. p. cr}}{\text{Tng} \times 80}$;

$\therefore$ layers in full bo $= \dfrac{\text{total traverse cr}}{\dfrac{\dfrac{1}{2} \times \text{sksg} \times \text{tng} \times 16 \times \text{cir. p cr}}{\text{Tng} \times 80}} =$

$\dfrac{\text{total traverse cr} \times 2 \times \text{Tng} \times 80}{\text{sksg} \times \text{tng} \times 16 \times \text{cir. p. cr}}$; $\therefore$

(61) $\text{lpi} = \dfrac{\dfrac{\text{total traverse cr} \times 2 \times \text{Tng} \times 80}{\text{sksg} \times \text{tng} \times 16 \times \text{cir. p. cr}}}{\text{radius full bo} - \text{radius bare bo}} =$

$\dfrac{\text{total traverse cr} \times 4 \times \text{Tng} \times 80}{(\text{dia. full bo} - \text{dia. bare bo}) \times \text{sksg} \times \text{tng} \times 16 \times \text{cir. p. cr}}$.

133. Reasoning as in your derivation of previous constants, from equation (60) and (61), for cone frames as in Fig. 6 derive

(62) tension constant = layers per inch × tension gear =

$\dfrac{\text{total traverse cone rack} \times 4 \times \text{tension driven gear} \times 80}{\left(\begin{matrix} \text{dia. full} \\ \text{bobbin} \end{matrix} - \begin{matrix} \text{dia. bare} \\ \text{bobbin} \end{matrix} \right) \times \dfrac{\text{skip shaft}}{\text{driver gear}} \times 16 \times \dfrac{\text{cir. pitch}}{\text{cone rack}}}$,

(63) layers per inch $= \dfrac{\text{tension constant}}{\text{tension gear}}$, and

(64) tension gear $= \dfrac{\text{tension constant}}{\text{layers per inch}}$.

Some Tension Train Combinations of Fig. 6			
	A	**B**	**C**
diameter of full bobbin	12″	10″	10″
diameter of bare bobbin	$1\frac{3}{4}''$	$1\frac{5}{8}''$	$1\frac{5}{8}''$
skip shaft driver gear, sksg	16	20	16
tension driven gear, Tng	68	64	68
tension gear, tng		26 to 59	
circumferential pitch of cone rack, cr	.3846	.3333	.3333
total traverse of cone rack	26″	28″	28″

Find the (a) *tension constants, tnc, and* (b) *lpi ranges of Fig.* 6 *with the combinations in the following three problems:*

134. A.   **135.** B.   **136.** C.

What number of teeth in tng ought to be tried on Fig. 6 for the lpi and combination in the following problems:

137. A. At least and as near as possible to 18.6?
138. C. Close as possible to but not over 29.4?
139. B. No heavier than and close as possible to 1.75 hank and 12.2 layer multiplier?
140. C. At least and as near as possible to 1.25 HR and 16.2 lay multiple?

Layers Per Inch, Tension Constants, Ranges, and Gears of the Variable Pulley Frame. Your study of the lay train of the variable pulley frame in Fig. 7 included clc sliding along cls and reversing the shock gear. What causes clc to slide is your next study. Integral with rvs is a 19-tooth spiral gear meshing with the *builder shaft driven gear, Bushg.* Bushg through the *builder shaft, bush,* is integral with the spiral *builder shaft driver gear, bushg,* shown at the upper left of Fig. 7. Meshing with bushg are the two spiral *builder screw gears, Busg,* shown also in Fig. 10. Each Busg is integral with its vertical *builder screw, bus,* shown horizontal in Fig. 7 and vertical, as it actually is, in Fig. 10. Threaded to each bus is its *firing gear, fig,* which meshes with the vertical *long gear, lng.* Until you study the taper train consider lng stationary and ∴ fig kept from revolving but free to slide vertically on lng as bus revolves. Pivotal on clc and free to slide clc on cls is the *clutch arm, cla,* which is integral with the *rocker shaft, rks,* shown also at the upper left and in Fig. 10. Integral with

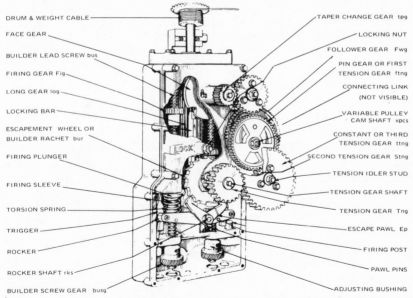

DRUM & WEIGHT CABLE
FACE GEAR
BUILDER LEAD SCREW bus
FIRING GEAR Fig
LONG GEAR log
LOCKING BAR
ESCAPEMENT WHEEL OR
BUILDER RACHET bur
FIRING PLUNGER
FIRING SLEEVE
TORSION SPRING
TRIGGER
ROCKER
ROCKER SHAFT rks
BUILDER SCREW GEAR busg

TAPER CHANGE GEAR tpg
LOCKING NUT
FOLLOWER GEAR Fwg
PIN GEAR OR FIRST TENSION GEAR ftng
CONNECTING LINK (NOT VISIBLE)
VARIABLE PULLEY CAM SHAFT vpcs
CONSTANT OR THIRD TENSION GEAR ttng
SECOND TENSION GEAR Stng
TENSION IDLER STUD
TENSION GEAR SHAFT
TENSION GEAR Tng
ESCAPE PAWL Ep
FIRING POST
PAWL PINS
ADJUSTING BUSHING

Figure 10.   The Parts of the Tension and Taper Trains at the Builder of Figure 7

rks is the double *escape pawl, Ep.* The *rocker,* however, is free to revolve on rks as a stud and its right and left *pawl pins* to contact Ep.

Thus motion from the lay train is transmitted to the tension train through the two bus which being driven by the same spiral bushg must revolve in opposite directions. But the two bus being of the same "hand," one fig must be traversing opposite to the other fig. As shown in Fig. 10 when the fig on the right traversed to its bottom, pushed down on its *firing sleeve,* compressed its *torsion spring,* forced its *trigger* off its *firing post,* and "fired" the right arm of the rocker down, fig on the left traversed to its top. When the right arm of the rocker was fired down its left *pawl pin* forced the right pawl of Ep down. Thus Ep through rks is reversing the motion from the lay train and the revolutions of bus and starting the right fig up and the left fig down in preparation for the next reversal.

As will be studied with the taper train the *variable pulley cam shaft, vpcs,* is under continuous stress to revolve. As shown in Figs. 7 and 10: integral with vpcs are the *variable pulley cam, vpc,* and the *first tension gear, ftng;* meshing with ftng is the *second tension gear, Stng,* which is integral with the *third tension gear, ttng;* and meshing with ttng is the *tension gear, Tng,* which through the tension gear shaft is integral with the *builder ratchet, bur.*

Thus bur is stressed continuously to revolve counterclockwise as viewed in Fig. 10 and does so when the rocker is fired and one pawl of Ep releases a tooth and the other pawl almost instantly catches and holds another tooth. The distance between pawls exceeds by $\frac{1}{2}$ tooth the distance between the tooth held and the tooth next to be caught.

141. From the foregoing description and your study of the lay train, answer and prove: What effect has each release by Ep on (a) RPM Dwg? Why? (b) Direction of traverse bo? Why? (c) Number of layers? Why? (d) What is the relation of the releases by Ep to the layers? Why?

(66) layers = revolutions bur × 2 × 19.

142. Also from the foregoing description and Fig. 7 prove that

$$(67) \quad \text{revolutions bur} = \frac{\text{revolutions vpc} \times \text{ftng} \times \text{ttng}}{\text{Stng} \times \text{Tng}}$$

143. From equation (67) show that (68) at each release of bur rev.

$$\text{vpc} = \frac{\frac{1}{2 \times 19} \times \text{Stng} \times \text{Tng}}{\text{ftng} \times \text{ttng}}$$ and ∴ when Fig. 7 is as in, for instance, combination A following, at each release the maximum rev. vpc = .007.

Each slight revolution of vpc through its *variable pulley cam follower arm, vpcfa,* screws the conical sides of the *driver variable pulley, vp,* closer together thereby decreasing the effective dia. vp, and the conical sides of the *driven variable pulley, Vp,* farther apart thereby increasing the effective dia. Vp.

144. From the foregoing and equation (68) answer: What effect through vpc does each release of bur have on (a) RPM vp? Why? (b)

RPM Vp? Why? (c) RPM vsl? Why? (d) RPM bo? Why? (cite the equation that proves your answer) (e) Traversing IPM bo? Why (cite the equation)?

The vpc is designed to shorten its throw by the same distance at each release of bur and to revolve 185° during a set.

145. Prove that during a set: from the foregoing and equation (67)

$$(69) \text{ rev. bur} = \frac{\dfrac{185}{360} \times \text{ftng} \times \text{ttng}}{\text{Stng} \times \text{Tng}}, \text{ from equations (66) and (69)}$$

$$(70) \text{ layers} = \frac{185 \times \text{ftng} \times \text{ttng} \times 2 \times 19}{360 \times \text{Stng} \times \text{Tng}}, \text{ and from equation (70)}$$

$$(71) \text{ lpi on full bo} = \frac{\dfrac{185 \times \text{ftng} \times \text{ttng} \times 2 \times 19}{360 \times \text{Stng} \times \text{Tng}}}{\dfrac{\text{dia. full bo}}{2} - \dfrac{\text{dia. bare bo}}{2}}.$$

146. From equations (60) and (71) for the variable pulley frame in Fig. 7 derive

(72) tension constant = layers per inch × tension gear =

$$\frac{185 \times \dfrac{\text{first}}{\text{tension gear}} \times \dfrac{\text{third}}{\text{tension gear}} \times 4 \times 19}{\left(\dfrac{\text{dia. full}}{\text{bobbin}} - \dfrac{\text{dia. bare}}{\text{bobbin}}\right) \times 360 \times \dfrac{\text{second}}{\text{tension gear}}}$$

and prove that formulas (63) and (64) are true.

Some Tension Train Combinations of Fig. 7				
	A	B	C	D
diameter of full bobbin	7″	7″	7″	$5\frac{1}{2}''$
diameter of bare bobbin	$2\frac{3}{8}''$	$2\frac{3}{8}''$	$2\frac{3}{8}''$	$2\frac{3}{8}''$
first tension gear, ftng	108	108	116	116
second tension gear, Stng	38	38	30	30
third tension gear, ttng	95	110	120	120
tension gear, Tng, range		38 to 67		

Find the (a) tension constants, tnc, and (b) lpi ranges of Fig. 7 with the combinations in the following four problems:

147. A.   **148.** B.   **149.** C.   **150.** D.

What number of teeth in Tng on Fig. 7 ought to be tried for the combinations and lpi in the following four problems:

151. A. 35?   **152.** B. 62?

153. C layer multiplier of 51.8 and HR close as possible to and no heavier than 1.70?

154. D near as possible to but no lighter than 3.00 hank with a 51.8 lm?

Finding Gears in Changing Layers Per Inch and Hank.

155. On any frame such as in Figs. 6 and 7 to change from a satisfactory present or old lpi to a new lpi, from formula (64), tnc and the layer multiplier remaining the same, derive

$$(73) \text{ new tension gear} = \frac{\text{old tension gear} \times \text{old layers per inch}}{\text{new layers per inch}}$$

and $\therefore$, lm also remaining the same

$$(74) \text{ new tension gear} = \frac{\text{old tension gear} \times \sqrt{\text{old hank}}}{\sqrt{\text{new hank}}},$$

Find the teeth in the tension gear that ought to be tried to give lpi as required under the satisfactory conditions in the following four problems:

156. 50 lpi if 40 teeth give 54 lpi.

157. At least and as near as possible to 65 lpi if 40 teeth give 50 lpi.

158. As heavy as and close as possible to .85 HR if 52 teeth run .70 HR.

159. No heavier than and close as possible to 1.65 hank when 43 teeth run 1.90 HR.

160. From a frame in your plant gather the data for and calculate its tnc, lpi range, tension gear for present and other lpi and hank as assigned by your instructor.

TAPER

Basic Formula.

161. If the lay and tension trains alone could build bo what would (a) the traverse of each layer equal (b) be the build of the ends of bo?

For the most production bo ought to be as near as the lay and tension trains alone would build it consistent with shortening each successive layer enough to prevent end coils sloughing. As in Fig. 11, a section along the center line of a full bo shows the shortening makes a straight line slope, except as will be studied later, and that

(75) taper = total shortening of traverse of bobbin.

Taper, Constants, Ranges, and Gears of Cone Frames.   In Fig. 6 the *builder screw bearings, bsb,* are integral with the bobbin carriage, can be adjusted vertically on it, and $\therefore$ traverse with bo. The right-handed upper

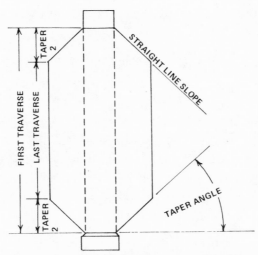

Figure 11.   Section Along Center Line of Full Bobbin of Roving

builder screw, **bus,** and the left-handed lower bus are integral with the square *builder rod,* **bur,** which is free to slide through a closely fitting square center hole in the *builder rod gear,* **Burg.** Thus bur revolves with Burg. The heights of bsb are so adjusted to the carriage that at the desired lower limit of the first down traverse in a set, upper bua escapes the restraint of upper buj and at the desired upper limit of the first up traverse lower bua escapes the restraint of lower buj. As emphasized in your study of tension each escape of a bua traverses cr away from the small end of Bc. Each traverse of cr, through the *taper gear,* **Tpg,** causes bus to revolve, the buj to be screwed closer together, upper bua to escape upper buj earlier than on the preceding down traverse of the carriage, and lower bua to escape lower buj earlier than on the previous up traverse.

162. Prove: from the foregoing that

(76) total shortening of traverse bo = shortening of traverse each buj during a set × 2; from Fig. 6 that

$$(77) \quad \text{rev. bus} = \frac{\text{rev. Tpg} \times 18}{\text{Burg}};$$

from formula (11), Chap. XX, Part One, and letting ttcr mean total traverse of cone rack, that

$$(78) \quad \text{rev. Tpg} = \frac{\text{ttcr}}{\text{Tpg} \times \text{cir. p. cr.}};$$

from equations (77) and (78) that

$$(79) \quad \text{rev. bus} = \frac{\text{ttcr} \times 18}{\text{cir. p. cr} \times \text{Tpg} \times \text{Burg}};$$

from equation (79) and formula (15), Chap. XX, Part One, that

(80) shortening of traverse each buj during a set =

$$\frac{ttcr \times 18 \times lead\ bus}{cir.\ p.\ cr \times Tpg \times Burg};$$

and from equations (75), (76), and (80) that

$$(81)\quad taper = \frac{ttcr \times 18 \times lead\ bus \times 2}{cir.\ p.\ cr \times Tpg \times Burg}.$$

163. From equation (81) for cone frames as in Fig. 6 derive

(82) taper constant = taper × taper gear =

$$\frac{total\ traverse\ cone\ rack \times 18 \times lead\ builder\ screw \times 2}{circumferential\ pitch\ cone\ rack \times builder\ rod\ gear},$$

$$(83)\quad taper = \frac{taper\ constant}{taper\ gear}, and$$

$$(84)\quad taper\ gear = \frac{taper\ constant}{taper}.$$

Some Combinations of the Taper Train of Fig. 6

	A	B
taper gear, Tpg	11 to 14	13 to 16
builder rod gear, Burg	12	14
lead of builder screw, bus	.1667"	.1667"
circumferential pitch of cone rack, cr	.3846	.3333
total traverse of cone rack	26"	28"

Find the (a) *taper constants, tpc, and* (b) *taper ranges of Fig.* 6 *with the combinations in the two following problems:*

164. A.   **165.** B.

166. On the 12" × 6" bobbin of Fig. 6 with combination A and the clinging fiber to be run it seems feasible to increase the last layer to $9\frac{1}{2}"$. What Tpg ought to be tried?

167. The slick 10" × 5" bobbins on Fig. 6 with combination B are inclined to slough with a 14-tooth Tpg. (a) What Tpg ought to be tried to correct this and hurt production the least? (b) How much will this change taper?

Taper, Constants, Ranges, and Gears of the Variable Pulley Frame. Your study of tension of Figs. 7 and 10 included (a) lng and fig not revolving during a layer; (b) continuous stress of vpcs to revolve and ∴ bur revolving $\frac{1}{2}$ tooth whenever at the end of a layer an fig fires; and (c) during a set the revolution of vpcs = $\frac{185}{360}$.

The builder weight is suspended from the builder cable wound on the *builder cable drum* which is integral with lng shown in Fig. 10 and in Fig. 7 upside down at lower left and horizontal at upper left. Meshing with lng is the *face gear* which is integral with the *taper gear, tpg.* Free to revolve upon vpcs as a stud is the eccentric *follower gear, Fwg,* which through the *connecting link* is, let us temporarily consider, completely, integral with ftng.

Hence, the continuous stress from the builder weight on lng to revolve and ∴ from lng (a) not only on vpcs, through ftng, to revolve but (b) also on each fig to revolve when at the end of a layer the tension train, through bus, causes an fig to fire.

168. From Fig. 7 select the correct word in each set of parentheses: due to its revolution a firing fig (a) (unscrews, screws) while the other fig (b) (screws, unscrews). What effect ∴ does each fig revolving at the instant its bus reverses direction of revolution have on (c) next traverse each fig (d) ∴ rev. each bus during next layer (e) ∴ rev. bos during next layer.

169. From your study of tension, the foregoing descriptions and problem, and Fig. 7 prove that: during a set simultaneous rev. fig =

$$\frac{\dfrac{185}{360} \times 115 \times 63 \times 55 \times 27}{50 \times tpg \times 27 \times 20} \text{ and } \therefore$$

(85) due to rev. fig. decreased simultaneous rev. bus =

$$\frac{185 \times 115 \times 63 \times 55 \times 27}{360 \times 50 \times tpg \times 27 \times 20}.$$

170. For the moment considering lng and bo not revolving, from Fig. 7 and formula (37), Chap. **XX**, Part One prove that: rev. bos =

$$\frac{\text{rev. bus} \times 20 \times 19 \times 42 \times 60 \times 40}{13 \times 19 \times 60 \times 4 \times 18 \times 27} = \frac{\text{rev. bus} \times 14}{10.53} \therefore \text{ from equation (85)}$$

during a set due to rev. fig., decreased rev. bos =

$$\frac{\dfrac{185 \times 115 \times 63 \times 55 \times 27}{360 \times 50 \times tpg \times 27 \times 20} \times 14}{10.53} ; \therefore \text{ from formulas (15), Chap. XX, Part}$$

One and (75) total shortening traverse bo =

$$\frac{14 \times 185 \times 115 \times 63 \times 55 \times 27 \times .5}{10.53 \times 360 \times 50 \times tpg \times 27 \times 20} = \text{taper}; \therefore$$

(86) taper constant = taper × $\dfrac{\text{taper}}{\text{gear}} = \dfrac{14 \times 185 \times 115 \times 63 \times 55 \times 27 \times .5}{10.53 \times 360 \times 50 \times 27 \times 20}$;

and ∴ formulas (83) and (84) are true.

171. Find the (a) taper constant and (b) taper range of Fig. 7 with a 32- to 35-tooth tpg range.

172. By how much does a 1-tooth increase from a (a) 32- (b) 34-tooth tpg on Fig. 7 change taper and which way?

173. What tpg on Fig. 7 ought to be tried to obtain a last layer as near as possible to and (a) at least $10\frac{1''}{8}$ on a $14'' \times 7''$ bo (b) not over $7\frac{3''}{4}$ on a $12'' \times 5\frac{1''}{2}$ bo?

Fwg and ftng are integral through, and except as modified by, the *connecting link* which has a circular hole in each end. One hole has a working fit with a round pin in ftng and the other a working fit with either of two round pins in Fwg. At the start of a set the pin in ftng is directly under vpcs and the pins in Fwg are to the right and left of vpcs. Because of the eccentricity of Fwg and the angle of the connecting link, at the start of a set if the connecting link is placed to work with the (a) left pin of Fwg, Fwg is released equally at each $\frac{1}{2}$ tooth release of bur, making a straight taper as in Fig. 10 (b) right pin, Fwg is released increasingly with each release of bur, making a convex taper with less liability to slough.

Finding Gears in Changing Taper.

174. On any frame as in Figs. 6 and 7 to change from a satisfactory present or old to a new taper, from formula (84), the constant remaining the same, derive

$$(87) \text{ new taper gear} = \frac{\text{old taper gear} \times \text{old taper}}{\text{new taper}}.$$

How many teeth in the taper gear ought to be tried to give taper as required under the satisfactory conditions in the following three problems:

175. $2\frac{1}{2}''$ if 20 teeth taper $2\frac{1}{4}''$?

176. $2\frac{7}{8}''$ if $3\frac{1}{4}''$ is tapered by 15 teeth?

177. Changing to slicker stock and lighter hank necessitates not over a 10″ last layer on a 14″ × 7″ bo now getting a $10\frac{1}{4}''$ last layer from 35 teeth?

PRODUCTION

Basic Formulas and Production Constants.

178. As with carding department machines previously studied derive

$$(88) \frac{100\%}{\text{hanks}} = \frac{\dfrac{\text{RPM front}}{\text{roll}} \times \pi \times \dfrac{\text{dia. front}}{\text{roll}} \times 60 \times \text{hours} \times \text{spindles}}{36 \times 840}$$

and ∴

$$(89) \text{ production constant, pc} = \frac{\pi \times \text{dia. front roll} \times 60}{36 \times 840}.$$

179. With minimum labor calculate pc for frames with front rolls of $1''$, $1\frac{1}{8}''$, $1\frac{3}{16}''$, $1\frac{1}{4}''$, and $1\frac{15}{16}''$.

180. From formulas (88) and (89) derive

(90) 100% hanks = production constant × RPM front roll × hours × spindles.

Percents of Production and Contraction.   As with machines previously studied 100% production at the delivery or front roll, f, must be modified by the percent of production, % p, and also on the roving frame by the percent of contraction, % c, previously studied with draft, to find the hanks at spindles, *sps,* or *spindle hanks, shks,* from the hanks at f or *front roll hank, fhks.*

Production in Hanks from RPM of Front Roll.

181. From formula (90) and the foregoing derive

$$(91) \quad \frac{\text{front}}{\text{roll}} = \frac{\text{production}}{\text{constant}} \times \frac{\text{RPM}}{\text{front}} \times \text{hours} \times \text{spindles} \times \frac{.01 \times \%}{\text{production}}$$
$$\text{hanks} \qquad \qquad \text{roll}$$

and

(92) spindle hanks = front roll hanks × (1 − .01 × % contraction)

Such abbreviations as *fhks/sp* meaning fhks per spindle (i.e., for each spindle); *shks/sp* meaning shks per spindle (i.e., at each spindle); *fhks/sph* meaning fhks per spindle hour (i.e., for each spindle during each hr.); and *shks/sph* may be used. The hank clock by which frame tenders are usually paid is driven by f and ∴ register fhks for each frame which are called also *clock hanks, chks,* or *frame hanks, fmhks.* Thus fhks = chks × spindles per frame × frames. The abbreviation *chks/h* meaning chks per hr., or fmhks/hr may be used.

Find the hanks abbreviated and under the conditions in the following examples and four problems:

EXAMPLE: *fhks/sph with* 1″ *f at* 186 *RPM and* 81% *p.*

By formula (91) fhks/sph = .006233 × 186 × 1 × 1 × .01 × 81 = .939.

EXAMPLE: (a) *fhks/sp and* (b) *fmhks with* 1″ *f at* 202 *RPM and* 79% *p for* 40 *hrs.*

(a) By formula (91) fhks/sp = .006233 × 202 × 40 × 1 × .01 × 79 = 39.79; (b) same as (a).

EXAMPLE: (a) *fmhks and* (b) *shks for* 3 108-*spindle frames with* 1″ *f at* 208 *RPM,* 78% *p, and* 3% *c for* 40 *hrs.*

(a) By formula (91) fmhks = .006233 × 208 × 40 × 3 × .01 × 78 = 121.35; (b) by formulas (91) and (92) shks = .006233 × 208 × 40 × 3 × 108 × .01 × 78 × (1 − .01 × 3) = 12713.

182. 100% fhks/sph with $1\frac{1}{8}''$ f at 265 RPM.

183. (a) chks and (b) shks for $5\frac{1}{2}$ 8-hr. days and 3 96-spindle frames with $1\frac{1''}{8}$ f at 280 RPM, 81.5% p, and 2.75% c.

184. (a) fhks/sph, (b) fhks/sp, (c) fmhks, and (d) shks for 3 40-hr. weeks of 3 frame tenders each on 4 82-spindle frames with $1\frac{3''}{16}$ f at 172 RPM, 84.5% p, and 3.25% c.

185. (a) fhks/sph, (b) fhks/sp, (c) chks, (d) shks/sph, and (e) shks for 3 8-hr. shifts per day for 1 5-day week for 2 96-spindle frames with $1\frac{15''}{16}$ f at 144 RPM, 80.5% p, and 4.8% c.

Production in Hanks from RPM of Flyer.

186. Prove: from formula (32) that RPM $f = \dfrac{\text{RPM fl}}{\pi \times \text{dia.}\, f \times \text{tpi}}$; $\therefore$ from formulas (89) and (91) that fhks $= \dfrac{\pi \times \text{dia.}\, f \times 60}{36 \times 840} \times \dfrac{\text{RPM fl}}{\pi \times \text{dia.}\, f \times \text{tpi}}$ $\times$ hrs. $\times$ sps $\times$ .01 $\times$ % p; and

(93) $\dfrac{\text{front}}{\substack{\text{roll} \\ \text{hanks}}} = \dfrac{\text{RPM flyer} \times \text{hours} \times \text{spindles} \times .01 \times \% \text{ production}}{\text{twist per inch} \times 504}$

Find the hanks abbreviated and under the conditions in the following four problems:

187. 100% (a) fhks/sph and (b) shks/sph, .75 tpi, 660 RPM fl, 3% c.

188. (a) fhks/sp and (b) fmhks, $1\frac{1}{3}$ tpi, 900 RPM fl at 77.7% p for 3 frames for 3 40-hr. weekly shifts.

189. (a) fhks/sp and (b) chks, 1.50 tm, 1.30 HR, 1200 RPM fl at 80.5% p for 4 frames for 3 8-hr. shifts $5\frac{1}{2}$ days per week.

190. (a) fhks/sph, (b) fhks/sp, (c) fmhks, and (d) shks with 59.81 tc, 24-tooth tg, at 1800 RPM fl, 79.8% p, and 4.8% c for 4 96-spindle frames for 3 8-hr. shifts per day for 1 5-day week.

Production in Pounds from RPM of Front Roll and Flyer.

191. From formulas (6) Chap. 1, (91), and (93) derive

(94) pounds $= \dfrac{\substack{\text{RPM} \\ \text{production} \times \text{front} \times \text{hours} \times \text{spindles} \times .01 \times \% \\ \text{constant} \qquad \text{roll} \qquad\qquad\qquad\qquad\qquad \text{production}}}{\text{hank roving}}$

and

(95) pounds $= \dfrac{\text{RPM flyer} \times \text{hours} \times \text{spindles} \times .01 \times \% \text{ production}}{\text{twist per inch} \times \text{hank roving} \times 504}$

Such abbreviations as lbs./sp, meaning lbs. per spindle, and lbs./sph, meaning lbs. per spindle hr. (i.e., for 1 spindle for 1 hr.) are common.

Find (a) *lbs./sph,* (b) *lbs./sp, and* (c) *lbs. under the conditions in the following seven problems:*

192. 100% for .70 HR from $1\frac{1}{8}''$ f at 216 RPM for 8 hrs. of 1 88-spindle frame.

193. 1.20 RH from $1\frac{1}{4}''$ f at 240 RPM and 78.3% p for 2 102-spindle frame for 5 days of 3 8-hr. shifts.

194. .90 HR from $1\frac{1}{8}''$ f at 270 RPM and 81.9% p for 4 96-spindle frames for 3 8-hr. shifts per day for 1 5-day week.

195. 1 frame of 88 sps, 900 RPM fl, 81.2% p for 8 hrs. on 1.20 hank with $1\frac{1}{3}$ tpi.

196. 2 8-hr. shifts per day for 1 5-day week of 2 96-spindle frames at 1200 RPM fl and 83.3% p on 1.60 hank and 1.90 tpi.

197. 1.48 HR and 1.50 tm at 1600 RPM fl and 79.1% p on 4 96-spindle frames for 3 44-hr. weekly shifts.

198. 28-tooth tg on 3 96-spindle frames of 54.69 tc, 1800 RPM fl, and 78.4% p running 2.5 hank for 3 8-hr. shifts for a $5\frac{1}{2}$-day week.

199. Equation

$$(96)\quad \frac{\text{approximate}}{100\% \text{ lbs./sph}} = \frac{2 \times \text{RPM fl}}{1000 \times \text{tpi} \times \text{HR}}$$

or "twice the flyer speed divided by a thousand times the twist times the hank" is often used. Show: (a) its derivation, (b) why it is easy to use and remember, (c) its + or − error in lbs. and %, and (d) its error if used for 6 88-spindle frames for 3 8-hr. shifts for a 5-day week.

Finding the Hours Per Set, Doffing Cycle, Percent of Production, and Creeling Cycle.   One meaning of *hours per set, hrs./set,* is the hrs. that bo actually revolves in being filled exclusive of *incidental stops, ist,* i.e., the hrs. between the start and end of a set to piece broken ends, clean, and otherwise service the frame. *Hours to doff frame, dhrs.,* is the part of an hr. between sets required to doff a frame full of full bobbins produced during a set, replace them with bare bobbins, and prepare the frame for the next set. *Doffing cycle, dfc,* is the hrs. from the start of one set to the start of the next. Often ist is calculated as a % for ist of dfc, *% ist of dfc. Creeling cycle, clc,* is the hrs. required for a spindle to consume its creeled raw stock whether a full can of sliver at a slubber or a full bobbin, single or double, of slubber roving at an intermediate.

200. Prove: that

$$(97)\quad \text{hours per set} = \frac{\text{pounds on full bobbin}}{100\% \text{ pounds per spindle hour}};$$

that dfc = hrs./set + % ist of dfc + dhrs.; ∴ that dfc − % ist of dfc = hrs./set + dhrs.; ∴ that dfc × (1 − .01 × % ist) = hrs./set + dhrs.; ∴ that

(98) $\dfrac{\text{doffing}}{\text{cycle}} = \dfrac{\text{hours per set} + \text{hours to doff frame}}{1 - .01 \times \% \text{ for incidental stops}}$, and since

(99) $\dfrac{\% \text{ of}}{\text{production}} = \dfrac{100 \times \text{hours per set}}{\text{doffing cycle}}$, that

(100) $\dfrac{\% \text{ of}}{\text{production}} =$

$$\dfrac{(100 - \% \text{ for incidental stops}) \times \text{lbs. on full bobbin}}{(\text{hrs. per set} + \text{hrs. to doff frame}) \times 100\% \text{ lbs. per spindle hr.}} \text{ ;}$$

and that

(101) $\dfrac{\text{creeling}}{\text{cycle}} =$

$$\dfrac{\text{doublings} \times \text{pounds on full creeled bobbin or in full can}}{100\% \text{ pounds per spindle hours} \times .01 \times \% \text{ of production}} \text{ .}$$

Find the (a) hrs. /set, (b) dfc, (c) % p, and (d) clc in the following example and five problems:

EXAMPLE: *2.75 lbs. on bo, 42 lbs. in can, 1.92 100% lbs./sph, 9% ist of dfc, and .183 dhrs.*

(a) By formula (97) hrs./set $= \dfrac{2.75}{1.92} = 1.432$, (b) by formula (98)

dfc $= \dfrac{1.432 + .183}{1 - .01 \times 9} = 1.77$, (c) by formula (99) % p $= \dfrac{100 \times 1.432}{1.77} = 80.9$

or by formulas (97) and (100) % p $= \dfrac{(100 - 9) \times 2.75}{(1.432 + .183) \times 1.92} = 80.7$, and

(d) by formula (101) clc $= \dfrac{42}{1.92 \times .01 \times 80.7} = 27.11$.

201. 46 oz. of .65 HR on full bo, 48 lbs. in full can, RPM $1\frac{1''}{8}$ f 124, 9.4% ist of dfc, and 12 min. to doff frame.

202. 27 oz. of 1.80 HR on full intermediate bo, 44 oz. on each of 2 slubber bobbins, 159 RPM $1\frac{1''}{8}$ f, 3% c, 12% ist of dfc, and 18 min. to doff.

203. 33 oz. of 1.25 HR tm 1.20 on full bo, 43 lbs. in full can, 750 RPM fl, 11.3% ist of dfc, and 17 min. to doff frame.

204. 4.6 lbs. of .70 HR 1.30 tm on full bo, 54 lbs. in full can, 950 RPM fl, 10.2% ist of dfc, and .267 dhrs.

205. 5.7 lbs. of 1.60 HR 1.50 tm on full bo, 54 lbs. in full can, 1200 RPM fl, 10.2% ist of dfc, and 15 min. to doff frame.

206. As assigned by your instructor, solve production problems involving the roving frames of your plant.

Chapter XIII

SPINNING FRAME CALCULATIONS

DRAFT

Basic Total Draft Formula. Since the delivery roll of a spinning frame is the *front roll, f,* and the feed roll is the *back roll, b,* from formula (3), Chap. III the formula for mechanical *total draft, td,* is

$$(1)\ \text{total draft} = \frac{\text{surface distance of front roll}}{\text{surface distance of back roll}}.$$

Total draft is changed by changing SD b without changing SD f.

Constants, Gears, and Ranges of Total Drafts. Fig. 1 has only one shaft between the front roll shaft and the back roll shaft. You can reason that this *conventional* train is the minimum train that can provide a readily changeable size of *draft gear, dg,* between f and b.

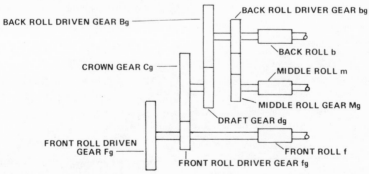

BACK ROLL DRIVEN GEAR Bg

BACK ROLL DRIVER GEAR bg

BACK ROLL b

CROWN GEAR Cg

MIDDLE ROLL m

MIDDLE ROLL GEAR Mg

DRAFT GEAR dg

FRONT ROLL DRIVEN GEAR Fg

FRONT ROLL f

FRONT ROLL DRIVER GEAR fg

Figure 1.   Conventional Draft Train

1. From formula (1) and from formula (30), Chap. XX, Part One for the conventional draft train as in Fig. 1 derive

$$(2)\ \frac{\text{total}}{\text{draft}} = \frac{\text{dia. front roll} \times \text{crown gear} \times \text{back roll driven gear}}{\text{dia. back roll} \times \text{front roll driver gear} \times \text{draft gear}}$$

2. From your study of constants in Chap. XX, Part One and from formula (2) show that if dg is the only changeable member of the train

$$\text{td} \times \text{dg} = \frac{\text{dia. f} \times \text{Cg} \times \text{Bg}}{\text{dia. b} \times \text{fg}}.$$

Hence, regardless of how td and dg change, td × dg = a constant. This is the total *draft constant, dc,* which is a labor saver in draft calculations.

3. For the conventional draft train as in Fig. 1 derive

$$(3) \quad \frac{\text{draft}}{\text{constant}} = \frac{\text{total}}{\text{draft}} \times \frac{\text{draft}}{\text{gear}} =$$

$$\frac{\dfrac{\text{dia. front}}{\text{roll}} \times \dfrac{\text{crown}}{\text{gear}} \times \dfrac{\text{back roll}}{\text{driven gear}}}{\dfrac{\text{dia. back}}{\text{roll}} \times \dfrac{\text{front roll driver}}{\text{gear}}},$$

$$(4) \quad \frac{\text{total}}{\text{draft}} = \frac{\text{draft constant}}{\text{draft gear}}, \text{ and}$$

$$(5) \quad \frac{\text{draft}}{\text{gear}} = \frac{\text{draft constant}}{\text{total draft}}.$$

Some Draft Train Combinations of Fig. 1

	A	B	C
dia. of front roll, f	1″	1″	1″
effective dia. middle roll, m, over apron	1.07″	1.1″	1.1″
dia. of back roll, b	$\frac{7″}{8}$	1″	1″
front roll driver gear, fg	42	23	23
crown gear, Cg	98	120	170
draft gear, dg	27 to 60	28 to 70	28 to 70
back roll driven gear, Bg	90	80	119
back roll driver gear, bg	26	33	33
middle roll gear, Mg	30	29	29

By formula (3) find dc for Fig. 1 with the combinations in the following three problems:

4. A.   **5.** B.   **6.** C.

What is the td range of Fig. 1 with the combinations in the following example and two problems:

EXAMPLE: *A?*

By formula (4) and dc found in a preceding problem: td $= \dfrac{240.00}{60}$

$= 4.00$; and td $= \dfrac{240.00}{27} = 8.89$.   **Answer:**   4.00 to 8.89.

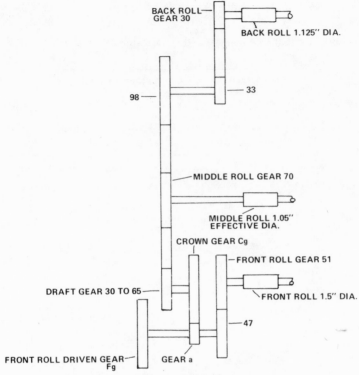

Figure 2.   Draft Train

7. B?   **8.** C?

For Fig. 1 *what* (a) *dg ought to be tried for the td and combination in the following example and four problems and* (b) *td this dg is expected to give:*

EXAMPLE: *As near as possible to and at least 6.50 with A?*

By formula (5) and dc from a preceding problem: (a) $dg = \dfrac{240.00}{6.50} =$ 36.9; ∴ a 37-tooth dg gives a td < 6.50 and a 36-tooth dg gives both a td > 6.50 and as near as possible to it. By formula (4) and (a): (b) td = $\dfrac{240.00}{36} = 6.67$. Answers: (a) 36-tooth (b) 6.67.

9. As near as possible to but not over 13.75 with b?

10. On C as close as possible to but no greater than 14.2?

11. With B if any different from 6.25 to be on the heavy side?

12. With C if any different from 30.00 to be on the light side?

13. For the conventional train in Fig. 2, designed for worsted and other such long staples, derive

(6) $\dfrac{\text{draft}}{\text{constant}} = \dfrac{\text{total}}{\text{draft}} \times \dfrac{\text{draft}}{\text{gear}} = \dfrac{1.5 \times 47 \times \text{crown gear} \times 98 \times 30}{1.125 \times 51 \times a \times 33}$

and prove that formulas (4) and (5) are applicable.

Some Draft Train Combinations of Fig. 2		
	A	**B**
gear a	32	18
crown gear, Cg	111	125

What is the (a) *dc and* (b) *td range of Fig.* 2 *with the combinations in the following two problems:*

    14. A?   **15.** B?

    16. For the train in Fig. 3 derive

(7) $\dfrac{\text{draft}}{\text{constant}} = \dfrac{\text{total}}{\text{draft}} \times \dfrac{\text{draft}}{\text{gear}} = \dfrac{1 \times 72 \times \text{crown gear} \times 116}{1 \times 23 \times a}$

and prove that formulas (4) and (5) are applicable.

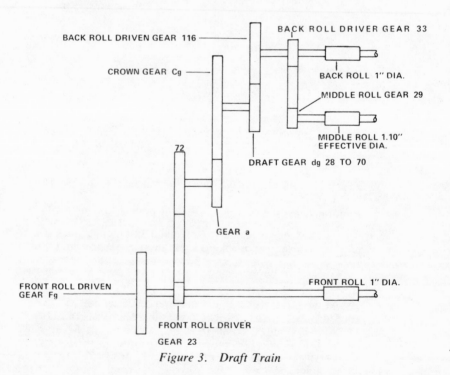

Figure 3.   Draft Train

Some Draft Train Combinations of Fig. 3			
	A	B	C
gear a	70	44	27
crown gear, Cg	100	122	149

What is the (a) *dc and* (b) *td range of Fig.* 3 *with the combinations in the following three problems:*

17. A?   **18.** B?   **19.** C?

20. For the train in Fig. 4 derive

(8) draft constant = total draft × draft gear =

$$\frac{\dfrac{\text{dia. front}}{\text{roll}} \times a \times B \times \dfrac{\text{constant}}{\text{driven gear}} \times 32}{\dfrac{\text{dia. back}}{\text{roll}} \times \dfrac{\text{front roll}}{\text{gear}} \times \dfrac{\text{constant}}{\text{driver gear}} \times d}$$

and prove that formulas (4) and (5) are applicable.

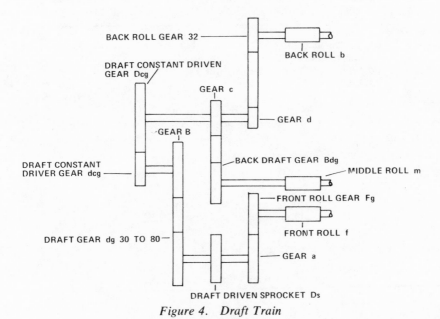

Figure 4.   Draft Train

What is the (a) *dc and* (b) *td range of Fig.* 4 *with the combinations in the following five problems:*

21. A?   **22.** B?   **23.** C?   **24.** D?   **25.** E?

Some Combinations of Fig. 4

	A	B	C	D	E
dia. of front roll, f	$1''$	$1''$	$1\dfrac{15''}{16}$	$1''$	$1\dfrac{3''}{8}$
effective dia. over apron middle roll, m	1.07″	1.07″	1.05″	1.07″	1.07″
dia. of back roll, b	$1''$	$1''$	$1\dfrac{1''}{8}$	$1''$	$1''$
front roll gear, Fg	40	40	36	43	51
gear a	53	53	26	66	57
gear B	126	126	126	98	98
draft constant driver gear, dcg	65	47	27	43	27
draft constant driven gear, Dcg	100	118	138	106	122
gear c	57	57	36	46	46
back draft gear, Bdg	61	78	50	43 to 78	43 to 78
gear d	18	18	18	15	15

Basic Intermediate Draft Formulas.   The *intermediate drafts, id*, of the spinning frame trains in Figs. 1 to 4 are *break or back draft, bd*, between b and m and *front draft, fd*, between m and f.

26. In Fig. 1: which roll is the (a) feed roll of bd (b) delivery roll of bd (c) feed roll of fd (d) delivery roll of fd?

27. From the preceding example and formula (2), Chap. III show that

$$(9)\ bd = \frac{SD\ m}{SD\ b}$$

$$(10)\ fd = \frac{SD\ f}{SD\ m}, \therefore$$

$$(11)\ bd \times fd = \frac{SD\ f}{SD\ b} = td \text{ and for such trains } \therefore$$

(12) total draft = back draft × front draft,

$$(13)\ back\ draft = \frac{total\ draft}{front\ draft},$$

$$(14)\ front\ draft = \frac{total\ draft}{back\ draft},$$

and substituting td from formula (4) into formulas (13) and (14) $\therefore$

$$(15)\ \text{back draft} = \frac{\text{draft constant}}{\text{front draft} \times \text{draft gear}}\ \text{and}$$

$$(16)\ \text{front draft} = \frac{\text{draft constant}}{\text{back draft} \times \text{draft gear}}.$$

Fixed Back Draft Trains.

28. From equations (9) and formula (30), Chap. XX, Part One for Figs. 1 and 3 derive

$$(17)\ \frac{\text{back}}{\text{draft}} = \frac{\text{dia. middle roll} \times \text{back roll driver gear}}{\text{dia. back roll} \times \text{middle roll gear}}$$

In the following example and two problems what is the (a) *bd and* (b) *fd range of Fig.* 1 *with the following combinations:*

EXAMPLE: *A?*

By formula (17): (a) bd = $\dfrac{1.07'' \times 26}{.875 \times 30}$ = 1.06; by formula (16): (b)

fd = $\dfrac{240}{1.06 \times 60}$ = 3.77 and fd = $\dfrac{240}{1.06 \times 27}$ = 8.39.

29. B?
30. C?
31. For Fig. 2 derive

$$(18)\ \text{back draft} = \frac{1.05'' \times 98 \times 30}{1.125'' \times 70 \times 33}$$

and find the (a) bd and fd range with combination (b) A and (c) B.

32. For Fig. 3 what is the (a) bd and its fd range with combination (b) A (c) B (d) C?

33. For Fig. 4 derive

$$(19)\ \text{back draft} = \frac{\text{dia. middle roll} \times c \times 32}{\text{dia. back roll} \times \text{back draft gear} \times d}$$

What are the (a) *bd and* (b) *fd ranges of Fig.* 4 *with the combinations in the following three problems:*

34. A?   35. B?   36. C?

Constants, Gears, and Ranges of Changeable Back Draft Trains.

37. By the same reasoning you derived the formulas for dc, for the back draft constant, bdc, of combinations D and E, Fig. 4 derive

(20) back draft constant = back draft × back draft gear =

$\dfrac{\text{dia. middle roll} \times c \times 32}{\text{dia. back roll} \times d}$,

$$(21) \text{ back draft} = \frac{\text{back draft constant}}{\text{back draft gear}}, \text{ and}$$

$$(22) \text{ back draft gear} = \frac{\text{back draft constant}}{\text{back draft}}.$$

What are the (a) *bdc* (b) *bd range and* (c) *fd ranges of Fig.* 4 *with the combinations in the following two problems:*

38. D?   **39.** E?

Draft and Back Draft Constants, Gears, and Precision.

How precise are the controls by a 1-*tooth change from the* (a) *smallest* (b) *largest draft of the combinations in the following six problems*

40. Fig. 1 A td?
41. Fig. 1 C td?
42. Fig. 3 A td?
43. Fig. 3 C td?
44. Fig. 4 A td?
45. Fig. 4 E td and bd?
46. From your answers to the preceding six problems select the correct word in each set of the following parentheses: The dg of each combination of Figs. 1 to 4 is (a) (directly, inversely) proportional to the td. The bdg of Fig. 4 is (b) (inversely, directly) proportional to the bd. In each such train the less the td the (c) (less, more) precisely it is controlled by a 1-tooth change in dg and the less the bd the (d) (more, less) precisely it is controlled by a 1-tooth change in bdg.

What (a) *gears give as near as possible to the drafts, under the conditions, on the combinations indicated in the following six problems* (b) *drafts are given by each such gear:*

47. Not over 6.25 td A, Fig. 2?
48. At least 22.50 td B, Fig. 2?
49. Heavy side of 8.50 td A, Fig. 3?
50. Light side of 60.00 td C, Fig. 3?
51. Not over 12.50 td and 1.50 bd D, Fig. 4?
52. Not under 45.00 td but not over 2.00 bd E, Fig. 4?

Finding Gears in Changing Drafts.

53. In changing from a present or old td which has been given satisfactorily by a present or old dg to a required or new td and new dg if the dc remains the same, for frames as in Figs. 1, 2, 3, and 4 show from formulas (3), (6), (7), and (8) that new td × new dg = old td × old dg and ∴

$$(23) \frac{\text{new draft}}{\text{gear}} = \frac{\text{old total draft} \times \text{old draft gear}}{\text{new total draft}}$$

54. By derivation similar to formula (23) for frames as combinations D and E, Fig. 4 derive

(24) $\dfrac{\text{new back}}{\text{draft gear}} = \dfrac{\text{old back draft} \times \text{old back draft gear}}{\text{new back draft}}$

What gears ought to be tried to give as near as possible to the drafts and under the conditions in the following example and three problems:

EXAMPLE: 11.45 *td if a 62-tooth dg drafts 9.5 td?*

By formula (23) new dg $= \dfrac{9.5 \times 62}{11.45} = 51.4.$ $\dfrac{9.5 \times 62}{51} = 11.55.$

$\dfrac{9.5 \times 62}{52} = 11.33.$ $11.55 - 11.45 = .10.$ $11.45 - 11.33 = .12.$

Answer: 51-tooth dg.

55. 23.25 td and not over 1.30 bd if a 25-tooth dg and 50-tooth bdg give 26.5 td and 1.40 bd respectively?

56. 1.60 bd and not under 21.50 td if a 45-tooth bdg drafts 2.00 and a 56-tooth dg drafts 28.00?

57. 10.55 td and 1.90 bd if a 43-tooth dg and a 48-tooth bdg draft 18.5 and 2.20 respectively?

58. As assigned by your instructor from the frames in your mill derive dc, td, dg, bdc, bd, and bdg formulas and solve current draft and draft change problems.

Contraction, Actual and Total Draft, Constants, Hank Roving, Counts and Gears.   Slippage between stock and rolls and waste extraction is usually negligible. But due to twist the length of end delivered by the front roll contracts.

59. From the foregoing, formula (5), Chap. III, your study of percentage and equations show: that (a) td $= \dfrac{ad}{1 - .01 \times \% \, c}$; $\therefore$ that (b)

$1 - .01 \times \% = \dfrac{ad}{td}$; $\therefore$ subtracting 1 from each side of equation (b) that

(c) $-.01 \times \% \, c = \dfrac{ad}{td} - 1 = \dfrac{ad}{td} - \dfrac{td}{td} = \dfrac{ad - td}{td}$; $\therefore$ multiplying both sides

of equation (c) by -100 that (d) $\% \, c = \dfrac{100 \times (td - ad)}{td}$; $\therefore$

(25) $\%$ of contraction $= \dfrac{100 \times (\text{total draft} - \text{actual draft})}{\text{total draft}}$;

from equation (a) that

(26) total draft $= \dfrac{100 \times \text{actual draft}}{100 - \% \text{ of contraction}}$;

$\therefore$ from formula (13), Chap. III and formulas (4) and (26) that (d) $\dfrac{dc}{dg} =$

$$\frac{.12 \times db \times gr.\ sl \times counts}{1 - .01 \times \% \ c} = \frac{\dfrac{100 \times db \times counts}{HR}}{1 - .01 \times \% \ c} \ ; \ and \ \therefore \ that$$

$$(27) \ \frac{draft}{gear} = \frac{(100 - \% \ of \ contraction) \times draft \ constant}{12 \times doublings \times grain \ sliver \times counts} =$$

$$\frac{(100 - \% \ of \ contraction) \times draft \ constant \times hank \ roving}{100 \times doublings \times counts}$$

By the most suitable formulas find what is required under the conditions of the following nine problems:

60. The $\%$ c with (a) 17.55 td and 16.50 ad (b) 43.26 td and 39.12 ad.

61. The $\%$ c if single 1.50 HR is drafted into 12.10s with a 524.64 dc and 60-tooth dg.

62. The $\%$ c if 7.50s is drawn from double .82 HR with a 742.42 dc and 39-tooth dg.

63. The $\%$ c when double .90 HR is drawn into 12.00s with a 28.25 td.

64. The $\%$ c if 106.00s is drawn from single 1.80 HR with 66.54 td.

65. The td required with (a) 32.56 ad and 3.7% c (b) 48.77 ad and 8.7% c.

66. The td required for drafting double 1.15 HR into 15.00s at 4.8% c.

67. The dg to draw single 55 gr. sl to 8s with 3041 dc at 2.9% c.

68. The dg to draw as near as possible to but no heavier than 10.50s from double 1.25 HR with 1556.72 dc at 4.9% c.

Finding Gears in Changing Actual Draft, Contraction, Doublings, Hank Roving and Counts.

69. Into formula (23) substituting the value of td from formula (26) and simplifying and cancelling for such as Figs. 1 to 4 derive

$$(28) \ \frac{new \ draft}{gear} =$$

$$\frac{\dfrac{old \ actual}{draft} \times \dfrac{old \ draft}{gear} \times (100 - new \ percent \ of \ contraction)}{new \ actual \ draft \times (100 - old \ percent \ of \ contraction)}$$

70. Into formula (28) substituting the value of ad from formula (6), Chap. III for such as Figs. 1 to 4 derive

$$(29) \ \frac{new}{draft} =$$
$$gear$$

$$\frac{\dfrac{old}{doublings} \times \dfrac{old}{counts} \times \dfrac{new}{hank \ roving} \times \dfrac{old}{draft \ gear} \times \left(100 - \dfrac{new \ percent}{of \ contraction}\right)}{\dfrac{new}{doublings} \times \dfrac{new}{counts} \times \dfrac{old}{hank \ roving} \times \left(100 - \dfrac{old \ percent \ of}{contraction}\right)}$$

Find the teeth required in the dg in making the changes or corrections indicated in the following eight problems:

		from					to		
	ad	counts	HR	% c	dg	ad	counts	HR	% c
71.	9.55			2.4	48	10.25			2.8
72.	30.44			7.4	26	29.50			8.6
73.		15.40	.85 single	7.1	44		14.90	same	same
74.		44.15	3.80 double	7.4	37		45.00	same	same
75.		21.60	.85 single	4.4	56		26.40	1.10 single	same
76.		16.80	1.00 single	7.7	51		same	.60 single	4.7
77.		9.75	.50 single	7.1	40		12.40	.80 single	7.7
78.		109.00	6.00 double	3.6	40		62.00	4.00 double	5.7

79. Tests show that a 50-tooth dg drafts 19.50s average from .98 average hank. The HR lightens to 1.04 average. What dg will keep the average counts no lighter than 19.70?

Finding Counts in Adjusting Draft Gears. It is helpful to know the effect on the counts of a 1-tooth adjustment in the dg.

80. Assuming the same doublings, HR, and % c from formula (29) for such as Figs. 1 to 4 derive

$$(30) \quad \text{new counts} = \frac{\text{old counts} \times \text{old draft gear}}{\text{new draft gear}}$$

Find the (a) counts and (b) change in counts resulting from the change in dg teeth in the following six problems:

	old counts	teeth in old dg	.	teeth in new dg
81.	9.50s	33		34
82.	9.50s	61		62
83.	23.40s	32		33
84.	23.40s	40		41
85.	56.30s	33		32
86.	56.30s	57		56

87. From your answers to the preceding six problems select the correct word in each set of the following parentheses: In such Figs. as 1 to 4 (a) the (coarser, finer) the counts the less the change in counts by a 1-tooth change in dg; the (b) (larger, smaller) the dg for the same counts the less the change in counts by a 1-tooth change in dg; (c) to "heavy 1 tooth" means to use a dg 1 tooth (larger, smaller).

88. You must spin 31.70s with 6% c from single 1.30 HR and a choice of using a dc of 896.76 or 1556.64 dc. The dg range is 26 to 60 teeth. (a) Which dc would you use? Why? What dg would you use to (b) start the frames (c) heavy 1 tooth if necessary?

89. As assigned by your instructor for the counts being spun in your plant calculate each counts if (a) heavied (b) lightened 1 tooth.

TWIST

Basic Formula. As in Fig. 5 the *main shaft, ms,* is integral with the *cylinder, c,* or one *pulley, p,* for every 2 or 4 *spindles, Sp.* Sp is integral with the *bobbin, bo,* and the *whorl, W,* which by the *tape,* acting as a belt, is driven

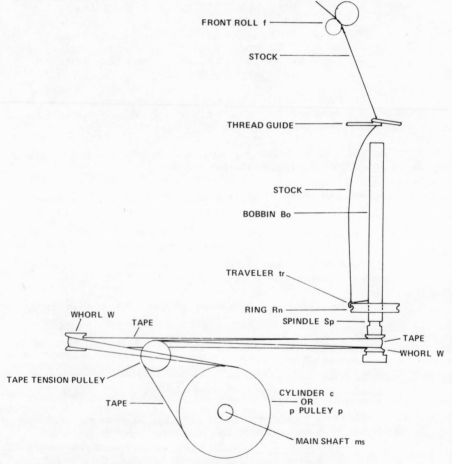

FRONT ROLL f

STOCK

THREAD GUIDE

STOCK

BOBBIN Bo

TRAVELER tr

RING Rn

WHORL W

TAPE

SPINDLE Sp

TAPE

WHORL W

TAPE TENSION PULLEY

TAPE

CYLINDER c
OR
p PULLEY p

MAIN SHAFT ms

Figure 5.   Twist Train Section at Spindle

from c or p. The stock is free to pass through the *traveler, tr,* and tr is free to revolve around its *ring, Rn.* As will be studied later RPM f and RPM Sp are constant.

90. If the stock passes directly from f to bo show that, for the first instant, the following standard may be true.

$$(31) \quad \frac{\text{twist}}{\text{per inch}} = \frac{\text{RPM spindle}}{\text{IPM front roll}} = \frac{\text{RPM spindle}}{\text{dia. front roll} \times \pi \times \text{RPM front roll}}.$$

Inaccuracies in the Basic Formula.

91. (a) But what continuous, orderly, and essential function of bo would not occur if the stock does pass directly from f through the thread guide to bo instead of through tr also? (b) And if the stock passes through tr but tr does not revolve what necessity does the stock lack? (c) What causes tr to revolve? (d) What are the functions of tr? Select the correct sign in the following parentheses: ∴ RPM tr always is (e) (=, >, <) RPM Sp.

92. Since, as you have studied, twist contracts the stock between f and bo and bo must wind the stock as bo receives it, show that: (a) IPM bo devoted to winding = IPM f × (1 − .01 × % c) = dia. f × π × RPM f × (1 − .01 × % c), ∴ (b) RPM bo devoted to winding = $\dfrac{\text{dia. f} \times \pi \times \text{RPM f} \times (1 - .01 \times \% \text{ c})}{\text{dia. bo} \times \pi}$, ∴ (c) RPM Sp devoted to twisting =

$$\text{RPM Sp} - \frac{\text{dia. f} \times \text{RPM f} \times (1 - .01 \times \% \text{ c})}{\text{dia. bo}} =$$

$$\frac{\text{dia. bo} \times \text{RPM Sp} - \text{dia. f} \times \text{RPM f} \times (1 - .01 \times \% \text{ c})}{\text{dia. bo}}, \text{ and dividing the}$$

sides of equation (c) by the corresponding sides of equation (a), ∴

$$(32) \quad \frac{\text{actual}}{\text{tpi}} = \frac{\dfrac{\text{dia. bo} \times \text{RPM Sp} - \text{dia. f} \times \text{RPM f} \times (1 - .01 \times \% \text{ c})}{\text{dia. bo}}}{\text{dia. f} \times \pi \times \text{RPM f} \times (1 - .01 \times \% \text{ c})}$$

$$= \frac{\text{dia. bo} \times \text{RPM Sp} - \text{dia. f} \times \text{RPM f} \times (1 - .01 \times \% \text{ c})}{\text{dia. bo} \times \text{dia. f} \times \pi \times \text{RPM f} \times (1 - .01 \times \% \text{ c})}.$$

What is the difference in standard tpi calculated by formula (31) *and actual tpi calculated by equation* (32) *with bo* (a) *bare and* (b) *full under the conditions in the following example and three problems:*

EXAMPLE: *RPM Sp 9400, RPM f 145, dia. f 1″, dia. warp bo bare* $\dfrac{31″}{32}$, *full 2″, % c 6.5?*

By formula (31): tpi = $\dfrac{9400}{1 \times 3.1416 \times 145}$ = 20.64. By formula (32):

$$\text{actual tpi with bare bobbin} = \frac{\dfrac{31}{32} \times 9400 - 1 \times 145 \times (1 - .01 \times 6.5)}{\dfrac{31}{32} \times 1 \times 3.1416 \times 145 \times (1 - .01 \times 6.5)} =$$

$$21.74 \text{ and actual tpi with full bobbin} = \frac{2 \times 9400 - 1 \times 145 \times (1 - .01 \times 6.5)}{2 \times 1 \times 3.1416 \times 145 \times (1 - .01 \times 6.5)} = 21.91.$$

$21.74 - 20.64 = 1.10$. $21.91 - 20.64 = 1.27$.   **Answer:**   (a) 1.10 (b) 1.27.

93. RPM Sp 4800, RPM f 190, dia. f $1\dfrac{1}{8}''$, dia. warp bo bare $1\dfrac{1}{16}''$, full $2\dfrac{1}{2}''$, % c 4.00?

94. RPM Sp 9600, RPM f 120, dia. f $1''$, dia. warp bo bare $1\dfrac{1}{4}''$, full $2\dfrac{3}{4}''$, % c 7.60.

95. RPM Sp 10800, RPM f 100, dia. f $1''$, dia. filling bo at last layer bare .48″, full 1.375″, % c 3.78?

96. From your answers to the preceding three problems select the correct word or words within each set of the following parentheses: The actual tpi calculated by equation (32) is always equal to or (a) (less, more) than tpi calculated by the standard formula. With warp wind tpi (b) (increases, decreases) with each additional layer. With filling wind tpi (c) (increases, is constant, decreases) with each upstroke and (d) (increases, is constant, decreases) with each down-stroke.

Ratio of RPM Spindle to RPM Cylinder, Pulley, or Main Shaft and Inaccuracies. On some frames each whorl is run from the cylinder by its own tape. On others, as in Fig. 5, four whorls are run from one pulley by one tape which is kept tight by a tension pulley. Since as you have studied, tpi is directly proportional almost solely to RPM Sp and RPM Sp is so high, accurately calculating RPM Sp: RPM ms is especially important.

97. From Chap. XX, Part One derive

$$(33) \quad \frac{\text{RPM of spindle}}{\text{RPM of main shaft}} = \frac{\text{dia. of cylinder or pulley} + \text{tape thickness}}{\text{dia. of whirl} + \text{tape thickness}}$$

What is RPM Sp: RPM ms in the following eight problems:

	dia. c or p	dia. whirl	tape thickness
98.	6″	$\dfrac{25''}{32}$	.0225″
99.	6″	$\dfrac{25''}{32}$	.0590″

100.	8″	$\dfrac{15″}{16}$	.0300″
101.	8″	$\dfrac{15″}{16}$	.0590″
102.	8″	$1\dfrac{1″}{8}$	.0300″
103.	8″	$1\dfrac{1″}{8}$	.0590″
104.	10″	$\dfrac{15″}{16}$	.0300″
105.	10″	$\dfrac{15″}{16}$	.0590″

106. From your answers to the preceding eight problems select the correct word in each set of the following parentheses: Granted that the other terms in formula (33) are unchanged the (a) (smaller, larger) the whorl the more tape thickness affects RPM Sp: RPM ms; the (b) (thicker, thinner) the tape the greater RPM Sp: RPM ms; the more the tape swells from humidity the (c) (greater, smaller) RPM Sp: RPM ms; and the more the tape stretches from tension and its slippage thereby reduced the (d) (greater, smaller) RPM Sp: RPM ms. Why?

107. From equation (32) state the effect on (a) RPM Sp: RPM ms of tape slippage (b) tpi of changes in RPM Sp: RPM ms.

Since RPM Sp: RPM ms calculated by formula (33) may differ from actuality often it is determined by using the speed indicator on ms and on several Sp not driven by the same tapes, calculating the average RPM Sp.

What would you consider a fairly reliable RPM Sp: RPM ms if the speed indicator on ms and on each Sp not run by the same tape reads as in the following three problems:

108. RPM ms 1156, RPM Sp 8201, 8311, and 8245?

109. RPM ms 992, RPM Sp 9600, 9642, 9744, and 9670?

110. RPM ms 1022, RPM Sp 8864, 8936, 8891, 8830, and 8952?

111. As assigned by your instructor, find by the speed indicator RPM Sp: RPM ms of frames in your plant.

Each machinery builder publishes RPM Sp: RPM ms, some of which are shown in the combinations that follow, found by tests to be fairly reliable.

112. Summarize the inaccuracies in using formulas (31) and (33) that may make tpi appear (a) greater (b) less than actual tpi.

Constants, Gears, and Ranges of Twist Per Inch.   Fig. 6 is of the simplest, sometimes called *conventional,* twist train.

113. From Fig. 6 and Chap. XX, Part One show that: (a) RPM Sp $=$ $\dfrac{\text{RPM ms} \times \text{effective dia. c}}{\text{effective dia. W}}$; (b) RPM f $= \dfrac{\text{RPM ms} \times \text{mss} \times \text{tg}}{\text{Js} \times \text{Fg}}$; substi-

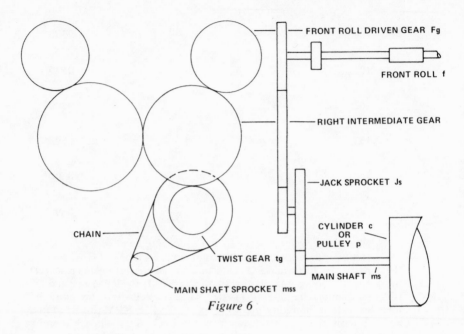

Figure 6

tuting the value of RPM Sp from equation (a) and RPM f from equation

(b) into formula (31) ∴ (c) $\text{tpi} = \dfrac{\dfrac{\text{RPM ms} \times \text{effective dia. c or p}}{\text{effective dia. W}}}{\dfrac{\text{dia. f} \times \pi \times \text{RPM ms} \times \text{mss} \times \text{tg}}{\text{Js} \times \text{Fg}}}$; and on

the right side of equation (c) cancelling RPM ms, substituting the value

of $\dfrac{\text{effective dia. c}}{\text{effective dia. W}}$ from formula (33) and simplifying, for the conventional train ∴

(34)

$$\frac{\text{twist}}{\text{per inch}} = \frac{\text{jack sprocket} \times \text{front roll driven gear} \times \dfrac{\text{RPM spindle}}{\text{RPM main shaft}}}{\text{dia. front roll} \times \pi \times \text{main shaft sprocket} \times \text{twist gear}}$$

114. From your study of constants in Chap. XX, Part One and from formula (34) show that if tg is the only changeable member of the

train $\text{tpi} \times \text{tg} = \dfrac{\text{Js} \times \text{Fg} \times \dfrac{\text{RPM Sp}}{\text{RPM ms}}}{\text{dia. f} \times \pi \times \text{mss}}$.

Hence however tpi and tg may change tpi × tg = a constant. This is the *twist constant, tc,* which is a labor saver in twist calculations.

115. For the conventional train as in Fig. 6 derive

(35) twist constant = twist per inch × twist gear

$$= \frac{\dfrac{\text{jack}}{\text{sprocket}} \times \dfrac{\text{front roll}}{\text{driven gear}} \times \dfrac{\text{RPM spindle}}{\text{RPM main shaft}}}{\text{dia. front roll} \times \pi \times \text{main shaft sprocket}},$$

(36) twist per inch $= \dfrac{\text{twist constant}}{\text{twist gear}}$, and

(37) twist gear $= \dfrac{\text{twist constant}}{\text{twist per inch}}$.

Some Twist Train Combinations of Fig. 6

	A	B	C	D
dia. of front roll, f	1″	1″	1″	1″
front roll driven gear, Fg	100	100	100	100
twist gear, tg	25 to 50	30 to 60	35 to 65	35 to 70
jack sprocket, Js	42	53	69	76
main shaft sprocket, mss	42	15	16	15
builder's RPM spindle:				
RPM main shaft	5.70	6.73	8.69	10.37

What is the tc of Fig. 6 with the combination in the following four problems:

116. A?   **117.** B?   **118.** C?   **119.** D?

What is the tpi range of Fig. 6 with the combinations in the following example and three problems:

EXAMPLE: *Combination A?*

By formula (36) and tc found in a preceding problem:

$\text{tpi} = \dfrac{181.44}{50} = 3.63$ and $\text{tpi} = \dfrac{181.44}{25} = 7.26.$ **Answer:** 3.63 to 7.26.

120. B?   **121.** C?   **122.** D?

In Fig. 6 what tg ought to be tried for the tpi and combinations in the following example and three problems:

EXAMPLE: *A 5?*

By formula (37) and tc found in a preceding problem:

$\text{tg} = \dfrac{181.44}{5} = 36.3$ **Answer:** 36- or 37-tooth.

123. B 20?   **124.** C 26?   **125.** D 45?
126. For the train in Fig. 7 show that formulas (34) to (37) apply. Why?

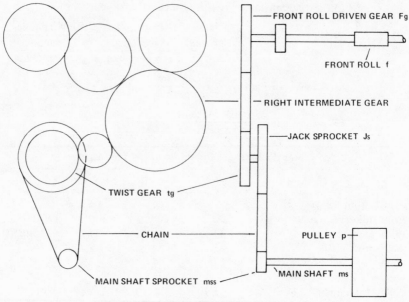

Figure 7.   Twist Train at Head End

Some Twist Train Combinations of Fig. 7		
	A	**B**
dia. of front roll, f	1″	1″
front roll driven gear, Fg	100	100
twist gear, tg	25 to 50	35 to 70
jack sprocket, Js	42	86
main shaft sprocket, mss	21	15
builder's RPM spindle: RPM main shaft	5.70	8.30

What is the (a) *tc and* (b) *tpi range of Fig. 7 with the combinations in the following two problems:*

127. A?   **128.** B?

129. On Fig. 7 what tg ought to be tried to insert (a) 13 tpi with combination A (b) 23 tpi with combination B?

130. For the train in Fig. 8 derive

(38) twist constant = twist per inch × twist gear

$$= \frac{57 \times \dfrac{\text{twist constant}}{\text{driven gear}} \times 120 \times 21 \times \dfrac{\text{front roll}}{\text{gear}} \times \dfrac{\text{RPM spindle}}{\text{RPM main shaft}}}{\text{dia. front roll} \times \pi \times a \times 18 \times \text{twist constant driver gear} \times 19}$$

and prove that formulas (36) and (37) are applicable.

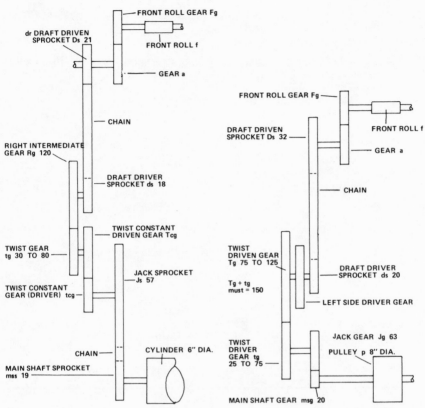

Figure 8.   Right-Side Twist
Train at Head End

Figure 9.   Right-Side Twist
Train at Head End

Some Combinations of Fig. 8			
	A	B	C
dia. of front roll, f	$1''$	$1\frac{3''}{8}$	$1\frac{15''}{16}$
front roll gear, Fg	40	28	36
gear a	53	28	26
twist constant driven gear, Tg	100	86	59
twist constant driver gear, tcg	36	50	77
builder's RPM spindle: RPM main shaft	5.15	5.15	5.15

What is the (a) *tc and* (b) *tpi range of Fig.* 8 *with the combinations in the following three problems:*

131. A?   **132.** B?   **133.** C?

134. On Fig. 8 what tg ought to be tried to insert (a) 46 tpi with combination A (b) 20 tpi with combination B (c) 6.5 tpi with combination C?

135. For the train in Fig. 9 derive

$$\text{tpi} = \frac{63 \times \text{Tg} \times 32 \times \text{Fg} \times \dfrac{\text{RPM Sp}}{\text{RPM ms}}}{\text{dia. f} \times \pi \times \text{a} \times \text{tg} \times 20 \times 20} \quad \text{and} \therefore$$

$$(39) \text{ twist constant} = \text{twist per inch} \times \frac{\text{twist driver gear}}{\text{twist driven gear}}$$

$$= \frac{63 \times 32 \times \dfrac{\text{front}}{\text{roll gear}} \times \dfrac{\text{RPM spindle}}{\text{RPM main shaft}}}{\text{dia. front roll} \times \pi \times \text{a} \times 20 \times 20},$$

$$(40) \ \frac{\text{twist}}{\text{per inch}} = \frac{\text{twist}}{\text{constant}} \times \frac{\text{twist driven gear}}{\text{twist driver gear}} \text{ and}$$

$$(41) \ \frac{\text{twist driver gear}}{\text{twist driven gear}} = \frac{\text{twist constant}}{\text{twist per inch}}$$

Some Combinations of Fig. 9

	A	B	C	D
dia. of front roll, f	1″	1″	$1\frac{3''}{8}$	$1\frac{3''}{8}$
front roll gear, Fg	43	43	51	51
gear a	66	66	57	57
builder's RPM spindle: RPM main shaft	10.04	8.36	7.84	6.97

---

136. What is the tc of Fig. 9 with each combination?

137. Select the correct word in each set of the following parentheses: The tpi is always (a) (directly, inversely) proportional to a driver tg and (b) (directly, inversely) proportional to a driven tg. Why?

What is the tpi range of Fig. 9 *with the combinations in the following example and three problems:*

EXAMPLE: *A?*

From Fig. 9: tg + Tg = 150 and ∴ (a) Tg = 150 − tg. By the preceding problem the largest tg and smallest Tg insert the least tpi. Hence and from formula (40), the tc which you found, and equation (a): the

least tpi $= 10.49 \times \dfrac{150 - 75}{75} = 10.49$. Reasoning similarly: the most

tpi $= 10.49 \times \dfrac{150 - 25}{25} = 52.45$.   **Answer:**   10.49 to 52.45.

138. B?   **139.** C?   **140.** D?

141. From formula (41) and Fig. 9 show that: $\dfrac{tg}{150 - tg} = \dfrac{tc}{tpi}$, $\therefore$

$tg = \dfrac{(150 - tg) \times tc}{tpi}$, $\therefore$ tg $\times$ tpi $= 150 \times$ tc $-$ tg $\times$ tc, $\therefore$

tg $\times$ tpi $+$ tg $\times$ tc $= 150 \times$ tc, $\therefore$ tg $\times$ (tpi $+$ tc) $= 150 \times$ tc, and $\therefore$

(42) twist driver gear $= \dfrac{150 \times \text{twist constant}}{\text{twist per inch} + \text{twist constant}}$.

On Fig. 9 how many teeth in tg and Tg ought to be tried to insert the tpi with the combinations in the following example and three problems:

EXAMPLE: *49 tpi with A?*

By formula (42) and tc from a preceding problem: tg $=$

$\dfrac{150 \times 10.49}{49 + 10.49} = 26.5$ and $\therefore$ tg $= 26$ or 27 and Tg $= 150 - 26 = 124$ or

$150 - 27 = 123$.   **Answer:**   tg 26, Tg 124 or tg 27, Tg 123.

142. 40 tpi with B?   **143.** 24 tpi with C?
144. 9.5 tpi with D?

Twist Constants, Gears and Precision.

How precise is the control of tpi by a 1-tooth change in the tg from the (a) *least* (b) *most tpi on the combinations in the following six problems:*

145. A, Fig. 6?   **146.** D, Fig. 6?   **147.** A, Fig. 7?
148. B, Fig. 7?   **149.** A, Fig. 8?   **150.** A, Fig. 9?
151. From your answers to the preceding six problems select the correct word in each set of the following parentheses: The (a) (larger, smaller) the tc and the (b) (more, less) the tpi the more precise the control of the tpi by a 1-tooth change in the tg.

Finding Twist Gears from Constants, Multipliers, and Counts.

152. From formulas (5), Chap. IV, Part Two and (37) derive for such trains as Figs. 6, 7, and 8 with only a twist driver gear

(43) twist gear $= \dfrac{\text{twist constant}}{\text{twist multiplier} \times \sqrt{\text{counts}}}$

and from formula (42) derive for Fig. 9

$$(44)\ \text{twist driver gear} = \frac{150 \times \text{twist constant}}{\text{twist multiplier} \times \sqrt{\text{counts}} + \text{twist constant}}$$

How many twist gear teeth ought to be tried to run the yarn on the trains with the combinations in the following six problems:

153. 15s 3.25 tm A, Fig. 6?
154. 20s 3.75 tm A, Fig. 7?
155. 100s 4.00 tm B, Fig. 7?
156. 5.4s 4.25 tm C, Fig. 8?
157. 26s 4.50 tm D, Fig. 9?
158. 110s 4.75 tm A, Fig. 9?

Finding Twist Gears in Changing Twist Per Inch, Multiplier, and Counts. If the tc is unchanged, frequently labor can be saved by computing required or new twist gears from known present or old twist gears.

159. From formula (35), assuming the same tc, show that: tc = new tpi × new tg, tc = old tpi × old tg; ∴ (a) new tpi × new tg = old tpi × old tg, and ∴, dividing both sides of equation (a) by new tpi, derive for Figs. 6, 7, and 8

$$(45)\ \text{new twist gear} = \frac{\text{old twist per inch} \times \text{old twist gear}}{\text{new twist per inch}}$$

160. Select the appropriate formula and by reasoning similar to that in the preceding problem derive for Fig. 9

$$(46)\ \frac{\text{new twist driver gear}}{\text{new twist driven gear}} = \frac{\text{old twist per inch} \times \text{old twist driver gear}}{\text{new twist per inch} \times \text{old twist driven gear}}$$

How many teeth in the twist gears ought to be tried to insert the tpi required in the following four problems:

161. 25 tpi if the 35-tooth driver and only tg inserts 21.5 tpi?
162. 19.5 tpi if 17.25 tpi are inserted by a 58-tooth driver and only tg?
163. 35 tpi if the teeth of the twist driver gear plus the teeth of the twist driven gear must always be 150 and a 30-tooth twist driver gear inserts 40 tpi?
164. 9.5 tpi if the total teeth of twist driven and twist driver gears always is 160 and a 93-tooth twist driven gear yields 6.75 tpi?
165. From the appropriate formulas, for frames with only a driver twist gear derive

$$(47)\ \text{new twist gear} = \frac{\text{old twist multiplier} \times \sqrt{\text{old counts}} \times \text{old twist gear}}{\text{new twist multiplier} \times \sqrt{\text{new counts}}}$$

and for frames with driver and driven twist gears derive

$$(48) \quad \frac{\text{new twist driver gear}}{\text{new twist driven gear}} = \frac{\dfrac{\text{old twist multiplier}}{\text{new twist multiplier}} \times \sqrt{\text{old counts}} \times \dfrac{\text{old twist driver gear}}{\sqrt{\text{new counts}} \times \dfrac{\text{old twist driven gear}}{}}}{}$$

How many teeth in the twist gears ought to be tried to twist as required in the following four problems:

166. 9.6s if the only and 60-tooth driver tg spins 7.2s same tm?

167. 30.00s, 4.75 tm if the 36-tooth driver and only tg spins 28.00s, 4.50 tm?

168. 8.9s, 3.6 tm on Fig. 9 if a 65-tooth tg spins 9.6s, 3.2 tm?

169. 110s, 4.75 tm on Fig. 9 if a 118-tooth Tg spins 95s, 4.50 tm?

170. As assigned by your instructor, sketch the twist train at the head end of a spinning frame in your plant; derive the tc, tpi, and tg formulas; calculate the tpi ranges and precision of controls; compare your calculated tpi with actual tpi; and from the present tg and counts calculate tg for proposed changes.

LAY

Basic Formula.   The *coils per inch, cpi,* is the average number of coils that a *ring, Rn,* integral with the *ring rail,* in 1 inch of up or down traverse, *trav. Rn, lays* onto bo; or that bo in 1 inch winds onto itself.

171. Show that

$$(49) \quad \frac{\text{average coils}}{\text{per inch}} = \frac{\text{revolutions of bobbin devoted to winding}}{\text{traverse of ring (in inches) during above revolution}}$$

Coils Per Inch and Constants.   Some *conventional* lay trains as in Fig. 10 receive power directly from the shaft integral with the *right intermediate gear, Rg;* while others receive power from Rg through the *left intermediate gear* which meshes with and has the same number of teeth as Rg.

172. (a) What difference in RPM *builder cam, bc,* is caused by being driven indirectly from Rg? (b) Is RPM bc constant or variable?

The function of each segment of bc, through various levers of the builder, is to traverse each ring so that it lays onto its bo during each traverse a layer of the desired cpi.[1]

173. Through what part of each rev. bc would each *segment* of bc in Fig. 10 act?

174. From your study of worms in Chap. XX, Part One show in

---

[1] Other mechanisms of the builder, which you ought to study in your spinning frame fixing training or otherwise, adjusted by trial and error, regulate such items as traverse Rn, shortening successive traverse Rn for one warp wind, and height of bo of successive traverse Rn of another warp wind and of filling wind.

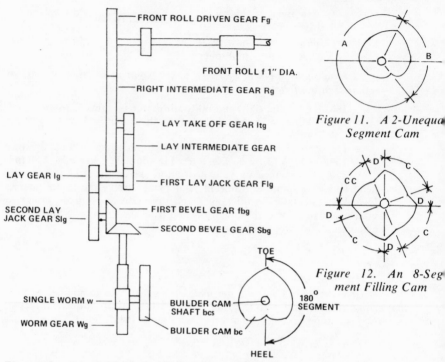

Figure 11. A 2-Unequal Segment Cam

Figure 12. An 8-Segment Filling Cam

Figure 10. Lay Train at Head End with a Heart Warp Cam

Fig. 10 that: rev. f $= \dfrac{\text{rev. bc} \times Wg \times Sbg \times Slg \times Flg \times Rg}{w \times fbg \times lg \times ltg \times Fg}$, $\therefore$ SD f $=$

$\dfrac{\pi \times \text{dia. f} \times \text{rev. bc} \times Wg \times Sbg \times Slg \times Flg \times Rg}{w \times fbg \times lg \times ltg \times Fg}$, $\therefore$ from your study of

contraction SD bo $= \dfrac{\pi \times \text{dia. f} \times \text{rev. bc} \times Wg \times Sbg \times Slg \times Flg \times Rg \times (1 - .01 \times \% \, c)}{w \times fbg \times lg \times ltg \times Fg}$,

$\therefore$ rev. bo devoted to winding $=$

$\dfrac{\dfrac{\pi \times \text{dia. f} \times \text{rev. bc} \times Wg \times Sbg \times Slg \times Flg \times Rg \times (1 - .01 \times \% \, c)}{w \times fbg \times lg \times ltg \times Fg}}{\pi \times \text{dia. bo}}$, and $\therefore$

from formula (49)

(50)   coils
        per inch

$= \dfrac{\text{dia. f} \times \text{rev. bc} \times Wg \times Sbg \times Slg \times Flg \times Rg \times (1 - .01 \times \% \, c)}{\text{dia. bo} \times w \times fbg \times lg \times ltg \times Fg \times \text{trav. Rn}}$

175. Similarly to deriving draft and twist constants show that dividing each side of formula (50) by rev. bc and $(1 - .01 \times \% \, c)$, multiplying each side by dia. bo, lg, and trav. Rn, and cancelling on the right side, each side becomes a *lay constant, lc;* and ∴ for Fig. 10:

$$(51) \quad \text{lay constant} = \frac{\frac{\text{coils per}}{\text{inch}} \times \frac{\text{dia.}}{\text{bobbin}} \times \frac{\text{lay}}{\text{gear}} \times \frac{\text{traverse}}{\text{ring}}}{\frac{\text{revolution}}{\text{builder cam}} \times \left(1 - .01 \times \frac{\text{percent}}{\text{contraction}}\right)}$$

$$= \frac{\frac{\text{dia.}}{\text{front}} \times \frac{\text{right}}{\text{intermediate}} \times \frac{\text{first}}{\text{lay jack}} \times \frac{\text{second}}{\text{lay jack}} \times \frac{\text{second}}{\text{bevel}} \times \frac{\text{worm}}{\text{gear}}}{\frac{\text{roll}}{\text{gear}} \quad \frac{\text{gear}}{\text{gear}} \quad \frac{\text{gear}}{\text{gear}}} \Big/ \frac{\text{front roll}}{\text{driven gear}} \times \frac{\text{lay}}{\text{take off}} \times \frac{\text{first}}{\text{bevel}} \times \text{worm}}{\text{gear} \quad \text{gear}},$$

(52) coils per inch

$$= \frac{\text{lay constant} \times \text{revolution builder cam} \times (1 - .01 \times \% \text{ contraction})}{\text{dia. bobbin} \times \text{lay gear} \times \text{traverse ring}}$$

and

(53) lay gear

$$= \frac{\text{lay constant} \times \text{revolution builder cam} \times (1 - .01 \times \% \text{ contraction})}{\text{coils per inch} \times \text{dia. bobbin} \times \text{traverse ring}}$$

Some Lay Train Combinations of Fig. 10

	A	B	C
front roll driven gear, Fg	100	72	100
right (or left) intermediate gear, Rg	196	120	166
lay take off gear, ltg	38	32	34
first lay jack gear, Flg	48	58	48
lay gear, lg	25 to 70	18 to 65	35 to 55
second lay jack gear, Slg	68	60	60
first bevel gear, fbg	25	30	30
second bevel gear, Sbg	25	23	30
worm gear, Wg	125	103	125

What is the lay constant of Fig. 10 with the combination in the following three problems:

176. A?   **177.** B?   **178.** C?

Segments and Revolution of Builder Cams.

179. With the symmetrical heart bc in Fig. 10 what rev. bc is required for 1 (a) up (b) down trav. Rn and (c) how does IPM of any trav. Rn compare with every other trav. Rn? Why?

What is cpi of Fig. 10 with a symmetrical heart warp bc and the combination under the conditions in the following example and two problems:

EXAMPLE: *A, first traverse Rn 8" at bare warp bo of 1" dia., with 30-tooth lg, and 5% c?*

By formula (52) and lc and rev. bc found in previous problems:

$$cpi = \frac{21044 \times .5 \times .95}{1 \times 30 \times 8} = 41.6$$

180. The same as preceding example except at full bo $1\frac{3''}{4}$ dia. and final traverse Rn $4\frac{1''}{2}$?

181. B, (a) trav. Rn 9" at bare warp bo 1.1" dia. (b) trav. Rn at full bo $2\frac{1''}{2}$ dia., 25-tooth lg, and 4% c?

182. C, (a) trav. Rn 11" at bare warp bo 1.5" dia. (b) trav. Rn 5" at full bo $3\frac{1''}{2}$ dia., 36-tooth lg, and 4% c?

183. By studying formula (52) and your answers to the preceding problems answer: What happens to cpi throughout full bo if rev. bc is the same for every trav. Rn and ratio of decrease in trav. Rn = ratio of increase in dia. bo?

Builder cams commonly have segments as follows: (a) 2 equal (Fig. 10) (b) 2 unequal (Fig. 11) (c) 8, 4 equal large alternated with 4 equal small (Fig. 12) (d) 4, 2 equal large alternated with 2 equal small (e) 6, 3 equal large alternated with 3 equal small.

184. Which segment in Fig. 11 causes the (a) slow trav. Rn (b) more cpi? Why? (c) What is the purpose of the small segment?

How many degrees are in the large and small segments to cause cpi during one trav. Rn to be the number of times more than cpi during the next trav. Rn with the cams in the following example and three problems:

EXAMPLE: *2 times with Fig. 11?*

$$A = 2 \times B, \therefore B = \frac{A}{2}, \therefore A + \frac{A}{2} = 360°, \therefore A = \frac{720°}{3} = 240°, \text{ and } \therefore$$

$$B = \frac{240°}{2} = 120°.$$

185. 3 times with Fig. 11?
186. 3 times with Fig. 12?
187. 3 times with a 6-segment cam?
188. 3 times with a 4-segment cam?

189. What is rev. bc if trav. Rn is caused by a (a) 270- (b) 240- (c) 210- (d) 180- (e) 135- (f) 90- (g) 67.5 degree segment?

190. By studying formula (52) select the correct word or words in each set of the following parentheses: If each segment of bc causes a constant IPM trav. Rn and each layer is parallel to the axis of bo, the actual cpi must (a) (be the same, vary) throughout each layer, (b) (equal, vary from) the average cpi, and (c) (may, may not) vary from one layer to another, but if all or a part of each layer is not parallel to the axis of bo the actual cpi of that layer must (d) (decrease, increase) toward the small dia. of that layer, (e) (decrease, increase) toward the large dia. Why? In any case the total coils in each layer (f) (equal, differ from) the average cpi, calculated by formula (52), × trav. Rn. Therefore, if the actual cpi throughout each layer not wholly parallel to the axis of bo equals the average cpi of that layer the part of the segment that causes trav. Rn which lays the non-parallel part of the layer must be so shaped as to (g) (increase, decrease) IPM trav. Rn toward the small dia. bo or (h) (increase, decrease) it toward the large dia. Why?

What is cpi laid by the (a) *slow* (b) *fast trav. Rn on Fig.* 10 *with the combinations under the conditions in the following examples and four problems:*

EXAMPLE: *A,* 270° − 90° *bc, trav. Rn* 8″ *at bare warp bo* $\dfrac{13″}{16}$ *dia.,* 40-*tooth lg, and* 8% *c?*

By formula (52): (a) $\text{cpi} = \dfrac{21044 \times .75 \times .92}{.8125 \times 40 \times 8} = 55.8$ (b) $\text{cpi} = \dfrac{55.8}{3} = $ 18.6.

191. A, 2-segment − 3: 1 bc, trav. Rn 8″ at bare warp bo 1″ dia., 47-tooth lg, and 6% c.

EXAMPLE: *B,* 6-*segment* − 3: 1 *bc, trav. Rn* $1\dfrac{5″}{8}$,*filling bo (quill)* *dia. bare average* .6″, *full* $1\dfrac{1″}{8}$, 65-*tooth lg and* 4% *c?*

$3 \times$ large segment $+ \; 3 \times \dfrac{\text{large segment}}{3} = 360°$, ∴ large segment =

$90°$, ∴ rev. bc of large segment $= \dfrac{90°}{360°} = .25$. Average dia. bo =

$\dfrac{.6″ + 1.125″}{2} = .8625″$. By formula (52) (a) $\text{cpi} = \dfrac{14313 \times .25 \times .96}{.8625 \times 65 \times 1.625} = 37.7$

(b) $\text{cpi} = \dfrac{37.7}{3} = 12.6.$

192. B, 6-segment − 3: 1 bc, trav. Rn $1\dfrac{11″}{16}$, filling bo (quill) dia. bare average .536″, full $1\dfrac{1″}{8}$, 50-tooth lg, and 5% c?

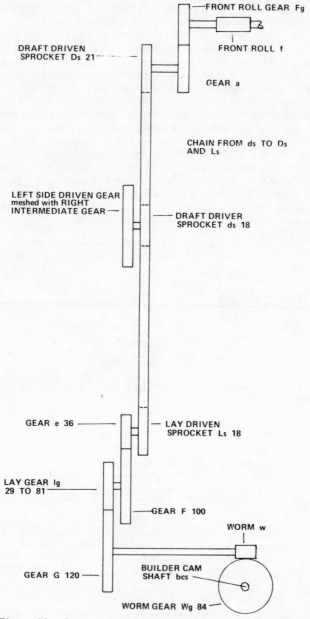

Figure 13.   Lay Train at Head End Viewed from Right Side

193. C, 2-segment − 3: 1 bc, trav. 11″ at bare warp bo 1.5″, 36-tooth lg, and 6.5% c?

194. C, 8-segment − 3: 1 bc, trav. Rn $2\frac{1}{4}''$ (filling wind) on warp bo dia. bare $1\frac{1}{16}''$ full $2\frac{3}{8}''$, 48-tooth lg, and 10% c?

195. For Fig. 13 derive

$$(54) \text{ lay constant} = \frac{\text{cpi} \times \text{dia. bo} \times \text{lg} \times \text{trav. Rn}}{\text{rev. bc} \times (1 - .01 \times \% \text{ c})}$$

$$= \frac{\text{dia. front roll} \times a \times 18 \times 100 \times 120 \times 84}{\text{front roll gear} \times 21 \times 36 \times \text{worm}}$$

and prove that formulas (52) and (53) apply.

Some Combinations of Fig. 13			
	A	B	C
dia. front roll, f	1″	$1\frac{3}{8}''$	$1\frac{15}{16}''$
front roll gear, Fg	40	28	36
gear a	53	28	26
worm, w	single	single	double

What is the lc of Fig. 13 with the combination in the following three problems:

196. A?   **197.** B?   **198.** C?

In Fig. 14 the *disc gear, Dsg,* is free to revolve upon the *builder cam shaft, bcs,* which is integral with the *output ring gear, Org,* and the *builder cam, bc.* The planet gear stud, integral with the *planet gear, pg,* is free to revolve in Dsg. The pg meshes with Org and the *fixed ring gear, frg,* which is integral with the samson of the frame and ∴ cannot revolve. The bcs is free to revolve in frg.

199. (a) Considering rev. f as −, what is the direction of rev. Dsg? (b) At the end of 1 rev. of Dsg by how many rev. would pg move Org if Org had 39 teeth? Why? Now suppose that clockwise the teeth of pg are numbered 1 to 13, of frg 1 to 39, and of Org 1 to 40. If at the start of a −rev. of Dsg tooth, 1 of frg is exactly aligned with tooth 1 of Org and tooth 1 of pg is pushing tooth 1 of frg (c) in which direction against which tooth of Org does tooth 1 of pg push? Why? At completion of 1 such −rev. Dsg (d) in which direction against which tooth of Org does tooth 1 of pg push, and ∴ (e) in which direction and by how many teeth has Org moved? Therefore (f) what is Org: pg?

200. From the preceding problem for Fig. 14 derive:

(55)   lay
constant

$$= \frac{\text{coils per inch} \times \text{dia. bobbin} \times \text{lay driver gear} \times \text{traverse ring}}{\text{revolution builder cam} \times \text{lay driven gear} \times (1 - .01 \times \% \text{ contraction})}$$

$$= \frac{\text{dia. front roll} \times a \times 20 \times 115 \times 40}{\text{front roll gear} \times 32 \times 21 \times 1},$$

(56)   coils
per inch

$$= \frac{\dfrac{\text{lay}}{\text{constant}} \times \dfrac{\text{revolution}}{\text{builder cam}} \times \dfrac{\text{lay driven}}{\text{gear}} \times (1 - .01 \times \% \text{ contraction})}{\text{dia. bobbin} \times \dfrac{\text{lay driver}}{\text{gear}} \times \dfrac{\text{traverse}}{\text{ring}}}$$

FRONT ROLL GEAR Fg

FRONT ROLL f

DRAFT DRIVEN
SPROCKET Ds 32

GEAR a

CHAIN from ds to Ds and Ls

LEFT SIDE DRIVEN GEAR
MESHED WITH LEFT
SIDE DRIVER GEAR

DRAFT DRIVER
SPROCKET ds 20

LAY DRIVER GEAR lg
25 TO 70

lg + Lg must = 95

LAY DRIVEN SPROCKET Ls 20

LAY DRIVEN GEAR Lg
25 TO 70

GEAR E 21
FIXED RING GEAR frg 39
PLANET GEAR pg 13
OUTPUT RING GEAR Org 40

BUILDER CAM bc

PLANET GEAR CENTER pc

P. CIR. Pg

P. CIR. Org

BUILDER CAM SHAFT bcs

CIR. pc

DISC

DISC GEAR Dsg 115

frg   Org   HOUSING integral with SAMSON

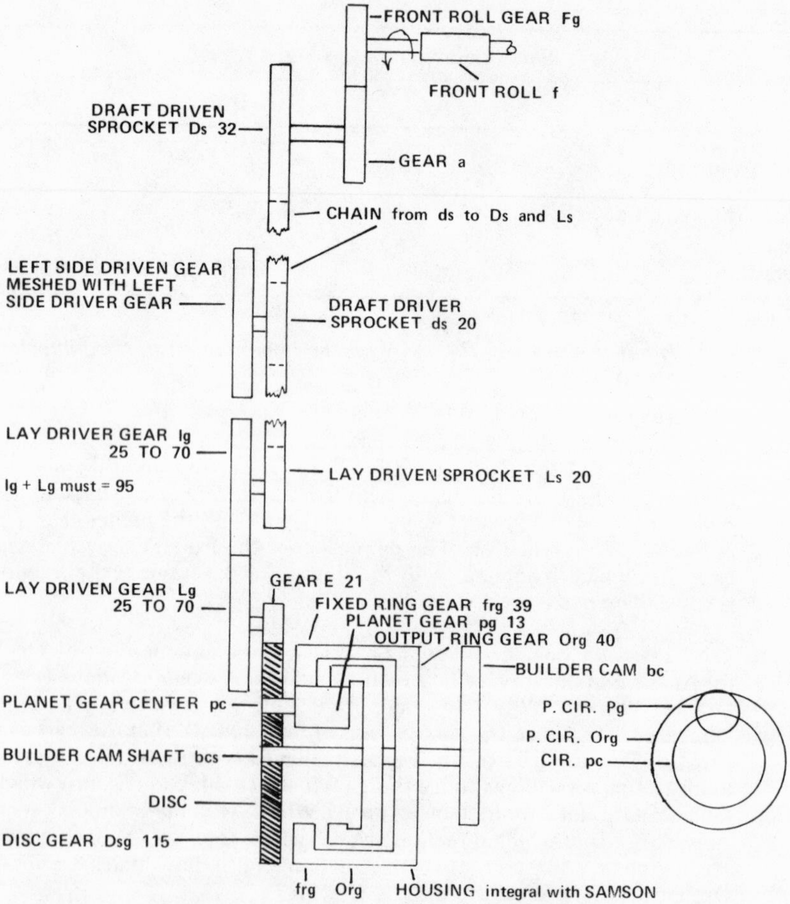

*Fig. 14. Lay Train with Epicyclic Double Internal-Ring Planet Spur Gear
Reducer at Dead End Viewed from Right Side*

(57) $\dfrac{\text{lay driver gear}}{\text{lay driven gear}}$

$$= \dfrac{\dfrac{\text{lay}}{\text{constant}} \times \dfrac{\text{revolution}}{\text{builder cam}} \times (1 - .01 \times \% \text{ contraction})}{\text{coils per inch} \times \text{dia. bobbin} \times \text{traverse ring}}$$

Some Combinations of Fig. 14

	A	B
dia. front roll, f	$1''$	$1\dfrac{3}{8}''$
front roll gear, Fg	43	51
gear a	66	57

What is the lc of Fig. 14 with the combinations in the following two problems:

201. A?   **202.** B?

Finding Lay Gears from Lay Constants.

203. What variable quantities on the right side of formulas (53) and (57) might have large changes made in them by large changes in (a) weight of yarn on and firmness of full bo without changes in counts, tpi, or total length of bo occupied by yarn (b) counts (c) tpi (d) correcting filling sloughing (e) number of and degrees in bc segments? Why?

After one or more such large changes as in the preceding problem how many teeth in the lay gear or gears ought to be tried on the frames with the combinations under the conditions to give the cpi on the slow trav. Rn in the following examples and six problems:

EXAMPLE: *Fig. 10, A, 2-segment* $- 2: 1$ *bc, 7% c, 8″ trav. Rn on bare warp bo.* $\dfrac{31''}{32}$ *dia., 30 cpi?*

Slow segment $+ \dfrac{\text{slow segment}}{2} = 360°, \therefore$ slow segment $= 240°, \therefore$

rev. bc $= \dfrac{240°}{360°} = \dfrac{2}{3}$. By formula (53) lg $= \dfrac{21044 \times \dfrac{2}{3} \times 93}{30 \times \dfrac{31}{32} \times 8} = 56.1, \therefore$ lg $=$

56 or 57.

EXAMPLE: *Fig. 10, B, 8-segment* $- 3: 1$ *bc, 4.85% c,* $1\dfrac{7}{8}''$ *trav. Rn, dia. quill bo bare average .568″ full* $1\dfrac{3}{4}''$*, cpi 21?*

$4 \times$ slow segment $+ \dfrac{4 \times \text{slow segment}}{3} = 360°, \therefore$ slow segment $=$

$67.5° \therefore$ rev. bc $= \dfrac{67.5°}{360°} = .1875$. Average dia. bo $= \dfrac{.568'' \times 1\frac{3}{4}''}{2} = 1.16''$.

By formula (53) lg $= \dfrac{14313 \times .1875 \times .9515}{21 \times 1.16 \times 1\frac{7}{8}} = 55.9, \therefore$ lg $= 55$ or 56.

204. Fig. 10, A, heart bc, 7.75% c, $8\frac{1}{2}''$ trav. Rn on bare warp bo dia. $1\frac{1}{16}''$, cpi 33?

205. Fig. 10, B, long segment of bc $210°$, 4.9% c, $9\frac{1}{2}''$ trav. Rn on bare tube warp bo average dia. $1\frac{1}{8}''$, cpi 28?

206. Fig. 10, C, 2-segment $-$ 3: 1 bc, combination warp wind, 7.75% c, $8''$ trav. Rn, dia. warp tube bo bare average $1.172''$, cpi 30?

207. Fig. 13, B, 4-segment $-$ 3: 1 bc, 3.55% c, $3\frac{3}{8}''$ trav. Rn, filling wind, warp tube bo dia. bare average $1.36''$ full $2\frac{7}{8}''$, average cpi 20?

EXAMPLE: *Fig. 14, A, 4-segment $-$ 3: 1 bc, 2.08% c, filling wind, dia. tube warp bo bare at top $1\frac{1}{8}''$ at bottom $1\frac{11}{32}''$, full $2\frac{7}{16}''$, trav. Rn $2\frac{7}{8}''$, average cpi 19?*

Rev. bc $= .375$, average dia. bo bare $= \dfrac{1\frac{1}{8}'' + 1\frac{11}{32}''}{2} = 1.23'', \therefore$ aver-

age dia. bo full $= \dfrac{1.23'' + 2\frac{7}{16}''}{2} = 1.83''$, trav. Rn $= 2\frac{7}{8}'' = 2.88''$. By formula

(57) $\dfrac{\text{lg}}{\text{Lg}} = \dfrac{210.13 \times .375 \times .9792}{19.0 \times 1.83 \times 2.88} = .77$, Lg $= \dfrac{\text{lg}}{.77}, \therefore$ lg $+ \dfrac{\text{lg}}{.77} = 95, \therefore .77 \times$

lg $+$ lg $= .77 \times 95, \therefore$ lg $= \dfrac{.77 \times 95}{1.77} = 41.3, \therefore$ lg $= 41$ or $42, \therefore$ Lg $= 54$ or 53.

208. Fig. 14, A, 4-segment $-$ 3: 1 bc, 2.26% c, filling wind dia. tube warp bo bare at top $1''$, at bottom $1\frac{1}{4}''$, full $1\frac{13}{16}''$, trav. Rn $2\frac{1}{8}''$, average cpi 21?

209. Fig. 14, B, 2-segment $-$ 7: 5 bc, % c 3.54, combination warp wind, dia. tube warp bo bare at top $1''$, at bottom $1\frac{1}{4}''$, full $1\frac{13}{16}''$, trav. Rn $6\frac{7}{8}''$, average cpi 17.7?

210. Fig. 14, B, 2-segment — 7: 5 bc, % c 3.54, combination warp wind, dia. tube warp bo at top $1\frac{1''}{8}$, at bottom $1\frac{11''}{32}$, full $2\frac{15''}{16}$, trav. Rn 9", average cpi 17?

Variation in Coils Per Inch on Bobbin.

Considering formulas (52) and (56) how many times greater are the average cpi at the bare bo than at the largest dia. bo in the following five problems:

211. Dia. tube warp bo bare average $1\frac{1''}{8}$, full $1\frac{13''}{16}$?

212. Dia. warp bo bare $\frac{31''}{32}$, full $1\frac{7''}{8}$?

213. Dia. tube warp bo bare average 1.23", full $2\frac{7''}{16}$?

214. Dia. quill bo bare average .568", full $1\frac{1''}{4}$?

215. Dia. tube warp bo bare average 1.23", full $2\frac{7''}{8}$?

Finding Lay Gears in Changing Coils Per Inch, Multiplier, and Counts.

Assuming the only changes required are in cpi and lay gears, frequently labor can be saved by computing required or new lay gears from satisfactory present or old lay gears.

216. With the foregoing assumption and reasoning similarly to deriving twist formula (45), from formulas (51) and (54) derive for Figs. 10 and 13

$$(58) \text{ new lay gear} = \frac{\text{old lay gear} \times \text{old coils per inch}}{\text{new coils per inch}}$$

and similarly to deriving formula (46), from formula (55) derive for Fig. 14

$$(59) \quad \frac{\text{new lay driver gear}}{\text{new lay driven gear}} = \frac{\text{old coils per inch} \times \text{old lay driver gear}}{\text{new coils per inch} \times \text{old lay driven gear}}$$

How many teeth in the lay gear ought to be tried to lay the average cpi required in the following four problems:

217. 40 cpi if the 38-tooth driver and only lg lays 50 cpi?
218. 52 cpi if the 46-tooth driver and only lg lays 40 cpi?
219. 40 cpi if the lay driver + lay driven gears must = 95 and a 28-tooth lay driver gear lays 50 cpi?
220. 52 cpi if the lay driver + lay driven gears must = 95 and a 42-tooth lay driver gear lays 40 cpi?

221. From the appropriate formulas, for frames with only a driver lay gear derive

$$(60) \quad \frac{\text{new lay}}{\text{gear}} = \frac{\text{old coil multiplier} \times \sqrt{\text{old counts}} \times \text{old lay gear}}{\text{new coil multiplier} \times \sqrt{\text{new counts}}}$$

and for frames with driver and driven lay gears derive

$$(61) \quad \frac{\dfrac{\text{new lay}}{\text{driver gear}}}{\dfrac{\text{new lay}}{\text{driven gear}}} = \frac{\dfrac{\text{old coil}}{\text{multiplier}} \times \sqrt{\text{old counts}} \times \dfrac{\text{old lay}}{\text{driver gear}}}{\dfrac{\text{new coil}}{\text{multiplier}} \times \sqrt{\text{new counts}} \times \dfrac{\text{old lay}}{\text{driven gear}}}$$

How many teeth in the lay gears ought to be tried to lay as required in the following three problems:

222. 36s if a 42-tooth driver and only lg lays 25s same cm?

223. 8.7s, 10 cm if a 60-tooth driver and only lg lays 9.3s, 15 cm?

224. 100s, 12 cm if the lay driver + lay driven gears must = 95 and a 60-tooth lay driver gear lays 81s, 10 cm?

225. As assigned by your instructor sketch the lay train of a spinning frame in your plant; derive the lc, cpi, and lg formulas; calculate cpi and compare your calculated cpi with actual cpi; and from present lg, cm, and counts calculate lg for proposed changes.

PRODUCTION

Basic Equations. Calculating 100% production of spinning frames and other spinning department machines starts with standard lengths (hanks with yarn on the cotton system) passing the delivery roll (f on spinning frames) multiplied, for machines with spindles, by the number of spindles, Sp, and unmodified by the operative's time that the machines are stopped.

226. From the foregoing derive

$$(62) \quad 100\% \text{ hks.} = \frac{\text{RPM } f \times \pi \times \text{dia. } f \times \text{hrs.} \times 60 \times Sp}{36 \times 840}$$

and formula (6), Chap. I, Part Two and equation (62) derive

$$(63) \quad 100\% \text{ lbs.} = \frac{\text{RPM } f \times \pi \times \text{dia. } f \times \text{hrs.} \times 60 \times Sp}{36 \times 840 \times \text{counts}}$$

Production Constants. Production constants, pc, save labor in calculating.

227. Similar to your derivation of draft, twist, and lay constants, from equation (62) or (63) derive

$$(64) \quad \text{production constant} = \frac{\pi \times \text{dia. front roll} \times 60}{36 \times 840}$$

228. With minimum calculating find pc for frames with $1''$, $1\frac{1}{8}''$, $1\frac{1}{4}''$, and $1\frac{3}{8}''$ f.

Percents of Production and Contraction. The *percent of production,* *% p,* is the percent of the operative's duty time that the machine runs. As studied with draft, twist, and lay, percent of contraction, *% c,* is the percent of length delivered by f that is lost in twisting.

Production in Hanks and Pounds from RPM of Front Roll. Such quantities as the following are frequent in calculating and recording production: *front roll hanks, fhks.,* meaning hks. just as delivered by f; *front roll hanks per spindle-hour, fhks./shr.,* meaning fhks to 1 spindle in 1 hr.; *spindle hanks, shks.,* meaning hks. as wound on the bobbin; *hanks per spindle-hour, hks./shr.,* meaning shks by 1 spindle in 1 hr.; and *pounds per spindle-hour, lbs./shr.,* meaning lbs. wound by 1 spindle in 1 hr. On each frame the *hank clock,* by which the operative is paid, is run by f and ∴ registers fhks for 1 spindle. Hence *clock hanks, chks,* are calculated like fhks but mean fhks × spindles per frame × frames; and *frame hanks, fmhks,* mean chks.

229. From the foregoing, equations (62) and (63), and formula (64) derive

(65) front roll hanks or clock hanks or frame hanks

$$= \frac{\text{production}}{\text{constant}} \times \frac{\text{RPM front}}{\text{roll}} \times \text{hours} \times \text{frames} \times .01 \times \frac{\text{percent of}}{\text{production,}}$$

(66) spindle hanks or hanks

$$= \frac{\text{production}}{\text{constant}} \times \frac{\text{RPM}}{\text{front}} \times \text{hours} \times \text{spindles} \times .01 \times \%p \times (1 - .01 \times \%c)$$

(67) pounds

$$= \frac{\text{production}}{\text{constant}} \times \frac{\text{RPM}}{\text{front}} \times \text{hours} \times \text{spindles} \times .01 \times \%p \times (1 - .01 \times \%c)$$

counts

In the following example and three problems find (a) 100% *fhks/ shr.* (b) *fhks/shr* (c) *chks* (d) *fmhks* (e) 100% *shks/shr* (f) 100% *hks/shr* (g) *hks* (h) 100% *lbs/shr* (i) *lbs/shr* (j) *lbs. of:*

EXAMPLE: 25.5s *by 2 252-spindle frames with* $1''$ *f at 150 RPM,* 80% *p, and* 4% *c for 8 hrs.*

By formula (65): (a) 100% fhks/shr = .0062333 × 150 × 1 × 1 × .01 × 100 = .0062333 × 150 = .93500 (b) fhks/shr = .93500 × .80 = .74800 (c) chks = .74800 × 8 × 2 = 11.968 (d) fmhks = 11.968. By formula (66): (e) 100% shks/shr = .93500 × (1 − .01 × 4) = .93500 × .96 =

.89760 (f) 100% hks/shr= .89760 (g) hks= .89760 × 8 × 2 × 252 × .80 =

2895.3. By formula (67): (h) 100% lbs./shr = $\dfrac{.89760}{25.5}$ = .03520 (i) lbs./

shr = .03520 × .80 = .028160 (j) lbs. = .028160 × 8 × 2 × 252 = 113.54.

230. 20.00s by 6 320-spindle frames with $1\frac{1''}{8}$ f at 160 RPM, 90% p, and 5% c for 12 hrs.

231. 24.00s by 9 228-spindle frames with $1\frac{1''}{4}$ f at 140 RPM, 92% p, and 6% c for 16 hrs.

232. 100.00s by 10 256-spindle frames with $1\frac{3''}{8}$ f at 45 RPM, 95% p, and 6% c for 40 hrs.

Production in Pounds from RPM of Spindle.

233. From formula (31) show that the approximate

$$\text{tpi} = \frac{\text{RPM Sp}}{\text{RPM f} \times \pi \times \text{dia. f} \times (1 - .01 \times \% \text{ c})} \therefore$$

$$(68) \text{ RPM f} \times \pi \times \text{dia. f} = \frac{\text{RPM Sp}}{\text{tpi} \times (1 - .01 \times \% \text{ c})}.$$

Substituting the right side of equation (68) into equation (63) prove that

$$100\% \text{ lbs.} = \frac{\dfrac{\text{RPM Sp}}{\text{tpi} \times (1 - .01 \times \% \text{ c})} \times \text{hours} \times 60 \times \text{Sp}}{36 \times 840 \times \text{counts}} \text{ and } \therefore$$

$$(69) \text{ pounds} = \frac{\dfrac{\text{RPM}}{\text{spindle}} \times \text{hours} \times \text{spindles} \times .01 \times \% \text{ production}}{504 \times \text{counts} \times \text{twist per inch} \times \left(1 - \dfrac{.01 \times \%}{\text{contraction}}\right)}.$$

In the following example and three problems find (a) 100% *lbs./shr* (b) *lbs./shr.* (c) *lbs. of:*

EXAMPLE: 2.50s, 5.00 *tpi by* 3 288-*spindle frames at* 3250 *RPM Sp,* 56% *p,* 3.7% *c for* 16 *hrs.*

By formula (69): (a) 100% lbs./shr. =

$\dfrac{3250}{504 \times 2.50 \times 5.00 \times (1 - .01 \times 3.7)}$ = .53569 (b) lbs./shr = .53569 × .56 = .29999 (c) lbs. = .29999 × 16 × 3 × 288 = 4147.1.

234. 20.00s, 19.70 tpi by 4 252-spindle frames at 9275 RPM Sp, 92% p, 6.8% c, for 3 8-hr. shifts.

235. 40.00s, 28.50 tpi by 14 240-spindle frames at 10500 RPM Sp, 95.5% p, 7.0% c for 40 hrs.

236. 32.50s, 4.50 tm. by 50 312-spindle frames at 11250 RPM Sp, 97.9% p, 3.6% c for 3 40-hr. weekly shifts.

237. Equation

(70) approximate 100% lbs./shr $= \dfrac{2 \times \text{RPM Sp}}{1000 \times \text{counts} \times \text{tpi}}$

or "twice the spindle speed divided by a thousand times the counts times the twist" is often used.

Show (a) its derivation (b) why it is easy to use and remember (c) its + or − error in lbs. and % (d) its error if used for lbs. in the preceding problem.

Creeling and Doffing Cycles. As used here the *creeling cycle* is the hours, including doffing and all other stops, required for a spindle to empty one of its roving bobbins regardless of doublings; and the *doffing cycle* is the hours, including doffing and all other stops, required for a spindle to fill its yarn bobbin.

238. From the foregoing show why

(71) creeling cycle
or hours to
empty 1 full $=$ $\dfrac{\text{pounds of roving on full bobbin}}{\text{doublings} \times \text{pounds per spindle hour}}$
roving bobbin

(72) doffing cycle or hours $=$ $\dfrac{\text{pounds of yarn on full bobbin}}{\text{pounds per spindle hour}}$
to fill 1 yarn bobbin

Find the (a) *creeling cycle hrs.* (b) *doffing cycle hrs. of the frames in the following example and three problems:*

EXAMPLE: Doublings 2; on full bo of roving 2 lbs., of yarn 4.80 oz.; lbs./shr .035783.

(a) By formula (71): creeling cycle hrs. $= \dfrac{2}{2 \times .035783} = 27.946$

or 27 hrs., 58 min. 4.80 oz. = .3 lbs. By formula (72) doffing cycle hrs. = $\dfrac{.3}{.035783} = 8.384$ or 8 hrs., 23 min.

239. Doublings 1; on full bo of roving 4.30 lbs., of yarn 2.08 oz; lbs./shr .038180.

240. Doublings 2; on full bo of roving 27 oz., of yarn 1.8 oz; lbs./shr .011875.

241. Single creeled; on full bo of roving 5.6 lbs; of yarn 9.0 oz.; lbs./shr .044582.

242. As assigned by your instructor, calculate production, including creeling and doffing cycles, for the spinning frames of your plant.

Chapter XIV

TWISTER, SPOOLER, & WARPER CALCULATIONS

TWISTER CALCULATIONS

Except for the drafting aspect, calculations concerning twisters have a close similarity to many of those made for spinning frames. Twist constants, twist gears and ranges of twists per inch can be found for a twister in exactly the same manner as found for a spinning frame.

Twist Constants, Twist Gears and Ranges of Twists per Inch.

For the conventional twist train shown in Figure 1 derive

$$(1)\ \text{TPI} = \frac{\dfrac{\text{dia. pulley (p)}}{\text{dia. whirl (w)}} \times \dfrac{\text{Twist sprocket}}{(\text{Ts})} \times \dfrac{\text{Large swing gear}}{(\text{Lsg})} \times}{\dfrac{\text{Main shaft sprocket}}{(\text{Mss})} \times \dfrac{\text{twist gear}}{(\text{tg})} \times \dfrac{\text{Small swing gear}}{(\text{Ssg})}}$$

$$\dfrac{\text{Roll gear (Rg)}}{\times 2 \times 3.1416}$$

PROBLEMS:

1. Calculate (a) the twist constant and (b) twists per inch range for the twist train in Figure 1.

2. Using the twist constant found in problem 1, calculate the twist gears needed to produce (a) 15 TPI; (b) 18 TPI; (c) 20 TPI.

3. The resulting count of a 4-ply yarn is 12.25s. Using a twist multiple of 4.0, what size twist gear should be used for the twist constant in Figure 1?

4. A fancy yarn is to be made by twisting together one end each of 24s, 36s, and 72s. If a twist multiple of 5.0 is desired, what twist gear should be used if the twist constant is 660?

5. What twist gear should be used to produce a 50s/5 ply yarn with a twist multiple of 6.0 and a gear train having a twist constant of 588?

6. A 30-tooth twist gear has been producing 32s/2. What change gear will be needed to insert the same amount of twist in 27s/3?

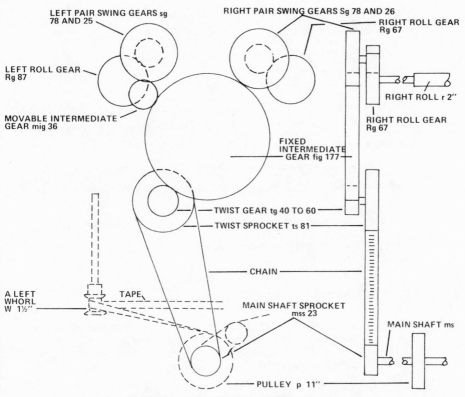

Figure 1.   Twist Train or a Ring Twister

7. A 32-tooth twist gear has been producing a 32s/2 yarn with a twist multiple of 6.0. What gear must be used to produce a 48s/3 yarn with a 4.0 twist multiple?

8. Similar to Figure 1, make a diagram of a twister in your plant and determine (a) the twist constant, (b) the twists per inch range, and (c) the twist gears needed for your range of yarn counts and twists per inch.

Production. When determining the production of a twister, primary consideration is given to the amount of yarn produced within a given period of time. The basic measure of twister production is the number of pounds of yarn produced by one spindle in one hour. This can be calculated by the following formula:

(2) 100% lbs. per spindle per hour

$$= \frac{\text{RPM front roll} \times \text{dia. front roll} \times 3.1416 \times 60}{840 \times 36 \times \text{counts of plied yarn}}$$

9. Calculate the 100% pounds per spindle per hour for the conditions listed below:

	(a)	(b)	(c)
Running time	1 hr.	8 hrs.	120 hrs.
Front roll diameter	$1\frac{1}{2}''$	$1\frac{1}{2}''$	$3''$
RPM front roll	164	146	120
Counts of plied yarn	40s	10s	2s

10. Allowing for a 15% loss in machine efficiency, how many pounds of 10s 3-ply yarn will a twister having 208 spindles produce in 8 hours if the $1\frac{1}{2}''$ front roll is turning 119 RPM?

11. What percentage of 100% production is realized on a 208 spindle twister if the $1\frac{1}{2}''$ dia. front roll is turning 88 RPM and it produces 207 lbs. of 20s 5-ply yarn each 8-hour shift?

12. To obtain 90% production, how many pounds of 36s 2-ply yarn must a 200 spindle twister produce in 8 hours if the $1\frac{1}{2}''$ front roll turns 75 RPM?

SPOOLER CALCULATIONS

Drum Speeds, Yarn Wound per Revolution, and Bobbin Run-off Time. Since the spooler is a drum type winder, that is one which drives the winding package by surface contact with a revolving cylinder or drum, first consideration should be given to the speed of the drum. From previous chapters you will remember:

$$(3)\ \text{RPM (of drum)} = \frac{\text{Motor Speed} \times \text{Dia. Motor Pulley}}{\text{Dia. Drum Pulley}}$$

PROBLEMS:

13. A spooler drum motor is found to be turning 1475 RPM. If the motor pulley diameter is 6″ and the drum pulley 7″ what is the speed of the drum?

14. The spooler in problem 13 has a drum $8\frac{3}{4}''$ in diameter. Calculate:

    a. Inches of yarn wound per drum revolution
    b. Yards wound per revolution
    c. Yards wound per minute

You will also remember from previous study that: Yds./bobbin = Wt/bobbin × counts × 840. Using the information you found in problems 13 and 14 determine:

15. How many minutes will be required to wind the yarn onto a cheese from a warp bobbin of 20s cotton yarn weighing .372 net pounds?

16. Warp bobbins in one plant contain .344 pounds of 17.25s polyester-cotton yarn. How many bobbins will be needed to produce a 39,848 yard cheese?

Production, Traveler Cycle Time, and Pounds per Machine per Hour.   In this chapter we will discuss only two of the many methods used to calculate spooler production. The first method assumes that the doffing of full packages takes place behind the traveler (after the automatic knotter rejects the full cheese). The second method is the case in which doffing is done ahead of the traveler. In order to minimize the wording in problems to follow, use the following symbols to designate some of the variables in making spooler calculations:

P = Production in pounds of yarn produced
M = Minutes machine is in operation (generally a 10% lost time factor is allowed here)
S = Number of spindles per machine
R = Number of rounds or cycles of the traveler necessary to wind the yarn from a full bobbin with no yarn breaks
BC = Number of full bobbins necessary to fill a spooler package
A = Number of full spinning bobbins per pound
$T = \text{Traveler cycle time} = \dfrac{\text{Yds. per bobbin}}{\text{Winding speed in Yds. per min.}}$
BB = Average number of yarn breaks (reties) per bobbin

Doffing Behind the Traveler.   Should each spindle wind at least part of the time during each cycle of the traveler, the formula for calculating spooler production would be:

$$(4)\ \text{Pounds} = \frac{M \times S}{A \times T \times (R + BB)}$$

This is usually not the case, however, since the traveler stops the winding process of any spindle containing a full package. Thus for any such spindles the winding process would be discontinued and the subsequent production lost for one complete cycle of the traveler. The total number of traveler cycles to produce a full package on any given spindle would be equal to $1 + (R + BB) \times BC$. Allowing for this probability the formula for calculating spooler production would be:

$$(5)\ P = \frac{M \times S \times \left[1 - \dfrac{1}{1 + (R + BB) \times BC}\right]}{A \times T \times (R + BB)}$$

17. Calculate the pounds of yarn produced by each of the three spoolers below:

	Spooler A	Spooler B	Spooler C
Spindles	234	234	288
Bobbins per pound	2.92	2.69	3.72
Winding speed in yds./min.	900	1200	1200
Yards per bobbin	2881	4450	4516
% of spindles with breaks or reties	14	20	30
Hours machine operated	120	120	120
Package weight in pounds	2.74	2.23	2.42

Doffing Ahead of the Traveler. Suppose the studies made at a certain plant indicate that a spooler operator can service 19.5 spindles per minute during each cycle of the traveler. Then the number of minutes of service time per traveler cycle would be determined as follows:

$$\text{Minutes service time} = \frac{\text{Number of spindles per machine}}{19.5}$$

Thus, the desired cycle time of the traveler could be determined by dividing the minutes of service time per cycle by the number of operators assigned to the machine.

18. Calculate the desired traveler cycle time for each of the following spoolers:
   a. 234 spindles, 3 operators
   b. 288 spindles, 4 operators
   c. 306 spindles, 3 operators

To determine the desired cycle time according to a particular yarn number, disregard the average breaks per bobbin and allow a time for doffing (Td) a full package before the knotter passes again. Thus,

$$(6) \ \text{Cycle time} = \frac{\dfrac{\text{lbs. of yarn}}{\text{bobbin}} \times \text{counts} \times 840 + \text{Td.}}{\text{winding speed YPM}}$$

19. Assume an average time for doffing (Td) of .25 minutes and calculate the desired cycle time for the following situations:

	Counts	lbs/bobbin	Winding speed	Spindles	Operators
a.	10s	.342	900 YPM	234	3
b.	26s	.308	1200 YPM	342	3
c.	20s	.329	1200 YPM	378	4

Before proceeding with spooler calculations, consideration must be given to the operator's personal time allowance, machine stoppage, and the yarn breaks expected during winding. These factors are usually determined by a series of studies made by industrial engineering staff and vary from plant to plant according to conditions at each plant.

To determine the number of times each spindle is serviced during a given hour (ts), prove that:

$$(7) \ \text{ts} = \frac{\dfrac{60 \ \text{min.}}{\text{hour}} - (\% \ \text{personal time} + \% \ \text{machine downtime})}{\text{traveler cycle time in minutes}}$$

and that:

$$(8) \ \frac{\text{lbs. per machine}}{\text{per hour}} = \frac{\text{ts} \times \text{No. of spindles} \times \dfrac{\text{yarn lbs.}}{\text{bobbin}}}{1.00 + \% \ \text{breaks}}$$

Assume a combined total lost time of 10% for personal time and machine downtime, use the information given in problem 19, and calculate the pounds per spooler under the conditions stated in the following problems:

    20. One hour, 14% breaks, data in 19 (a).
    21. Eight hours, 30% breaks, data in 19 (b).
    22. One hundred and twenty hours, 20% breaks, data in 19 (c).

WARPER CALCULATIONS

From your studies of previous chapters you will be able to determine any formula needed in making calculations pertaining to a warper.

PROBLEMS:

    23. Draw a diagram of the gearing of a warper in your plant, develop the necessary formula, and determine the maximum possible production in yards per minute.

    24. If a certain section beam containing 437 ends will hold 520 lbs. of 26s yarn, how many yards long will the beam be?

    25. A style requiring 5,672 ends of 26s is to be slashed from 13 section beams. Standard beams containing 437 ends are available. In order to slash this style how many ends must the necessary match beam contain?

    26. If the net weight of 14.25s yarn on a section beam containing 453 ends is known to be 492 lbs., how many yards are there in each end on the beam?

    27. A warp containing 2,268 ends is to be slashed from a set of six section beams. The warper will accommodate up to 672 ends. How many ends should be put on each section beam?

    28. A full cheese of 14.25s yarn weighs 2.75 lbs. How many 13,000 yard section beams could be warped without running any cheese empty?

Chapter XV

LOOM CALCULATIONS

Picks Per Minute

PROBLEMS:

1. While the crankshaft on a loom is making one complete revolution, how many picks does the loom put into the cloth? Why?

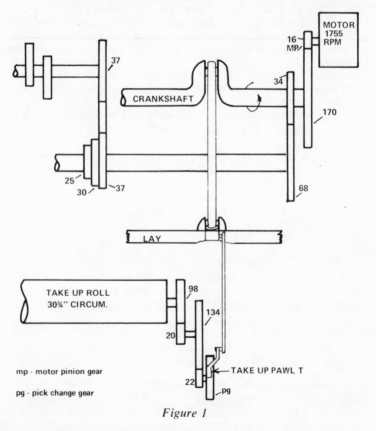

Figure 1

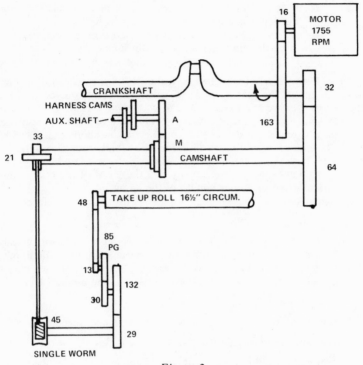

Figure 2

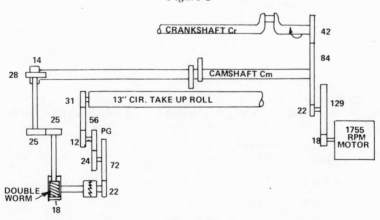

Figure 3

    2. Calculate the number of picks per minute the loom in Figure 1 is making.

    3. In order to run the loom in Figure 1 as near 175 picks per minute as possible, what size motor pinion gear should we use?

    4. How many picks per minute does the loom in Figure 2 make?

5. What size motor pinion gear would be necessary to obtain at least 193 picks per minute on the loom in Figure 2?

6. If a 19-tooth pinion gear were used on the loom in Figure 3, what would be the effect on the picks per minute?

Picks Per Inch and Pick Change Gears.   On the ratchet take-up motion shown in Figure 1 the *take-up pawl, T,* is so arranged that each time the lay sword moves forward the pawl turns the *pick change gear, pg,* forward one tooth. The pick change gear is a ratchet gear; therefore, we can consider the take-up pawl a one-tooth driver gear, because a one-tooth gear in making a complete revolution would move the gear with which it meshes only the distance of one tooth. Since the take-up pawl moves forward and then back each time the loom makes a pick, we can say that the RPM of the one-tooth gear, T, is the same as the picks per minute of the loom.

Let ppm stand for the number of picks per minute. Therefore:

(1) RPM of T = ppm.

Now let us consider the take-up roll. If we let tr stand for the take-up roll and let ppi stand for the number of picks per inch, then the number of picks per minute that tr takes up is the number of picks per inch multiplied by the number of inches the surface of tr travels in one minute. Hence,

(2) ppm = ppi $\times$ surface speed of tr.

We also know from our discussion of RPM and surface speeds that:

(3) surface speed of tr = RPM of tr $\times$ circumference of tr.

Therefore, substituting the right side of equation (3) in place of surface speed of tr in equation (2) we have:

(4) ppm = ppi $\times$ RPM of tr $\times$ cir of tr.

Therefore:

(5) RPM of tr $= \dfrac{\text{ppm}}{\text{ppi} \times \text{cir. of tr}}$.

Now let us consider the train of gears. Notice that the take-up roll gear turns at the same speed as tr. From our study of gear trains and omitting the word "of" after RPM, s.s., etc., we know that:

(6) $\dfrac{\text{RPM } T}{\text{RPM tr}} = \dfrac{\text{pg} \times 134 \times 98}{T \times 22 \times 20}$

Substituting from equations (1) and (5) into equation (6) we have:

(7) $\dfrac{\text{ppm}}{\dfrac{\text{ppm}}{\text{ppi} \times \text{cir. tr}}} = \dfrac{\text{pg} \times 134 \times 98}{T \times 22 \times 20}$

Cancelling in equation (7) we have:

(8) ppi $\times$ cir. tr $= \dfrac{\text{pg} \times 134 \times 98}{T \times 22 \times 20}$

From this we see that:

$$(9) \quad \text{ppi} = \frac{\text{pg} \times 134 \times 98}{T \times 22 \times 20 \times \text{cir. tr}}.$$

Contraction After Leaving the Take-Up Roll.   The cloth, while in contact with the take-up roll, is in a state of tension. After it leaves the take-up roll it is no longer under tension and the warp tends to draw up or contract. Therefore, there are more picks per inch in the finished cloth than there are in the cloth before it has left the take-up roll. Thus, we see that in order to determine the number of picks per inch the cloth on the cloth roll, we must subtract a slight amount from the circumference of the take-up roll. Experience has shown that, on the average, about $2\frac{1}{2}\%$ is the right amount to deduct. Therefore,

$$(10) \quad \text{ppi} = \frac{\text{pg} \times 134 \times 98}{T \times 22 \times 20 \times (\text{cir. tr} - 2\frac{1}{2}\% \text{ of cir. tr})}.$$

From this we can determine the formula for finding the driven pick change gear.

$$(11) \quad \text{pg} = \frac{T \times 22 \times 20 \times (\text{cir. tr} - 2\frac{1}{2}\% \text{ cir. tr}) \times \text{ppi}}{134 \times 98}.$$

To shorten our formula we can write it thus:

$$(12) \quad \text{pg} = \frac{T \times 22 \times 20 \times .975 \times \text{cir. tr} \times \text{ppi}}{134 \times 98}$$

EXAMPLE: *The loom in Figure 1 is to make cloth with 64 ppi. What size pick change gear must we use?*

$$\text{pg} = \frac{1 \times 22 \times 20 \times .975 \times 30.75 \times 64}{134 \times 98} = 64.28. \text{ The pick change}$$

gear must have 64 teeth.

7. What size pick change gear must be used on the loom in Figure 1 to obtain (a) 48 ppi, (b) 72 ppi?

8. Using formula (10) find how many picks per inch will be inserted by a 32-tooth pg.

Pick Constants.   The use of pick constants greatly shortens the figuring of picks per inch and pick change gears. From formula (12) we see that:

$$(13) \quad \frac{\text{pg}}{\text{ppi}} = \frac{T \times 22 \times 20 \times .975 \times \text{cir. tr}}{134 \times 98} = \frac{1 \times 22 \times 20 \times .975 \times 30.75}{134 \times 98} = 1$$

We can see that the quotient of pg divided by ppi always equals a certain fixed number. This number is called the pick constant. Therefore, the constant of this loom is 1. Letting pc stand for pick constant, we obtain from formula (13) the following useful formulas:

(14) $\text{pc} = \dfrac{\text{pg}}{\text{ppi}}$

(15) $\text{pg} = \text{pc} \times \text{ppi}.$

9. What size pick gear shall we use to obtain 29 picks per inch on the loom in Figure 1?

10. If the pc of a loom with a driven pg is 2, what size pg shall we use to obtain $9\frac{1}{2}$ ppi?

11. Following the same method used in working out formula (13) for the loom in Figure 1, show the following formula to be true for the loom in Figure 2.

(16) $\dfrac{\text{pg}}{\text{ppi}} = \dfrac{32 \times 33 \times 1 \times 29 \times 30 \times 13 \times .975 \times 16.5}{64 \times 21 \times 45 \times 132 \times 48} = \dfrac{1}{2}$

12. (a) On a loom with a driven pick gear, does increasing the size of the pick gear increase or decrease the picks per inch?

(b) Therefore, a driven pick gear is (directly, inversely) proportional to the picks per inch.

13. What size pg would be required to obtain 64 ppi on the loom in Figure 2?

14. Prove the following formula for finding the pick constant for the loom in Figure 3 to be correct:

(17) $\dfrac{\text{pg}}{\text{ppi}} = \dfrac{24 \times 42 \times 14 \times 2 \times 22 \times 12 \times .975 \times 13}{84 \times 28 \times 18 \times 72 \times 31} = 1.$

15. If on the loom in Figure 2 the 30-tooth gear that drives the pick gear is replaced by a 15-tooth gear, what size pick gear will then be required to obtain 64 ppi?

16. If the single worm gear on the loom in Figure 2 is changed to a double worm and the other gears remain as shown, what size pg will then be needed to obtain 40 ppi?

17. Suppose that in Figure 3 the pick change gear and the 24-tooth driver gear are interchanged so that the pick change gear becomes a driver and the 24-tooth gear a driven gear.

Rearrange the formula worked out in problem 14 and prove the following formula true:

(18) $\text{ppi} \times \text{pg} = \dfrac{84 \times 28 \times 18 \times 72 \times 24 \times 31}{42 \times 14 \times 2 \times 22 \times 12 \times .975 \times 13} = 576.31$

18. Now show that when the pg is a driver gear the following formulas are true:

(19) $\text{pc} = \text{pg} \times \text{ppi},$

and

(20) $\text{pg} = \dfrac{\text{pc}}{\text{ppi}}$

19. Using the conditions set up in problems 17 and 18, find the driver pick gear required to obtain 18 ppi.

20. Using the conditions set up in problems 17 and 18, find how many picks per inch would be obtained by using a 24-tooth pg.

Suppose we wish to change from the cloth being made at present on a loom to a cloth with a different number of picks per inch, and we wish to find the driven pg required for the new cloth:

Using equation (14): $pc = \dfrac{present\ pg}{present\ ppi}$, also $pc = \dfrac{required\ pg}{required\ ppi}$.

Since the left sides are equal, the right sides must be equal. Therefore, $\dfrac{present\ pg}{present\ ppi} = \dfrac{required\ pg}{required\ ppi}$. Hence,

(21) $required\ pg = \dfrac{present\ pg \times required\ ppi}{present\ ppi}$.

21. If a loom is making 34 ppi with a 20-tooth driven pg, what size pg will make 26 ppi? Use formula (21).

22. If a loom is making 42 ppi with a 35-tooth driven pg, what size pg will make 30 ppi?

23. Prove that if a loom has a driver pick gear:

(22) $required\ pg = \dfrac{present\ pg \times present\ ppi}{required\ ppi}$.

24. If a loom is making 45 ppi with a 16-tooth driver pg, what size gear must we use to obtain 32 ppi?

25. A 20-tooth driver pick gear is making 60 ppi. What size gear will make 80 ppi?

26. Make diagram showing the driving motion and take-up motion for each type loom in your plant. For each type loom find (a) the picks per minute, (b) the pick constant, and (c) the picks per inch with its present pick gear.

Cam Gearing. There are many kinds of cam arrangements. The simplest arrangement is to place the cam directly on the cam shaft. Looking at Figure 3 we see that one RPM of cam shaft Cm = 2 RPM of crank shaft Cr. Hence, a cam on the cam shaft would be up every two picks, which is the condition required for plain weaving with two harnesses.

It is therefore evident that when it becomes necessary to have harnesses up (or down) only every three, four, five and six picks as in weaving twills and sateens, another arrangement is necessary. Figure 2 shows one arrangement of an auxiliary cam shaft, to which the cams are attached, adaptable to any of the above weaves. It is evident that with a weave requiring harnesses up (or down) every two picks, the crank shaft Cr must revolve twice as fast as gear A which is on the auxiliary shaft; requiring harnesses up (or down) every three picks, the crank shaft must revolve three times as fast as A; up (or down) every four picks, four times as fast as A, and so on. Hence:

RPM Cr = number of harnesses × RPM A.

Also $\dfrac{RPM\ Cr}{RPM\ A} = \dfrac{64 \times A}{32 \times M}$. Combining these two equations we have:

$\dfrac{number\ of\ harnesses \times RPM\ A}{RPM\ A} = \dfrac{64 \times A}{32 \times M}$. Cancelling we have:

(23) number of harnesses $= \dfrac{2 \times A}{M}$, or

(24) $M = \dfrac{2 \times A}{\text{number of harnesses}}$.

M has three "steps" as shown. M and the auxiliary shaft are so arranged that A can be brought into mesh with any of the steps on M. A can be changed.

EXAMPLE: *If A has 30 teeth, how many teeth must the largest step of M have to make a 2-harness plain weave?*

Using formula (24): $M = \dfrac{2 \times 30}{2} = 30.$

27. If A has 30 teeth, how many teeth must the middle step of M have to weave a 3-harness twill?

28. If A has 30 teeth, how many teeth must the smallest step of M have to weave a 4-harness twill?

29. Work out the following formula for finding A:

(25) $A = \dfrac{M \times \text{number of harnesses}}{2}$.

30. If the steps of M remain as in the preceding example and as in problems 27 and 28, and the loom is to weave a 5-harness sateen, (a) what is the smallest number of teeth that A can have to make this weave and (b) with what step on M must A mesh?

31. If M is to remain as in the preceding example and problems, (a) what is the least number of teeth A may have and (b) with what step of M must A mesh to weave a 6-harness sateen?

32. Suppose we wish to have enough steps on M to weave everything from 2 to 6-harness weaves without changing A. (a) How many steps on M will be needed? (b) What will be the number of teeth in each step of M to keep the number of teeth in A as small as possible? (c) How many teeth will there be in A?

33. If the looms in your weave room are equipped to make twills, make a diagram of the gearing and calculate the sizes of gears necessary to make everything up to 6-harness work.

Throw of Cams.   Consider Figure 4. From our study of levers we see that the treadle is a lever, the shed of the harness is the resistance distance, the throw (or difference between the largest and smallest radius) of the cam is the power distance and the center of the stud, f, is the fulcrum. Hence, considering the front harness, q:

$\dfrac{\text{throw of cam}}{\text{shed}} = \dfrac{\text{length of treadle f to p 2}}{\text{total length of treadle}}$. Therefore:

(26) throw of cam $= \dfrac{\text{length of treadle f to p 2} \times \text{shed}}{\text{total length of treadle}}$.

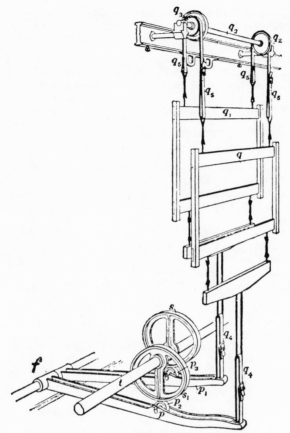

Figure 4.   Shedding Motion of a Loom
(Courtesy and special permission of
International Textbook Co.)

34. What must be the throw of the cam to obtain a shed of 3″ if the treadle is 30″ long and the point of contact of the cam and treadle is 18″ from the center of the stud?

35. On a certain loom the points of contact of the cams and the treadles are 15″ from the center of the stud. The front harness requires a shed of 4″ and the back harness needs a shed of at least $4\frac{1}{2}^{\prime\prime}$. What must be the throw of each cam if the front harness treadle is 22″ long and the back harness treadle is 20″ long?

36. On another loom the points of contact of the cams and treadles are 15″ from the center of the stud. The front harness requires a shed of $3\frac{3}{4}^{\prime\prime}$ and the back harness a shed of 5″. The front treadle is 24″ long and the back treadle is 23″ long. Find the required throw of each cam.

Production and Percent of Production. Suppose we wish to find how many yards will be produced in one hour by a loom running 150 picks per minute making cloth with 50 picks per inch if there is no stoppage.

150 picks per minute ÷ 50 picks per inch = 3 inches per minute.
3 inches per minute × 60 minutes per hour = 180 inches per hour.
180 inches per hour ÷ 36 inches per yard = 5 yards per hour.

37. Hence, prove the following formula for 100% production:

$$(27) \quad \frac{100\% \text{ production}}{\text{in yards per hour}} = \frac{\text{picks per minute} \times 60}{\text{picks per inch} \times 36}$$

38. How many yards of 52 pick drill will be produced in 2 hours by a loom running 177 picks per minute?

39. If a loom is run 204 picks per minute and is making 48 pick goods, how many yards will the loom weave in 8 hours if it runs continuously?

40. What is 100% production per hour for a loom running 210 RPM and making 37″ 3.95 68 × 40 3-harness drills?

41. If the loom in problem 40 produces an average of 8.05 yards per hour, what is the percent production?

42. Hence, prove the following formula to be true:

$$(28) \quad \% \text{ production} = \frac{\text{actual yards per hour}}{100\% \text{ yards per hour}} \times 100.$$

43. What is the percent production of a loom running 190 ppm if it actually produces 62 yards of 38 pick goods in 8 hours?

44. If a loom running 182 RPM and making 80 × 80 fabric produces only 26.84 yards in an 8-hour shift, what is the % production?

45. A certain loom is running 266 RPM and is making a cloth with 24 ppi. Assuming 93% production and 550 yards per roll find how many hours it takes to fill up a roll.

Production from Pick Clocks. In most plants each loom is equipped with a pick clock which records in whole numbers the loom production in thousands of picks. The pick clock readings are used as a means of calculating loom efficiency on % production.

EXAMPLE: *Suppose we have a loom running 176 RPM and the pick clock shows 77 (thousands of picks) at the end of an 8-hour shift. What is the percent production?*

$$176 \frac{\text{picks}}{\text{minute}} \times 60 \frac{\text{minutes}}{\text{hour}} \times 8 \frac{\text{hours}}{\text{shift}} = 84,480 \frac{\text{picks}}{\text{shift}} \text{ at } 100\%$$

production.

77,000 ÷ 84,480 = .9114 or 91.14%. Hence, prove the following formula for finding percent production to be true

$$(29) \quad \% \text{ production} = \frac{\text{actual picks on clock}}{100\% \text{ picks}} \times 100.$$

47. A certain loom running 163 RPM shows a pick clock reading of 71 at the end of the shift. What is the % production?

47. If a loom running 145 RPM runs 88% production for 8 hours, what number will the pick clock record?

48. If a certain loom, by running continuously for 8 hours, could pick 94,080 times, but at the end of the shift showed only 85 on the pick clock, (a) What would be the speed of the loom, and (b) What would be the % production?

49. A certain weaver has as part of his loom assignment five looms on the same style of cloth, and each loom is running 165 RPM. At the end of the shift the pick clocks on these looms read 69, 69, 68, 70 and 69 respectively. What is the % production on this style for the shift?

50. If the cloth in problem 49 contains 34 ppi, how many total yards did the five looms produce that shift?

51. A weaver runs a set of 24 looms. Eight of the looms run 180 picks per minute (ppm) and the rest run a higher speed of 205 ppm. (a) What is the total possible picks this weaver could run in an 8 hour shift? (b) A total of all pick clocks on the set at the end of the shift is 1993 (thousands of picks). What is the percent of production for the shift? (c) The same style of sheeting is on all 24 looms and the picks per inch is 88. How many yards of cloth did these looms weave during the shift?

52. There are 31 looms in a weaver's set. All of these looms run 193 ppm. During an 8 hour shift, 3 of these looms are taken out of the weaver's set for a training session which lasts 3 hours. The total picks on all 31 looms is 2555 (thousands of picks). (a) What is the weaver's efficiency for the shift if you allow for the training downtime? (b) What would be her efficiency if the 3 training looms were considered a part of her job for the entire shift?

53. The weaving department of a plant contains 842 looms. The speed in picks per minute of the looms vary as follows: 300 looms — 195 ppm, 242 looms — 224 ppm, 100 looms — 148 ppm, and 200 looms — 178 ppm. The 242 looms with the faster speed weave plain sheeting with 83 picks per inch, and the balance of the looms weave drapery material with 66 picks per inch. The weaving department operates 3 shifts per day of 8 hours, 6 days a week. (a) Calculate the yards of sheeting material the plant will produce in one week based on a 93% weaving efficiency for this type cloth. (b) How many yards of drapery material will be woven in one week if the estimated efficiency for this type cloth is 87%?

Part One

ANSWERS

Chapter I   Reading Numbers

1. 122, one hundred twenty-two; **2.** 236, two hundred thirty-six; **3.** 999, nine hundred ninety-nine; **4.** 1,122, one thousand one hundred twenty-two, or Eleven hundred twenty-two; **5.** 2,236, two thousand two hundred thirty-six or twenty-two hundred thirty-six; **6.** 9,999, nine thousand nine hundred ninety-nine, or ninety-nine hundred ninety-nine; **7.** 11,122, eleven thousand one hundred twenty-two; **8.** 32,236, thirty-two thousand two hundred thirty-six; **9.** 99,999, ninety-nine thousand nine hundred ninety-nine; **10.** 111,122, one hundred eleven thousand one hundred twenty-two.

11. 532,236, five hundred thirty-two thousand two hundred thirty-six; **12.** 999,999 nine hundred ninety-nine thousand nine hundred ninety-nine; **13.** 1,111,122, one million one hundred eleven thousand one hundred twenty-two; **14.** 6,532,236, six million five hundred thirty-two thousand two hundred thirty-six; **15.** 9,999,999, nine million nine hundred ninety-nine thousand nine hundred ninety-nine; **16.** 11,111,122, eleven million one hundred eleven thousand one hundred twenty-two; **17.** 76,532,236, seventy-six million five hundred thirty-two thousand two hundred thirty six.

18. 99,999,999, ninety-nine million nine hundred ninety-nine thousand nine hundred ninety-nine; **19.** 143,256,793, one hundred forty-three million two hundred fifty-six thousand seven hundred ninety-three; **20.** 650,763,941, six hundred fifty million seven hundred sixty-three thousand nine hundred forty-one; **21.** 769,832,456, seven hundred sixty-nine million eight hundred thirty-two thousand four hundred fifty-six; **22.** 3,896,743,226, three billion eight hundred ninety-six million seven hundred forty-three thousand two hundred twenty-six; **23.** 11,456,666,732, eleven billion four hundred fifty-six million six hundred sixty-six thousand seven hundred thirty-two; **24.** 27,567,-891,429, twenty-seven billion five hundred sixty-seven million eight hundred ninety-one thousand four hundred twenty-nine.

25. 1,001, one thousand one; **26.** 10,001, ten thousand one; **27.** 100,000, one hundred thousand; **28.** 500,009, five hundred thousand nine; **29.** 1,000,000, one million; **30.** 900,000,000, nine hundred million; **31.** 90,120,304, ninety million one hundred twenty thousand three hundred four; **32.** 9,000,000,002, nine billion two; **33.** 100,001,001,001, one hundred billion one million one thousand one; **34.** 4,475; **35.** 32,000; **36.** 1,046,400; **37.** 1,416,550; **38.** 22,280,-000,000; **39.** 22,000; **40.** 37,929,000; **41.** 9,140,900,000.

Chapter II   Addition of Whole Numbers

1. 5; **2.** 7; **3.** 9; **4.** 11; **5.** 13; **6.** 15; **7.** 17; **8.** 18; **9.** 15; **10.** 21; **11.** 24; **12.** 27; **13.** 85; **14.** 79; **15.** 78; **16.** 89; **17.** 189; **18.** 999; **19.** 1940 looms; **20.** 2329 yards.

21, 1818 pounds; **22.** 1920 looms; **23.** 3450 yards; **24.** 3281 pounds; **25.** $22,441; **26.** 422,664 yards; **27.** 211,400 drop wires; **28.** 10,287 pounds; **29.** 111,672 pounds; **30.** 205,772 pounds of yarn, 3163 pounds of waste.

Chapter III   Subtraction of Whole Numbers

1. 4; **2.** 4; **3.** 11; **4.** 12; **5.** 15; **6.** 23; **7.** 63; **8.** 112; **9.** 12; **10.** 43; **11.** 25; **12.** 41; **13.** 0; **14.** 4; **15.** 7; **16.** 6; **17.** 4; **18.** 5; **19.** 7; **20.** 9; **21.** 9; **22.** 6; **23.** 15; **24.** 11; **25.** 10; **26.** 30; **27.** 44; **28.** 101; **29.** 250 more; **30.** 674 yards; **31.** 24,730 pounds; **32.** 6 pounds; **33.** 9 pounds; **34.** 6 yards; **35.** 3013 pounds; **36.** 203 years; **37.** 78 years; **38.** 292,430 yards; **39.** 8212 yards; **40.** 453 pounds.

Chapter IV   Multiplication of Whole Numbers

1.   30; **2.** 36; **3.** 42; **4.** 24; **5.** 27; **6.** 36; **7.** 42; **8.** 70; **9.** 25; **10.** 80; **11.** 9; **12.** 5; **13.** 0; **14.** 0; **15.** 0; **16.** 36; **17.** 22; **18.** 36; **19.** 39; **20.** 69; **21.** 28; **22.** 88; **23.** 1107; **24.** 3192; **25.** 2523; **26.** 72,968; **27.** 66,612; **28.** 89,991; **29.** 720 ounces; **30.** $33,000.00; **31.** 12,000 yds; **32.** 984 dents; **33.** 44,620 bobbins; **34.** 640 ounces; **35.** 280,000 yards; **36.** 133,000 pounds; **37.** 114,240 yards; **38.** 1,484,520 heddles; **39.** 770,000 heddles; **40.** $62,832.00; **41.** 87,360 picks; **42.** 199,200 picks.

Chapter V   Division of Whole Numbers Without Final Remainders

1. 2 pounds; **2.** 4 yards; **3.** 3; **4.** 8 yards; **5.** 8; **6.** 2 boxes; **7.** 7; **8.** 9; **9.** 2; **10.** 1; **11.** 7 bobbins; **12.** 1; **13.** 6; **14.** 9; **15.** 10; **16.** 9; **17.** 1; **18.** 1; **19.** 71; **20.** 234; **21.** 132; **22.** 811; **23.** 1470; **24.** 206; **25.** 199; **26.** 1005; **27.** 239 pounds; **28.** 288; **29.** 90,040; **30.** 90,919; **31.** 42 looms; **32.** 43 weeks; **33.** 36 inches; **34.** 89 pounds; **35.** 268 frames; **36.** 50; **37.** 40; **38.** 25; **39.** 20; **40.** 10; **41.** 5; **42.** 4; **43.** 2; **44.** 1; **45.** 3 days; **46.** 4 pounds; **47.** 52,080 yards; **48.** 1 ounce; **49.** 96 yards.

Chapter VI   Multiples, Prime Numbers and Factors

1. 2, 2, 2, 3, 5; **2.** 2, 2, 2, 2, 2, 2, 2; **3.** 2, 3, 5, 5; **4.** 5, 5, 7; **5.** 2, 3, 5, 7; **6.** 3, 9, 7; **7.** 2, 2, 3, 3, 3, 5; **8.** 239; **9.** 2, 2, 2, 3, 5, 7; **10.** 7, 11, 13; **11.** 2, 2, 2, 3, 11, 13; **12.** 2, 2, 2, 3, 7, 11, 17; **13.** 48; **14.** 24; **15.** 90; **16.** 126; **17.** 1001; **18.** 144; **19.** 360; **20.** 1092; **21.** 720; **22.** 504.

Chapter VII   The Meaning of Fractions

49. $10\frac{11}{16}$; **50.** $225\frac{37}{201}$; **51.** $116\frac{141}{1000}$; **52.** $17\frac{222}{2000}$; **53.** $\frac{57}{16}$; **54.** $\frac{1680}{840}$;

55. $\frac{57}{16}$; **56.** $\frac{57}{16}$ of an inch; **57.** $\frac{1680}{840}$; **58.** $\frac{840}{120}$; **59.** $\frac{12}{840}$; **60.** $\frac{1}{7}$ of a pound; **61.** 2;

62. 4; **63.** 6; **64.** 6; **65.** $\frac{1}{2}$; **66.** $\frac{3}{4}$; **67.** 4; **68.** 9; **69.** $\frac{97}{11}$; **70.** 25.

Chapter VIII   Reduction of Fractions, Cancellation and Division with Fractional Remainders

1. $\frac{3}{75}$; **2.** $\frac{27}{36}$; **3.** $\frac{84}{96}$; **4.** $\frac{125}{100}$; **5.** $\frac{42}{120}$; **6.** $\frac{1}{2}$; **7.** $\frac{1}{2}$; **8.** $\frac{1}{4}$; **9.** $\frac{1}{3}$; **10.** $\frac{1}{3}$; **11.** $\frac{1}{3}$;

12. 5; **13.** $\frac{1}{5}$; **14.** $\frac{1}{5}$; **15.** 5; **16.** $\frac{1}{3}$; **17.** 13; **18.** $\frac{1}{13}$; **19.** $\frac{12}{7}$; **20.** $\frac{1}{3}$; **21.** $\frac{1}{9}$; **22.** $\frac{5}{11}$;

23. $\frac{9}{16}$; **24.** $\frac{7}{9}$; **25.** $\frac{63}{95}$; **26.** $\frac{37}{53}$; **27.** 11; **28.** $\frac{25}{3}$.

29. $\frac{7}{18}$; **30.** $\frac{27}{350}$; **31.** $\frac{1}{11}$; **32.** $\frac{5}{187}$; **33.** $\frac{9}{4}$; **34.** $\frac{23}{4}$; **35.** $\frac{78}{11}$; **36.** $\frac{120}{13}$; **37.** $\frac{76}{7}$;

38. $\frac{157}{12}$; **39.** $\frac{129}{5}$; **40.** $\frac{1003}{100}$; **41.** 3; **42.** 3; **43.** 4; **44.** $1\frac{3}{4}$; **45.** $3\frac{1}{3}$; **46.** $3\frac{4}{5}$; **47.** $9\frac{3}{16}$;

48. 5; **49.** $99\frac{1}{7}$; **50.** $8\frac{8}{9}$; **51.** $2\frac{128}{561}$; **52.** $15\frac{1}{2}$; **53.** $3\frac{9}{10}$ pounds; **54.** $\frac{5}{8}$ grains; **55.** 15

yards; **56.** $22\frac{1}{2}$ dents; **57.** $14\frac{2}{5}$ ounces; **58.** $58\frac{1}{2}$ grains.

Chapter IX   Addition and Subtraction of Fractions and Mixed Numbers

1. 1; **2.** $1\frac{3}{4}$; **3.** $2\frac{1}{2}$; **4.** $5\frac{1}{2}$; **5.** 3; **6.** $4\frac{1}{4}$; **7.** $4\frac{1}{3}$; **8.** $2\frac{35}{48}$; **9.** $\frac{13}{22}$; **10.** $26\frac{23}{40}$;

11. $\frac{37}{160}$; **12.** $\frac{131}{504}$; **13.** $\frac{239}{630}$; **14.** $\frac{513}{1400}$; **15.** $21\frac{281}{780}$; **16.** $13\frac{1}{2}$ pounds; **17.** $46\frac{3}{4}$

pounds; **18.** 46 pounds; **19.** 46 pounds; **20.** 3; **21.** $\frac{1}{2}$; **22.** $\frac{1}{2}$; **23.** $\frac{7}{8}$; **24.** $1\frac{15}{16}$;

25. $\frac{1}{4}$; **26.** $\frac{9}{16}$; **27.** $7\frac{10}{21}$; **28.** $20\frac{88}{95}$; **29.** $18\frac{131}{180}$; **30.** $5\frac{12}{31}$; **31.** $7\frac{2}{9}$; **32.** $418\frac{1}{2}$

pounds; **33.** $5\frac{3}{4}$ pounds; **34.** $1\frac{9}{16}$ inches; **35.** $3\frac{7}{12}$ yards.

Chapter X   Multiplication of Fractions

1. $2\frac{1}{2}$; **2.** 3; **3.** $1\frac{3}{4}$; **4.** $3\frac{1}{2}$; **5.** $2\frac{1}{2}$; **6.** 5; **7.** $\frac{1}{2}$; **8.** $\frac{1}{2}$; **9.** $1\frac{1}{4}$; **10.** $3\frac{3}{4}$; **11.** 3;

12. 5; **13.** $33\frac{1}{3}$; **14.** $\frac{5}{28}$; **15.** $13\frac{1}{3}$; **16.** $1\frac{4}{5}$; **17.** $4\frac{1}{2}$; **18.** $26\frac{1}{4}$; **19.** 3024; **20.** 11,766;

21. $6\frac{3}{4}$; **22.** $225\frac{5}{24}$; **23.** (a) 14 ounces, (b) 11 ounces; **24.** (a) 24 inches, (b) 27

inches; **25.** 4000 grains; **26.** (a) 45 min., (b) 40 min; **27.** 85,680 yards; **28.** 58

pounds 7 ounces; **29.** $\frac{3}{4}$ pound; **30.** 890 dents; **31.** \$3.36; **32.** 2224 ends; **33.** $895\frac{1}{5}$

RPM; **34.** \$96.00; **35.** $8\frac{5}{14}$ pounds; **36.** 471 pounds; **37.** 216 pounds copper,

36 pounds tin, 9 pounds zinc.

Chapter XI   Division of Fractions and Reduction of Complex Fractions

1. $\frac{3}{8}$; **2.** $\frac{1}{4}$; **3.** $\frac{1}{8}$; **4.** $\frac{1}{8}$; **5.** $\frac{3}{8}$; **6.** $\frac{3}{8}$; **7.** $\frac{3}{4}$; **8.** $\frac{5}{8}$; **9.** $\frac{5}{8}$; **10.** $\frac{3}{4}$; **11.** 1; **12.** $\frac{1}{4}$; **13.** 1;

14. $1\frac{2}{3}$; **15.** $\frac{3}{4}$; **16.** $2\frac{1}{4}$; **17.** $\frac{3}{4}$; **18.** $\frac{7}{8}$; **19.** $\frac{3}{8}$; **20.** $\frac{5}{8}$; **21.** $\frac{1}{4}$; **22.** $\frac{3}{8}$; **23.** $\frac{5}{16}$; **24.** $\frac{5}{24}$;

25. $\frac{7}{80}$; **26.** $\frac{9}{16}$; **27.** $\frac{23}{27}$; **28.** $\frac{97}{240}$; **29.** $2\frac{117}{2200}$; **30.** $1\frac{1}{4}$; **31.** $2\frac{3}{8}$; **32.** $1\frac{1}{4}$; **33.** $2\frac{1}{8}$;

34. $5\frac{1}{7}$; **35.** $6\frac{7}{24}$; **36.** $4\frac{1}{50}$; **37.** $1\frac{1}{100}$; **38.** 2; **39.** 4; **40.** 16; **41.** 24; **42.** $2\frac{2}{3}$; **43.** $2\frac{6}{7}$;

44. $2\frac{14}{17}$; **45.** 8; **46.** 90; **47.** 14; **48.** 2; **49.** 2; **50.** 6; **51.** 3; **52.** 10; **53.** $6\frac{1}{2}$; **54.** $\frac{3}{14}$;

55. $\frac{91}{216}$; **56.** $9\frac{1}{27}$; **57.** $\frac{1}{2}$; **58.** $15\frac{7}{8}$ pounds; **59.** $\frac{3}{8}$ pounds; **60.** (a) $2\frac{9}{16}$ inches;

(b) 80 ends; **61.** $3\frac{11}{16}$ yards; **62.** $52\frac{1}{4}$ grains; **63.** 304 yards; **64.** 32 hours; **65.** $\frac{5}{16}$

pounds; **66.** $70\frac{6}{31}$ yards; **67.** $72\frac{8}{59}$ yards; **68.** $22\frac{2}{5}$ dents; **69.** $22\frac{1}{2}$ tpi.

Chapter XII   The Meaning of Decimals; Addition and Subtraction of Decimals

1. $\frac{9}{10}$; **2.** $\frac{4}{5}$; **3.** $\frac{7}{10}$; **4.** $\frac{3}{5}$; **5.** $\frac{1}{2}$; **6.** $\frac{2}{5}$; **7.** $\frac{3}{10}$; **8.** $\frac{1}{5}$; **9.** $\frac{1}{10}$; **10.** $\frac{99}{100}$; **11.** $\frac{49}{50}$;

12. $\frac{97}{100}$; 13. $\frac{91}{100}$; 14. $\frac{77}{100}$; 15. $\frac{3}{4}$; 16. $\frac{1}{2}$; 17. $\frac{9}{20}$; 18. $\frac{1}{4}$; 19. $\frac{11}{100}$; 20. $\frac{1}{10}$; 21. $\frac{9}{100}$;

22. $\frac{7}{100}$; 23. $\frac{3}{50}$; 24. $\frac{1}{20}$.

25. $\frac{1}{25}$; 26. $\frac{3}{100}$; 27. $\frac{1}{50}$; 28. $\frac{1}{100}$; 29. $\frac{999}{1000}$; 30. $\frac{499}{500}$; 31. $\frac{99}{100}$; 32. $\frac{977}{1000}$;

33. $\frac{4}{5}$; 34. $\frac{3}{4}$; 35. $\frac{1}{2}$; 36. $\frac{499}{1000}$; 37. $\frac{39}{100}$; 38. $\frac{1}{4}$; 39. $\frac{101}{1000}$; 40. $\frac{1}{10}$; 41. $\frac{99}{1000}$;

42. $\frac{81}{1000}$; 43. $\frac{3}{40}$; 44. $\frac{1}{20}$; 45. $\frac{1}{40}$; 46. $\frac{1}{100}$; 47. $\frac{9}{1000}$; 48. $\frac{1}{200}$.

49. $\frac{1}{1000}$; 50. $\frac{9}{10,000}$; 51. 10.1; 52. 12.2; 53. 25.29; 54. 1.84; 55. .5;

56. 7.05; 57. 19.08; 58. 2000.0202; 59. .5; 60. 7.50; 61. 8.402; 62. 80.4; 63. 99.7;
64. $5.01; 65. $6.66; 66. $1.59; 67. $2.69; 68. $22.89; 69. $28.07; 70. $557.11;
71. $1906.06; 72. $10.105; 73. $19.199; 74. $10 or $10.00; 75. $90 or $90.00;

76. $10,596.00; 77. $10\frac{1}{2}$ cents; 78. $10\frac{1}{2}$ cents; 79. 14 dollars 56 cents; 80. 5146

dollars and $56\frac{7}{10}$ cents; 81. 16.22; 82. 102.009; 83. 162.169; 84. $156.47;

85. .1760 pound; 86. 4.121; 87. $.95; 88. .1091; 89. .0618 pound; 90. $17.27.

Chapter XIII   Multiplication of Decimals

1. 6; 2. 15.54; 3. 15.0953; 4. 174.328; 5. 2690.35695; 6. 3.927; 7. 27;
8. 81; 9. 1; 10. 1; 11. .0001; 12. .008; 13. .01; 14. .0001; 15. 10,000; 16. 10,000;
17. 5200; 18. 314.16; 19. 437,500; 20. 20; 21. 83; 22. 70; 23. 5.2; 24. .031416;
25. 7; 26. .000840; 27. 76.92; 28. .00120; 29. 3001.5 pounds; 30. 18,009
pounds; 31. 11,106 pounds; 32. 1478.4 pounds; 33. 1320 pounds; 34. 57.5
pounds; 35. 62.5 yards; 36. 891 dents; 37. 2148 ends; 38. 1050.625 yards;
39. 3007.5 knots; 40. 121 teeth; 41. $6700.00; 42. $18,753.00; 43. $2357.96;
44. $66.75; 45. $3.00; 46. $1248.00; 47. $532.50; 48. $400.32; 49. $1,262.50;
50. $1856.25; 51. $11.00; 52. $153.81.

Chapter XIV   Division of Decimals and Reduction of Fractions
to Decimals.

1. 3.33; 2. 2.50; 3. 1.33; 4. .50; 5. .125; 6. .125; 7. .25; 8. .50; 9. .625;
10. .75; 11. .875; 12. 1.125; 13. 1.25; 16. 28.17; 17. 1.27; 18. 1120; 19. 20.25
pounds; 20. 4.5 yards; 21. 15 belts; 22. 14 minutes; 23. 640 picks; 24. 35 inches;
25. 22.8 dents; 26. 1407.6 yards; 27. 25.83 tpi; 28. 19.2 yards; 29. 1.06 cuts;
30. 39.33 cuts; 31. 21 weeks.

Chapter XV   Equations, Analysis, Formulas and Polynomials

2. 853.3; **3.** 4; **4.** 7; **5.** 16; **6.** 23.1s; **7.** 8477; **8a.** 20.0; **8b.** 30.05s; **9.** inches $=$ 36 $\times$ yard; **10.** 1 skein $= 120 \times$ 1 yard; **11.** pounds $= \dfrac{\text{ounces}}{16}$; **12.** yards $= 840 \times$ hanks; **13.** grains $= 7000 \times$ pounds; **14.** hours $= \dfrac{\text{minutes}}{60}$; **15.** cotton yarn numbers $= \dfrac{1000}{\text{weight in grains of 120 yards}}$; **16.** $2 \times (3 - 1) = 4$; **17.** $2 \times (3 - 1) = 4$.

18. $2 \times (3 + 1) = 8$; **19.** $5 = 5 \times (5 - 4)$; **20.** $4 = 4 \times (5 - 3 - 1)$; **21.** $3 \times (3 + 4 - 6) = 3$; **22.** $6 = 2 \times (15 - 13 + 1)$; **23.** $108 = 4 \times (125 - 75 - 23)$; **24.** $20 \times (3 - 2 - 1) = 0$; **25.** $a \times (3 - 1) = 4$; **26.** $2 \times b \times (3 - 1) = 4$; **27.** $2 \times (c + 1) = 8$; **28.** $5 = (25 - 20) \times d$; **29.** $6 = (15 - 13 + 1) \times yz$; **30.** $108 \times a = 4 \times bc \times (125 - 75 - 23)$; **31.** $20 \times c \times d \times (3 - 2 - 1) = 0$.

32. $20 \times y \times (3 \times c \times d - 2 \times c - d) = 0$; **33.** $\dfrac{1}{2} \times (3 - 1) = 1$; **34.** $(6 - 2) \times \dfrac{1}{4} = 1$; **35.** $\dfrac{2}{4} \times (3 - 1) = 1$; **36.** $(c + 1) \times \dfrac{2}{3} = 1$; **37.** $5 = \dfrac{5d}{m} \times (5 - 4)$; **38.** $6 = \dfrac{y3}{f} \times (15 - 13 + 1)$; **39.** $d = \dfrac{4 \times ef}{e \times f} \times (125 - 75 - 23)$; **40.** $\dfrac{20 \times y}{c} \times \left(\dfrac{3 \times a \times d}{b \times r} - \dfrac{2 \times a}{b} - \dfrac{d}{r} \right) = 0$; **41.** $\dfrac{1}{2} \times (3 - 1) = 1$; **42.** $1 = \dfrac{1}{(3 + 4)} \times (3 + 4)$; **43.** $1 = \dfrac{5 \times y}{(p + c)} \times (s + 2 \times a)$; **44.** $6 + 8 = 14$; **45.** $12 - 9 = 3$; **46.** $30 + 35 = 70 - 7 + 2$; **47.** $\dfrac{2}{2} + \dfrac{6}{2} = \dfrac{6}{3} - \dfrac{12}{3} + \dfrac{18}{3}$; **48.** $\dfrac{144 + 180}{70 - 42} = \dfrac{81}{7}$.

49. $a \times b + a \times c = 14$; **50.** $a \times b - a \times c = 3$; **51.** $30 + 5 \times b = 10 \times b - b + 2$; **52.** $\dfrac{a}{a} + \dfrac{a \times b}{a} = \dfrac{a \times b}{b} - \dfrac{b \times c}{b} + \dfrac{b + d}{b}$; **53.** $\dfrac{a \times b \times c \times e + a \times b \times d \times e}{f \times h - fg} = Z$; **54.** $3 \times 3 + 2 \times 3 \times 4 + 4 \times 4 = 49$; **55.** $5 \times 5 - 2 \times 3 \times 5 + 3 \times 3 = 4$; **56.** $a \times a + 2 \times a \times b + b \times b = 49$; **57.** $c \times c + 2 \times c \times d + d \times d = 36$; **58.** $a \times a - 2 \times a \times b + b \times b = 4$; **59.** $r \times r - 2 \times r \times s + s \times s = 25$; **60.** $\dfrac{10 \times 4}{7} + \dfrac{10 \times 5}{7} - \dfrac{10 \times 6}{7} = 4\dfrac{2}{7}$; **61.** $\dfrac{63}{13} - \dfrac{45}{13} + \dfrac{27}{13} - \dfrac{18}{13} = 2.08$; **62.** $\dfrac{a \times b}{e + f} + \dfrac{a \times c}{e + f} - \dfrac{a \times d}{e + f} = g$; **63.** $s = \dfrac{b \times b}{r} + \dfrac{2 \times b \times p}{r} + \dfrac{p \times p}{r}$; **64.** $X = \dfrac{y + y}{y + z} - \dfrac{2 \times y \times z}{y + z} + \dfrac{z \times z}{y + z}$.

65a. $qr = \dfrac{P + 50 - (sw - 5)}{mc} - \dfrac{P - sw}{mc} = \dfrac{55}{mc}$; **65b.** $+.016$; **66a.** CRPM =

$$\dfrac{\text{RPM f} \times \text{dia. f}}{2} - \dfrac{\text{RPM f} \times \text{dia. f}}{\dfrac{3}{4}} = \text{RPM f} \times \text{dia. f} \times \left(\dfrac{1}{2} - \dfrac{1}{\dfrac{3}{4}}\right) = \text{RPM f} \times$$

dia. $f \times \left(-\dfrac{5}{6}\right) = -\dfrac{5 \times \text{RPM f} \times \text{dia. f}}{6}$; **66b.** -140; **66c.** decreases; **67.** 10; **68.** 7;

69. 10; **70.** $\dfrac{c - b}{4}$; **71.** 15; **72.** $\dfrac{b}{3}$.

Chapter XVI   Percentages

1. $41.21; **2.** 44,011 yards; **3.** 29.38 tpi; **4.** 437.5 pounds; **5.** 89.7%;
6. 75%; **7.** .5%; **8.** .8%; **9a.** .5%; **9b.** .56%; **10.** 96%; **11.** 5%; **12.** 15%; **13.** 12.5%;
14. 12.5%; **15.** 4.8%; **16.** 6.6%; **17.** 126,303 pounds; **18.** 5460 pounds; **19.** 49.6
yards; **20.** 152.8 pounds; **21.** 12.5; **22.** 64.2 yards. **23.** 48.9 inches; **24.** 7.7%;
25. 5%; **26.** seconds, 18,948.6 yards; shorts, 7,105.7 yards; firsts, 447,659.7
yards; **27.** water, 994.5 pounds; tallow, 867 pounds; starch, 229.5 pounds;
glycerine, 433.5 pounds; ash, 25.5 pounds; **28.** 60%; **29.** 918 bales; **30.** sheeting, 294 looms; drills, 336 looms; sateens, 210 looms; **31.** 12 fixers; **32.** 59.78
yards; **33.** $26.42; **34.** 666.67 yards.

Chapter XVII   Measures of Weight, Length, Time and Volume

1. 437.5 grains; **2.** 7 skeins; **3.** 600 minutes; **4.** 63 yards, $25\dfrac{13}{16}$ inches;

5. 58 yards, $30\dfrac{5}{8}$ inches; **6.** 18 hours, 21.6 minutes; **7.** 25 pounds, 11.2 ounces;

8. 7560 inches; **9.** 19,250 grains; **10.** 9240 yards; **11.** 2.55 hours; **12.** $10\dfrac{2}{3}$ yards;

13. $9\dfrac{7}{16}$ pounds; **14.** 2 pounds, 12 ounces; **15.** 7 yards, 24 inches; **16.** 5 hours,
5 minutes; **17.** 7.5 pounds; **18.** 9.25 pounds; **19.** 9.33 hanks; **20.** 15.5 hanks;
21. 570 pounds; **22.** 34 pounds 7 ounces; **23.** 583 feet, 7 inches; **24.** 454 pounds,
13 ounces; **25.** 3 hours, 25 minutes; **26.** 110 yards, 32 inches; **27.** 242 feet;
28. $1721\dfrac{1}{4}$ pounds; **29.** 15 yards of 16 ounce; 19 yards, 12 inches of 12 ounce;

30. 3 feet, $8\dfrac{1}{4}$ inches.

31. 3.1416 inches; **32.** 6.2832 inches; **33.** 785.4 inches; **34.** 5.6942 yards;
35. $7\dfrac{1}{2}$ inches; **36.** 5 feet; **37a.** 6 feet; **37b.** $2\dfrac{1}{2}$ inches; **38.** $5\dfrac{1}{4}$ inches; **39.** 9;
40. 16; **41.** 81; **43.** 100; **44.** 144; **45.** 324 square inches; **46.** 144; **47.** 1296;

48. 1746 square inches; **49.** 181.5 square inches; **50.** 72; **51.** 9 square feet; **52.** $1957\frac{1}{2}$ square feet; **53.** $11\frac{2}{3}$ square feet; **54.** 1056 square inches; **55.** $28\frac{1}{2}$ square feet; **56.** $1135\frac{1}{4}$ square inches; **57.** $278\frac{2}{3}$ square feet; **58.** 54.03 square feet; **60.** 153.94 square inches; **61a.** 7.07 square feet; **61b.** 10,178.8 pounds.
    62. 12.5664 square feet; **63.** 1296 cubic inches; **64.** 1728 cubic inches; **65.** 2 gallons; **66.** 7.48 gallons; **67.** 90 gallons; **68.** 432 gallons; **69.** 254 cubic feet; **70.** 10,500 pounds; **71.** 409.06 cubic feet; **72.** 54.55 inches; **73.** 54.978 square feet; **74.** 62.832 square feet; **75.** 51.836 square feet; **76.** 158.63 gallons; **77.** 282 pounds; **78.** 1451.43 gallons.

Chapter XVIII   Square Root

1. 5; **2.** 6; **3.** 7; **4.** 8; **5.** 9; **6.** 10; **7.** 11; **8.** 12; **9.** 9.75; **10.** 19; **11.** 23.75; **12.** 16.25; **13.** 2.4; **14.** 1.2; **15.** $1\frac{1}{3}$; **16.** $1\frac{1}{4}$; **17.** 1; **18.** $\frac{3}{4}$; **19.** $\frac{2}{3}$; **20.** $\frac{3}{5}$; **21.** $\frac{1}{2}$; **22.** $\frac{1}{4}$; **23.** .1; **24.** .3; **25.** .4; **26.** .9; **27.** 1; **28.** less; **29.** greater; **31.** 15; **32.** 16; **33.** 21; **34.** 35; **35.** 105; **36.** .93; **37.** 2.94; **38.** .89; **39.** 35.23; **40.** 10.53; **41.** 17.97; **42.** 4.0308; **43.** 4.3008; **44.** 4.5550; **45.** 5.6418; **46.** 6.5520; **47.** .44721; **48.** .42426; **49.** 12.49; **50.** 1.19583.

Chapter XIX   Ratio and Proportion

12. 17,440 pounds; **13.** 2334.72 hanks; **14.** 4712.4 pounds; **15.** 5880; **16.** 52 yards; **17.** 12,845.5 pounds; **18.** 92.5%; **19.** \$100.41; **20.** 120 hours; **21.** 18,544 yards; **22.** 48 hours; **23.** \$108.00; **24.** 40.8 yards; **25.** 253 yards; **26.** 36.36 hours; **27.** 3150 ends; **28.** 1.17 yards per pound; **29.** \$105.26; **30.** 4704 spindles; **31.** 47.83 pounds.

Chapter XX   Mechanical Calculations — Conventional Power Trains

1a. $\pi \times 3' \times 1 = 9.425'$; **1b.** $\pi \times 3' \times 5 = 47.12'$; **2a.** $\pi \times 20'' \times 10 = 628.3''$; **2b.** $\pi \times 20'' \times 60 = 3770''$; **4a.** $30'' \times \pi \times 50$; **4b.** $30'' \times \pi \times 50$; **4c.** $\dfrac{30'' \times \pi \times 50}{6'' \times \pi} = \dfrac{30 \times 50}{6}$; **4d.** $\dfrac{30 \times 50}{6} \div 50 = \dfrac{30}{6}$; **5a.** $25'' \times \pi \times 36$; **5b.** $25'' \times \pi \times 36$; **5c.** $\dfrac{25'' \times \pi \times 36}{8'' \times \pi} = \dfrac{25 \times 36}{8}$; **5d.** $\dfrac{25 \times 36}{8} \div 36 = \dfrac{25}{8}$; **6a.** $28'' \times \pi \times 40$; **6b.** dia. B $\times \pi$; **6c.** $\dfrac{28'' \times \pi \times 40}{\text{dia. B} \times \pi} = 112$; **6d.** $\dfrac{28'' \times 40}{112}$; **6e.** $28'' \div \dfrac{28'' \times 40}{112} = \dfrac{112}{40}$; **6f.** $\dfrac{28'' \times 40}{112} \div 28 = \dfrac{40}{112}$; **7a.** inversely; **7b.** directly; **7c.** is not.

9. 600; **10.** 16″; **11a.** 3″, 7540, 628.3, 133; **11b.** 5″, 12566, 1047.2, 222; **11c.** 8″, 20106, 1675.5, 356; **12a.** 4″, 15708, 1309.0, 208; **12b.** 7″, 27489, 2290.8, 365; **12c.** 10″, 39270, 3272.5, 521; **12d.** 13″, 51051, 4254.3, 677; **14a.** +402; **14b.** +4.7; **15a.** 4″; **15b.** $(219 - 208) = 11$, $(786 - 781) = 5$; **15c.** $(11 \div 208) - (5 \div 781) = .046 = 4.6\%$; **16a.** opposite to; **16b.** backward; **16c.** negative minus −; **17a.** $-\dfrac{18 \times 225}{6.5} = -623$; **17b.** $-\dfrac{4'' \times (-623)}{18.25} = 137$; **18a.** 13195; **18b.** 1047; **18c.** −10053 or 10053 LH; **18d.** −1466 or 1466 LH.

21a. 6.2832″; **21b.** .31416″; **21c.** .31416″; **21d.** 3.1416; **21e.** 1″; **22.** .2618″; **24a.** 5; **24b.** 1; **24c.** 5; **24d.** 1; **25.** 133.4 RH; **27.** 1857.7 RH; **29.** .45″; **30.** 25.1; **31b.** left; **31c.** right +; **33a.** −; **33b.** +; **33c.** +; **33d.** −; **33e.** −; **33f.** $[-8 - 0] \times 1 \times .1667'' = -1.33''$; **33g.** $[-8 - 0] \times (-1) \times .1667'' = 1.33''$; **33h.** approach; **34a.** $[27.6 - 0] \times .5'' = 13.8''$; **34b.** down; **34c.** $[-1472 - (-1406)] \times .5'' = [-1472 + 1406] \times .5'' = -66 \times .5'' = -33''$ up; **34d.** $[-1339 - (-1396)] \times .5'' = [-1339 + 1396] \times .5'' = 57 \times .5'' = 28.5$ down; **36.** 18; **37.** 60; **40a, b, c,** none; **40d.** no carrier teeth in equations; **41a.** other; **41b.** other; **41c.** one; **41d.** driver; **41e.** driver; **41f.** driven; **41g.** directly; **41h.** driver; **41i.** driver; **41j.** inversely; **41k.** driven; **43a.** $\dfrac{\text{rev. H}}{\text{rev. L}} = \dfrac{\text{E} \times \text{dia. J} \times \text{dia. L}}{\text{G} \times \text{dia. I} \times \text{dia K}};$

43b. $\text{RPM H} = \dfrac{\text{RPM L} \times \text{E} \times \text{dia. J} \times \text{dia. L}}{\text{G} \times \text{dia. I} \times \text{dia. K}};$

43c. $\text{IPM H} = \dfrac{\text{RPM L} \times \text{E} \times \text{dia. J} \times \text{dia. L} \times \pi \times \text{dia. H}}{\text{G} \times \text{dia. I} \times \text{dia. K}}.$

44a. 2.25; **44b.** 1.80; **45a.** 1.83; **45b.** 2.17; **46a.** 942.5; **46b.** 1028.2; **47a.** 761.2; **47b.** 978.7; **48a.** 418.9; **48b.** 457.0; **50d.** 1.25; **50e.** 1.75; **50f.** 24; **50g.** 36; **51a.** product; **51b.** quotient; **52a.** 5026.6; **52b.** 335.1; **52c.** 251.3; **52d.** 14″; **52e.** 16″; **54.** when they most nearly (a) are perpendicular to each other (b) coincide; **55a.** stem center; **55b.** $7\dfrac{1''}{2}$; **55c.** $\dfrac{3''}{8}$; **55d.** 1st or 2nd; **55e.** 50 lbs; **56a.** 40″. **56b.** bearing on floor; **56c.** 2 tons; **56d.** $\dfrac{5''}{8}$; **57a.** 1st and 2nd; **57b.** .8″; **58a.** 3rd; **58b.** 6.6″.

60a. where p. dia. pg meets p. cir. rg; **60b.** where p. dia. pg meets p. cir. sg; **60c.** p. dia. pg; **60d.** pc; **60e.** p. rad. pg; **60f.** 2nd; **61a, b, c.** +; **d, e, f.** −; **63a.** where p. dia. pg meets p. cir. sg; **63b.** p. dia. pg; **63c.** p. rad. pg; **63d.** 2nd; **64a.** −; **64b.** +; **64c.** +; **64d.** +; **64e.** −; **64f.** −; **66a.** same; **66b.** same; **68a.** $\dfrac{1}{3}$; **68b.** $\dfrac{2}{1}$.

70a. 11; **70b.** $\dfrac{4}{1}$; **71a.** 13; **71b.** .841; **71c.** .773; **71d.** −18.75 in same direction; **72a.** 13; **72b.** .875; **72c.** .785; **72d.** −39.8; **73a.** 13; **73b.** 285; **73c.** 258; **73d.** 242.25; **74a.** 1:2; **74b.** 40; **76a.** p. rad. rg − p. rad. sg; **76b.** p. rad. spg; **76c.** 3rd; **76d.** +; **76e.** −; **77a.** p. rad. rg − p. rad. sg; **77b.** p. rad. rpg; **77c.** 1st; **77d.** −; **77e.** +; **78a.** no; **78b.** same; **78c.** opposite; **80a.** 1 ahead; **80b.** 99 ahead; **80c.** 99 backward; **81a.** $-\dfrac{14}{1}$; **81b.** 132.7 opposite; **81c.** $\dfrac{30}{28}$.

Part Two

ANSWERS

Chapter I   Lap, Sliver, Roving, and Single Yarn Sizing Systems

1a. 1.0; **1b.** 1.0; **2a.** 2.0; **2b.** 2.0; **3a.** 2.5; **3b.** .50; **4a.** 3.25; **4b.** .25; **5a.** .50; **5b.** .50; **6a.** .143; **6b.** .05; **7a.** 1.0; **7b.** .10; **8a.** .143; **8b.** .01; **9a.** 1.0; **9b.** .071; **10a.** .125; **10b.** .020; **11a.** .30; **11b.** .005; **12a.** .50; **12b.** .25; **13a.** .10; **13b.** 10.0; **14a.** 2.0; **14b.** 200; **15.** 13s; **16.** 1.3s.

17. 10s; **18.** 14.3s; **19.** .525 run roving; **20.** 6.25s run; **21.** 5.33s cut; **22.** 10s met; **24.** smaller; **26.** 250 den; **27.** 300 grx. **28.** 600 tex roving; **29.** 6.0s tex; **30.** 150 tex; **31.** 3.0s dram roving; **33.** larger; **36.** 1.2; **37.** 12; **38.** 21; **39.** 3.8; **40.** 18.1; **41.** 31; **43.** 167; **44.** 180; **45.** 44; **46.** 405; **47.** 4.1; **49.** 53.1; **50.** 17.7; **51.** 5.9; **52.** 11.8; **53.** 6.25; **54.** 394; **59.** 17.7; **60.** 5.7; **61.** 133; **62.** 55.6; **63.** 107; **64.** 68.9; **66.** .20 hr; **67.** 1.20 hr; **68.** .91 hr; **69.** .019 hr; **70.** .12 hr.

71. 2.50 hr; **72.** 5.0; **73.** 10.0; **74.** 26.3; **75.** 70; **77a.** .20; **77b.** .25; **77c.** .40; **77d.** .50; **77e.** .80; **77f.** 1.00; **78a.** 1.25; **78b.** 1.50; **78c.** 1.75; **78d.** 2.00; **78e.** 2.50; **78f.** 4.00; **79a.** 4.00; **79b.** 5.00; **79c.** 8.00; **79d.** 10.00; **79e.** 12.50; **79f.** 20.00; **80a.** 10.00; **80b.** 12.50; **80c.** 16.00; **80d.** 20.00; **80e.** 40.00; **80f.** 100.00; **81.** .84; **82.** 42.90; **83.** 8.40; **84.** 133; **85.** 42.10; **86.** 53.20; **87.** 49.20; **88.** 740; **91.** 43.0s; **92.** 18.1s; **93.** 23.0s; **94.** 22.4s; **95.** 23.3s; **96.** 9.9s; **98.** 7660; **99.** 6510.

100. 12002; **101.** 204; **102.** 56228; **103.** 62681; **104.** 42950; **105.** 23990; **106.** 10234; **108.** 297; **109.** 519; **110.** 362; **111.** 427; **112.** .257; **114.** 316; **115.** 454; **116.** 8101; **117.** 6193; **119a.** 16; **119b.** 14.5 **119c.** 15.8; **120a.** 86; **120b.** 71 lbs. 8 oz; **122a.** 64.5; **122b.** 546.9; **123a.** 4813; **123b.** 193; **123c.** 6.4; **124a.** 59.8; **124b.** 27.1; **124c.** 272.5.

Chapter II   Ply Yarn Calculations

2. 5; **3.** 10; **4.** 17.5; **5.** 7; **6.** 20; **7.** 16; **8.** 15; **9.** 14; **10.** 20; **11.** 4.5; **12.** 13.9; **13.** 12.9; **14a.** lower; **14b.** more; **14c.** more; **14d.** lower; **15.** 1.67; **16.** 1.83; **17.** 1.53; **18.** 1.00; **19.** 5.46; **20.** 9.80; **21.** 10.00; **22.** 8.00; **24.** 20.0; **25.** 120.0; **26.** 30.0; **27.** 100.0; **28.** 42.9; **29.** 19.2; **30.** 21.2; **31.** 15.9.

Chapter III   Actual Draft Calculations

2. 125; **3.** 4; **4.** 7.5; **5.** 87.5; **6.** 52.5; **7.** 108; **8a.** <; **8b.** <; **8c.** <; **10.** =;
11. 10.37; **12.** 1.018; **13.** 72.40; **14.** 5.117; **16.** 109.4; **17.** 145.8; **18.** 123.8;
20. 8.774; **21.** 12.05; **22.** 10.00; **24.** 1.035; **25.** 1.040; **26.** 1.039; **28.** 36.0;
29. 96.0.
      30. 85.00; **33.** 5.040; **34.** 9.375; **35.** 11.52; **36.** 8.700; **37.** 10.58; **38.** 5.818;
40. 20.63; **41.** 72.73; **42.** 71.90; **43.** 33.75; **44.** 42.00; **45.** 17.78; **46.** 18.20;
47. 2.145; **48.** 2.214; **49.** 1.770; **50.** 34.99; **51.** 15.1 oz. lap; **52.** 17.0 oz. lap;
53. 50.0 gr. sl; **54.** 68.4 gr. sl; **55.** 52.8 gr. sl; **56.** 63.8 gr. sl; **57.** 48.0 gr. sl;
58. 150 gr. top; **59.** 47.6 gr. sl; **60.** 1846 gr. lap; **61.** 1704 gr. lap; **62.** 897.3 gr.
lap; **63.** 39.8 gr. sl; **64.** 74.1 gr. sl.
      65. 83.3 gr. sl; **66.** 137.4 gr. top; **67.** 1.15 hr; **68.** 1.70 wsd; **69.** 1.71
hr; **70.** 3.08 hr; **71.** .60 hr; **72.** .957 hr; **73.** 1.60 hr; **74.** 10.60s; **75.** 2.50 wsd;
76. 36.00's wsd; **77.** 6.38 run roving; **78.** 1.43 cut roving; **79.** 7.35s cut;
80. 2.00s ctn; **81.** 71.0 gr. sl.

Chapter IV   Lay and Twist Calculations

1a. inversely, **1b.** divided, **1c.** into, **1d.** divided, **1e.** into, **1f.** reciprocal;
5a. .006897; **5b.** 145; **6a.** .003764; **6b.** 265; **7a.** .006588; **7b.** 152; **8a.** .006502;
8b. 154; **9a.** .008584; **9b.** 116; **10a.** .003411; **10b.** 293; **13a.** .01004; **13b.** 99.6;
14a. .01476; **14b.** 67.7; **15a.** .009980; **15b.** 100.
      17a. 804; **17b.** .02081; **17c.** 48.0; **18a.** 296; **18b.** .01170; **18c.** 85.5;
19a. 174; **19b.** .1275; **19c.** 7.84; **20a.** 242; **20b.** .009587; **20c.** 104; **21a.** 260;
21b. .01719; **21c.** 58.1; **22a.** 227; **22b.** .03383; **22c.** 29.6; **23a.** inversely;
23b. directly; **23c.** inversely; **23d.** multiplied; **23e.** divided; **26.** .55; **27.** .88;
28. 1.79; **29.** 3.00; **30.** 6.72; **31.** 4.75; **32.** 12.1; **33.** 17.0; **34.** 17.8; **35.** 26.0;
36. 35.2; **37.** 35.7; **38.** 14.8; **39.** 14.5; **40.** 22.4; **42a.** 5.37s tex, 31.1 tm; **42b.** 13.4;
43a. 59.9s wsd, 4.50 tm; **43b.** 34.8; **44a.** 19.4s tex, 43.3 tm; **44b.** 9.8.

Chapter V   Cloth Calculations

1. $5\frac{1}{3}$; **2.** 3.5; **3.** $933\frac{1}{3}$; **4.** 12; **5.** 530.3; **6.** 17.6; **7.** 24,500; **9.** 2.53;

10. 1.576; **11.** 4.32; **12.** 3.60; **13.** 1.66; **14.** 4.05; **15.** 3980; **16.** 2250; **17.** 1680;
18. 2560; **19.** 2208; **20.** 714; **21.** 912; **22.** 872; **23.** 1048; **24.** $6\frac{1}{2}$; **25.** $7\frac{2}{3}$; **26.** 50″;
27. 43.48; **28.** 20.90; **29.** 841; **30.** 40.26; **31.** 1366; **32.** 18.70; **33.** 32″; **34.** 77.13;
35. 46.32; **36.** 37.50.
      37. 854; **38.** 492; **39.** 524; **40.** 6.29; **41.** 5.47; **42a.** 3.048; **42b.** 3.048;
42c. 2.344; **43.** 7.7%; **44.** 8735.24; **45.** 5654.45; **46.** 8696.87; **47.** 2015.62;
48. 139 yds; **49.** 1.289; **50.** 1892.57; **51.** 13.511; **52.** 11.1%; **53.** 7.7%; **54.** 1968;
55. 21.34; **56.** 45.55; **57.** 16s; **58.** 15.6s; **59.** 6.3%; **60.** 7.7%; **61.** 3640; **62.** 176;
63. 38.77; **64.** 49.01 inches; **65.** 30s; **66.** 22s; **67.** 6.1%; **68.** 9.1%; **69.** 3624;
70. 30s; **71.** 161 denier; **72.** 59.2; **73.** 12.7%; **74.** 14.3%; **75.** 25.71; **76.** 9s;
77. 9s; **78.** 165.5; **79.** 165.5; **80.** 335.2.

Chapter VI   Statistical Quality Control Calculations

1. xn. 4 n8, Σ × 578.5 lbs., x̄ 72.3 lbs., median 72 lbs., mode 72 lbs;
5. n10, Σ × 16.66 yds., x̄ 1.67 yds., median 1.67 yds., mode 1.67 yds; 6. n10,
Σ × 162.9%, x̄ 16.3%, median 16.0%, mode 12.0%; 8(1a). 8 grs, 8(1b). 13.3%,
8(2a). 2 lbs, 8(2b). 2.8%, 8(3a). .05 yds, 8(3b). 3.0%, 8(4a). 12.6%, 8(4b). 77.3%;
9a. =, 9b. =. 10. 0; 11a. left; 11b. right; 12c. 100; 12d. 65.9 lbs, 12e. 21.2,
12f. +1; 13. 0; 14. .76 lbs; 15. .0135 yds; 16. 6.84 lbs; 17. 1.95 grs; 18a. 2.58
grs./yd; 18b. .17 grs./yd; 19a. .73 lbs; 19b. .03 lbs; 20a. .015 yds./lbs; 20b. .0015
yds./lb; 21a. 1.78 grs./yd; 21b. .17 grs./yd; 22a. σ 2.02 lb./in., σ e5 1.72 lbs./in;
22b. σ 3.33 lbs./in., σ e5 2.87 lbs./in; 24a. 0; 24b. 0; 25a. 4.58 grs; 25b. 4.30 grs;
26a. 1.05 lbs, 26b. 1.01 lbs; 27a. .808 yds; 27b. .898 yds; 28. 10.4 lbs;
29a. 3.90 grs; 29b. 3.56 grs; 30a. 1.27 lbs; 30b. 1.11 lbs; 31a. 7.57 lbs; 31b. 6.51
lbs; 32a. 45; 32b. 3; 35a. .86; 35b. 1.7 grs./yd; 36a. .29; 36b. .86 lb; 37a. .28;
37b. .56 lb; 38a. .0045; 38b. .0135 yds./lb; 39a. .684; 39b. 2.05 lbs; 40a. .588;
40b. 1.76 grs./yd; 41a. .46; 41b. 1.38 lbs./in; 42a. .77; 42b. 2.31 lbs./in; 44a.
71.4 lbs; 44b. 73.2 lbs; 45a. 1.657 yds./lb; 45b. 1.684 yds./lb; 46a. 153.9 lbs./in;
46b. 156.7 lbs./in; 47a. 2.45; 47b. .417 grs; 47c. 49.8 grs. 20.1s; 47d. 52.2 grs,
19.2s; 48a. 63.9 lbs; 48b. 67.9 lbs; 49a. 41.8 lbs./in; 49b. 46.4 lbs./in; 50a. 11.0;
50b. 15.1 ends down per 1000 sp. hrs; 53. b; 53c. no.

55. 130 yds. of sliver; 56. 1.04 yds. of lap. 57. 96 yds. of sliver; 58. 5.8 yds.
of roving; 59a. 120; 59b. 240 yds. of yarn; 60a. 1 yd; 60b. 2.36; 60c. over-all;
61a. Σ × 205, 198, 199, 200, 193, 197, 203, 203, 207, 192 grs., r4w 2, 1, 3, 4, 3,
3, 2, 3, 3, 2 gr.; 61b. 5, 3, 3, 4 grs.; 61c. 5, 5, 4, 5, grs.; 61d. 26 grs.; 61e. 1.26
grs.; 61f. 49.9 grs.; 61g. 2.53; 61h. 34 grs.; 61i. 1.83 grs.; 61j. 3.67; 62. 1.33;
63. .50; 64. 1.66; 65a. 2.29; 65b. .57; 65c. 1.71; 65d. 54.5; 65e. 57.5 grs./yd.;
65f. .81;

66a. cause may be in drawing; 66b. cause not in drawing. 66c. Σ × 237,
240, 212, 233, 251, 226, 224, 240 grs., r4w 4, 3, 6, 4, 5, 6, 4, 5, grs.; 66d. 7, 5,
8, 12 grs.; 66e. 8, 8, 9, 7 grs.; 66f. 37 grs.; 66g. 2.24 grs.; 66h. 58.2 grs.; 66i. 3.85;
66j. 64 grs.; 66k. 3.88 grs.; 66l. 6.67; 66m. 2.36; 66n. 8.57. 66o. Σ × 167, 166,
163, 166, 161, 163, 164, 165 grs., r3w 2, 1, 1, 2, 3, 3, 4, 2, grs.; 66p. 18 grs.;
66q. 1.33 grs.; 66r. 54.8 grs.; 66s. 2.43; 67a. 3%; 67b. no.; 67c. 9 and 18 show
greatest r.; 67d. 2.91 grs.; 67e. 54.8 grs.; 67f. 5.31; 67g. pickers.

Chapter VII   Picker Calculations

1a. to f. finisher; 2. more; 4a. increased; 4b. increased; 5a. decreased;
5b. inversely; 6a. decreases; 6b. increases; 9a. 9.27″; 9b. 9.36″; 9c. 9.54″;
11. 2.54; 12. 3.52; 15. 1.60; 16. 3.17; 17. 3.56; 18. 3.93; 19. 4.61; 24. 780.0;
25. 18.2; 26. 25.3; 27. 29.8; 28. 31.3; 29. 36.1; 30. 41.6; 32a. 40.6; 32b. 43.3.
33a. 32.6; 33b. 48.9; 35a. 35.5; 35b. 27.0; 35c. 29.5; 36a. 31.4; 36b. 29.3;
36c. 25.1; 37. dia. dp, dia. fp, or both; 38. $9\frac{1}{2}″$ fp; 39. 8″ fp; 40. $4\frac{1}{2}″$ dp; 41. 5″ dp;
42. new dia. dp ×; 43. new dia. fp = 33, as 3″ dp and 11″ fp; 44. 57.38; 45. 52.0;
46. 29.2; 47. 26.8; 49. 28.4; 50. 22.9; 51. 22.8; 52. 20.0; 54. $7\frac{1}{2}″$ ep; 55. 9″ ep;
56. $9\frac{1}{2}″$ ep; 57. 52.0; 58. 54.2; 63. .002900; 64. 3227; 65. 20010; 66. 144,800;

68. 90.24; **69.** 72171; **70.** 18044; **71.** 998; **72.** 17; **75.** 301; **76.** 72.2; **78a.** 8″; **78b.** 2564; **79a.** 8″.

79b. 8.3; **81.** $6\frac{1}{2}$″; **82a.** 8″; **82b.** 569; **84a.** on a straight line between centers; **84b.** whole; **88a.** .9783; **88b.** 1.460; **89a.** 37.33 to 74.66; **89b.** 55.70 to 111.4; **90a.** 56; **90b.** 86.64 yds; **91a.** 59; **91b.** 61.18 lbs; **92a.** 71; **92b.** 67.64 lbs; **93a.** 46; **93b.** 68.96 lbs; **96.** 59; **97.** 67; **98.** 46; **101a.** 6.59; **101b.** 9.1 min; **102a.** 3.15; **102b.** 19.0 min; **103a.** 9.19; **103b.** 6.5 min.

Chapter VIII   Card Calculations

2a. decreased; **2b.** increased; **3a.** increased; **3b.** inversely; **6A.** 1595.4; **6B.** 2373.9; **7A.** 49.9 to 160; **7B.** 59.3 to 158; **8Aa.** 1.6; **8Ab.** 14.5; **8Ba.** 1.5; **8Bb.** 9.9; **9a.** larger; **9b.** smaller; **10a.** 26 or 27; **10b.** 20; **10c.** 10 or 11; **11a.** 31 or 32; **11b.** 19 or 20; **11c.** 10 or 11; **14.** 24 or 25-tooth; **15.** 13- or 14-tooth; **16.** 19-tooth; **18a.** product; **18b.** divided by; **18c.** product; **20a.** ft 1.037, lb 185.5 to 4451, cyd 1.880, dfd .01572 to .1179, ct 1.102, cct 1.062, cdt 1.170. **20b.** 1.136; **21a.** stock shortened; **21b.** another intermediate draft < 1.

23. 116.08; **24.** 99.00; **25.** 101.5; **27a.** 15-tooth; **27b.** 61.9; **28a.** 29-tooth; **28b.** 79.5; **29a.** 35-tooth; **29b.** 78.2; **30a.** 3.9; **30b.** 3.9; **31a.** directly; **31b.** same; **33a.** 15; **33b.** 56.3; **34a.** 25; **34b.** 75.0; **35a.** 27; **35b.** 54.2; **36a.** 28; **36b.** 68.2; **37a.** 21; **37b.** 82.4; **38a.** 13; **38b.** 52.6; **39a.** 20; **39b.** 63.7; **40a.** fine control of cleaning and waste; **40b.** powers rest of card after cyl; **40c.** belt thickness; **42a.** 7″; **42b.** 430; **43a.** 7.25; **43b.** 487; **44a.** 7.5; **44b.** 706; **45a.** more; **45b.** fs; **47a.** 3.00″; **47b.** 2.16; **48a.** 5.00″; **48b.** 3.59; **49a.** 11.00″.

49b. 3.74; **50a.** 15.5″; **50b.** 4.22; **51a.** 4.00″; **51b.** 4.25; **53a.** .144; **53b.** .180; **53c.** .216; **54a.** .143; **54b.** .173; **54c.** .216; **54d.** .259; **55A.** 7.19 to 54.0; **55B.** 7.72 to 32.1; **56a.** 25; **56b.** 10.8; **57a.** 2.5″; **57b.** 17.3; **58a.** 4.25″; **58b.** 25.3; **60a.** vertical cylinder touching cir. can; **60b.** 1 layer of as many coils as the ratio rev. tube: rev. can; **63c.** 20.1; **63d.** 21.1; **64a.** 15a and b; **64b.** In fig. 4, rpg = spg = pg; **66.** 37.1; **67.** 57.2; **68.** 61.9; **69.** 67.7; **73.** 16.8; **74.** 24.5; **76a.** .02429; **76b.** .02358; **78.** 1038; **79.** 1385; **80.** 21186; **81a.** 35; **81b.** 17.6.

81c. 24.0; **82a.** 27; **82b.** 21.9; **82c.** 27.9; **83a.** 23; **83b.** 23.6; **83c.** 3267; **84a.** 5.0″; **84b.** 32.4; **84c.** 52.4; **85a.** 2.75″; **85b.** 11.8; **85c.** 18.5; **86a.** 4.50″; **86b.** 21.8; **86c.** 28.1; **87a.** 23; **87b.** 22.4; **87c.** 3424; **88a.** 29; **88b.** 33.8; **88c.** 18,145; **90.** 1023; **91.** 19197; **92.** 29.74; **93.** 30.0; **94.** 32.48; **99a.** .388640; **99b.** 154.385; **99c.** .556728; **99d.** 107.773; **100a.** .372079; **100b.** 161.256; **100c.** .600908; **100d.** 99.8489; **101a.** .466368; **101b.** 128.654; **101c.** .474918; **101d.** 126.338; **102a.** .528484; **102b.** 113.532; **102c.** .482177; **102d.** 124.436; **103a.** .625640; **103b.** 95.9018; **103c.** .446707; **103d.** 134.316; **104a.** .727611; **104b.** 82.4616; **104c.** .526306; **104d.** 114.002.

Chapter IX   Drawing Frame Calculations

1a. >; **1b.** >; **1c.** deeper; **1d.** less; **1e.** larger; **3.** 3.000; **4.** 3.984 to 10.15; **5a.** .064; **5b.** .376; **5c.** .047; **5d.** .116; **6a.** indirectly; **6b.** directly; **6c.** smaller; **7a.** dg 30, Fdg 85; **7b.** 8.50; **8a.** dg 47, Fdg 86; **8b.** 5.49; **9a.** dg 33, Fdg 86; **9b.** 7.81; **10a.** dg 61, Fdg 86; **10b.** 4.23; **11a.** dg 26, Fdg 87; **11b.** 10.0; **13.** 5.023 to 9.941; **14a.** .093; **14b.** .302; **14c.** .152; **14d.** .262; **15a.** dg 29, Bdg 33; **15b.**

9.53; **16a.** dg 40, Bdg 37; **16b.** 7.74; **17a.** dg 49, Bdg 36; **17b.** 6.15; **19A.** 290.3;
19B. 429.1; **19C.** 441.4; **19D.** 630.5.

20A. 3.540 to 6.048; **20B.** 5.233 to 8.940; **20C.** 5.383 to 11.32;
20D. 7.689 to 16.17; **21Aa.** .044; **21Ab.** .124; **21Da.** .095; **21Db.** .404; **22a.** 70;
22b. 4.15; **23a.** 55; **23b.** 7.80; **24a.** 41; **24b.** 15.4; **25a.** inversely; **25b.** smaller;
25c. larger; **25d.** smaller; **28.** 45 or 46; **29.** 47; **30.** 44; **32A.** ltc .9253, lt .915
to .991, bdc 1.204, bd 1.20 to 2.52, md 1.018, fdc 2.448, fd 1.61 to 8.00, ctc
65.78, ct .967 to 1.10; **32B.** ltc 1.131, lt 1.03 to 1.12, bdc 1.055, bd 1.06 to
2.21, md 1.212, fdc 2.346, fd 1.54 to 7.67, ctc 65.45, ct .963 to 1.09; **33a.** product; **33b.** divided by; **33c.** product; **34a.** >; **34b.** <; **34c.** <; **35a.** 4.343,9%;
35b. 11.06, 9%; **37.** bd 1.326 to 1.527, mid 1.205 to 2.849, fd 2.286 to 3.143, ct
.8877 to 1.146; **38a.** 5.756, 14.6%; **38b.** 8.057, 60.4%; **40.** bmd 1.103, fd 1.000;
40A. fmdc 7334; **40B.** fmdc 10841; **40C.** fmdc 10841; **40D.** fmdc 15487.

41. lt .9800 to 1.000, bd 1.111 to 1.556, fmd A 2.130 to 5.093, fmd B
3.148 to 7.528, fmd C 3.148 to 9.266, fmd D 4.497 to 13.24, ct A .9694 to
1.008, ct C .9971 to 1.038; **44.** 13.48; **45.** 10.87; **46.** 6.934; **47.** 11.37; **49a.** dg
36, Fdg 87, Bdg 52; **49b.** gr sl 60.6, bd 2.01, fd 3.54; **50a.** dg 28, Fdg 87, Bdg
80; **50b.** gr sl 69.3, bd 1.15, fd 6.70; **52a.** Bdg 29, dg 39, Fdg 38 or 39; **52b.** gr
sl 67.9, bd 1.16, mid 1.92, fd 2.71, or 2.79; **53a.** Bdg 35, dg 43, Fdg 42;
53b. gr sl 56.9, bd 1.41, mid 1.62, fd 3.00; **55a.** dg 50, brg 30; **55b.** gr sl 66.7, bd
1.11, fmd 4.89; **56a.** dg 51, brg 40; **56b.** gr sl 65.1, bd 1.48, fmd 5.31; **57a.** dg
39, brg 42; **57b.** gr sl 64.1, bd 1.56, fmd 6.62; **58a.** dg 72, brg 40; **58b.** gr sl
57.9, bd 1.48, fmd 5.38; **61.** 15″ 27 to 42, 16″ 29 to 47, 18″ 38 to 49, 20″ 38 to
44; **63.** 15″ 25, 16″ 29, 17″ 35, 18″ 42; **65.** 15″ or 16″ 26 and 20, 18″ or 20″ 22
and 29.

68. makes actual SD > SD; **68b.** negligible; **68c.** makes $\dfrac{\text{actual SD cr}}{\text{SD cr}} =$
$\dfrac{\text{ef dia. cr}}{\text{dia. cr}}$; **70a.** wl cr = 3.201 × dia. cr.; **70b.** 6.40; **86a.** 3.59″; **86b.** 3.53″;
87a. 33.3″; **87b.** 32.0″; **88.** 34.2; **90a.** <=; **90b.** >; **90c.** <=; **90d.** >; **92a.** 7353.3;
92b. 55543; **93.** 138.2; **94a.** 4339.6; **94b.** 29162; **96a.** 19.00; **96b.** 127.7;
97. 32501; **98.** 146334; **99a.** 145.6; **99b.** 149.7; **100a.** 30470; **100b.** 237666;
102. cf 1.18, dff 1.63, cc 507, dfc 36.9; **103.** cf 2.10, dff 2.16, cc 171, dfc 27.8;
104. cf 1.14, dff 1.43, cc 632, dfc 41.9; **105.** cf 1.36, dff 3.22, cc 354, dfc 18.6;
106. cf 1.13, dff 2.59, cc 529, dfc 23.1; **107.** cf 1.69, dff 2.01, cc 285, dfc 29.9.

Chapter X   Sliver Lapper Calculations

1a. =; **1b.** +; **1c.** constant; **1d.** constant; **1e.** increasing; **1f.** constant;
3. td and dc .9331; **6.** A 144.97, B 147.31, C 179.08, D 181.97; **7.** A 2.014
to 3.295, B 2.046 to 3.348, C 2.487 to 4.070, D 2.527 to 4.136; **8.** Aa .029
b .073., Ba .029. b .074., Ca .035. b. .090, Da .036. b .092.; **9a.** inversely;
9b. larger; **9c.** less; **10a.** 68; **10b.** 2.13; **11a.** 53; **11b.** 2.78; **12a.** 51; **12b.** 3.51;
13a. 45; **13b.** 4.04; **15.** 42; **16.** 57; **17.** 45; **18.** ct .9225 dt 1.012.

19a. lt .9890, fd 1.000, tct 1.009, ct 1.003; **19b.** A and C 1.041, B and D
1.058; **20a.** $\dfrac{181.95}{\text{dg}}$; **20b.** .02, A and B 1.93 to 3.16, C and D 2.39 to 3.90;
23a. >; **23b.** <; **23c.** >; **23d.** <; **23e.** >; **25.** 1.00; **26.** 3.90; **27a.** 58.3; **27b.** 49.4;
28a. 46-tooth; **28b.** 950.4; **29a.** 43; **29b.** 1109; **30a.** 50.6; **30b.** 1201; **32.** 43;
33. 62 or 63; **34.** 57; **35.** FPM bdm fig. 1 = 4.8552 × mp, FPM bdm fig. 2 =

$\dfrac{17310}{Bds}$; **36a.** 131.10 to 203.92; **36b.** 274.76 and 279.19; **38.** 21.234 hks., 2165.9 lbs; **39.** 482.75 hks., 53296 lbs; **40a.** 4355 hks, 512191 lbs; **40b.** 4286.3 hks, 504064 lbs.

43a. kls; **43b.** Klg; **44a.** kig.; **44b.** $\dfrac{67 \times 57}{kg}$; **46a.** maybe .857; **46b.** 142.8 to 299.9; **46c.** .170 to .357; **47a.** 24; **47b.** 250 yds; **48a.** 29; **48b.** .246 hk.; **49a.** 26; **49b.** 14.8 lbs.; **50a.** 35; **50b.** 25.7 lbs.; **52.** cf 8.73, cc 6.87, dff 17.1, dfc 3.51; **53.** cf 7.40, dff 14.8, dff 17.1, dfc 3.51; **54.** cf 11.8, dff 23.6, cc 5.08, dfc 2.54; **55a.** 75; **55b.** 101.

Chapter XI Comber Calculations

2. reduce .5%; **3.** % no is correct; **6.** 47.5; **7.** 64.9; **8.** 18; **9.** 50.2; **10.** 73.1; **13a.** .36364; **13b.** .909 to 1.43; **14a.** .40509; **14b.** 1.01 to 1.03; **15a.** Lr 45, Fr 16, 1.023; **15b.** Lr 38, Fr 15, 1.026; **17a.** .45200; **17b.** 5.88 to 7.23; **18a.** .44403; **18b.** 6.66 to 8.88; **19a.** 7.23; **19b.** 6.66; **21.** .993 to 1.04; **22a.** .974 to 1.01; **22b.** 1.01 to 1.05; **23a.** 47-tooth 1.014; **23b.** 90-tooth .9954; **23c.** 91-tooth 1.025.

25. 1.01 to 1.14; **26.** .961 to 1.06; **27a.** 46-tooth dbg 1.050; **27b.** 48-tooth ttg 1.024; **29a.** 6.8967, 4.35 to 7.50; **29b.** 8.2760 5.22 to 9.00; **30a.** 6.60 to 8.81; **30b.** 7.84 to 10.5; **30c.** 9.65 to 12.9; **31a.** 1.0455; **31c.** 1.1429; **32a.** 1.0869; **32b.** 1.4236; **34a.** 392.17, 3.69 to 6.36; **34b.** 470.60, 4.43 to 7.63; **35.** 1.0200; **36.** 1.0214; **37a.** .093771, 3.94 to 5.25; **37b.** .11135, 4.68 to 6.24; **37c.** .13705, 5.76 to 7.67; **39a.** 1.015; **39b.** 1.011.

40a. 1.0323; **40b.** 1.0327; **40c.** 1.1583; **40d.** 1.0319; **43.** product; **45a.** .074510, 40.1 to 69.1; **45b.** .089412, 48.1 to 83.0; **46a.** min and max 1.38; **46b.** min and max 1.66; **49a.** 278.95; **49b.** 290.57; **50a.** 312.85; **50b.** 325.89; **51a.** 278.73; **51b.** 290.35; **53a.** 46.9 to 62.6; **53b.** 55.7 to 74.3; **53c.** 68.6 to 91.5; **53d.** 48.9 to 65.2; **53e.** 58.1 to 77.4; **53f.** 71.5 to 95.3; **54.** min and max 1.4; **56.** Cg 25, dg 43 or 44; **57.** Cg 25, dg 42; **59.** bsg 24 Fg 38 dg 43; **60.** bsg 25 Fg 26 dg 56; **61.** bsg 24 Fg 26 dg 49. or bsg 25 Fg 26 dg 47; **63.** 22.7; **65a.** 41.4; **65b.** 44.3; **65c.** 37.1; **65d.** 52.7; **68.** 4200; **69.** 4900; **70.** 5250; **71.** 6300; **72c.** straight line between centers of kig and Kg; **72d.** whole, **72e.** min., 72f Kg; **73a.** 1.08; **73b.** 1.92; **74.** 31-tooth; **75.** 28-tooth; **76.** 42-tooth; **77.** 27-tooth; **80a.** .0059841; **80b.** .0099992; **81.** 42.5; **82.** 279.1; **83.** 60.2; **84.** 477.3; **87a.** .00011133; **87b.** .00013360; **88a.** .46488; **88b.** .48425; **89a.** .52138; **89b.** .54310; **90a.** .46452; **90b.** .48387; **91.** 27.6; **92.** 33185; **93.** 38.9; **94.** 37593; **97a.** .24785; **97b.** .27798; **97c.** .24766; **98.** 321.6; **99.** 446.4; **100.** 475.4; **101.** 503.1; **102.** 567.6.

Chapter XII Roving Frame Calculations

4. 190.15; **5.** 249.32; **6.** 316.00; **7.** 2.44 to 6.79; **8.** 3.84 to 13.85; **9.** 4.86 to 12.64; **10a.** 34; **10b.** 5.59; **11a.** 21; **11b.** 11.87; **12a.** min .06, max .73; **12b.** min .08, max .49; **14a.** 250.00; **14b.** 4.17 to 17.86; **15a.** 503.05; **15b.** 8.38 to 20.12; **17a.** 180.49; **17b.** 2.51 to 6.01; **18a.** 242.96; **18b.** 3.37 to 8.10; **19a.** 884.39; **19b.** 12.28 to 29.48; **20a.** td and fd; **20b.** bd.; **20c.** fd inversely; **22a.** 1.98 to 5.52; **22b.** 3.17 to 11.45.

23a. 1.32; **23b.** 3.16 to 13.53; **23c.** 6.35 to 15.24; **24b.** td unchanged, fd changed, opposite; **25a.** 58.68; **25b.** 1.05 to 2.35; **25c.** 12.04 to 2.07; **25d.** 4.86 to 12.64; **26a.** 84.54; **26b.** 1.76 to 1.10; **26c.** 5.46 to 1.42; **26d.** 7.36 to 1.91; **26e.** 26.80 to 6.98; **28a.** 28b can, without, either, or; **28c.** cannot, without, either or or; **28d.** independent of, of; **28e.** dependent upon, both; **31. bdc** 59.92   fdc 292.66   dc 17536   bd 1.17 to 2.14   fd 3.33 to 10.45   td 3.90 to 22.36.

32. bdc 200.00   fdc 360.00   dc 72000   bd 2.56 to 6.45   fd 3.91 to 12.00   td 10.03 to 77.42; **33a.** .07; **33b.** 1.19; **34a.** .03; **34b.** .19; **35.** td (a) .18, (b) .95, bd (a) .01, (b) .03; **36.** bd (a) .03 (b) .14, fd (a) .04 (b) .36, td (a) .04 (b) .76; **37a.** 47; **37b.** 1.25; **38a.** 59; **38b.** 8.53; **39.** dg 32, bdg 38, td 27.64, bd 2.22; **40.** bdg (a) 29, bd (b) 2.07 fdg (a) 31 td (b) 19.51; **41.** bdg (a) 72, bd (b) 2.78, fdg (a) 28, td (b) 35.71; **44.** dg 56, bdg 35; **45.** dg 28, bdg 44; **46.** bdg 42, fdg 22.

47. bdg 28, fdg 24; **50.** dg 35; **51.** dg 46; **52.** dg 73; **53.** bdg 33, fdg 25 or bdg 34, fdg 24; **54.** dg 39 or 40; **55.** dg 25; **57.** 38 or 39; **58.** 32 or 33; **59.** bdg 34, fdg 38 or 39; **60.** bdg 42, fdg 37 or 38; **61.** bdg 76, fdg 69; **62.** (a) constant, (b) constant; **64a.** .55; **64b.** 1.22; **65a.** 1.18; **65b.** 1.73; **66a.** .49; **66b.** 1.27; **67a.** 1.11; **67b.** 2.86; **68a.** .024; **68b.** .151; **68c.** increase; **71.** 29.07; **72.** 50.07; **73.** 40.38.

74. .765 to 1.321; **75.** 1.065 to 1.727; **76.** 1.063 to 1.553; **77.** 31- or 32-tooth; **78.** 40- or 41-tooth; **79.** 26- or 27-tooth; **81.** (a) tc 19.48, tpi .325 to .649, (b) tc 29.64, tpi .494 to .988, (c) tc 41.50, tpi .692 to 1.383; **82.** (a) tc 54.69, tpi .912 to 2.486, (b) tc 59.81, tpi .997 to 2.719; **83.** (a) 22- or 23-tooth, (b) 28- or 29-tooth; **85.** 53; **86.** 41; **87.** 41; **88.** 35 or 36; **89.** 42 or 43.

92. not be wound; **96.** (a) 170.48 (b) 3.79 to 8.52; **97.** (a) 175.91, (b) 5.50 to 9.77; **98.** (a) 339.26, (b) 7.71 to 13.05; **99.** (a) 252.14, (b) 7.64 to 11.46.

100. 27; **101.** 27; **102.** 29; **103.** 32; **106.** (a) nothing, (b) reverse, (c) + to −, or − to +; **108.** (a) decrease, (b) direct, (c) constant, (d) increase, (e) over, (f) decrease, (g) under, (h) less, (i) always, (j) same; **110.** (a) always, (b) of, (c) none, (d) the same, (e) faster, (f) than, (g) as, (h) slower, (i) same; **112.** 4.691; **113.** (a) 262.7, (b) 6.25 to 14.59; **114.** (a) 328.4, (b) 8.21 to 18.24; **115.** (a) 370.6, (b) 10.90 to 20.59; **116.** 22; **117.** 21; **118.** 32; **120.** 25; **121.** 23; **122.** 38; **123.** 25;

125. (a) 14, (b) $\frac{1}{14}$, (c) 4, (d) $\frac{1}{4}$; **126.** (a) 27.6 to 64.5, (b) 13.8″ to 32.3″;

127. (a) 22.1 to 49.1, (b) 11.1″ to 24.6″; **128.** (a) 19.6 to 37.0, (b) 9.8″ to 18.5″; **129.** (a) more, (b) more, (c) directly.

130. (a) constant, (b) decrease, (c) be constant, (d) layer, (e) away from, (f) small, (g) set; **131.** (a) traverse away from small end of Bc, (b) reduces, (c) reverses, (d) reverses, (e) adds 1; **134.** (a) 560.6, (b) 9.50 to 21.6; **135.** (a) 642.0, (b) 10.9 to 24.7; **136.** (a) 852.6, (b) 14.5 to 32.8; **137.** 30; **138.** 29; **139.** 30; **140.** 42; **141.** (a) reverse, (b) reverse, (c) adds 1, (d) equal; **144.** (a) none, (b) reduces, (c) reduces, (d) reduces (49), (e) reduces (56); **147.** (a) 2280, (b) 34 to 60; **148.** (a) 2640, (b) 39.4 to 69.5; **149.** (a) 3918, (b) 58.5 to 103.1; **150.** (a) 5799, (b) 86.6 to 152.6; **151.** 65 or 66; **152.** 42 or 43; **153.** 58; **154.** 65; **156.** 43 or 44; **157.** 30; **158.** 48; **159.** 46; **161.** (a) first traverse, (b) flat; **164.** (a) 33.8″, (b) 2.41″ to 3.07″.

165. (a) 36.0″, (b) 2.25″ to 2.77″; **166.** 14-tooth; **167.** (a) 15-tooth, (b) −.17″; **168.** (a) screws, (b) screws, (c) shortens, (d) decreases, (e) decreases; **171.** (a) 136.1, (b) 3.89″ to 4.25″; **172.** (a) −.129″, (b) −.114″; **173.** (a) 35-tooth, (b) 32-tooth; **175.** 18; **176.** 17; **177.** 33; **179.** 1″ .006233, $1\frac{1}{8}$″ .007012, $1\frac{3}{16}$″

.007402, $1\frac{1''}{4}$ .007791, $1\frac{15''}{16}$ .012076; **182.** 1.858; **183.** (a) 211.2, (b) 19719;
184. (a) 1.076, (b) 129.1, (c) 1549, (d) 127031; **185.** (a) 1.400, (b) 168.00,
(c) 336.1, (d) 1.333, (e) 30714; **187.** (a) 1.746, (b) 1.694; **188.** (a) 124.9, (b)
374.6; **189.** (a) 148.0, (b) 591.8.

190. (a) 1.146, (b) 137.2, (c) 549.0, (d) 50170; **192.** (a) 2.164, (b) 17.31,
(c) 1523; **193.** (a) 1.220, (b) 146.4, (c) 29871; **194.** (a) 1.723, (b) 206.7,
(c) 79389; **195.** (a) .9063, (b) 7.250, (c) 638.0; **196.** (a) .6524, (b) 52.19,
(c) 10021; **197.** (a) .9294, (b) 122.7, (c) 47112; **198.** (a) .5734, (b) 75.69,
(c) 21799; **199.** (c) + .000016 lb. + .8%, (d) + 1 lb; **201.** (a) 2.15, (b) 2.59,
(c) 83.0, (d) 43.2; **202.** (a) 2.72, (b) 3.43, (c) 79.3, (d) 11.2; **203.** (a) 2.33,
(b) 2.94, (c) 79.3, (d) 61.1; **204.** (a) 1.86, (b) 2.37, (c) 78.5, (d) 27.8;
205. (a) 7.27, (b) 8.37, (c) 86.9, (d) 79.2.

Chapter XIII   Spinning Frame Calculations

4. 240.00; **5.** 417.39; **6.** 879.57; **7.** 5.96 to 14.91; **8.** 12.57 to 31.41;
9. (a) 31-tooth, (b) 13.46; **10.** (a) 62-tooth, (b) 14.19; **11.** (a) 67-tooth, (b) 6.23;
12. (a) 29-tooth, (b) 30.33; **14.** (a) 379.73, (b) 5.84 to 12.66; **15.** (a) 760.21,
(b) 11.70 to 25.34; **17.** (a) 518.76, (b) 7.41 to 18.53; **18.** (a) 1006.86, (b) 14.38
to 35.96; **19.** (a) 2003.94, (b) 28.63 to 71.57; **21.** (a) 456.62, (b) 5.71 to 15.22;
22. (a) 745.16, (b) 9.31 to 24.84; **23.** (a) 1424.04, (b) 17.80 to 47.47.

24. (a) 791.04, (b) 9.88 to 26.37; **25.** (a) 1451.74, (b) 18.15 to 48.39;
26. (a) b, (b) m, (c) m, (d) f; **29.** (a) 1.25, (b) 4.77 to 11.93; **30.** (a) 1.25, (b) 10.05
to 25.13; **31.** (a) 1.19, (b) 4.91 to 10.64, (c) 9.83 to 21.29; **32.** (a) 1.25, (b) 5.93
to 14.82, (c) 11.51 to 28.77, (d) 22.90 to 57.26; **34.** (a) 1.78, (b) 3.21 to 8.55;
35. (a) 1.39, (b) 6.70 to 17.87; **36.** (a) 1.19, (b) 14.96 to 39.89.

38. (a) 105.00, (b) 1.35 to 2.44, (c) 4.05 to 19.53; **39.** (a) 105.00, (b) 1.35
to 2.44; (c) 7.44 to 35.84; **40.** (a) .07, (b) .32; **41.** (a) .18, (b) 1.08; **42.** (a) .11,
(b) .64; **43.** (a) .41, (b) 2.47; **44.** (a) .07, (b) .49; **45.** td (a) .23, (b) 1.56, bd,
(a) .01, (b) .05; **46.** (a) inversely, (b) inversely, (c) more, (d) more; **47.** (a) 61,
(b) 6.23; **48.** (a) 33, (b) 23.04; **49.** (a) 62, (b) 8.37; **50.** (a) 33, (b) 60.73; **51.** td
(a) 64, (b) 12.36, bd (a) 70, (b) 1.50; **52.** td (a) 32, (b) 45.37, bd (a) 53, (b) 1.98;
55. 28-tooth dg, 54-tooth bdg; **56.** 56-tooth bdg, 72-tooth dg; **57.** 75-tooth dg,
56-tooth bdg; **60.** (a) 6.0, (b) 9.6; **61.** 7.7; **62.** 3.9; **63.** 5.6.

64. 11.5; **65.** (a) 33.81, (b) 53.4; **66.** 27.41; **67.** 55- or 56-tooth; **68.** 88-
tooth; **71.** 44 or 45; **72.** 26 or 27; **73.** 45 or 46; **74.** 36; **75.** 59; **76.** 31 or 32;
77. 50; **78.** 46; **79.** 53; **81a.** 9.22s; **81b.** −.28; **82a.** 9.35s; **82b.** −.15; **83a.** 22.69s;
83b. −.71; **84a.** 22.83s; **84b.** −.57; **85a.** 58.06s; **85b.** +1.76; **86a.** 57.31s;
86b. +1.01; **87a.** coarser; **87b.** larger; **87c.** larger; **88a.** 896.76; **88b.** 34- or
35-tooth; **88c.** 35- or 36-tooth; **91a.** winding; **91b.** twist; **91c.** IPM bo; **91d.** to
cause sp to devote some RPM to winding and the rest to twisting; **91e.** <;
93a. 0; **93b.** .17; **94a.** 1.84; **94b.** 1.98; **95a.** .68; **95b.** 1.12; **96a.** more; **96b.** increases; **96c.** increases; **96d.** decreases; **98.** 7.49.

99. 7.21; **100.** 8.30; **101.** 8.09; **102.** 6.95; **103.** 6.81; **104.** 10.37; **105.** 10.09;
106a. smaller; **106b.** thinner; **106c.** smaller; **106d.** greater; **107a.** decrease;
107b. changes in the same direction; **108.** 7.14; **109.** 9.74; **110.** 8.70; **112a.** contraction, winding, and tape thinning; **112b.** tape thickening and slipping;
116. 181.44; **117.** 756.92; **118.** 1192.88; **119.** 1672.44; **120.** 12.62 to 25.23.

121. 18.35 to 34.08; **122.** 23.89 to 47.78; **123.** 37- or 38-tooth; **124.** 45-
or 46-tooth; **125.** 37- or 38-tooth; **127a.** 362.87; **127b.** 7.26 to 14.51;

128a. 1514.73; **128b.** 21.64 to 43.28; **129a.** 27- or 28-tooth; **129b.** 65- or 66-tooth; **131a.** 1443.40; **131b.** 18.04 to 48.11; **132a.** 861.25; **132b.** 10.77 to 28.71; **133a.** 377.01; **133b.** 4.72 to 12.57; **134a.** 31- or 32-tooth; **134b.** 43- or 44-tooth; **134c.** 58-tooth; **136A.** 10.49; **136B.** 8.74; **136C.** 8.18; **136D.** 7.28; **137a.** inversely; **137b.** directly.

138. 8.74 to 43.70; **139.** 8.18 to 40.90; **140.** 7.28 to 36.40; **142.** tg 26 Tg 124 or tg 27 Tg 123; **143.** tg 38 Tg 112 or tg 39 Tg 111; **144.** tg 65 Tg 85 or tg 66 Tg 84; **145a.** .07; **145b.** .28; **146a.** .35; **146b.** 1.32; **147a.** .15; **147b.** .55; **148a.** .31; **148b.** 1.20; **149a.** .23; **149b.** 1.55; **150a.** .28; **150b.** 2.42; **151a.** smaller; **151b.** less; **153.** 14 or 15; **154.** 21 or 22; **155.** 37 or 38; **156.** 38 or 39; **157.** tg 36 Tg 114 or tg 37 Tg 113; **158.** tg 26 Tg 124 or tg 27 Tg 123; **161.** 30 or 31; **162.** 51 or 52; **163.** driver 33 or 34, driven 117 or 116; **164.** driver 54 or 55, driven 106 or 105; **166.** 51 or 52; **167.** 32 or 33; **168.** tg 60 or 61, Tg 90 or 89; **169.** tg 28 or 29, Tg 122 or 121; **172a.** reverses sign; **172b.** constant.

173. $\dfrac{360°}{180°} = .5$; **176.** 21044; **177.** 14313; **178.** 17576; **179a.** .5; **179b.** .5;

179c. =.; **180.** 42.3; **181a.** 27.8; **181b.** 12.2; **182a.** 14.2; **182b.** 13.4; **183.** stays constant; **184a.** A; **184b.** A; **184c.** bind layers; **185.** 270, 90; **186.** 67.5, 22.5;

187. 90, 30; **188.** 135, 45; **189a.** $\dfrac{270}{360} = .75$; **189b.** $\dfrac{2}{3}$; **189c.** $\dfrac{7}{12}$; **189d.** .5;

189e. .375; **189f.** .25; **189g.** .1875; **190a.** be the same; **190b.** equal; **190c.** may; **190d.** increase; **190e.** decrease; **190f.** equal; **190g.** decrease; **190h.** increase; **191a.** 39.5; **191b.** 13.2; **192a.** 48.5; **192b.** 16.2; **193a.** 20.7; **193b.** 6.9; **194a.** 16.0; **194b.** 5.3.

196. 31800; **197.** 33000; **198.** 16792; **199a.** +; **199b.** 0; **199c.** −40; **199d.** −39; **199e.** −1; **199f.** 40:1; **201.** 210.13; **202.** 210.39; **203a.** cpi dia. bo; **203b.** dia. bo; **203c.** dia. bo %c; **203d.** trav. Rn cpi; **203e.** rev. bc; **204.** 32 or 33; **205.** 26 or 27; **206.** 43 or 44; **207.** 83 or 84; **208.** lg 51 or 52, Lg 44 or 43; **209.** lg 37 or 38, Lg 58 or 57; **210.** lg 25 or 26, Lg 70 or 69; **211.** 1.6; **212.** 1.9; **213.** 2.0; **214.** 2.2; **215.** 2.3; **217.** 47 or 48; **218.** 35 or 36; **219.** driver 32 or 33, driven 63 or 62.

220. driver 36, driven 59; **222.** 35; **223.** 93; **224.** driver 53 or 54, driven 42 or 41. **228.** 1″ .006233, $1\frac{1}{8}″$ .0070125, $1\frac{1}{4}″$ .0077917, $1\frac{3}{8}″$ .0085708.

230a. 1.122; **230b.** 1.0098; **230c.** 72.706; **230d.** 72.706; **230e.** 1.0659; **230f.** 1.0659; **230g.** 22,103; **230h.** .053295; **230i.** .047966; **230j.** 1105.1; **231a.** 1.0908; **231b.** 1.0035; **231c.** 144.50; **231d.** 144.50; **231e.** 1.0254; **231f.** 1.0254; **231g.** 30973; **231h.** .042725; **231i.** .039307; **231j.** 1290.5; **232a.** .38569; **232b.** .36641; **232c.** 146.56; **232d.** 146.56; **232e.** .36255; **232f.** .36255; **232g.** 35269; **232h.** .0036255; **232i.** .0034442; **232j.** 352.69; **234a.** .050115; **234b.** .046106; **234c.** 1115.4; **235a.** .019650; **235b.** .018766; **235c.** 2522.2; **236a.** .027776; **236b.** .027193; **236c.** 50905; **237c.** +.000016 lb., +.8%; **237d.** 408%; **239a.** 112.624; **239b.** 3.405; **240a.** 71.053; **240b.** 9.474; **241a.** 125 hrs., 37 min. **241b.** 12 hrs., 37 min.

Chapter XIV   Twister, Spooler, and Warper Calculations

1a. 826.14; **1b.** 20.65 − 13.77; **2a.** 55; **2b.** 46; **2c.** 41; **3.** 59; **4.** 38; **5.** 31; **6.** 40; **7.** 48; **9a.** .383; **9b.** 1.09; **9c.** 134.6; **10.** 472.59; **11.** 60.5%; **12.** 56.1 lbs;

13. 1264 RPM; **14a.** 27.49″; **14b.** .76 yds; **14c.** 965; **15.** 6.49 Min.; **16.** 8;
17a. 134,092; **17b.** 117,118; **17c.** 97,503; **18a.** 4 min; **18b.** 3.69 min.; **18c.** 5.23
min.; **19a.** 4.0 min.; **19b.** 5.85 min.; **19c.** 4.85 min.; **20.** 948 lbs.; **21.** 5,983 lbs.;
22. 138,415 lbs.; **24.** 25,988 yds.; **25.** 428.; **26.** 13,000; **27.** 378; **28.** 2.

Chapter XV   Loom Calculations

1. one; **2.** 165.18; **3.** 17-tooth; **4.** 172.27; **5.** 18-tooth; **6.** Increase 7.13
ppm.; **7a.** 48-tooth; **7b.** 72-tooth; **8.** 31.86; **9.** 29-tooth; **10.** 19-tooth; **12a.** increases; **12b.** directly; **13.** 32-tooth; **15.** 16-tooth; **16.** 40-tooth; **19.** 32-tooth;
20. 24 ppi; **21.** 15-tooth; **22.** 25-tooth; **24.** 22- or 23-tooth; **25.** 15-tooth; **27.** 20;
28. 15; **30a.** 50; **30b.** middle; **31a.** 45; **31b.** smallest; **32a.** 5; **32b.** 30, 20, 15,
12, 10; **32c.** 30; **34.** 1.8″; **35.** 2.73″, 3.38″; **36.** 2.35″, 3.26″; **38.** 11.35; **39.** 56.66;
40. 8.75 yds.; **41.** 92%; **43.** 93%; **44.** 88.5%; **45.** 32.02; **46.** 90.5; **47.** 61; **48a.** 196
RPM; **48b.** 90.3%; **49.** 87.12%; **50.** 281.86; **51a.** 2265, 600; **51b.** 87.97%;
51c. 629.1; **52a.** 92.32%; **52b.** 88.97%; **53a.** 145,774; **53b.** 344,520.